THE MAMMOTH

Special Ops

*Also available*

# THE MAMMOTH BOOK OF
# Special Ops

Richard Russell Lawrence

RUNNING PRESS
PHILADELPHIA · LONDON

9 8 7 6 5 4 3 2 1
Digit on the right indicates the number of this printing

Library of Congress Cataloging-in-Publication Data is available on file

ISBN-13: 978-0-78671-826-9
ISBN-10:  0-7867-1826-9

This book may be ordered by mail from the publisher. Please include
$2.50 for postage and handling.
But try your bookstore first!

Running Press Book Publishers
2300 Chestnut Street
Philadelphia, PA 19103-4371

Visit us on the web!
www.runningpress.com

# CONTENTS

# INTRODUCTION

The *Mammoth Book of Special Ops* presents over forty accounts of unconventional warfare from the Vietnam War to recent military operations in Iraq.

The accounts are drawn from the years 1966–2006. Two-thirds of them come from 1990 onwards, and they feature first-hand accounts of operations both by special forces and by regular troops conducting special operations. The *Mammoth Book of Special Ops* includes accounts of special operations by Australian, Israeli, Pakistani and Russian forces as well as American and British forces.

In the book, you'll find accounts describing missions behind enemy lines, Long Range Reconnaissance, counter-insurgency, counter-terrorism, hostage rescues, maritime operations, snipers, pathfinders, Close Air Support, close quarter battles and peacekeeping.

Civilians are included, too. For example, at the Beslan school siege in 2004 Russian Special Forces watched over open sights while terrorists held over 1,000 people hostage. Many of the hostages were children who were kept without food or water for three days (*Beslan School Siege*).

The value of good reconnaissance and local intelligence is

apparent in accounts throughout (*Mosul, Fallujah, Operation Barras, Marine Snipers in Nam, Tiger Country*).

The bravery of the troops shines through. *Custer's Last Stand* is an account of a Green Beret patrol in Vietnam during 1970, where the US Special Forces patrol had to be rescued. When an officer with the relieving force reached them, he said, "Motherfucker, this looks like Custer's last stand!" More recently, two British patrols were cut off and surrounded at Majar al-Kabir in 2003. The paras fought their way out but six military policemen were killed, and the incident has been called the British "Black Hawk Down" (*Majar al-Kabir*).

Unconventional fighting has its place here, too. During the Tet Offensive in 1968, the unexpected and unconventional tactics of the North Vietnamese and Viet Cong made a definite contribution to the result of the war. Although the North Vietnamese and Viet Cong lost 50,000 men in the Tet Offensive, they achieved their political goals (*The Tet Offensive*). And at Nasiriyah in 2003 an Iraqi Infantry Division fought in an unconventional manner and the individual units of a US Marine Task Force fell into a series of traps set for them. The Marine units had to respond in equally unconventional ways, while its senior commanders were unable to understand what was happening (*Ambush Alley*).

Mysteries are also solved. Numerous different sources reveal what really happened to the SAS patrol Bravo Two Zero during the First Gulf War in 1991. Ten years later, an investigator discovered exactly who compromised them and what they really did. (*Whatever Happened to Bravo Two Zero?*)

Finally, the changing nature of military operations in recent years is also shown. Unconventional tactics are required when fighting against unconventional opponents. As one soldier said, in Iraq in 2004:

This is a guerrilla war . . . to win this war, we've gotta fight as guerrilla warriors. The more we raid and patrol and seize the initiative, the closer we'll come to winning this war.

# MOSUL (2004)

## Counter IED patrol

*In 2003–4 Mike Tucker spent fourteen months with US forces on special operations in Iraq.*

*Tucker is a former US Marine infantry veteran with special operations experience. After his service with the US Marines he lived in Thailand for five years; then he took an MA degree. As a journalist he has specialized in investigating war crimes. In 2002 he went behind Burmese army lines with Karen guerillas, but in 1992 he had actually fought on the same side as the Karen guerillas when they raided a Burmese army slave labour party near Shotoh mountain, across the border from North West Thailand.*

*On 18 July 2003 he entered northern Iraq. Among the Kurds he documented previously unreported atrocities, including massacres at Gizi and Soriya.*

*On 27 September he was attached to various units as an embedded writer. He was posted around Mosul in northern Iraq. He was not given combatant status but he was given a*

*9mm Beretta sidearm and was told not to hesitate to use it.
Every combat commander told him to stay close to their men
when they moved; never to get in front of them; and always to
tell them when he saw the enemy.*

On 3 October Tucker joined a Counter IED foot patrol.
IEDs are Improvised Explosive Devices, usually roadside
bombs detonated by insurgents. They are often placed on
the Coalition's main supply routes to damage their convoys.
To Tucker, it was like being a human mine-detector walking through Mosul, looking suspiciously at every gold and
green palm-oil can to check if it had wires sticking out of it.
The wires could be tied to grenades, plastic explosives or
TNT within the cans.

When on foot, the patrolling soldiers regarded heaps of
plastic bags, market refuse and empty plastic jugs with
suspicion, checking them for signs like loose scattered dirt.
That could indicate a freshly dug hole which might contain
former Iraqi army artillery rounds daisy-chained together
with baling wire, to ensure that the explosion had greater
power to kill or maim. First Sergeant Nathan Fulks called
them "Hope it ain't me patrols". He had patrolled in the
Kurdish hills during the First Gulf War, when their greatest fear had been stepping on a mine. He compared the
danger from mines to the threat from IEDs.

The patrol that rolled out at dawn on 3 October had an
additional purpose: to deceive the insurgents into thinking
everything was normal when in fact a special operation was
being planned. After the patrol, the US forces would circle
around their base and immediately enter the tight narrow
streets to kill or capture insurgents whom ground intelligence had informed them were in the area. The raid was
made by the Scout platoon of HHC Company of the Third
Battalion of Five Hundred and Second Infantry Regiment
(3–502) of the Hundred and First Airborne Division (the
Screaming Eagles).

Raising his M203 in the pouring rain, a sergeant waved
them through. A specialist opened the gates and they rolled
out in four trucks. The lead and tail trucks mounted fifty-

calibre machine guns, while the middle two mounted Squad Automatic Weapon (SAW) – light machine guns.

The trucks had sandbags packed against their wooden sides for protection against ambushes. In the distance they could see the spires of Muslim minarets, ancient Assyrian domed temples and bombed-out Ba'athist buildings. The men scanned their sectors looking for Rocket Propelled Grenade (RPG) gunners rushing out of an alley or around a street corner. They scoped the minarets of mosques and the streets and rooftops for snipers. Their eyes were always busy but their weapons were on safe.

People were beginning to appear on the streets: Arab women with their heads covered in black scarves and wearing long billowing black dresses, children heading to school, Kurdish men in baggy trousers with sashes around their waists, Kurdish women in silk and colourful cotton dresses. Vendors' stalls were piled high with apples, oranges and heaps of onions. Donkeys and horses meandered along the cracked concrete sidewalks.

They turned onto a main street, where they were held up by horse-drawn carts.

By this time, they were patrolling on foot. They checked out every palm-oil tin very carefully. One member of the team examined the tin to see if there were any wires sticking out of it or any disturbed dirt around it. Finally, he lifted it with a stick. It was empty.

The other members of the team watched their surroundings carefully. IEDs are sometimes command detonated; they can be set off by remote control by an insurgent who is actually nearby within sight, so the team was alert for anyone looking out of a window or peeping around a corner.

They continued walking watchfully. Every dawn, patrols of scouts or men from the mortar sections rolled out on Counter IED patrols in heavily armed trucks heading for the dusty rubble-strewn and sewage-ripe streets of Mosul. They were glared at by some Iraqis, cheered by others and ignored by the rest.

Many of the men thought that foot patrols built rapport with the locals and brought good real-time ground intelligence: "eyes on the ground".

The patrol had spread out with ten metres between each man. By the time they reached their trucks, their flak jackets were heavy with rain.

Specialist Joe Thoman told Tucker about a counter IED patrol that had been ambushed on 13 September. It was a very dark night, a little after eight in the evening. All the streetlights had breen shot out. The two-truck patrol had been preventing black market sales of propane gas. The street was only just wide enough for their trucks.

Thoman was on the SAW on the lead truck, while specialist Hurt was driving the trail truck. As they turned a corner there were blasts behind them, multiple explosions. Although they were ordered to drive through, they dismounted and went back to their trail truck. It was covered in smoke with sparks coming from underneath.

Gordy from the trail truck had been hit and had jumped off. People were appearing in the streets and on the rooftops. The scouts fired warning shots; if people kept popping up or approaching, they shot them.

Sergeant Morales had been on the lead truck. When he reached Hurt he found that Hurt's lower right leg had been mangled and his right foot had been blown off. Morales put a wire tourniquet on Hurt's wounded leg; meanwhile Thoman tried to keep Hurt from going into shock by getting him to focus. Thoman and Staff Sergeant Chapman grabbed Hurt and got him onto the lead truck. They drove to an intersection where a Black Hawk helicopter set down. It was the One Hundred and First Division's "Eye in the Sky", which took him to the nearest airfield. When it got there, Hurt's blood pressure was down to ninety-five.

They went back to the trail truck and discovered the IED had blown the whole floor off it. They checked out some screaming coming from a nearby house; it was an Iraqi civilian who been hit by shrapnel from the IED blast.

After that incident the patrols were enlarged to a minimum of four vehicles. At least two of the vehicles were heavily armed with fifty-calibre machine guns and MK19s. At 9:30 on 3 October they rolled out again to make the raid. Children waved at them and shouted greetings, and Tucker replied in Arabic. Women were emptying buckets of dirty water into the streams of raw sewage, and the smell reminded Tucker of elephant dung in Burma. Trash fires were burning in oil-drums on the sidewalks. Men in two-piece suits with kaffiyehs around their necks warmed their hands over the fires.

The scouts remained vigilant until they stopped near a two-storey building. They dismounted while the machine-gunners stood fast. As they reached an alley corner near a T intersection, Morales said, "Watch the balconies, watch the rooftops." Tucker looked up and saw Iraqis coming out on the balconies as they secured the alleys around the two-storey building.

Another truck manned by the mortar section had joined the scouts to guard their rear. They checked the gate to the courtyard for any signs of wires or detonating cord. Then they jabbed it open with the barrel of a gun. Their interpreter greeted an Iraqi who came out to meet them. The interpreter told the soldiers that he had no objection if they searched his house and asked him questions. Their officer told them to clear the house and separate the men from the women.

The purpose of the raid was to kill or capture the insurgents who had planned and carried out the ambush that had nearly killed Hurt. An Iraqi woman told them that the mother of one of the insurgents lived across the street, so they crossed the street, taking care to secure each new area they entered. The interpreter identified the insurgent's mother. At first she denied that he had been there. They made their way straight up to the rooftop. Tucker noticed some muddy footprints on the roof of an adjoining building. The footprints looked scuffed up, as if they had been dug in just before someone leapt. The woman they had been talking to continued to deny that her son had been there. When she was threatened with arrest she offered to take them to him. Their officer told them that they were moving out "hasty raid. On foot."

The interpreter took the mother out to the trucks while the scouts stopped at each alley corner and checked both ways before crossing. They covered each other while their officer spoke into his I-Com radio. When they came to a wider street, they slowed to join their trucks.

The interpreter met them with the mother, who indicated a blue steel door in a high concrete wall. The door had a latch but there was no house number. The mother knocked on the door and was admitted, followed by the scouts. Inside it was like a candle-lit cave with a small kerosene heater burning brightly. Two Arab men and a boy were there. The men were aged about thirty. One of them admitted that he had planned the ambush on 13 September. They took him back to the Strike Brigade Holding area where insurgents were detained and interrogated.

Their officer came out with the captured insurgent. Lieutenant Thomas told his team leaders: "Hasty raid, we know where the second one is. The guy talked; he gave up everything. Let's roll."

At about one o'clock they drove out of the Strike Brigade's base. Tucker was in the lead truck with Sergeant Lotto's team. They passed a herd of water buffalo as they crossed the river Tigris and re-entered Mosul.

In Mosul, they had to negotiate heavy traffic, with Iraqis trying to weave between their trucks. Iraqi police halted the traffic at intersections and waved them through as two Kiowas swooped overhead, heading east at a height of 200 metres.

At the intersection where the Black Hawk had picked up Hurt they turned north, then turned in through a pair of old, crumbling brick gates. They halted, jumped out and formed a crescent-shaped perimeter around the open doorway of an auto repair shop. A big, heavy man in a short-sleeved khaki shirt and black trousers came out, and Sergeant Lotto levelled his rifle at him. The man put his hands up immediately and spoke quickly, wide-eyed. The interpreter confirmed that they had caught their man. The insurgent had already admitted that he threw the grenades and the IED that nearly killed Hurt and wounded Gordy and Chapman.

They took both insurgents back to the Strike Brigade Holding area. In their opinion, the insurgents were heading for the "Guantanamo slim-diet plan" after they had been interrogated.

At 3:30 in the afternoon they dropped the insurgents off at the Division Holding Centre. They dusted themselves off, cleared their weapons and checked for any rounds in the chambers. After a welcome meal in the "chow" tent, Tucker was told that he looked too conspicuous in his civilian gear. Because he didn't look like a scout, he might be mistaken for a member of Special Forces and a sniper or insurgent might aim at him first. They lent him a pair of their fatigues.

Tucker went out on several more patrols with the Scout and Mortar platoons of 3–502. On 9 October he was talking to the HHC Company's commander Captain Daniel Morgan, who explained:

"The culture here makes it interesting. You might think that the Arabs are at ease with you, but they may just be blowing smoke. So much is a face game. Are they telling you something just because it will save them face? They'll tell you things that don't always pan out. For every twenty things, you may get two. It's worth it. Those two things will help you win the war."

He nodded quickly, gulping down the last of his coffee.

"You get some evil perpetrators off the street," he continued. "We've nailed key Ba'athists, former generals. There are three kinds of insurgents we've nailed here: former Ba'athist Party regime loyalists who want the status quo back. They want a Ba'athist dictatorship back in place. Saddam gave them whatever they wanted. Women, cars, houses, you name it. Then you've got *fedayeen* Saddam. These are former Iraqi Army, and also simply Iraqis whose allegiance is still to Saddam. The second group has rudimentary military skills. The first group often hires the second group. They also hire foreign fighters – Syrian mercenaries, for example. And your third group – al-Quaeda and al-Ansar Islam terrorists. Al-Quaeda and al-Ansar Islam are building up cell networks through the *fedayeen*."

Tucker paused, getting it down, and Morgan sipped from his coffee. He'd heard reports up north of al-Quaeda's connections to al-Ansar Islam and the *fedayeen* from Kurdish military intelligence, but no American in-country had ever stated as such to him.

"Al-Quaeda and al-Ansar Islam are coordinating with *fedayeen* Saddam?"

"Yes," the captain said, shrugging his shoulders, speaking in a calm, matter-of-fact tone. "Which is where the mosques come into play. It's very much a reconnaissance and intelligence war, and Special Operations will have an increasingly large role to play. I bet I can count on one hand the generals from WWII, Korea, and Vietnam who can tell me how to fight this war. By no means in any previous war was an infantry company commander, like myself, fighting like a CIA case officer. Moreover, we've done over two-dozen raids that were strictly joint Special Operations raids with CAG. We've done the planning – they've given me the ability to say no. The future is down that road – merging line units with Special Operations on a broader scale. All 18th Airborne Corps – 82nd Airborne, Screaming Eagles, and 10th Mountain will strike and kill our enemies in Iraq and Afghanistan with greater effectiveness if we integrate our Special Operations elements with our line units. And a vital part of all this, of course, is building strong, solid, human intelligence networks. Habitual relationships between Special Ops, line units, and human intelligence networks must be formed. Working with the Special Operations community, for instance, we use UAVs for aerial recon, real-time recon. As advanced as our technological recon assets are, like UAVs, however, the human intelligence cannot be replaced. There is simply no substitute for eyes-on reconnaissance. Which is why, in this war, your scouts and snipers are invaluable. Many times I've gotten Intel with a picture and a ten-digit grid location, exact target location, and been told not to recon – that the human, eyes-on recon, was unnecessary. I disobeyed those specific orders not to obtain eyes-on reconnaissance and I got the eyes-on recon. I confirmed, via eyes-on recon, that the reports were wrong, denied the intelligence, got human Intel on the perpetrators, and still carried out the operations. And nailed the perpetrators. I always tell the young lieutenants, and the men, of course, do not avoid reconnaissance. Reconnaissance is absolutely crucial to victory."

## Chopper raid to capture arms north of Mosul

*On 21 October Tucker was told that third platoon Bravo Company would be raiding by air assault seven klicks (kilometres) north of Nimrud. Their targets would be a cache of three thousand mortar rounds and an insurgent cell leader and his assistant. Intelligence was aware that* fedayeen *had been telling imams at the mosques that they had many weapons and they were ready to spread them around.*

*On 22 October they took off in three Black Hawk helicopters, escorted by Kiowa warrior gunships.*

*Third platoon Bravo Company was commanded by Second Lieutenant Bromberger. After landing they discovered that they were in the wrong position and they would have to search for the arms cache by foot. Specialist Kemp had a mine detector strapped to his back. He was at the head of a vee-shaped formation of minesweepers, which were five metres apart.*

Gun trucks rolled up in support from Delta Company Third Battalion Five Hundred and Second Regiment. A crowd of some thirty people was watching them 300 metres away.

Tucker joined Kemp and the other infantrymen who

were acting as minesweepers. The Kiowas were still overhead when Kemp reported that he had found something.
Bromberger told Kemp to stay still. Kemp handed Bromberger the headphones from his mine detector so that he
could confirm the contact. He did so and marked the spot
with a white stake. Then he gestured to his men to continue
their search.

They inched their way forwards through deep thick dirt.
As they swept the ground dust drifted up on them. One of
the other minesweepers called out that he was getting
strong signals. Again the lieutenant marked the position
with a white stake. They made another contact ten feet
further on. Bromberger decided that it was time to start
digging. When Kemp had dug down six feet, his shovel
touched something. Kemp carefully lifted his shovel out.
He was able to pull out a white plastic case which contained
six 82mm mortar rounds. They could see more cases piled
underneath.

They set to work to dig up the arms cache. After digging
all day they found 2,400 60mm mortar rounds and 600
82mm mortar rounds. Each round could have been made
into an IED.

They also raided the nearby village where they discovered Rocket Propelled Grenades (RPGs), mortar sights,
cleaning rods for mortar tubes, magazine pouches, yellow
detonation cord, bandoliers packed with 7.62mm calibre
bullets and magazines filled with 7.62 ammunition. In
addition they found a machine gun bipod, maps and brand
new wooden stocks for AK-47s in freshly painted green
wooden crates.

The information about the arms caches had come from
Kurdish sources. Tucker came to the conclusion that most
of the Coalition's successes in northern Iraq were based on
information from Kurdish sources. All the Kurds' information was gathered without satellites, radio and telephone
interception or sophisticated gadgets like Unmanned Aerial
Vehicles (UAVs). Instead they used the traditional techniques of hardcore reconnaissance on the ground, patrols and
raids.

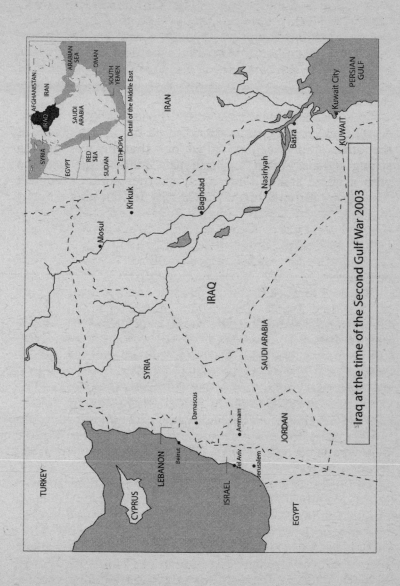

Iraq at the time of the Second Gulf War 2003

# MAJAR AL-KABIR: BRITISH PATROLS IN TROUBLE (2003)

*In February 2003 the chief of the British General Staff, General Sir Mike Jackson, predicted that, in Iraq: "The post-conflict situation will be more demanding and challenging than the conflict itself which could be relatively swift and with low casualties." British, US and other Coalition forces were seeking to impose order upon a country the size of France with a population of 22.4 million.*

*The Royal Military Police (RMP) is the British army's law enforcement unit. Once the war was won the RMP changed from being a rear echelon unit to being the "tip of the divisional spear". Their most important task was rebuilding the Iraqi police force.*

*156 Provost Company (RMP) was in a battle group with the First Battalion of the Parachute Regiment (1 PARA). 1 PARA was deployed at Amarah, in Maysan province, based in a camp at Abu Najir. The local population regarded them as invaders who had destroyed their infrastructure.*

*As well as 156 Provost Company (RMP), units of the Army Air Corps (AAC) were based with 1 PARA at Abu*

Najir.The heat had grounded their Lynx helicopters but their Chinooks were still able to fly.

On 1 May President Bush had declared that the war was won. Operation (Op) Telic was the British army's deployment in Iraq and was reduced in size. Two-thirds of the RMP force was sent home, including fifty RMPs and their commanding officer, Major Bryn Parry-Jones. Lieutenant Richard Phillips was in command of the twenty-five RMP who stayed in Iraq. They were due to be sent home early in July. 1 PARA was due to be replaced by the first battalion of the King's Own Scottish Borderers.

The RMP responded to reported incidents such as murders and kidnappings. They patrolled, manned vehicle checkpoints and trained the Iraqi police force. They tried to gain the Iraqis' trust by cajoling them and displaying a non-aggressive attitude. They usually left their rifles in their vehicles.

8 platoon of C Company of 1 PARA was divided into two "multiples". The multiples' call signs were Two Zero Alpha and Two Zero Bravo. They were due to patrol into Majar al-Kabir to show a "strong presence" because Majar al-Kabir was a volatile town where every local had access to weapons. Indeed, the locals saw it as their right to hold weapons.They were angry both because of shortages and the searches for weapons. They were inclined to protest at the invasion of their homes and because they wanted to keep their weapons.

The interim authority had decreed an amnesty under which locals might hand in their weapons. On 22 June the men of Two Zero Alpha were at the police station in Majar al-Kabir to collect weapons. No weapons had been handed in and the men were sunbathing. Private "Grif" Griffiths was doing stag (sentry duty) on the roof when scores of men appeared around the corner. Some of them were armed and they were all chanting: "La, La Amerika!" (No, no, America!). Griffiths alerted his sunbathing mates and Lieutenant Ross Kennedy, the officer comanding, ran into the courtyard. His men began dressing hurriedly. Stones began to break the windows. The naked paras got their kit together while the crowd wrecked the paras' vehicles – a Land Rover and a DAF truck. Two Zero Alpha's second in command (2IC) fired some warning shots over the crowd. Lieutenant Kennedy requested the Quick Reaction Force (QRF) via the satellite phone. He then climbed up on the roof to order his 2IC to cease fire. The QRF arrived and the crowd was pushed back by the column of Scimitar armoured cars and armed Land Rovers.

The same day, C Company's commander, Major Chris Kemp, had a meeting with local leaders in which he warned them that patrols would continue and that they would return on 24 June.

On the evening of 23 June, Sergeant Simon Hamilton-Jewell RMP met with his commanding officer, Lieutenant Richard Phillips RMP, to discuss a tour of Iraqi police stations which his section was due to make the next day. On 24 June, in response to the increased threat, both "multiples" of 8 platoon were due to visit Majar al-Kabir.

At 0630–0700 a patrol drove through Majar al-Kabir in two WMIKs (heavily armed open-top Land Rovers). When they returned, they reported that the town was "eerily quiet" and that the locals had given them "death stares".

The commander of the battle group was Lieutenant Colonel Tom Beckett, who was due to meet local officials that morning. His main effort in the post-war period had been restoring law and order, rebuilding schools and repairing water and electricity supplies. Beckett's own description of the situation was "benign but fragile". While he was away, Major Stuart Tootall was in charge of the battle group.

The area around Majar al-Kabir was flat. This restricted HF and VHF radio signals. Even within range there were black spots where communication was impossible. The paras were each equipped with Portable Role Radios (PRRs); they also had portable VHF radio and iridium satellite phones. The satellite phones connected directly to the Ops room but were diverted to voicemail if the company's phone was in use. The RMPs were not equipped with personal radios and their only means of communication were the radios in their vehicles.

The RMP duty Ops room representative was Warrant Officer (W/O) Matthew "Bob" Marley. Sergeant Hamilton-Jewell had informed him of his section's proposed journey. He was due to reach Al Uzayr by 1400 and to return to Abu Najir at 1700. Their first intended stop-off point was the police station at Majar al-Kabir. The RMPs were unaware of the paras' task.

At 0900 Two Zero Alpha and Two Zero Bravo left Abu Najir for Majar al-Kabir.

At 0910 C section, 156 Provost Company RMP left the camp at Abu Najir for its tour of police stations. After its first call at Majar al-Kabir, it would proceed to Al Uzayr via Qalat Salih.

The paras' ammunition was limited to 100 rounds per man for their personal rifles and 200 rounds for their General Purpose Machine Gun (GPMG). The full wartime load was six times this allowance. Their Pinzgauer vehicles were Austrian-made four-wheel-drive turbo-charged small trucks.

The RMPs were only carrying 50 rounds per man and had three Land Rover vehicles.

The paras were aware of the threat from Rocket Propelled Grenades (RPGs), so they varied the distance between their vehicles, occasionally swerving from side to side. It was scrubland with salt deposits and frenzied dogs on both sides of the road. Twenty minutes later they could see the town through the heat haze. But Lieutenant Ross Kennedy was unaware that Sergeant Hamilton-Jewell's RMP section would be in Majar al-Kabir.

Majar al-Kabir had a population of approximately 60,000. It was approximately 4km in length by 3km from east to west. The poor shared mud huts, while the more affluent class lived in cubular houses which had flat concrete roofs and were painted white. The locals had been hardened by resistance to Saddam and believed that they had liberated themselves. Saddam's supporters, the Ba'athists, had fled before the British arrived.

The attack on the police station two days before had

expressed the locals' rejection of both the new occupancy and the gun amnesty. There had been no shooting but it had been a warning. If the British returned, resistance would go up to the next level.

8 Platoon were due to meet up with a local militia known as Fawj ad-Dwaara (FAWJ). They were collabora-tors but had the reputation of being a trigger-happy outfit. The Iraqis called firing in the air "happy fire". At 0930 8 platoon reached the militia headquarters. Ten minutes later, the RMP section arrived at the police station. C Section, 156 Provost Company RMP was commanded by Sergeant Simon Hamilton-Jewell. With him were Corpor-al Russ Aston, Corporal Paul Long, Corporal Simon Miller, Lance Corporal Ben Hyde and Lance Corporal Thomas Keys. All RMPs were non-commissioned officers (NCOs). An interpreter was waiting for them, a local named Joseph.

At the militia headquarters, the paras split into their two multiples. Two Zero Alpha would make a foot patrol while Two Zero Bravo remained at the militia headquarters. Two Zero Alpha moved out in staggered file, within five metres of each other, constantly turning to look back at the FAWJ militia as if they were unsure of where they would be or who they might threaten.

At 1000 a four-wheel-drive vehicle drew to a halt by Lieutenant Kennedy. The militia commander, Talal Abid Ahmed Zubaida, got out and told Kennedy: "You can't go into the town." Then he explained: "It's not safe. Bad men. You will be shot at."

Kennedy's men had been shot at usually at least once a week. Only the day before his company commander and the militia leader had agreed that the British would "show a presence". It appeared that their interpretations of what this meant in practice were different.

Zubaida insisted: "If you go then you cannot take my men with you. The town is too dangerous." They agreed a compromise: that they would go in their vehicles and the militia would follow in theirs. Kennedy called Sergeant Robertson and briefed him on the change of plan, which also involved a change of route.

Two Zero Bravo would patrol in their Pinzgauer vehicles. They would cross the town's southern bridge and enter the souk – a labyrinth of bazaars, stalls and booths. Two Zero Alpha would remain at the militia headquarters with the DAF truck.

Two Zero Bravo's vehicle patrol drove off from the militia headquarters at 1010. They crossed the southern bridge over the river into the town. By 1015 they were driving into the souk. The narrow streets were filled with youths who pushed right up against the vehicles.

The loudspeakers on the mosques began to broadcast:

They are coming to search for weapons, to tear our houses apart. We musn't let them. Arm yourselves, they want to fight us. La, La, Amerika!

The crowd took up the chant: "La, La, Amerika!" The mob was two hundred strong and becoming increasingly hostile; they were beginning to throw stones.

By 1020 the crowd was getting louder. Sergeant Robertson knew that he could not use his satellite phone in a built-up area.

Sheikh Kadhum al-Fraijy, a tribal leader, described afterwards:

There was a patrol in the market and the people started throwing stones at them. The children were pulling at the soldiers' arms and trying to grab their weapons.

Back at the police station forty or fifty Iraqi policemen in civilian clothes were following their standard operating procedure. Faced with policing a town that had as many weapons as it had citizens, they merely remained in the building. Kennedy was also faced with an angry mob outside militia headquarters and he had lost radio communication with his patrol.

Meanwhile the RMP section had been at the police station for half an hour. Hamilton-Jewell, Aston and Hyde were inside the building with the Iraqi police. Long, Miller and Keys were outside with their Land Rovers. The military policemen's rifles and body armour were in their vehicles. At the militia headquarters hundreds of children were throwing rocks at the men of the Two Zero Alpha multiple, who crouched behind their vehicles.

The crowd around Two Zero Bravo were beginning to thump the bonnets of the paras' vehicles with their fists. Sergeant Robertson ordered his men to dismount: "Debus, debus and push them back. We need a cordon around the vehicles, and hold it."

Paras from both vehicles got out and started shoving the crowd back. The men from the second vehicle noticed that the militia were no longer with them. Robertson and Dolman had spotted the ringleaders. They had a riot gun which fired plastic bullets. They hoped that shooting the ringleaders with the riot gun would make the crowd back off.

The crowd didn't back off. Robertson noticed a gap in the crowd but a white four-by-four drove toward their vehicles and blocked the route. Robertson marched up to its driver with their interpreter. Through the interpreter, he told the driver to move it. The driver just shrugged. Robertson grabbed him by the shirt and pressed him against the side of the vehicle. The Iraqi got into his vehicle and drove it away.

Meanwhile the crowd had closed in again and they were continuing to throw stones. Robertson himself fired the first warning shots from his A2 (SA80 Mark II) assault rifle. Further warning shots were fired with their GPMG and Minimi light machine gun. The Iraqis turned and the street partially cleared. Most of Two Zero Bravo climbed back onto their vehicles, although Lynch and Hull stayed on their feet with Robertson and Dolman.

Suddenly they were under fire. Dolman dived for cover behind a garden wall. At least three of them had been the targets of aimed shots. They had just spotted where the rounds had come from: "Enemy, first floor!", when the volume of gunfire drowned the sound of their communication with each other. Robertson and Dolman fired at the man they had seen in the window. Robertson shouted at Lynch and Hull: "Get back on the Pinz and give us some covering fire!"

Two more gunmen broke from cover and shot at Dolman. Lynch and Hull opened fire and the gunmen went down. It was 1030.

Ahmed Younis said:

The market was very crowded. I threw myself onto the ground and shouted to everyone to run away or get down. The shooting lasted for about five minutes but there were bullets going everywhere. They were firing on automatic. I couldn't believe it when they started shooting.

Sheikh Shejar said:

The Iraqi side fired first. Later they went to the police station and attacked there. The mob wanted to shelter at the police station and use it as a base to attack the British.

At the police station Hamilton-Jewell, Aston and Hyde heard the gunfire and broke off their meeting. The RMPs did not know that Iraqis had been killed in the souk – the situation had become a blood feud in which the victims would require blood in return. The responsibility belonged to all the tribesmen in town, not just the victims' families and members of their own tribe, because lives had been taken by outsiders. According to custom, outsiders' lives were required in return.

At the militia headquarters, the paras of the Two Zero Alpha multiple recognized the difference between the sound of Two Zero Bravo's weapons and AK-47s. One of the militia tried to tell them it was "happy firing" but the paras' assault rifles had a higher-pitched sound and they kept them on single shot. In their experience the Iraqis always fired on automatic.

Lieutenant Kennedy knew that the Two Zero Bravo multiple was in a contact situation and he wanted to make sure they were extracted. He ordered his men to "mount up".They climbed into the DAF truck and Kennedy told his men: "Right, nobody overreact. Cover your arcs and keep an eye on those with weapons." He ordered Griffiths and Ritchie up into the firing positions but reminded them, "Only fire if you can identify armed targets."

The Iraqis chased Two Zero Bravo through the souk but were frustrated when the paras mounted their vehicles and drove away. The Iraqis headed north for the crossroads.

At the police station, Hamilton-Jewell ordered his men to bring their vehicles into the compound. Some of the Iraqi police left promising that they were going to investigate. Some of the mob began to notice the RMPs.

The loudspeakers were broadcasting: "Arm yourselves; the British are attacking. Fight for your freedom!"

Two Zero Alpha in the DAF had reached the north east corner of the crossroads. They were in contact and were returning fire. Lieutenant Kennedy ordered his men to "debus, debus." This was a standard operating procedure under heavy fire. His 2IC told them to "split left and right!" They were taking so much incoming fire that those nearest the DAF dived for cover underneath it. The driver had taken cover on the opposite side of the road. Their GPMG laid down suppressing fire, which enabled the driver to get back to the DAF. They spotted Iraqis advancing towards them down the main street, but held them back by charging towards them. Other paras advanced in pairs. The Iraqi gunmen retreated but it was hard to tell them from bystanders. The Coalition's rules of engagement were only to shoot at those carrying weapons. When the Iraqis were not firing, they hid their rifles.

*       *       *

Lieutenant Kennedy told his 2IC: "We're going to re-mount and extract to the edge of town. Comms are fucked, we'll have to exfil."

His driver told him that the truck would have to be jump-started. Kennedy told two of his men to hold off the Iraqis while the rest pushed. They moved the truck forwards but not, at first, enough to start the engine.

The Two Zero Bravo paras could hear Two Zero Alpha's

contact but they couldn't see them. They looked for an exit from the main street. As soon as they found one they began to look for their officer and the rest of his men.

In fierce heat and under enemy fire, the men of Two Zero Alpha were still pushing their truck while two of them engaged the enemy. One of them was the GPMG gunner, who was one of the last aboard when they finally got the engine started. The other man who had been engaging the enemy took the firing position above the driver's cabin.

Two of the British targets had eluded the Iraqis. The mob closed in on the remaining British target: the RMPs in the police station. Hamilton-Jewell told the interpreter that he needed the remaining Iraqi policemen to stand facing the mob. But once the Iraqi police saw the size and temper of the crowd they retreated into the back of the police station. The Iraqi policemen began to work the bars out of one of the windows so they could climb out and escape.

The Two Zero Bravo paras were far from getting clear. They were receiving incoming fire from both sides of the river as well as in front of and behind them. In fact, they were in a state of all-round defence and they were running low on ammunition. Robertson managed to get through to the ops room on the satellite phone. He told the duty officer: "We are in a heavy contact. We've killed several enemy already and we're starting to run low on ammunition. No casualties." He reported that they were surrounded and requested the QRF "Somewhere near the centre of town, on the eastern side of the river, north of the souk."

After he had reported that "there's hundreds of guys firing at us" he asked, "Where's Mr Kennedy?" He was told that the ops room hadn't heard from him and that they presumed he was with Robertson. Robertson told them that Kennedy had been at the militia headquarters but that they had "lost comms". The ops officer promised to send help.

Two Zero Alpha was driving north. When they were about 2km away from the police station, Kennedy tried to get through on the satellite phone. The ops room told the Army Air Corps to get a Chinook on standby at the

Helicopter Landing Site (HLS). The QRF had already been alerted. Warrant Officer Marley, the RMP duty ops room representative told the duty officer that he had a section scheduled to pass through the town that morning. He couldn't confirm because he didn't have comms. They might have already left for their next destination.

Sergeant Jason Rogers from the Airborne Reaction Force (ARF) reported and was informed what was going on. It was a nightmare scenario. Two lightly armed multiples were outnumbered and trapped in a volatile town and, possibly an RMP section, too. Their lives depended on effective communications and men and assets being available immediately but ammunition and medical supplies had been packed away because they were due to return to the UK in two weeks' time. They had not even been allowed to keep their personal morphine phials beyond the war phase of Op Telic.

At 1045 the Field Surgical Team at Abu Najir had been alerted. An Immediate Response team prepared to leave from the Helicopter Landing Site (HLS). At the police station most of the Iraqi police had left. Their chief begged the RMP to leave with them. One of the RMP told him: "It's our duty to stay."

At 1050 Kennedy got through to the ops room on the satellite phone. He was told what had happened to Bravo and was sent back in to help extract them. At the base Major Stuart Tootall, the acting commander of the battle group, delayed sending off the QRF while he reviewed his assets.

Robertson was told that Two Zero Alpha had managed to get to the edge of town but had been ordered back in to help extract them. Robertson ordered his driver to get their Pinz running. The next moment an RPG hit its fuel tank and the Pinz exploded.

In the courtyard of the police station, one of the RMP's Land Rovers had been set on fire. The few remaining Iraqi policemen were still pleading for the RMP to leave with them. Hamilton-Jewell told them that he needed a radio because theirs had been destroyed in the Land

Rover. The Iraqis offered to telephone the police at Qalat Salih.

Major Stuart Tootall was organizing the despatch of all available forces. He ordered C Company's commander to take everything available from B Company and the support company down to Majar al-Kabir to assess the situation and report back.

Two Zero Alpha in the DAF got as far as 500 metres from the police station before they came into contact. Bullet holes appeared in the cabin door, an indicator light was smashed and the windscreen cracked. They returned fire with interest but they could do nothing about the RPGs. When "RPGs" were reported they all dived out but the driver stayed in the vehicle. One RPG was on target but it was deflected by a drooping electrical cable which altered the grenade's direction; the shower of sparks struck the DAF. The driver got out but could not find enough cover to give him a firing position.

Two Zero Bravo had lost their second Pinz in flames. They were too far inside Majar al-Kabir to escape on foot, so Robertson asked the interpreter where they could hide until the Airborne Reaction Force (ARF) arrived. He told his men, "Buddy up, we're going to fire and manoeuvre then lay low." He added they should "check mags" because he knew they were getting low on ammunition.

They zigzagged along the cratered streets, keeping the river Majar on their left-hand side. They saw a Dushka up ahead. (This is the Russian equivalent of .50 calibre Browning heavy machine gun.) When it fired, the crouching paras could feel the ground shake.

They were pinned down by some gunmen, including one with an RPG. Robertson asked to be told when the RPG man was ready to fire. "He's in the aim, Sergeant . . . Now!" Robertson stood up from cover and shot him. The other Iraqis who had pinned them down exposed themselves and were put down by single shots. The paras took the chance to move.

Two Zero Bravo, Two Zero Alpha and the RMP section were within 400 metres of each other but were unable to communicate with each other.

At the HLS there were two Chinooks. Neither was sufficiently armoured for combat operations. One of the Chinooks had its rotors spinning. The pilot of the other was a female flight lieutenant, and the ARF was aboard her Chinook. She had been briefed and was methodically going through her preflight checks when the pilot of the other Chinook came over to ask her what was happening. He was Wing Commander Guy van den Berg, commander of 27 Squadron, RAF. He had just arrived from Basra in the Chinook that still had its rotors spinning. She told him what was happening and asked if she could take his Chinook because it would be quicker. He told her that he would take the ARF.

The medics were already aboard the Chinook that was running, but the medics were surprised when Sergeant Rogers' men came across from the female flight lieutenant's Chinook. It was unusual for medics and paras to be aboard the same helicopter.

An Army Air Corps Gazelle helicopter was sent out to locate Two Zero Alpha and Two Zero Bravo and to provide both multiples with an aerial comms link to the ops room. The Gazelle's call sign was Gaz One. Gaz One had also been told to "have a look at the police station" (for the RMPs). It was 1105.

Part of the additional forces Major Tootall had managed to find was a Manoeuvre Support Group (MSG), commanded by Colour Sergeant Luke. It saw Gaz One fly above them as they took on additional ammunition supplies. The Headquarters of 1 (UK) Division was notified of the alarming situation in Majar al-Kabir.

At 1110, Colour Sergeant Luke told the men of his Manoeuvre Support Group that they were going back into Majar al-Kabir again. Some of them had made the morning patrol. They were equipped with WMIKs armed with a .50 cal and a GPMG but they only had peacetime amounts of ammunition for them: 100 rounds for the .50 and 400 for the GPMG. Each WMIK had a crew of three, a driver and a commander (IC Wagon). The IC Wagon sat in the front and fired the GPMG. The .50 cal gunner sat behind him.

Two Zero Bravo took over an Iraqi house and told the occupants to lie on the floor. Robertson persuaded the house owner to go out to find out where the gunmen were. The paras were down to a single magazine or a mag and a half each. From inside the house, the satellite phone's signal was only just strong enough to get through to the ops room. Ops were able to tell him that the ARF and QRF were on their way and that there was an MSG heading towards them. They promised to keep the line open and asked if he had comms with Gaz One yet. Robertson told them: "We're trying. We're in a house on the eastern side of the river. There's wasteland to the north of us; we were being RPGed, we had to debus and find a hide. The crowd are milling around the wagons." He was told the Chinook would be there "any minute".

Robertson divided Two Zero Bravo into two sections. He told Dolman that, if they got overrun, he was to take the five men of his section into the other building. Robertson would take the men of the remaining section into an outhouse. Dolman told his men to "get full mags on now. Top up the rest". Dolman got comms with Gaz One.

Only one of the RMPs was an experienced infantryman. Lance Corporal Thomas Keys was an ex-para who had been in Operation Barras in 2000. Then he had more than 600 rounds for his GPMG, but on 24 June 2003 he was armed as a policeman with 50 rounds for his assault rifle. Lance Corporal Keys trained his sights on the entrance to the police station. Although Tom Keys had been in combat, he was the youngest member of the section. His twenty-first birthday was due in four days.

Corporal Simon Miller had already received multiple gunshot wounds while he was in the courtyard of the police station. His RMP comrades pulled out his shell dressings and applied them to staunch the flow of blood. Then they bandaged his left shoulder, right arm, lower back and right thigh.

Outside the police station an elderly man asked the gunmen to stop shooting. In respect they did so. He thanked them. He told them: "I am going to go inside, so do not shoot." He passed through the doorway, where Keys' rifle covered his steps.

Aboard the Chinook, they dipped to avoid an RPG. Van den Berg aligned the helicopter to make a pass and their appearance sparked mayhem on the ground. Men climbed frantically onto the rooftops to shoot at them. "It's Mogadishu down there"; "Look at them having a good hose"; "Fuck's sake, it's like Black Hawk Down." One of them saw a plume of black smoke which might have been one of the RMP Land Rovers. But they only knew about the para multiples anyway.

The men of Two Zero Alpha and Two Zero Bravo could hear the Chinook. It was a problem for multiple Bravo because Gaz One told them that they needed to identify their position.

Van den Berg began to set the Chinook down. Iraqis on the ground opened fire before they had to turn their backs on the blast from the twin turbine-driven rotors. They hit the Chinook with their first bursts. Sergeant Rogers thought it was a Negligent Discharge and got to his feet in fury. Then he was hit in the thigh. A second, heavier, burst of firing shredded the Chinook's armourless skin. They all hit the deck. Van den Berg pulled the Chinook hard right to avoid another RPG round, then climbed away. He rejected Rogers' request that he land the uninjured to assist Two Zero Alpha and Two Zero Bravo because the Chinook had taken too much fire and might be unable to lift off. After it landed, they found that it had one hundred bullet holes.

On the ground the men of Two Zero Bravo heard the sound of the Chinook flying away. They had used their mini-flares to tell the Chinook where they were. By doing so, they had given away their position to the Iraqis, who were looking for them. "Enemy closing to the rear, Sergeant." "Get on that back door." A para rushed forward to see Iraqis climbing over a crumbling wall: "Enemy front." They hit their assailants with head and body shots. As one assailant was thwarted, another took his place.

In the police station the elderly man saw the body of Si Miller and presumed he was dead. Corporal Russ Aston had also been hit by a long-range shot. The elderly man was trying to act as a mediator but the ringleaders outside told him he had to leave because they wanted to kill the soldiers inside. He protested that the men in the police station had not caused the trouble. They threatened to kill him as well if he did not leave.

Ops had to tell Robertson that the ARF had been "badly shot up with heavy casualties. The pilot aborted and is heading back." The QRF could be another twenty minutes. "We're running out of time here . . . what else can I say?"

Hundreds of locals had joined the crowd outside Two Zero Bravo's house. Their chants were reverberating. Robertson asked Joseph, the interpreter, what the crowd were singing. Joseph listened and told him: "Mr Robbo, they are singing that they want to chop your testicles off."

Steve Oellerman, one of the "heavy call signs" (hardened paratroopers), pointed out two Iraqis whom they recognized from the FAWJ militia. Robertson hoped that they might be taking the paras' side. The two Iraqis approached, waving a piece of white cloth.

Robertson gestured for them to approach but told his men to keep their sights on them. They came closer. Robertson must have felt relief until they raised their weapons. Robertson fired, knocking one of them down; the other fled.

Aboard the Chinook, the floor of the cargo hold had become a field surgery. Both the walls and floor were spattered with blood. One of the medical team, Gavin Macullum, had been hit. A round had gone clean through his right calf. At first he ignored his wound and began treating the more seriously injured. After a while his calf became numb.

There were so many wounded that the medics just treated those nearest to them; exposing wounded areas, compressing bullet entry areas and getting drips up.

At the hospital in Majar al-Kabir, medical staff were counting the Iraqi casualties. Some blamed the British for causing the fighting by shooting their friends without warning. One of them told Dr Firas Fasal: "There are British soldiers at the police station as well." Dr Fasal decided not to go there immediately but called for an ambulance from Amarah to help evacuate casualties.

At the police station, the ringleaders were repeating their threats to kill the elderly man unless he left.

In the ops room, they had requested US air support but they were told that no Cobra helicopter gun ships were close enough to provide support. They were trying to do all they could to prevent the battle group from sustaining what would be its first casualties in Op Telic. They warned their nearest field hospital to expect casualties.

About 1135, the pilot of Gaz One could see Two Zero Bravo engaged around the house where it had sheltered. He could also see Two Zero Alpha engaged north of the police station. He did not notice the riot outside the police station.

Robertson decided that it was time to escape from the house. He told Dolman that they would try to find cover in some dead ground so that Dolman's section could also get away. They knew that: "We can't put down much suppressive fire. Every round's got to find a target."

It was a classic example of "fire and manoeuvre": one soldier fired while the other made ground. The Iraqi interpreter, Joseph, showed impressive coolness under fire. He was a veteran of the Iran–Iraq war.

The Iraqi gunfire came suddenly but its aim was erratic. They took casualties from the paras' covering fire but they kept pouring in the rounds. Robertson's section dived into an irrigation ditch full of polluted water. They pressed themselves against one of the banks of the ditch. As they did so, their radios got wet and cut out.

At 1138, Major Kemp and Company Sergeant Major Grant Naylor had got far enough to set up an Incident Command Post (ICP). Colour Sergeant Luke's MSG was driving into Majar al-Kabir. At the same moment as they spotted paras from Two Zero Alpha they came into contact. They identified the source of the AK fire: a concrete building 50 metres back from the main street.

Colour Sergeant Luke summoned his vehicle commanders. He told them that they would approach from some waste ground. The lead "wagon" destroyed the building with its .50 cal. The vehicle commander told his gunner to cease fire then ordered him to "locate and engage targets on the left flank". Other .50 cal gunners engaged targets until they spotted what they thought were "C Company call signs . . . in those ditches. Eleven o'clock." Dolman's section caught up with Robertson and his men. More Iraqis blocked their path. Their boots were muddy, but the paras' reactions were still faster than those of the Iraqi gunmen in front of them. Most of them were down to half a mag and they had left their bayonets behind.

There was so much noise from the sound of the Scimitar armoured vehicles of the Household Cavalry Regiment (HCR), the WMIKs of the MSG, Iraqi Dushka, RPGs and AK-47s, Robertson's men could barely hear his orders. The Iraqis were using megaphones to exhort their men to fight.

Back at the ops room, Tootall was told that the ARF had landed safely back at the HLS and that some "fast air", two F-15s, were approaching. He asked if they could get comms with a Forward Air Controller (FAC). Eventually, he contacted Gaz One to ask him if he could act as FAC. Gaz One had to tell him that he was unable to guide the F-15's munitions onto targets because he was not FAC trained.

Without an FAC, the F15s were restricted to some low passes and firing "chaff". They did not deter the Iraqis but it cheered up the QRF. The Iraqis were being driven back except in front of Two Zero Alpha and Two Zero Bravo. Both platoon multiples were still in contact.

8 Platoon's 2IC asked the HCR Scimitars to advance down the high street. The vehicle commanders ignored his request because they regarded the threat from RPGs as too great. At 1140 they moved up to positions within firing distance of Two Zero Alpha and Two Zero Bravo. Robertson watched the strikes of the HCR's weapons, fearful of a

"blue on blue". They had fought off the Iraqis for so long it would be sickening to take casualties from "friendly fire" at this stage.

At the police station, the delay brought about by the elderly Iraqi was coming to an end.

Back at the HLS, the RAF ground crew were examining the bullet holes in the damaged Chinook. They identified the larger holes made by rounds from a Dushka as well as holes made by rounds fired from AK-47s. One round had missed the gearbox by three inches. If it had struck the gearbox, the helicopter would have crashed. The ground crew pitied the next people to fly in it.

They lifted the most seriously wounded man from the ARF, Private Damien Mason. An AK round had taken out a piece from his skull. Three men carried his stretcher while three medical staff held the drips and monitoring equipment which was keeping him alive. Once they had stabilized him they would have to fly him to Basra in the shot up Chinook. Sergeant Rogers went, too, as the round that had hit him in the thigh had missed his femoral artery by millimetres.

Robertson was unsure that the QRF had any idea of Two Zero Bravo's position, but he knew that they only had enough ammunition to give them one more fighting withdrawal. The next "bound" would have to take them to safety. He scribbled the details of his position for the HCR and handed it to Private Freddy Ellis. "Drop your webbing and run across there," he told Ellis.

At 1145 Private Ellis set off: "Run, mate, run." He zigzagged across the featureless ground, while the men of Two Zero Bravo sniped any exposed Iraqi heads they could see. Ellis made it to the row of British armoured vehicles.

Dr Fasal began to walk from the hospital to the police station.

The details Ellis gave to the HCR enabled them to engage the Iraqis without hitting the men of Two Zero Bravo, who were finally able to withdraw through Two Zero Alpha's position. The HCR laid down covering fire as Two Zero

Bravo finally reached safety.

Dr Fasal's visit to the police station did not take long. He drove an ambulance towards the British vehicles at the northern end of Majar al-Kabir. The British vehicles had formed a Fire Support Base (FSB). The locals were still making suicidal charges towards it.

The crew of one of the WMIKs of the MSG spotted an Iraqi pedalling a bicycle towards them with an RPG balanced on his shoulder. The Iraqi called to some children to run with him. The WMIK crew were dismayed by the situation but they did not allow the threat to the FSB to get any further.

Major Kemp reported to Tootall that Two Zero Bravo were all accounted for. Tootall asked about Two Zero Alpha and was told that they were with the QRF. Everyone was relieved except for WO Marley, the RMP representative. By then Marley's CO, Lieutenant Phillips, was with the QRF.

At 1200 Major Kemp informed Tootall that Dr Fasal had told him there were four British hostages at the police station. Major Kemp asked Dr Fasal to facilitate their release. He agreed and left for the police station.

At 1230, Dr Fasal returned. He told Major Kemp he had seen three dead British soldiers at the police station. The numbers did not make sense immediately. WO Marley requested a TACSAT message be sent to Al Uzayr for Sergeant Hamilton-Jewell to radio in on his arrival. Gaz One was replaced over Majar al-Kabir by Gaz Two.

Meanwhile W/O Marley was still trying to find out if any one had had contact with his missing section. Finally Tootall asked Kemp: "Can you confirm at the police station? We are missing six RMPs here, repeat six RMPs." Kemp acknowledged the request and told Tootall that there was "still a very heavy contact in progress here though."

When Kemp next spoke to Tootall he had to tell him, "There are six dead at the police station." Dr Fasal would collect the bodies and Lieutenant Phillips would have to identify his men. When they heard about the six dead

RMPs, the men of Two Zero Alpha were stunned. They had been no more than 100 metres from the police station: "We were just there, on that fucking crossroads." They wanted to go back in. This time it was the British who wanted blood.

By 1250 Bravo and Alpha were reunited in the vicinity of the ICP. Dr Fasal brought the bodies of Sergeant Hamilton-Jewell, Corporal Long and Corporal Aston to the ICP, where they saw that the RMPs had thirty or more wounds to their heads and bodies. Dr Fasal returned with the bodies of Corporal Miller, Lance Corporal Hyde and Lance Corporal Keys. At least one of them had been shot near his sexual organs. Others had been hit with rifle butts and stamped on. The bodies were transferred to British ambulances.

At 1308 Lieutenant Colonel Beckett arrived and was briefed by Major Kemp.By 1340 all Coalition Forces had been accounted for. Lieutenant Colonel Beckett ordered all personnel to withdraw.

Up to one hundred people had died at Majar al-kabir, six of them British.

The British Special Investigations Branch (SIB) investigated what had happened. There were two other investigations: 1 PARA conducted their own and a report was prepared for Permanent Joint Headquarters (PJHQ).

They interviewed numerous witnesses, and Iraqi accounts of what happened to the RMPs vary. Salah Mohammed al-Wahele said:

> I was among the crowd (at the police station). I heard the shots and I wanted to see what was happening. I saw people who had guns and were firing on the British. There were more than four hundred there.

Sheikh Kadhum al-Fraijy:

> Shots were fired. The military police came out from the police station. One of their bullets came out accidentally. One person was killed and the family of this person heard about it.

They went to the police station to avenge the killing of their brother. The RMP did fire at the police station.

Their interpreter said that after the RMP had "taken their light weapons to defend themselves" there was "continuous shooting". He added: "The shots became nearer in single and consecutively."

Salah Mohammed al-Wahele added: "The soldiers fired shots and the people fired back. Then they attacked the building."

After he had called the police in Qalat Salih to warn them about the "grave situation and the big mob", the interpreter said that "the British advised me not to worry about them but to take care of myself and get in a safer place."

Abbas Baiphy was one of the last Iraqi policemen to leave the RMPs. He said: "We knew that we would be killed too because the people thought that we were collaborators. But they refused to come with us."

Salam Mohammed, a police trainee, said: "I am so ashamed we left them. They told us to save ourselves though they refused to run away. There was no way they could escape."

The militia leader Zubaida claimed that he had tried to negotiate a peaceful settlement but that the RMPs had refused to hand over their weapons. Salam Mohammed added: "They were murdered in cold blood. The British were shot in the head several times. The executioners were standing right in front of them."

Dr Fasal said of Hamilton-Jewell:

He was standing in the doorway and it looked like he was trying to protect the others. I was just doing my job. I was trying to bring peace. Often I think if I had got to them sooner, I might have brought life.

Ali al-Ateya, who worked at the hospital, said:

I didn't think they would be killed. When I returned with my doctor friends, I saw the bodies in the room. The men were dressed in their desert uniforms except helmets – those had been removed and were strewn around the floor. One of the bodies was upright against a wall, others were lying about the floor in different positions. Each one had been shot in the head more than once. The blood was still warm and wet, as though the killings had only just happened.

Lieutenant Colonel Beckett continued with his "softly, softly" approach. Senior officers from 1 Para met with the council of local elders and there was a leaflet drop. The leaflet stated:

We will not punish anyone since this would be the method of Saddam Hussein. We will return to set up good relations with you because our concern is to build up a peaceful Iraq. Do not let rumours ruin our good relations.

While there was no British presence in the town, the police station was burnt to the ground.

The Board of Inquiry into the incident commended Lieutenant Colonel Beckett for withdrawing after the bodies had been recovered by the Iraqi doctor. The decision had made him extremely unpopular with his men.

# WHATEVER HAPPENED
# TO BRAVO TWO ZERO? (1991)

*On 22 January 1991, five days into the ground phase of the first Gulf War, a Special Forces patrol was inserted deep behind Iraqi lines. In the desert of Northern Iraq, a team of eight men from Twenty-Second Regiment Special Air Service (22 SAS) was sent to help find Scud missiles which were threatening the Coalition.*

*The mission was compromised on its second day. It was unable to contact its base of operations or use its emergency beacons. Three of the team died, four were captured and one escaped to the Iraqi–Syrian border.*

*It became famous because of books written by two of the team. One was written by the patrol leader. He used the pen name "Andy McNab". This is not his real name. The other was written by the escapee who wrote as "Chris Ryan". This is not his real name either. Their books became best sellers and have been the subject of television dramatizations.*

*The team was McNab, the patrol leader, Vince Phillips, Ryan, Bob Consiglio, Mal, Dinger, "Legs" Lane and*

Michael "Kiwi" Coburn. Vince Phillips was the second in command.

After McNab and Ryan's accounts were published, all members of United Kingdom Special Forces had to sign a confidentiality agreement. Michael "Kiwi" Coburn later wrote his own account of what happened. In McNab's account he was referred to as "Mark". According to Coburn, they were dropped in the wrong place by the Royal Air Force and their senior officers refused to allow a rescue mission.

In McNab and Ryan's accounts, the second in command of the patrol was blamed for compromising the patrol and was accused of being negative and indecisive. He was also held responsible for failing to pass on a message. This may have been the cause of the patrol splitting up. The second in command, Vince Phillips, was one of those who died.

Coburn wanted to investigate what really happened to Bravo Two Zero and to Vince Phillips. Phillips was the most experienced soldier of them all. He had served in the Parachute Regiment and the Royal Marine Commandos for eleven years before his nine years with the Special Air Service. He was, in fact, senior to McNab. He was not in command of the patrol because he was from A squadron and this was a B squadron operation.

In December 2000 Coburn won a court case against United Kingdom Special Forces for the right to publish his account. In court both Coburn and another member of the team, Mal (called "Stan" in McNab's account), stated that both Ryan and McNab had distorted the facts. In the same court case, the Commanding Officer (CO) of 22 SAS condemned McNab's book as "untruthful" and described Ryan's "selling out" of Phillips as "disgusting". Coburn's lawyer, Grant Illingworth, said that the "truth has been obscured and distorted".

Michael Asher is a former paratrooper and member of 23 SAS. (23 SAS is the territorial, part time, regiment of UK Special Forces.) In 2001 Asher visited Iraq himself to find out what really happened to Bravo Two Zero. Asher speaks Arabic and has considerable desert experience. He also interviewed Peter Ratcliffe, who had been the Regimental Sergeant Major (RSM) of 22 SAS at the time. Ratcliffe described

*Ryan and McNab's books as "cheap war fiction". He added that members of 22 SAS who know their real identities regard them with "contempt or ridicule or both".*

General Sir Peter de la Billiere was the Commander of the British Forces in the first Gulf War. He described how Special Forces became involved in what began as a very high technology assault. The Iraqis had begun firing Scud missiles at targets in Israel. Scud missiles were Soviet designed missiles capable of carrying a 2,000-pound conventional warhead from 100 to 180 miles. De la Billiere:

> When they got in there the Scud war against Israel began in earnest, and it was quite clear that unless this was contained we were going to see Israel coming into the war with all the political dangers and effects that that was likely to bring with it, and so it was critical to stop this. You have one job, one job to do, and that is get those Scuds out of the battle.

The Scuds were being launched from around the road that leads from Baghdad to Jordan through the northern Iraqi Desert. They were known as the "Main Supply Routes" (MSRs). The mission was to make for the MSR, locate the Scuds, cut their communications and put them out of action.

De la Billiere described the task of the Special Forces was to be "eyes on the ground": "You can't beat a pair of eyes on the ground. We know that from using Special Forces in Europe."

At their briefing, the CO of B squadron 22 SAS told them: "We will be the deepest squadron and you the furthest patrol in Iraq."

The yeoman of signals told them: "There will be two other patrols operating in your area, one on each of these Main Supply Routes (MSRs). All will have squadron call-signs; yours is Bravo Two Zero."

On a map he indicated two other MSRs south of the one Bravo Two Zero would be watching. The CO of B squadron continued:

Now I know it looks like you're out on a bit of a limb but if another Scud lands in Tel Aviv or somewhere similar and the Israelis enter the war, the Coalition could collapse. The fall-out would probably destabilize the whole region. Regimental Head Quarters (RHQ) put forward the plan to observe the northern MSRs with the hope of catching a Transport Erector Launcher (TEL) on the move. Preventing the launch of one Scud could be vital. Any sightings of a Scud are to be reported on the SATCOM immediately and you will have fighter-bombers on "No notice to move" readiness 24 hours a day.

Airborne Warning & Control System (AWACS) is also providing 24-hour coverage of the Area of Operations (AO) for any major problems. If all else fails a call on the Tactical Beacon (TACBE) using your call sign will be intercepted immediately. You will have a reply within 20 seconds and Combat Search and Rescue (CSAR) will deploy to your assistance. As you are 350 klicks (kilometres) from the Saudi border, I have decided that your Escape & Evasion (E & E) plan should take you north to Syria. It is a lot closer and the CIA have safe houses in the populated frontier villages. They will be identifiable by white material draped from the windows.

Your cover story, should you require one, is that you are a pilot rescue team sent into Iraq to search for, locate and rescue downed Coalition pilots. That gives you a plausible reason for being so far behind enemy lines.

Their CO had changed their E & E from the standard plan, which would have been to head south for the Saudi border. He was apparently unaware that they would be out of range of AWACS which were not patrolling that far north.

After he left, the members of the team discussed their plans. First, they discussed their transport options. They would have preferred using Land Rover 110s. These were the long-wheel-base version of the Land Rover vehicles, which they called pinkies.

The patrol leader said that he knew that there were no

pinkies available but he thought there were some short-wheel-base Land Rovers.

The short-wheel-base Land Rovers were known as dinkies. Vince Phillips told him that there was only one dinkie left. He doubted that they could fit all eight of them plus their kit into a "three-quarter-sized" Land Rover. Ryan also doubted that they could hide it while they were in their Observation Position (OP).

Asher asked the former RSM of 22 SAS, Peter Ratcliffe, if Bravo Two Zero had been badly prepared for their operation. Ratcliffe:

> They turned down the idea of taking vehicles. That, in my opinion, was their biggest mistake. Both the Boss (Commanding Officer) and I advised them strongly to do so, but McNab rejected the advice. That was really the cause of everything that went wrong. As for preparation, they had access to the same data that everyone else had at that time – no more nor less. The satellite images they had weren't the best because they didn't show depressions, but with experience McNab should have known they would be there. As far as the weather goes, the met boys predicted that it would be much milder and no one serving in the Regiment had fought in the Iraqi desert before, so we had no experience. As you know, predicting the weather is never easy – the point is that we were all in the same boat.

The most significant point that Radcliffe made was that no one serving in the regiment had fought in the Iraqi desert. The conditions there were to prove as deadly as the enemy.

The desert of Iraq is not like the desert of Saudi Arabia or Kuwait. It is not made of sand but of hard earth and rocks and it is very cold both day and night in winter. All their desert training appears to have been in conditions similar to the desert of Saudi Arabia.

Team member "Legs" Lane was the signaller in charge of their principal communication device. He liaised with the yeoman of signals about codes and radio frequencies.

Their principal communication device was a PRC 319 radio set, which had a duplex antenna. This was a coil of wire that could be hidden in trees or laid flat on rocks. The 319 had a burst capacity that enabled it to send encrypted messages in a fraction of a second. This reduced the chance of their being located by Radio Direction Finding (DF).

They were also equipped with a SATCOM/TACSAT set, which transmitted in real time and was likely to give away their position by DF. It was a large set which had to be carried in two halves. Coburn and "Bob" Consiglio shared this load. They also had four TACBE handheld devices. These sent off a signal with their call sign to any Airborne Warning & Control System Aircraft (AWACS) that were within range. It could also be used as a radio to contact any other Coalition aircraft that were within its range (about 70 km).

The patrol was taken by C130 aircraft to their Forward Operating Base (FOB). A Chinook helicopter took them from the FOB to the Forward Air Refuelling Point. They took off from the Forward Air Refuelling Point at last light on 22 January 1991.

It was two hours (187 miles) to their Drop Off Point (DOP) near the northernmost of the three Iraqi Main Supply routes (MSR). Their flight plan had to avoid all known Anti-Aircraft (AAA) positions. They dropped off Bravo One Zero first. Bravo One Zero was to cover the southern of the three MSRs. At 2000 hours Bravo Two Zero touched down.

They immediately lay down in the cold desert in an all-round defence perimeter until the Chinook helicopter took off. Then each member of the team picked up 95 kilos (209 pounds) of equipment and began the march to their Lying Up Position (LUP). They left the rest of their equipment in a cache at the DOP.

At FOB they received a signal informing them that Bravo Two Zero had been successfully despatched.

Bravo Three Zero aborted at their DOP and returned to base. Bravo Three Zero was intended to cover the central

MSR.

McNab checked their position using his handheld Magellan Global Positioning System (GPS). He found that they were closer to the northern MSR than they had intended to be.

Each man was equipped with the standard issue Bergen rucksack to carry their personal equipment. In addition to their own equipment, weapons and rations for ten days they brought 25 kilos each of fibre sand bags, camouflage nets, full-sized shovels, anti-personnel mines, plastic explosives, jerry cans of water and spare batteries for the radios. The sand bags, camouflage nets, shovels and mines were for digging an OP into the bank of a wadi (dried-up stream or river bed).

Four of them were armed with the Belgian-made 5.56mm light machine guns, which the British called Minimis and the Americans Squad Automatic Weapons (SAW). The others were armed with M16 rifles fitted with M203 40mm grenade launchers.

Each of them had a 66mm single shot rocket launcher.

By using his GPS, McNab found a spot matching the description of the LUP they had planned to use. It provided good cover but was a poor defensive position. They found a better position in a nearby wadi. After they had ferried the rest of the equipment from the DOP to the LUP, they laid up for the rest of the night taking turns to do "stag" (sentry duty).

That first night they realized it was much colder than they had expected. They had not even brought sleeping bags. They also must have realized that it would be impossible to dig an OP in the very hard earth by the MSR. They had practised digging an OP in the sand of the Saudi desert; in fact they had expected conditions in Iraq to be the same as those in the Saudi desert.

At dawn on 23 January the patrol leader checked to see if they had left any tracks and to lay anti-personnel mines 50 metres away from their position. On his recce he saw that they were near a settlement. It was identifiable by trees, a water tower and a building. In fact it was only 2 km from their DOP. He wrote a situation report (sitrep) which he ordered to be sent off by radio.

They spotted an S60 AAA twin gun battery 800 to 1,000 metres away. According to Coburn, they assumed that the AAA position had a garrison of platoon strength. They agreed that that there was "an Iraqi platoon bashered up a squirrel's fart away". The MSR they had been sent to watch was an unsealed desert track system 600 metres away. When they tried to send the sitrep on the PC 319 they could not get any acknowledgement. They tried recalibrating the frequencies and adjusting the aerial, but by the end of the day they were not receiving any messages at all. There were three possible reasons for this: the set was damaged, the transmitting station was down, or they had been given the wrong frequencies.

The back-up was the SATCOM/TACSAT. They knew this was dangerous because they could be detected by DF, but they couldn't get anything on the SATCOM/TACSAT either.

The patrol leader said:

If we still have not established comms by midday tomorrow we will prepare to evacuate this location and head south at last light to the co-ordinates where the crabs were supposed to drop us. Once there, secure and cache the stores, then myself and one other will return to the actual DOP and between us we should be able to rendezvous with the heli and get our new radio. In the meantime, we carry on with the routine and keep trying the comms. If this fucks up and we end up pulling out, at least no one can say we didn't try.

"Crab" was inter-service slang for the RAF.

In March 1991 the CO of 22 SAS told them: "You were given the wrong frequencies; they couldn't work that far north."

They never discovered why the SATCOM/TACSAT didn't work.

The night of 23/24 January, the men of Bravo Two Zero did a night recce. They saw a tented encampment nearby, which could have been Bedouin or military. Back at FOB, a signaller reported that Bravo Two Zero was over its lost comms threshold. The officer on duty concluded that Bravo Two Zero was not in trouble or they would have used the SATCOM/TACSAT. Anyway the only available helicopter was busy resupplying A & D squadrons that night. Then a signaller reported that Bravo Two Zero had been given the frequencies for the border area around Kuwait City.

When Bravo Two Zero had tested its equipment back at base, they had only made a local test. If they had made a longer range one, it might have revealed the problem.

At midday the patrol leader told them to try the SATCOM/TACSAT. At first they received nothing, then Legs got a partial message on the guard net. He thought that he could get a message back. The patrol leader told him to tell them they were moving to the Emergency Rendezvous (ERV) tonight to receive a new set. He told them to make sure the message about the AAA position went as well.

"Legs" Lane got the message away but did not receive any acknowledgement of its receipt. This was worrying because it should have been automatic within two minutes of FOB receiving a message. Then they lost contact on the guard net.

At 1600 they were trying to re-establish contact when they heard the sound of a small bell and the bleating of goats. They saw a small boy herding goats. At FOB a signaller received their message. He tried to reply with the correct frequencies but there was no acknowledgement to his reply. The signaller reported that Bravo Two Zero had been in contact on the guard net but that they hadn't acknowledged his reply. The message said that there was an S60 AAA emplacement by their position.

Then FOB received a message: COMPROMISE. RE-QUIRE IMMEDIATE EXFIL.

Bravo Two Zero had been seen and required immediate exfiltration (emergency pick-up). A colleague of the officer on duty remarked that he wouldn't send a heli anywhere near that AAA position.

The men of Bravo Two Zero thought that the small boy

herding the goats had seen them. They began to dump all
their non-essential kit and clear off. There was still an hour
of daylight left.

In 2001 Asher met the small boy they thought had seen
them. He found the settlement near Bravo Two Zero's
LUP. The first person he met was the boy, Adil, who
was then twenty-one. He told them:

I was about ten years old then, I took the sheep up to the
wadi edge, but I didn't go into it. It is true I looked down
into the wadi but I didn't see any foreign soldiers there. I
now know they were there, of course, but I didn't see them
at the time and didn't know anything about it until my uncle
told me later.

His uncle was Abbas Bin Fadhil, who was the first person
who saw the soldiers. Abbas Bin Fadhil was a Bedouin who
had served in the Iraqi Special Forces during the Iran–Iraq
war. The settlement near Bravo Two Zero's LUP belonged
to him.

Abbas Bin Fadhil confirmed a number of details, including the S60 AAA position. He also told Asher that he had
heard their helicopter when it dropped them off. He recognized the sound of its twin engines. The DOP was only
2km away. Abbas Bin Fadhil told Asher what happened:

In 1991 there was a very cold winter. The wind was terrible.
This house is on a hill, as you can see, so one day – it was 24
January; I know the date because a lot happened on that day
– I decided to park it [the bulldozer] down in the wadi, out
of the wind. I was afraid the fuel would freeze up. I drove it
down there – it only takes a few minutes from the house –
and right up to the end of the wadi, where there is a
sheltered place. When I got there I saw two armed men
peering at me over the rocks, not more than ten metres
away, one on the side of the wadi in front of me and one
below to my left. They were wearing camouflage jackets and
shamaghs over their faces, and I had no idea who they were.

They could have been Iraqi commandos, or special troops of the Intelligence Service, or enemy fliers who had crashed. They could have been sheep-rustlers. Whoever they were, I decided to pretend I hadn't seen them. I looked at the ground, avoided eye contact, and reversed the bulldozer out of the wadi-end. Then I just turned it round and drove straight back to the house.

The men of Bravo Two Zero had heard the sound of Abbas' bulldozer. They knew a tracked vehicle was coming towards them. They thought it would be at least an Armoured Personnel Carrier (APC), so they prepared their 66mm single shot rocket launchers.

Because Abbas Bin Fadhil had avoided eye contact with them, the men of Bravo Two Zero weren't sure that he had seen them. They held their fire, but they knew that they really had been compromised this time. They tried the SATCOM/TACSAT. Coburn got nothing but static. "Legs" Lane tried the 319. He sent out their pre-arranged code word for a compromise on the guard net:

Zero Bravo, Zero Bravo, this is Bravo Two Zero transmitting blind, patrol compromised, require immediate exfil, repeat patrol compromised, require immediate exfil.

They sorted out their bergens and booby-trapped their stores. Then they moved out and headed south down the wadi. There was about a quarter of an hour of daylight left. They were covering each other in pairs when Coburn saw some of the leading men waving their hands in the air.

Abbas Bin Fadhil had gone back to his house. He got out his AK-47 and began loading it. Abbas Bin Fadhil was not concerned about the war. As far as he was concerned, armed strangers were threatening his home where there were women and children.

His father came in and asked him what he was doing. Bin Fadhil told him he was going to find out what the strangers were doing. His father, who was over seventy, went to fetch his own rifle. It was a bolt-action Brno single shot rifle that was as old as he was. Abbas' brother Hayil came in. After he had been told what was happening, he, too, went and got his AK-47.

Abbas, his father and his brother went back to the wadi. Abbas Bin Fadhil:

> When we got to this point, I saw eight men down there. I suspected they were foreigners, but I still couldn't tell for certain. They saw me, but I was holding my AK-47 down by my side so they couldn't see it.

Asher asked him why they didn't attack Bravo Two Zero while they were sitting ducks. Abbas Bin Fadhil:

> There were two reasons. First we only had rifles, and there were rocks to hide behind in that wadi. They could have got behind the rocks and we would never have been able to kill them. There were eight of them and only three of us – my father was an old man, and I have a crippled ankle and can't run, so we wanted to be sure of our ground before we did anything. The second thing was we still didn't know who they were, and if we'd shot them and they turned out to be Iraqis we could have got into big trouble. Remember, they'd seen us but hadn't done anything, and it's very hard to just shoot someone down in cold blood, whoever they are. So for now we just watched.
>
> Soon – it was late afternoon, about five-thirty or so – they started moving south down the wadi in single file. They were carrying packs that looked very heavy, and were spaced about ten metres apart. We didn't do anything, but just walked parallel with them along the wadi to see where they would go.

Abbas Bin Fadhil felt that he still had to find out who the men were:

> They were moving fast and we knew we had to do something before they got away but we still didn't know who

they were. We decided to fire two warning shots over their heads to find out who they were.

This was standard Bedouin practice when encountering strangers.

I fired two quick shots over the strangers' heads with my AK-47 and immediately they went down. By God, they were fast. They started shooting back straight away, so of course we knew they were enemies. We were lying flat out on the ground about 300 metres from them, and had taken off our red shamaghs so as not to present good targets. It must have been quite difficult for them to see exactly where we were. Hayil and I were putting down fire on automatic and my father was struggling with his old rifle. Suddenly they fired rockets in our direction – two rounds, which just exploded harmlessly in the desert. At the time I thought they were mortar shells, but later we found the used rocket-launchers.

He continued:

A smoke grenade went up, or maybe more than one, and under the cover of the smoke they pulled out. From what we could see they seemed to do it in a very disciplined way, working in pairs with one firing and the other retreating. We were still firing, but couldn't see them properly until they went over the rim of that ridge, heading south-west. Actually, we only saw five of them going over the hill, and we thought maybe we'd hit the other three.

Abbas said that he fired about four magazines, about 120 rounds. Hayil said that he fired about eighty. They couldn't say how many shots their father fired because his rifle was old. Abbas Bin Fadhil:

They ran off south west, and believe me they were moving really fast.

We decided not to follow them because it was getting dark and anyway I can't walk far with my bad leg. If we had wanted to we could have tracked them quite easily enough, as the ground was quite greasy, but we were defending our home and the main thing was that they'd gone. When the Iraqi army came later, they did open the packs and they found all sorts of stuff – a radio, medical equipment, food, a flag and a map – everything you can think of but at that time all we found here apart from the packs was a clip of tracer rounds, spent rocket launcher cases, and a pool of blood.

Abbas sent the boy Abdil to the nearest Iraqi army post which was about 15km away. He had to send the boy on foot because of petrol rationing. The soldiers did not arrive until 1 a.m. on 25 January.

As Coburn climbed the opposite side of the wadi he heard the sound of a 12.7mm DSHKA heavy machine gun. As he struggled to get his pack off, he was aware of a tracer round hitting the gravel beside him. According to Coburn, the DSHKA was mounted on an APC 600 metres away; there were also two white Toyota pick-ups. The troops from the pick-ups were 400 metres away lying prone, firing in their direction. Apart from the DSHKA, the incoming fire was inaccurate.

Coburn was also aware of bursts of AAA fire overhead. Dinger yelled at him that the S60s were "having a go at them".

Back at FOB B squadron was organizing a rescue mission but they were ordered to stand down until they had more information about the situation. The officer who countermanded the rescue mission insisted that they wait until they knew more. "Then we can organize something rationally."

Coburn and Dinger caught up with Bob and Mal. A few minutes later they joined McNab, Ryan, Vince and Legs at the base of a small escarpment. McNab told them that they had reached the end of the wadi when the APC and the pick-ups appeared. They had tried to bluff their way out with a wave but it was answered by incoming 7.62mm fire. They tried signalling an AWACS with their TACBEs but there was no response.

They decided to head south for the secondary rendezvous (RV) because the Iraqi troops they had contacted were heading in the same direction as their emergency rendezvous (ERV). They hoped that they could signal an approaching Chinook with their TACBEs. If there was no helicopter there, they would box west for a few klicks (kilometres), then north again and make for Syria, according to the E & E they had been given.

An hour later, they seemed to have shaken off the Iraqis. When they were near the ERV they made another attempt to signal an AWACS with their TACBEs. They carried on to the secondary RV. There was no sign of a helicopter, so they decided it was time to head for the Syrian border, which was 200km away. They saw three probable Scud launches that night.

Mal was the first to suffer from heat exhaustion. They had stop for a few minutes while he recovered. Ryan took the lead position, followed by Mal. Vince Phillips came third in front of McNab, who was followed by Bob, Dinger and Legs. Coburn was "tail-end Charlie".

As he was checking behind them, Coburn noticed figure-of-eight vapour trails in the sky to the south east. He realized that it must be Coalition jets in a holding pattern, awaiting their turn to make an attack run-in. He told McNab that he thought they should be in range of their TACBEs.

McNab tried twice. The second time he got a response; it was weak and broken off but they hoped the pilot would at least report the contact.

Their response was, "Let's tell the others," – followed by, "Where are the others?"

They found Bob, Dinger and Legs all kneeling, waiting for them, but there was no sign of Ryan, Mal or Vince Phillips. McNab insisted that he had passed a message on to Ryan to halt and tried to contact him on his TACBE but there was no response. In the hope that the others were laid up somewhere waiting for them, they pushed on.

They had to risk crossing the MSR. Then they began looking for somewhere to use as an LUP during the day. They had to use some gravel knolls about 20km north of the MSR. According to Coburn's Magellan GPS, he estimated that they had covered 75 klicks the previous night. They put this down to "someone trying to put a 7.62 up your arse".

They were still hopeful that the jet pilot would report their contact. In fact, the pilot had forgotten about it; he only remembered and reported it three days afterwards.

McNab allowed them to brew up some hot tea on one of their mini cooker hexamine blocks. Once they had cooled down, the icy cold began to penetrate their inadequate clothing. They needed sleep but suffered from uncontrollable fits of shivering. They huddled together to share their body warmth. The result was fitful bouts of sleep, which lasted perhaps five to ten minutes each. They had to rotate the men on the end. They combined the rotation with changing the sentry, taking an hour's "stag" at a time.

During the afternoon it began to snow. About four o'clock in the afternoon they decided to move off. Visibility was so poor that they were unlikely to be seen.

The snowstorm was coming from the north so they were walking directly into it. The wind chill was so bad that lying in a ditch seemed preferable. They found a ditch which allowed them to turn their backs to the wind. Another brew of tea also helped, and Coburn shared a sachet of mixed fruit that he had brought with him.

By four in the morning, the storm had calmed down enough for them to continue. Just before dawn they reached the main Baghdad–Syria trunk route. A steady stream of civilian traffic was cruising up and down the highway. The four-wheel-drive vehicles cruising past them were just what they needed. They found an LUP in a shallow wadi 1km from the road.

They heard another goat herder coming towards them. They hoped that the goats and their attendant would pass them by, but four of the animals came into their wadi. Then they saw a wizened old Bedouin man draped in a completely black Arab robe standing over them. He gave a wide toothless grin and began to babble in some unknown tongue that didn't even sound like Arabic.

The only two words of Arabic McNab knew were *hadj* and *souk*. *Hadj* is a respectful form of address for an old man and *souk* means "market". So he asked him, *"Hadj, where the souk?"* The old man replied and pointed to the south. Eventually the old man walked off to the north.

They decided to risk breaking cover while it was still light, in case the goat herder told anyone about them. They saw two Iraqi four-ton trucks pull off the highway near their LUP. McNab decided that they should hijack a vehicle, trying the wounded man routine. Two of them would be on the road; one of them would pretend to be really injured while the other would wave down a vehicle. With their shamags on, at night, they might get away with their deception. Then the rest of them would come out of hiding and help themselves to a four-wheel-drive vehicle.

They agreed that big round headlights meant that it was a truck and they should ignore it. A car would have small round headlights and they should stop it. When a suitable pair of headlights appeared, Bob leant on McNab and they walked onto the road. In the glare of the headlights, McNab let Bob fall to the ground and waved his arms. As soon as the car stopped, Dinger, Legs and Coburn leapt from their hiding place to take control of the vehicle, a taxi with five passengers. One of them was a policeman, so the soldiers decided to take him with them.

Back at FOB, the CO 22 SAS had just been told about the message that the jet pilot had forgotten. He wanted to know why Bravo Two Zero was heading north. The commanding officer of of B squadron had to tell him that he had told them to head for Syria because it was so much closer than Saudi Arabia.

CO 22 SAS decided that they would try to clear up their own mess rather than ask the Americans to send out a Combat Search & Rescue (CSAR) mission. This amounted to posting Bravo Two Zero as MIA (missing in action), informing all ground call signs of the fact and notifying their own heli ops to monitor all frequencies for possible transmissions if they were operating north of the Saudi border.

McNab, Bob, Dinger, Legs and Coburn were crammed inside the taxi with the Iraqi policeman. They tried to ask him what they would find at the border post. They interpreted his frightenened response as indicating that there were "shitloads of troops" on the border.

They were enjoying being in a heated car after their recent experience. Coburn wanted them to turn off the main road onto a track that led to the border, whereas McNab wanted to dump the car "then leg it the last couple of clicks to the border."

They reached the outskirts of the town of Krabilah, which included the crossing point. They were thinking of ditching the car when they passed a sign that said "Checkpoint" in both Arabic and English. They stopped the car. The checkpoint was 700 metres ahead. According to Coburn's Magellan GPS they were about 16 klicks from the border.

McNab told the policeman to drive through the checkpoint and pick them up the other side. The others thought it was crazy but they all got out. They were actually within an Iraqi brigade position.

They managed to bypass the roadblock before a hail of automatic fire and red tracer came streaking over their heads. They broke to their left and returned fire. Two vehicles drove up behind the Iraqi position and their headlights illuminated scores of troops on the ground before they discharged more troops.

McNab and the others made for some derelict houses while the Iraqi fire was still being directed towards their old position. An air raid siren went off, followed by AAA fire as the ground shook from Coalition bombs.

This diversion allowed them to cut east towards the Euphrates. They paused as some troop carriers passed; then they reached a warren of clay and stone houses. They reached the river and filled their water bottles before moving along the bank of the river.

Coburn noted that he had only had a couple of M16 magazines left in his Minimi. The Minimi had an interchangeable housing that could take belt-fed (linked) ammunition or M16 magazines.

According to Coburn's Magellan GPS they were only six klicks from the border. They could see the red hazard lights on a telecommunications device, which was actually on the border itself.

They crossed a field of crops. The crops were so high that the soldiers couldn't see more than a couple of metres ahead. Their path was blocked by a stream flowing into the Euphrates. They were just about to check out the other side when they heard sporadic firing from the rear of the patrol. A long burst from Dinger's Minimi followed.

Tracer began coming from every direction including the far side of the stream ahead of them. They had walked into a dug-in Iraqi position. Coburn and Bob returned fire with their Minimis. Coburn noticed that the incoming fire was going over their heads. He fired his remaining ammunition in the direction of the greatest concentration of Iraqi fire, then he dashed to the bank of the stream and threw himself down the bank. He slid to the bottom where he found McNab waiting. McNab asked him where the others were. Coburn told him that he thought Bob, Dinger and Legs must have withdrawn back towards the river. Bob Consiglio had been "tail-end Charlie". He was left on his own.

In 2001 Asher met an Iraqi who claimed that he was one of the men who fought with Bravo Two Zero that night. He was a local citizen called Subhi. He told them that at about two o'clock in the morning of 27 January they saw a man running towards them down the track towards his group. The running man must have been Bob Consiglio. Subhi's group were seven armed local citizens who had been rounded up to help the police encircle the area. They had been told that the foreign soldiers had been seen down there.

They shouted at him to stop. He shouted back something in a weak voice, then turned as if to to go back. The Iraqis opened fire. One of the rounds probably hit a grenade in his equipment because it exploded and continued to burn. He was screaming. It lasted for quarter of an hour. None of them understood English and they didn't go near him until it was light.

Then the police came and took the body away. It was badly burned. He had taken a bullet in the mouth, which must have spun him around; another bullet had probably ignited the grenade.

Back by the stream, Coburn found that he had lost his last magazine: he was out of ammunition. They had to climb back up the bank of the stream because it had a concrete weir across it. They reached the bank of the Euphrates but there was no sign of the others. McNab had run out of ammunition. Coburn and McNab dumped their weapons in the reeds of the Euphrates and everything except their water bottles, the Magellan GPS and some freeze-dried food.

They began to crawl on their hands and knees across the flat cropland. After an hour they had passed three Iraqi positions but had only covered about 100 metres.

The ground was no longer in their favour and was forcing them back towards the main road. They tried to re-cross the stream they had been beside before. Coburn was at the top of the far side; he had paused to listen when he heard the sound of an AK-47 being cocked. He threw himself to the ground and saw McNab haring back to safety before a hail of fire erupted from foxholes all around him.

From the bank of the stream, Coburn could see soldiers standing up, looking for them. A vehicle drove up to the Iraqi position and its headlights shone down the banks of the stream. Coburn began to inch himself away. It took him an hour to get 20 metres but at least he was out of the glare of the headlights.

He only had about eighty minutes until daylight and needed some fresh cover. He thought there was another ditch 30 metres away. He spotted a ditch that ran between two of the Iraqi foxholes and managed to get into it. It was about half a metre deep. Coburn began crawling towards the Iraqi foxholes to try to get past them. He was five metres from the nearest one when an Iraqi soldier climbed out of one of the foxholes and jumped into his ditch. Coburn only had a knife with which to defend himself. He raised himself to his feet. The Iraqi noticed the movement and jumped backwards in fright. He cocked his AK-47, yelled and fired on full automatic. Two of his comrades opened fire seconds later.

Coburn felt no pain, only shock, as if someone had hit his ankle with a sledgehammer. A brief wave of nausea swept over him before the pain took over. He put his hands over his head and was hit a second time in the right tricep. The bullet missed his head by inches. The firing probably continued for a minute before the Iraqis realized that he was no longer a threat.

He was surrounded by screaming Iraqis, jubilant over their success, firing their AK-47s into the air. When they stopped celebrating, they started kicking him and hitting him with their rifle butts. He was almost unconscious when the beating stopped. Then he was dragged to a Toyota pick-up.

Another group of soldiers started beating him again until an officer arrived and ordered them to search him. He was put in the back of the pick-up. His arms were tied to the sides of the vehicle. Three soldiers leapt into the back of the pick-up to guard him. He was jolted by the movement of the vehicle and the muzzle of an AK-47 kept hitting him on the temple.

Coburn was taken into a building to be questioned. He tried to limit his answers to his name and rank but they hit him on his injured leg with a rifle butt. They told him that unless he co-operated he would not receive any medical attention. He told them that he was in the Parachute regiment and that he was a medic attached to a pilot rescue team. He was asked where the others were and was told that the Iraqis knew there were eight of them. He said that they had become separated.

Eventually he was taken to another room and left on a medical examination trolley. The Senior Non-Commissioned Officer (SNCO) and his subordinates punched him, hit him with their rifle butts and threatened him with decapitation.

Three men arrived; two of them were wearing grey suits. One of them, who was wearing a dirty white coat, turned out to be a doctor. The doctor told Coburn that he would not be entitled to medical treatment unless he answered the policemen's questions. He answered meekly and the doctor gave him some dressings, putting one around Coburn's injured arm and the other around the outside of his right boot. Coburn asked for water and was given a cup of cold water. Then he was left in the charge of the SNCO; Coburn expected them to beat him but they didn't.

The following evening, the same three men came back with the policeman from the taxi. They demanded that he tell them where the rest of his "criminal accomplices" were. Coburn said:

> I swear to you that I do not know. When we left the taxi there was lots of shooting; it was so dark. I was very frightened. I'm only a medic. I became separated and I haven't seen them since.

One of the policemen hit him on the side of the head; the other asked him in a reasonable voice why he was continuing to lie to them. Then he accused Coburn of being a member of an Israeli commando team. If he admitted it, they would treat his wounds. Coburn couldn't see his questioner so he denied the allegations, insisting that he really was a medic, not a commando.

The questioning continued with a lot of anti-American–Israeli rhetoric. According to Coburn, he was in so much pain that if they had beaten him, he would have been incapable of a coherent response. Coburn lost track of time.

All this time Coburn had been handcuffed. After the policemen left, Coburn he was taken to a nearby room which was being used as a field hospital. The first doctor came back and examined the wound in his arm; he told Coburn it was a clean entry and exit wound, "not a problem". Before he did anything else, the doctor gave Coburn an anaesthetic.

When Coburn came round he was in a small ambulance. He was relieved to find that his foot had not been amputated, though any attempt to move his foot caused intense pain. He was on his way to Baghdad. The vehicle stopped and a crowd was allowed to reach him. He was slapped, kicked and punched on his stretcher before he was taken into an underground military base to shelter from an air raid.

When they arrived in Baghdad, he was taken to a complex guarded by soldiers in red berets: the Iraqi Republican Guard. They told him that he was the only survivor "from the soldiers in the north". Coburn asked them how many bodies had been found. Four, they replied, but two were in hospital.

He was left alone. Time passed slowly until one day he was drugged by a very hostile anaesthetist. When he woke up, he was being slapped in the face by policemen who questioned him along the same lines as before. After half an hour this group left.

Coburn's leg was in a cast. He could see his injured foot, which was swollen and yellow. Any attempt at moving his ankle joint was intensely painful.

He was moved into a cell with a window. Iraqi soldiers were able to look in at him. They made high-pitched victory screams or throat-cutting gestures through the window. Sometimes they aimed their guns at him through the window and fired the weapon's action. His guards never allowed these tormentors into his cell.

He was given bread and rice to eat. He found that the rice had a lot of grit in it, so each mouthful had to be searched very carefully to preserve his teeth.

Three weeks later, two men were shown into his cell. As soon as he had confirmed his identity, one of them hit him on the nose with his clipboard. They asked him, "What is your unit?"

Coburn stuck to his "medic" cover story and was hit again. Then the Iraqi said: "We know everything. You flew into Iraq in two Chinook helicopters, which we heard; you were dropped next to the northern MSR, in the wrong position. There were eight of you."

Coburn was shocked. He thought someone else must have been caught. If his story and theirs did not correspond he could be in deeper trouble. To gain time he replied: "I am sorry, sir, I cannot answer that question."

The Iraqi beat him for another minute, then said:

Andy Mcnab, Vince Phillips, Bob Consiglio, Steve Lane . . . we have been told everything. Everyone is happy now; all your friends are being well looked after. You see, you cannot lie to us any more.

You are in the SAS. You are a commando, an assassin in Iraq. You are here to find our missiles and to call American planes to destroy them. Also, to blow up our fibre-optic cables. That is the truth, isn't it?

Coburn admitted it. He only had time to decide that what he knew was three weeks old and of unknown value. He was told that the Iraqis had three of his "friends" in another prison. They kept asking him questions about SAS operations in Iraq. He began making up answers. The Iraqis became quite genial.

Apart from the sound of distant small-arms fire one night, things became routine again. Then the bombing of the city intensified for a week. Suddenly the bombing stopped. One of his regular guards came in and said:"Five days, you go. It is over."

The Iraqi doctor came to see Coburn again. He told him that the stitches in his wound should have been removed. He cleaned the wound and told Coburn that he would never run again. Coburn remains grateful to that doctor for saving his foot and the degree of mobility he enjoys at present.

In the middle of the night, a representative of the Red Crescent and two armed civilians came to move him to another building, where conditions were better than those he had experienced for the past five weeks. After waiting for two hours he was given a meal and some hot tea.

Since he had been captured he had been wearing the same

clothes. He was given fresh clothes. Then he was helped into the corridor, hopping unsteadily. There were twenty other prisoners. They were put on a bus which had its curtains drawn. After a ride of no more than twenty minutes, the bus stopped. The curtains were drawn back and they could see they were in the parking lot of a large, modern hotel. A member of the International Red Cross helped him into the hotel.

Coburn recognized one of his fellow wounded prisoners: his A squadron sergeant major, who had been "bumped" while doing a recce of an Iraqi installation. Their vehicle, a pinkie, had been shot up. The sergeant major was hit in the back of the leg. The other two men in the pinkie tried to carry the wounded man but he ordered them to leave him. They applied a tourniquet to his leg and the Iraqis had found him at first light.

The sergeant major told Coburn that they had received a message that Bravo Two Zero was MIA about ten days after it had deployed. Coburn was incredulous about the delay before they were posted MIA.

McNab appeared. Coburn asked him: "What about Dinger, Bob, Mal and the rest? Where are they?"

McNab replied:"Bloody Dinger and Mal were released yesterday, weren't they, jammy bastards." McNab continued:

Anyway I saw you hit the deck and bomb burst into the wadi . . . so I shot down the wadi a hundred metres, turned north again and crossed the road. Can't have been that far from the border when it started to get light so I looked for a LUP, found a small culvert and hid in it waiting for last light.

Fucking ragheads found me first, though, didn't they? Dragged me out of the culvert and took me to a garrison on the border. That's where I saw that they had caught Dinger as well.

Coburn asked him about Bob or Legs. McNab continued:

Don't know. Dinger was with Legs when he was picked up and said that Legs was in a bad way. Anyway they started beating up on me, trying to get me to talk, but I held out for a week or so. By that time I knew they had Mal as well and all of us were getting severe hidings.

I made the decision to tell them everything. It wasn't worth one of us getting beaten to death for.

Coburn chipped in:

The Iraqi comms must have been well knackered because it took them near on three weeks to click that I was part of the patrol. I thought that I had bluffed my way out of it. The old secret police weren't too happy when they realized that I had been lying to them all along.

McNab added: "When we arrived in Baghdad, the guards here let us all stay in the same cell."

While they were waiting for their flight out of Iraq, Coburn was able to check the Red Cross's list of the names of those due for repatriation. Those who had already been accounted for were struck through in red, including Mal and Dinger. The names of Robert Consiglio, Vincent Phillips and Stephen Lane were unmarked. The real name of Chris Ryan was missing.

The next day they were flown back to Saudi Arabia in a Swiss Boeing 727 aircraft. From Riyadh, they were flown to Akrotiri Air Force Base, Cyprus, in an RAF medivac plane.

At Akrotiri Coburn was reunited with Mal and Dinger. Coburn asked Dinger what had happened to him:

When that last contact blew up, we had shit flying in from all directions and I lost sight of the rest of you completely. We hit a bunch of Iraqis almost straight away. I emptied the Minimi into the lot of them from about five feet, bloody brilliant it was. Anyway Legs and I bomb-burst down towards the river, expecting to have Bob and the rest of you somewhere behind in tow, but once we got there we realized that we were alone. We began to move up the bank towards the north when we heard a follow-up squad behind us, shooting up everything and anything that moved. Our only option left was the river. There was a small boat chained to the bank but we couldn't release it, drawing attention to ourselves – shooting the padlock off would have had them on us in seconds. I mean, we had all just about gone down with hypothermia only a few hours before, you know? But Legs was positive, he made the decision, so we ditched all our kit and waded on in into the water.

Coburn knew that the Euphrates was over 600 metres wide there. He thought it must have been like an Arctic swim in those conditions. Dinger continued:

It was worse, mate, believe me. At first we had swum out only about 60 or 70 metres, then hit high ground. Not being able to see a thing, we thought initially that maybe the river narrowed there and that we had made it across. Of course it turned out to be a small island, too small to hide on, so we had to go back in again. I didn't want to, I was shattered, but Legs sorted me out and we jumped back in again. God it was cold, the current was so strong we were swept well downstream.

We tried to stay next to each other as much as possible, talking and encouraging one another across, but about 50 metres or so from the far bank. Legs stopped talking. I managed to get a hold of him and drag the two of us to the bank, but he could hardly stand up. I wasn't in much better condition myself.

Anyway, we managed to get ourselves out of the water and into a small farmer's shed nearby. Both of us were in rag order but Legs was becoming really lethargic. Hypothermia was setting in. For the remainder of the night, I tried as best I could to keep him and myself warm, lying on top of one another. It was so fucking cold, you know?

Anyway, come morning, Legs was totally incoherent. He was slipping away, I knew it. The only thing I could do for him now was get him to a hospital. There were some farmers working in the fields about, so I dragged Legs out of the shed and got their attention. They dropped their farm tools and buggered off somewhere, looking for the soldiers, I suppose. Legs couldn't understand me. I tried to tell him that I was sorry, that I couldn't help him any more and that he needed to get to hospital. Before I knew it, they were all over us; I couldn't make a break even had I wanted to. The rest of it's history.

Last I saw of him, he was being loaded into the back of an ambulance on a stretcher. After that I was getting so much of a kicking that I wasn't able to take a lot of notice.

Coburn asked Mal what had happened to the other half of the patrol: Mal, Vince and Ryan.

According to Mal, they didn't realize the split had occurred for half an hour. Ryan scanned the area with the Night Vision Aid (NVA) and tried the TACBE. They waited another half an hour in the hope that the rest of the patrol would come along. Then they decided to continue north, with Ryan leading, followed by Vince and Mal.

Before first light they laid up in a shallow trench, freezing cold but not too bad until it began to snow. Because they thought they were virtually in contact with hostile forces, they observed Standard Operating Procedure; this meant no fire or hot drinks.

By last light they were all in a bad way. As they got ready to move it became apparent that Vince's condition was serious. He couldn't even hold his weapon properly. Ryan was also struggling. Mal was the least affected.

Mal led, followed by Ryan and Vince. The sleet and snow were bad enough but the wind chill was the critical factor. They carried on, trying to keep warm and alert, but there was no relief from the wind.

At some point during the night of 24 January, they

became separated from Vince. Mal admitted they weren't paying enough attention. Ryan yelled at Mal that he couldn't see Vince. This happened several times. Each time they would stop, retrace their steps and there he would be, trudging along. Finally he didn't appear. They stumbled about for thirty minutes looking for him, virtually blind.

Ryan made the decision to go on; Mal acquiesced. They carried on all night, with Mal in the lead and Ryan following. At first light, they laid up, but later that day another goat herder stumbled on to them.

Mal and Ryan argued about what to do but Mal wanted to try to communicate with the goat herder to get some information. Mal took matters into his own hands by simply going up to him and speaking to him.

By means of drawing on the ground and pointing, the goat herder indicated that there was a habitation with a vehicle nearby. Mal decided to follow the herder. Ryan reluctantly accepted this. Mal gave him his belt and the equipment attached to it and hid his M16 under his shirt as best he could.

They walked for a couple of hours until they came to a small house with a couple of four-wheel-drive vehicles parked outside. Mal's weapon was still hidden when a man came out. He saw Mal, yelled at someone inside and made a run for the vehicles. As Mal pulled his weapon out, soldiers began coming out of the house. Mal said that he shot the man who had made a run for the four-wheel-drive vehicle. Then he shot the first three soldiers to come out of the house. At that point he ran out of ammunition; he crawled into the nearest vehicle but he couldn't find the keys.

Then there was a silence as the firing stopped and Mal saw the barrel of an AK-47 pointing at him through the broken windscreen. But the Iraqi didn't fire. He and his comrades beat Mal up for at least an hour. He was taken to an interrogation centre run by the secret police and the Republican Guard, and stuck to a version of the pilot rescue cover story. After about two weeks someone came with the full story of the patrol. After his story was exposed as false, he received a beating which lasted most of an entire night.

He was taken from the interrogation cell to the military prison where he was put in the cell with McNab and Dinger.

In 2001 Michael Asher was shown the place where Phillips' body had been found by a Bedouin. He built a cairn of stones as a memorial. In case they might object, he asked the local Bedouin for their permission. They replied:"Why not? He deserved it." They added: "They were real men, those soldiers, to have endured the conditions here in winter. Heroes, every one."

In his own account, Ryan stated that he waited until 1830 for Mal to return. Then he began to walk south. After fifteen minutes he saw the headlights of two vehicles approaching. He hit one with his 66mm rocket. He hit the other with a 40mm grenade from his M203. He sprayed the men from the back of the vehicles with his M16. He did not mention any of this at his debriefing in the United Kingdom.

He continued to move by night and lay up by day. For five days he went without food. On 30 January he climbed the border fence at Al Qaim. He had walked 186 miles.

Asher concluded that their real heroism was in surviving the desert but that McNab and Ryan's heroism was marred by what they wrote afterwards.

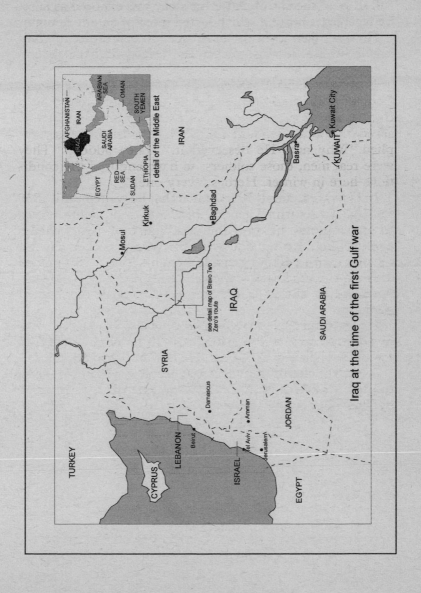

detail of the Middle East

see detail map of Bravo Two Zero's route

Iraq at the time of the first Gulf war

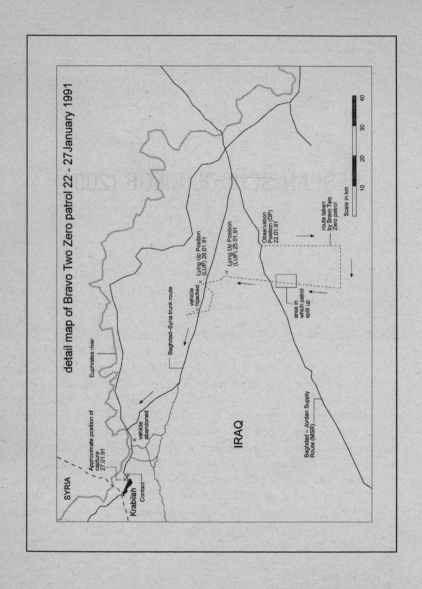

detail map of Bravo Two Zero patrol 22 - 27 January 1991

# BESLAN SCHOOL SIEGE (2004)

## 3 September 2004

*On Wednesday 1 September 2004, gunmen took more than 1,000 men, women and children hostage at a school in the town of Beslan in the Russian Federal Republic of North Ossetia. Russian authorities said that the hostage-takers were making unclear demands. The authorities did not know exactly how many people were being held hostage in Middle School Number One. Wednesday 1 September was the first day of the new school year, when traditionally parents and family members attended an opening ceremony at their children's school.*

*During the assembly gunmen arrived and started shooting, then herded everyone into the school. It was estimated that there must have been 1,500 people present. When the shooting started some were able to get away. Perhaps 1,200 people were taken hostage. Conditions were very hot and security forces and media representatives rushed to the spot. Ten thousand Russian special forces and Interior Ministry troops ringed Beslan Middle School Number One.*

*In* The Times, *on 5 September, Jeremy Page and Clem Cecil reported:*

When their chance of freedom came with a massive explosion that shook School Number One, many of the children found that they could not escape.

Forced to strip to their underwear and sit shoulder-to-shoulder for three days with their knees tucked under their chins, their legs were numb and would not respond to the instinct to flee.

Hungry and dehydrated after being denied food and water by their captors, they stumbled aimlessly and weakly, their way further hampered by the debris and dust from the blast falling all around them.

The stronger ones reached the windows and began to break the glass with their fists, cutting and scratching their hands, arms and faces in their frantic efforts to get out.

And as they ran, crying and fearful, gunmen in the upper floors of the school began shooting at them.

Fatima, 15, dazed and clearly in shock, seemed to know little of her escape. "I don't know what caused the blast, I just remember a huge bang," she said.

"I tried to get up but I couldn't walk or see anything. Somebody grabbed me and then I cannot remember anything until I got to hospital."

Vitaly Makiyev, 11, was shaking as he told how policemen carried him from the building. When the gunmen arrived on Wednesday morning, Vitaly had run back into the school building, thinking he would be safe there.

"They held us for three days and they didn't give us any food or water," he cried.

Rosa Dudiyea told the Kommersant newspaper that the hostage-takers had at first pretended to be Russian and lured some children into the building with sweets.

"A military lorry appeared in front of the school building. people wearing camouflage and masks jumped out – I could only see their eyes and beards,"she said.

"They opened fire. Everyone started running about. Some people, including myself, managed to hide behind a fence.

"Several gunmen stayed outside, near the entrance. They started screaming in very good Russian, 'Russians, Russians, come here, don't be afraid!' One of the terrorists tried to lure children with chocolate."

A woman teacher who was freed with her three-year-old daughter on the second day of the siege, but forced to leave her older children behind, said that as many as 1,500 people had been in the school when the siege began.

"It happened within two or three minutes," she told *Izvestiya* newspaper. "We had begun to form a line in the school yard to listen to the headmistress's September 1 speeches when suddenly we heard shots.

"We were herded into the sports hall. The doors into the hall were locked. People in masks broke the windows and leapt through them and then they broke the doors down. In the hall they ordered us to sit on the floor and began quickly to mine the room.

"Two large explosive devices were put in the basketball nets and then through the hall they led wires that they attached to smaller explosive devices. The whole place was mined within ten minutes."

Atsamas Ketsoyev, 14, told *The Times:* "There were bombs laid out all around the gymnasium – some were hanging from the ceiling and there was one big bomb in the middle of the room. There were two women wearing explosive belts. There was also a man standing with his foot on something like a pedal or a button."

Around this, said Atsamas, the half-naked children were forced to sit, crammed together "with our knees under our chins".

It was hot and many had difficulty breathing even after the hostage-takers – who never removed their masks – ordered male hostages to smash windows.

The teacher who was freed said that the terrorists had frequently fired shots to stop children crying and prevent people talking. "The younger classes were terrified. They often asked to go to the toilet. They took them to the toilet in groups. If the younger ones cried the fighters shot in the air and shouted at them to be quiet. Then the young ones were silent.

"There were six or seven fighters in the hall. Two at one end, two at the other. Two or three walked around the hall. I can't say how many there were, although when we went to the toilet I saw in the corridor there were many of them – some lying down, some walking around.

"On the first day they brought a few buckets of water from the loo. People in masks gave the babies powdered milk in cold, unboiled water."

The teacher said that women with very young children were later moved upstairs because the crying of the babies irritated the gunmen.

She said: "A frightened child in the hall made a noise and one of the fighters seized a child and threatened to kill it if the noise didn't stop.

"One of the terrorists grabbed a child who was crying and said, 'If this noise doesn't stop I'll shoot you.'"

She continued: "The terrorists said that they only demanded one thing – that troops should be taken out of Chechnya. In general they spoke little and mostly in whispers, but we heard that.

"Mostly they explained things with gestures. By their speech it was possible to make out there were Chechens and Ingush among them."

The teacher said that during the night some of the children became more frightened and would wake crying from fitful dozes. She added: "The young ones began to cry every now and then, and the fighters shot into the air and enforced silence.

"In the morning they told us they wouldn't give us any more water because the authorities were refusing to negotiate. When the children were taken to the loo some tried to drink from the tap. The fighters stopped this."

Some children among those who escaped said they had become so thirsty they drank their own urine. Others had ripped leaves off pot plants in the school and eaten them.

Male hostages were held apart from the women and children and some were forced to "work" – boarding up windows and throwing out the corpses of those killed when the school was seized.

One teenager escaped when he jumped from a window out of which he had just thrown a body. He broke his leg but managed to hide until nightfall when he crawled to safety.

Hostages said they believed that the terrorists had murdered some of the wounded.

Zalina Dzandzarova, freed on the second day of the siege, said she believed that two suicide bombers had killed themselves on Wednesday, detonating their explosive belts in the corridor, where male hostages were being kept. Mrs Dzandarova said: "They took some of the injured out of the gym and finished them off right there."

The siege continued until Friday 3 September. Valery Andreyev, regional head of the Federal Security Services (FSB), stated:

I want to point out that no military action was planned. We were planning further talks.

Reporters Alan Hamilton and Michael Evans described what happened next:

There was a plan. a careful, softly-softly plan of delicate negotiation. But then there were two loud explosions, the plan was blown clean out of the window, and chaos reigned.

For what happened next, there was no plan. Ten thousand Russian special forces and Interior Ministry troops ringed Beslan No. 1 School. They had been there for three days, and hoped for a peaceful outcome. So too did the hundreds of distraught parents held at arm's length by the security cordon; their wait was hourly becoming more painful.

There were already a dozen or so dead within the school, victims of the opening moments of the three-day hostage crisis. A bus carrying four doctors was sent into the school to collect their bodies. Its mercy mission had, by all accounts, been agreed with the hostage-takers within.

Four Russian military helicopters circled overhead, powerless to influence the rapidly unfolding events on the ground.

At 1.08 p.m. local time – a hot early afternoon in Besian – several things happened within a matter of a few short, action-charged minutes. Two explosions were heard within the school.

One witness claimed that a woman hostage-taker with explosives strapped to her waist had blown herself up accidentally; another witness said a bomb taped to a ceiling inside the school accidentally fell, setting off an explosion.

Young hostages, already deprived of food and water and in a high state of stress, appear to have been panicked by the explosion and made a frantic bolt for freedom.

Another explosion had blown a hole in the school wall. Suddenly a river of young children poured out, some from the gash in the brickwork and some through windows. Most were in their underwear; some were naked.

The air inside the school had been foetid and stiflingly hot. All looked quite terrified.

The situation then took a terrible turn. The hostage-takers inside the school opened fire on the fleeing children, apparently with every intention to kill. A few ran; many more were carried by soldiers to waiting ambulances. Some children were covered in blood from head to foot, their lower limbs a mess of burns and blast injuries. Some collapsed on to waiting stretchers; others ran to parents, pouring bottled water down their throats after three days of intense heat and having apparently been reduced to drinking their own urine.

Russian forces had no plan to cope with such an outcome. But at that moment they decided that their only option, with hapless children under fire, was to use maximum force to storm the school in an effort to free those still held inside. Local civilians, many of them armed, joined in the gun battle.

The Russians were hampered by an almost total lack of information. They had no idea how many children were inside, and they did not know how the terrorists were deployed. The hostage-takers, by contrast, were well prepared, having laid mines on the gymnasium floor and hung grenades from ceilings. They even had an escape route in the event of a full-frontal assault.

As the Russians stormed the building, the hostage-takers split into groups and fought the troops on at least three fronts inside the building. As darkness fell last night, one group of terrorists was still engaging troops from the school basement. Within minutes of the first explosions it became clear that traumatized children, some as young as five, were not the only ones to escape.

In the utter confusion of that first assault, as many as 13 terrorists may have escaped from the school building, and were reported to be heading for the railway station in the south of the town.

They found refuge in a house. On the horizon a short distance from the school, mushroom clouds of explosive smoke drifted high on the still air as Russian tanks surrounded their hideout.

The fact that they had managed to flee the immediate area underlined the pathetic failure of the authorities to seal off the school.

Back at the school, the sound of a gun battle within was punctuated every half-minute by the louder explosion of a grenade, or a tripped booby-trap. More young hostages were brought out and rushed to a fleet of ambulances and private cars which ferried them to hospital. Several were at best unconscious; they may have already died.

Another wave of special forces assaulted the school, soldiers kicking in the few remaining undamaged windows to gain entry. As no further major explosion had been heard from within, hopes rose that there would be more survivors. But by now the stream of walking wounded hostages had been reduced to a trickle, and then dried up.

Then the casualty figures, unreliable in the extreme,

began to mount. Reports said that five hostage-takers were dead, and that 158 children had been taken to hospital. Then the dead rose to seven, and those in hospital to more than 300.

The fleet of ambulances could not cope with the torrent of the injured, and appeals went out for private cars to ferry victims to local hospitals. At one stage two dozen badly injured children lay on stretchers, covered in blood and being comforted by parents who gave them water.

As the gun battle continued within the school, the roof of the school gym was seen to be on fire, and there were fears that embers from the burning rafters could worsen the injuries of those still inside.

Order at the scene then broke down completely. Hundreds of people broke through the security cordon and invaded the school in search of their still-missing children, oblivious to the dangers of the gun battle, a burning roof and the threat of booby-traps. The authorities appeared completely to have lost control of events.

Two hours after the initial assault, the gunfire within the school had become sporadic although the sound of exploding grenades still contributed a regular and deadly rhythm. Three hours after the original assault, reports filtered out that the bodies of 100 hostages had been found in the gym.

At the same time Russian forces captured and led out one of the hostage-takers. He and his captors were immediately swamped by what looked perilously like a lynch mob of those parents and townsfolk who had flooded into the school grounds.

Official Russian government statements from Moscow claimed that troops had now taken full control of the school building. Evidence on the ground told a different story, with the crackle of small-arms fire still being heard from within.

It went on for hours. Russian troops had found themselves in the worst possible position, fighting a suicidal and determined foe within the confines of a tightly enclosed space. That was never part of their plan.

Dmitry Beliakov was with a Russian Special Forces (Alfa) Assault team:

At 7 a.m. on Friday I was with Alfa special forces – Russia's answer to the SAS – when the radio call came through, loud and clear: "You are not in reserve any more. Get ready."

As a *Sunday Times* photographer, I was granted special access to Alfa when they were sent to tackle the hostage crisis in Beslan. I listened as the unit was ordered to prepare 30 men to storm the school where hundreds of men, women and children were being held hostage. During the next 45 minutes the commanders of Alfa – one of two elite units dispatched to the Ossetian town of Beslan – discussed tactics and options.

I never heard anyone question whether they were going to storm the building. The only question was when and how the assault should take place. The commanders clearly believed that the only way to rescue the people inside was to attack.

The officers were calm and professional as they gave their orders: "You will be responsible for evacuation; you for machinegunners. If a commander is wounded you will do this and you will go there."

We had arrived in Beslan at 1 a.m. the day before. Alfa's first mission had been to link up with the crack troops from the interior ministry. Eventually they found them camped out in the dark, in a derelict radio training college. It was opposite the school where the hostages where being held. Only 100 yards and a railway track lay between us and the building.

I could make out a dead man lying outside the school, next to an electricity pylon. In his mid-thirties, he had obviously been shot and was covered in blood. His body slowly baked in the 29°C heat. By the end of that day the smell of his rotting corpse would fill our nostrils.

At first light, I and three soldiers crept round the school in a horseshoe shape to try to get to grips with the territory. It was confusing: there were lots of people wearing camouflage and carrying Kalashnikovs. Some were local police, others were just local people with weapons.

As we made our way round the school we came to a narrow alley and had to crawl to avoid the sniper fire. I could not see the snipers, but I could hear and feel their bullets behind my ears. Twice when we ran from one corner of the building to another, I heard loud booms as rocket-propelled grenades were launched at us. Clouds of dust and rubble enveloped me.

In every house and garden we saw armed local people watching. They tried to help the Russian soldiers as best they could, describing the layout of the school complex and pointing out the various buildings.

We knew the hostage takers were well armed – just how well suddenly became clear when I saw dust from their bullets flick up behind the feet of the officer in front of me. The Chechens were training their sniper rifles on us.

To get out of range we would have to scale two nearby fences. The first Alfa man jumped onto the first fence and aimed covering fire at the rebels while we three others threw ourselves over. I have never jumped so fast in my life. Back in the radio college we examined the school windows to try to determine the location of the snipers – all the while ducking to make sure that we were not visible. They fired at us several times through the windows anyway. We stayed in the college until the end of the day, when we were ordered to evacuate to the town centre and Alfa unit headquarters.

Next morning the orders were given. The interior ministry forces were to back up the security ministry special forces, who would act as the frontline strike troops.

Alfa waited for their orders. Finally we were taken to an old five-storey apartment block 50 yards from the school, from which all the residents had been evacuated. The soldiers installed themselves in a fourth-floor flat.

The windows of the whole block were soon full of snipers and Alfa machinegunners. Nikolai, a 34–year old sniper who has spent 15 years with special forces, kept watch, trying to pick off the Chechen snipers. The radio would crackle with a coded command: "Light house one" was the order, instructing him which floor to fire at.

Suddenly, at 1:02 p.m., we heard a powerful explosion. We were used to the bangs, as the Chechens were firing rocket-propelled grenades into our building, but I saw Nikolai with a mad look on his face dash into his sniper position – a table with a chair on top fixed with sandbags.

"These bastards are blowing up the school," he shouted. Then there was another explosion and two other Alfa men opened fire on the school, covering hostages who were fleeing from out of its windows.

Through a broken door I saw a shocking scene: the hostages, some of them almost naked, running, in shock and covered in blood. A middle-aged woman was bleeding badly from her head and a near-naked girl, about 14, was running for her life. Everyone was covered in blood as they tried to cross the playground to get to garage buildings where they could take cover.

Throughout the afternoon powerful blasts continued to shake the area. Much of the school was under government control by 7 p.m. By the end of the day three men from the Alfa unit had been killed – prompting commanders to call for tanks, which fired upon the school to try to take out the remaining rebels. It was about 8.45 p.m. when we left the compound and returned to Alfa headquarters. I found that two of the men I had accompanied earlier had suffered shrapnel wounds.

Back at base we drank in silence to the memory of their fallen comrades and dead hostages. We were very depressed; as the Russians say, "below the floor".

## On 7 September Ben Hoyle reported:

The only hostage-taker captured in the Beslan school siege claimed last night that the raid was ordered by the Chechen rebel leader Asian Maskhadov and radical warlord Shamil Basayev to "provoke a war across the Caucasus".

Speaking in a slurred and halting voice the man, who appeared to be from the Caucasus and is believed to be called Nur-Pashi Kulayev, described how he had been involved in the raid.

He said: "They gathered us in a forest, a person known as 'commander', said that we must seize a school in Beslan. They said this task was ordered by Maskhadov and Basayev."

The chief investigator of the Northern Caucasus prosecutor's office said that the hostage-takers had also taken part in an armed raid in Ingushetia in June that left up to 90 dead and was "organized by Basayev" – the first time he has been linked to last week's attack by a public official.

The captured suspect also told Russian state television that there were Uzbeks, Arabs and Chechens among the hostage-takers, but it was not clear whether he was speaking under duress.

Umar Sikoyevi, the suspect's lawyer, claimed that the group's leader had not told the hostage-takers what their mission was before the raid. After the seizure a fierce argument broke out, with several terrorists saying that seizing children as hostages was wrong. Their commander shot and killed the dissidents' leader, then detonated the suicide belts worn by two women raiders by remote control to re-establish order, Mr Sikoyevi claimed.

Russian media claimed large quantities of arms and explosives had been smuggled into the school in the months before by concealing them in building materials.

When they launched their operation last Wednesday, the hostage-takers would have known that they had access to enough military equipment to withstand a long siege. Ruslan Aushev, a former President of Ingushetia and the only mediator to enter Middle School No 1 during the three-day standoff, said that negotiations with the hostage-takers had been going on when fighting erupted:

"We gave the order to stop firing but there was a third force, these popular militias who decided to liberate the hostages on their own. The hostage takers said: 'You are shooting at us, it's the attack. We are going to blow everything up.' Everything went wrong due to these stupid civilians."

Russian security sources said that the planners of the raid were believed to have scouted at least two schools in Beslan.

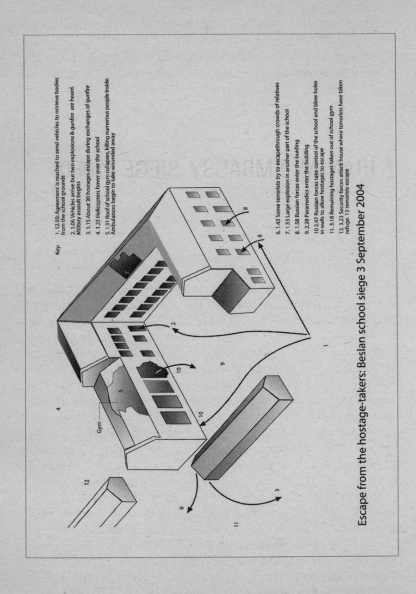

Key:

1. 12.50 Agreement is reached to send vehicles to retrieve bodies from the school grounds

2. 1.06 Vehicles arrive but two explosions & gunfire are heard. Military assault begins

3. 1.15 About 30 hostages escape during exchanges of gunfire

4. 1.25 Helicopters hover over the school

5. 1.31 Roof of school gym collapses, killing numerous people inside. Ambulances begin to take wounded away

6. 1.43 Some terrorists try to escape through crowds of relatives

7. 1.53 Large explosion in another part of the school

8. 1.58 Russian forces enter the building

9. 2.28 Paramedics enter the building

10. 2.47 Russian forces take control of the school and blow holes in walls to allow hostages to escape

11. 3.18 Remaining hostages taken out of school gym

12. 3.23 Security forces attack house where terrorists have taken refuge. 13 terrorists escape

Escape from the hostage-takers: Beslan school siege 3 September 2004

# IRANIAN EMBASSY SIEGE (1980)

*The SAS (Special Air Service) was formed in North Africa in 1941, to attack airfields behind enemy lines. It was disbanded at the end of WWII. The SAS was reformed during the 1950s for counter insurgency service in Malaya, Oman, Yemen and Borneo. During the 1970s its duties expanded to include anti-terrorist operations.*

*Palestinian terrorists took members of the Israeli Olympic team hostage at the Munich Olympics in 1972. The hostages died during a rescue attempt by the German police; immediately afterwards, the SAS was ordered to form an anti-terrorist unit to rescue hostages. An anti-terrorist unit unit was to be on duty at all times, trained for situations in which terrorists and their hostages were in a confined space.*

*In 1980, individual SAS troopers were armed with Hechler & Koch MP5 sub-machine guns and Browning 9mm pistols. In addition they used stun grenades and wall blasting charges. They called them "flash bangs" and "Harvey wallbangers". Once they were inside a building, their standard technique was to open a door, throw a flash bang into the room, close the door then burst in immediately after the explosion.*

*On 30 April 1980, Police Constable Trevor Locke was on*

*duty outside the Iranian Embassy in Knightsbridge, London.
He was a member of the Diplomatic Protection Group. He was
standing outside the front door, in uniform but unarmed. At
11.25 a.m. he heard gunfire. He only had time to send a
warning through his lapel radio before he was grabbed by some
gunmen and pulled inside the building. Chris Cramer, a BBC
producer, was inside, trying to obtain a visa. Cramer, Locke
and twenty-four others became hostages.*

PC Locke:

> I remember the gun going off, Brp! Very close. I fell back; I
> thought I'd been shot. Within minutes they had secured the
> building.

Cramer:

> This little tiny Arabic looking guy with a kafir and kind of
> little bulgy eyes started to hop around the room with a pistol
> and this bright green hand grenade in one hand, which
> certainly got my attention.

A police anti-terrorist squad moved into the building next
door to gather information. 6 Troop, B squadron, SAS, was
the anti-terrorist unit on duty at their headquarters in
Herefordshire. At 11.48 they were alerted and drove up
to London.

Within minutes, armed police and news teams surrounded the building. A police unit began negotiations
with the gunmen. The gunmen identified themselves as
Kuzistanis, and their leader identified himself as Salim.
They were protesting against the ill-treatment of Kuzistanis by the Iranian regime led by the Ayatollah Khomeini.
They demanded an autonomous state of Kuzistan and the
release of 91 Kuzistanis held prisoner in Iran. John Dellow
was the Deputy Assistant Commissioner of the Metropolitan Police Force. Dellow:

> What we were concerned about was finding out how serious

was their intent, isolating them, making sure that we talked to them nicely and hoped that they were going to come out and let us have the hostages and things would calm down, but all the indications in this one were that this was rather more serious than that.

The next day, 1 May, the hostage, Chris Cramer, became ill and was released. Before he was allowed to leave, PC Locke told him:

> OK, Chris, but don't forget once you get out you've got to tell them on the outside, there are six of them, they've got two machine pistols, three Brownings, a snub nosed forty-five, hand grenades and spare ammunition. You've got to tell them on the outside. He said: "Don't worry, I'll do that."

He was able to pass on the information. When the SAS troop arrived, they immediately made contact with the caretaker of the building. He told them that the ground and first floor windows were armoured. The police ordered the Gas Board to start drilling in the street outside to drown out the sounds made by the anti-terrorist squad's operations. Planes were diverted to fly low over the building.

After dark, 6 Troop, B squadron, SAS entered the building next door to the embassy. They identified a potential entry point through the skylight on the embassy roof. They also pre-positioned abseil ropes in case they were needed. The police fitted microphones and keyhole cameras for surveillance.

The gunmen demanded that they should be allowed to broadcast their demands, then they might release the hostages. They asked for an autonomous state of Kuzistan and the release of 91 Kuzistanis held prisoner in Iran. The Jordanian, Algerian and Iraqi ambassadors were to negotiate on their behalf. Their demands were broadcast but they did not release any hostages.

By 5 May, the sixth day, negotiations were breaking down. PC Locke:

They got us to sit facing the wall with our hands behind the back of our heads. They were clicking these guns. I could feel the hairs on the back of my neck standing proud with fear and I thought they were really going to do it.

At 6.50 p.m. they shot the Iranian press officer and pushed his body out of the front door.

The SAS Assault team was divided into two sections. They were designated Red and Blue. Red was responsible for the top three floors, while Blue was responsible for the lower three floors. They planned a simultaneous assault from the front and back onto all six floors of the building. Robin Horsfall was a member of the Red section of the SAS Assault team. He and another trooper were to abseil from the roof down to an outside balcony on the second floor, which would be their assault position. Horsfall:

We weren't going to go in unless anyone was killed, but if anyone was killed it was highly likely we would. That had come straight from Downing Street as far as we were concerned. We knew that [Prime Minister] Margaret Thatcher's policy was 'We do not negotiate with terrorists' and we had already been given the nod that if anyone was killed we were going in . . . We moved closely up to the building; we got onto the back door and the roof. The ropes were attached and prepared. Everyone was ready to go. The next stage was for everyone to move on to their assault positions.

The assault was authorized. Negotiations continued to distract the gunmen. The negotiators were actually talking to Salim, who was saying: "We are listening to suspicious movement . . . there is suspicion; just a minute, I'll come back, I'm going to check . . ."

At 7:18 p.m. TV cameras saw men in black, wearing balaclavas and respirators, moving about on the roof. What they were filming was the SAS Blue and Red sections moving to their assault positions on the balconies. Robin

Horsfall was abseiling down to the third floor rear windows. Horsfall:

I looked and there was Tom hanging from his rope. He'd got his glove caught in his abseil equipment. The curtains had caught fire from the flames from one of the stun grenades that had gone in. The flames had started to sweep up the window and you could hear him screaming down the radio. I looked up and there was absolutely nothing I could do. I thought, if someone doesn't cut him down he's going to burn to death. The guys on the roof are looking down over the edge at him. As he's pushing himself away from the flames, he's pushing himself beyond the balcony, so if they cut him down at the wrong moment he'd fall forty feet down to solid concrete. They're trying to cut the rope when he was on the in-swing; they succeeded in getting him down and saving his life.

As a hostage appeared, crawling on the front balcony, PC Locke saw Salim go for his gun. Locke:

I ran as hard as I could towards him and I managed to hit him with my shoulder in the hip and ran him back nearly eight to ten feet towards an office door. I had him, we were facing towards the door and he was going nowhere. [I heard a voice say] "Trevor, get away." I let go of him and I rolled over to look at the door where the voice came from; and there he was; this guy standing there who knew me personally as Trevor and I didn't know him from Adam. He was dressed in black overalls with this futuristic-looking gun and balaclava. I rolled over and immediately I heard BRRP! I looked back and there was Salim lying absolutely lifeless. He had a line of bullet holes going at a diagonal from his eye across his chest.

Mac was another SAS trooper in Blue team. He was one of two troopers who were chasing a gunman through the smoke filled corridors. Mac:

We put a smoke grenade in, lots of smoke, we go in but we can't find him, but we know he's in there, torches come across; both the torches hit the guy at the same time and he's lying there: a couple of rounds, bang, bang, job done.

The flash bangs had started fires throughout the building. Hunting the gunmen was difficult because it was almost impossible to distinguish them from the hostages. The SAS troopers began to get everyone out of the building. As the hostages came down the staircase, close together, there were gunmen among them. Only the hostages knew who they were. Horsfall:

Up on the stairs there was a voice that shouted: "He's a terrorist! He's a terrorist!" and we saw someone stumble down the stairs. But if the guys on the stairs had opened fire there was a danger of a bullet going through him and hitting someone behind and nobody could actually open fire.

Mac:

Someone shouted, "Grenade!" He had a grenade in his hand. As he came clear, at the bottom of the staircase, there was me and two others. We fired a burst each and the guy had twenty-seven bullet holes in him. There was no drama. His body just went pfft! He was on the ground, dead.

During the confusion one hostage was shot by a gunman. Only one gunman survived. He was caught trying to hide among the hostages. It was the first time the SAS had acted openly or, as its founder put it: "the first time it had hunted its fox in public." That evening, the Prime Minister, Margaret Thatcher, congratulated them.

# MARINE SNIPERS IN NAM (1966–7)

*In 1966 John J. Culbertson was a sniper with the Second
Battalion, Fifth Regiment (2/5) US Marines. He served with
the legendary sniper Tom Casey.*

*According to Culbertson, the Viet Cong were using small
patrols of infantry, with three man sniper cells attached, to
ambush the daily Marine sweeps from their firebase at Phu Loc
6 north of An Hoa.*

*First they would wait until a patrol walked along a trail
bordering a rice paddy. Once the patrol had been seen by Viet
Cong sympathizers, information about its numbers and the
direction of its march would be passed to the Viet Cong. Then
the Viet Cong would select a prepared ambush site further
down the trail. They preferred to use hides where they could
preset distances into their scopes.*

*They would begin their attack by sniping the most important
patrol members: first the point man, then the radio man,
followed by the non-commissioned officer or officer in charge
of the patrol. Sometimes they might open an attack by setting
off a command-detonated mine or booby-trap. This was supposed to confuse the patrol members and cause panic and
confusion further down the column. The radio man was a*

*vital target because he could call up air support or the fire-*
*base's powerful artillery. An Hoa's 105mm and 155mm guns*
*were powerful enough to penetrate the strongest bunkers.*

*After they had fired their sniper weapons at individual*
*targets, the Viet Cong would rake the kill zone with automatic*
*fire from their AK-47 rifles. They would try to pick off any*
*wounded or exposed Marines; then they would break off the*
*engagement before they received any return fire.*

*The Marines reacted to these ambushes by attaching coun-*
*tersniper teams to the patrols. When the patrol was ambushed,*
*the snipers would be marching in the middle of the column.*
*Upon contact they would deploy to return accurate fire on the*
*Viet Cong marksmen. Alternatively they might drop off the*
*patrol's main body and take up a position where they could*
*scan the treelines and hillsides. With binoculars and rifle*
*scopes, they could pick up movement in the deep jungle.*

*The Marines were organized into two-man teams: a shooter*
*and a spotter. The shooter was equipped with a M1-D sniper*
*rifle with a telescopic sight (scope). The spotter had an M-14*
*rifle and binoculars.*

On 10 June 1966 Sergeant Tom Casey joined the Fifth
Marine sniper platoon, which was being formed on Hill 35
south of Chu Lai. On one of his first patrols he tested the
marines' countersniper tactics. He was dropped off as his
patrol rounded a hillside surrounded by jungle. He took up
position in a camouflaged hide, then waited as the patrol
moved across the paddy dikes towards a treeline 500 metres
away. Casey's rifle swept the open fields until the first shots
from a Viet Cong sniper cell broke the silence and wounded
a Marine.

Casey focused his sights on the area where the muzzle
blast had flared. When the sniper came up for a second shot,
Casey aimed a yard high and squeezed the trigger. The
30.06 bullet from his Garand sniper rifle penetrated the
sniper's layer. He fired a second time as soon as his rifle had
settled, then a third time. The strike was audible. The Viet
Cong sniper was knocked back from his hole's parapet and
dashed against his partner with a bloody wound in his chest.

There was no more Viet Cong fire. Tom Casey and his spotter, Lance Corporal Vaughn Nickell, got up from their leafy hide and rejoined their comrades on the trail. Tom Casey knew that if there had been two Viet Cong sniper teams he and Nickell might have been killed themselves.

During the next few days Casey and Nickell worked with first Alpha and then Bravo companies of First Battalion, Fifth Marines. They killed a Viet Cong sniper who exposed too much of his upper torso when his team ambushed Casey's patrol. Nickell shot him from two hundred metres offhand (standing) after the first flight of bullets flew harmlessly overhead. Casey and his spotter prevented half a dozen other ambushes from proving fatal.

In November 1966 the gun pits of the Eleventh Marines 155mm howitzer battery was being attacked by Viet Cong suicide troops known as sappers. These attackers crawled through the paddies and muddy clay right up to the wire of the camp at Chu Lai. They shoved box mines and crude bamboo bangalore torpedoes through the Marines' wire obstructions. After they had set them off, the sapper commander would send his demolition teams directly at the artillery pieces to destroy or disable the guns with additional explosive charges. They had managed to cause extensive damage to several of the howitzers.

Casey deployed the Marines of the sniper platoon in pairs to act as outpost sentinels and ambush teams. Casey and Nickell found a small crevasse-like fold in the earth about a kilometre out. They scanned back and forth along sections of the camp's wire, looking for movement. They did not notice anything until their night vision improved, but after fifteen minutes Casey heard a scratching sound. It sounded like something was being dragged or pulled through the dirt towards the Marines lines. They peered in the direction of the sound until they could just make out the shape of men crawling towards the wire: Viet Cong sappers, but they were so close that if Casey fired he and Nickell might be hit by Marine counterfire from the security bunkers. The security bunkers were armed with M-60 machine guns and M-79 grenade launchers.

The sappers reached the wire before Casey decided what to do. He asked Nickell: "Tell me, you still got those two Willy-Pete grenades you carry on you?" Nickell handed Casey a grenade of the type he wanted.

They each threw one of the white phosphorus grenades together. The Viet Cong sappers were exposed by the brillant white light of the exploding grenades, and the sappers immediately blew their initial charges. Then the Viet Cong shouldered their weapons and tried to fight their way into the perimeter.

After five minutes of tracer, explosions and chaos, the Marines' machine guns and high-explosive grenades drove the remnants of the Viet Cong sapper platoon back. Two Viet Cong soldiers stumbled by Casey and Nickell's hide. They never saw Casey and Nickell before the snipers shot the Viet Cong sappers at point blank range. Shortly afterwards the snipers yelled out, "Marine patrol coming in."

On 13 November 1966 Sergeant Tom Casey was given permanent command of Fifth Marine Regimental Sniper Platoon. He was given the task of training all new sniper recuits, keeping the teams fit for combat and rotating ambush teams and patrols. He led as many ambushes as he could himself – ensuring that his men acquired the techniques of night movement, noise discipline and the sense to know when to fire or when silence and caution were necessary.

On 3 January 1967 Casey, with Ron Willoughby as his spotter, was accompanying a patrol from Hotel Company 2/5, led by Sergeant Manny Ybarra. They were in an area which was new to them, twenty five miles southwest of Da Nang. They had dropped off the column and were looking for it when they spotted a file of soldiers step out of the treeline and turn away from the snipers' hillside hide out and follow the Hotel Company patrol. Casey whispered: "Man, those men are armed, and I can see weapons even at this distance. We got to warn the patrol or those bastards will sneak up on their rear and cut them off from us."

Willoughby replied: "I make them about 500 metres at

the rear and 600 metres when their point man crosses that big dike trail up ahead. See if you can target the length of their column, and you'll hit somebody and then Sergeant Ybarra will be forewarned. What do you think?"

Casey wasn't pleased but he rested his rifle on a branch and dialled in 600 metres of elevation. The wind was blowing directly into his face. He dismissed it as a negligible factor. He aimed dead on the leading Viet Cong. He reckoned that if his estimate of the distance was wrong he would hit the man behind the leading Viet Cong. He allowed up to forty-five inches for bullet drop but he knew that he was shooting down a slope, so the target could appear closer than it really was – perhaps as far as 800 metres. The column was seven soldiers and a black-clad woman who might have been a Viet Cong nurse. She was definitely a combatant and they were all armed.

He kept his target in his crosshairs until he had taken up all the trigger slack and the rifle had discharged. The blast and concussion from the rifle broke the eerie silence of the jungle. When the rifle settled back onto the point man, there was a gap behind him and a figure sprawled on the trail. All the other members of the patrol had scattered into the treeline.

An hour later Ybarra and his patrol came towards their hillside and waved for the snipers to join them. He admitted they had "saved our chilli when you shot that gook. I owe you boys a couple of Shlitz beers when we get back to An Hoa. Remember, don't never come back the same way as you go out." Casey had noticed that the patrol had approached their hillside from a different side of the rice valley to that which they had taken before.

On 24 January 1967, Willoughby and Casey, with four other snipers, were ordered to go on an operation to search out and destroy the experienced R-20th Main Force Battalion of the Viet Cong in the area known as the Arizona Territory. Two reinforced Rifle Companies of the 2/5 Marines were chosen to do this. One of the two was Hotel Company which was based at the river outpost of Phu Loc 6, six miles northeast of An Hoa.

Hotel Company had been making daily patrols around the Arizona Territory's villages and hamlets. Their purpose was to make the Marines' presence known and to try to win the hearts and minds of the local villagers. The local villagers' leaders were being interrogated by the Viet Cong, who would torture or kill anyone who showed sympathy towards the Americans, especially teachers or doctors.

As soon as the Marines had left, the Viet Cong would return to the village and resume their pressure on the villagers. It was a situation which the Marines were losing, unless they could force the Viet Cong main force into a conventional battle in which they could inflict sufficient casualties to allow the small Marine patrols to resume their pacification of the villages.

The regular Communist forces were highly elusive. Their strategy was to bleed the US Marine and Army patrols in order to wear out the resolve of the US public. Culbertson's opinion was that the North Vietnamese and Viet Cong leaders knew that the war was misunderstood in the US. In particular, the North Vietnamese general Vo Nugyen Giap knew that the war was becoming unpopular with an increasingly misinformed population who had lost interest in anything outside the continental United States. Culbertson reckoned that the Vietnamese must have been thrilled by the daily features in the US newspapers which described riots and unrest among anti-war protesters on nearly every college campus in America.

It was the opinion of the Marine sniper that the North Vietnamese and Viet Cong leaders hoped that bleeding the American military for long enough would create considerable distrust of the US President and his generals among the fathers and mothers of the killed and wounded. If they could do this, perhaps, the US population as a whole would grow tired of the conflict and pull out.

Culbertson considered that General Giap was a shrewd and brutal tactician. His military operations against the French had resulted in their total rout and destruction at Dien Bien Phu in 1954. His northern Viet Minh had been the forerunners of the southern Viet Cong. They had cut off the French forces, then destroyed their elite airborne and Foreign Legion units piecemeal.

In 1967 Giap intended to use the Viet Cong to spearhead major pitched battles against the Americans. From these battles he would learn the finer points of his opponents' strategy. Eventually, he hoped to deprive the US of the will to continue the struggle. His ultimate strategy would be to send North Vietnamese regular Army (NVA) units into South Vietnam. Not only would they cross the Demilitarized Zone (DMZ) but they would also come down the complex of jungle paths which would become known as the Ho Chi Minh Trail. The trail ran through the neighbouring states of Laos and Cambodia.

Giap expected that the Army of the Republic of Vietnam would collapse by the early 1970s without their better-trained and equipped American allies. What the North Vietnamese leaders feared was a direct US attack on the north. Their dilemma was to decide whether to hold back their best troops to guard against this or to commit them to the battle to bleed the Americans in the south. Ho Chi Minh agreed with his leading general that they should inflict as many casualties as possible on the Americans to lessen their determination. Their own people would suffer greatly, but they would hide their own losses so that their enemy never discovered how close to victory they really were.

At Phu Loc 6, northeast of An Hoa, the sniper platoon was told that two teams of snipers would be attached to Hotel and Foxtrot companies for the operation against the Main Force of the Viet Cong Battalion in Arizona Territory. Sergeant Tom Casey was not happy about this because he would not be allowed to go with his snipers himself. Lieutenant Colonel Airheart, the commanding Officer of 2/5 Marines, considered Casey to be a "bush-smart NCO" and he wanted him at Headquarters "when the lead started cutting into his Marines". Operation Tuscaloosa would begin with the two companies advancing to the Song Thu Bon river. Foxtrot would take the main highway north of the river. Hotel would march off the west side of Phu Loc 6 and cross at Liberty Bridge. Hotel and Foxtrot would join up in the vicinity of the firebase at My Loc 2 where they would be within range of its heavy artillery. They could also receive air support from the First Marine Air Wing at Da Nang.

John J. Culbertson was a Private First Class (PFC) in third platoon, Hotel Company 2/5 Marines. He was third platoon's "shooter" (designated marksman). At 1800 a Viet Cong sniper took two shots at the entrance to the command post bunker. No one was hit but the platoon commander, Second Lieutenant Smith, was extremely annoyed because this had become a regular event: "Dammit, it's that mal-adjusted VC son of a bitch Six O'clock Charlie taking target practice at my hootch again. Captain Doherty [CO of Hotel Company] wants this pint-sized asshole put to sleep. Where is my shooter? Culbertson, you psycho, Okie bastard! Where are you when I need you?"

Culbertson was actually grazed on his shoulder by Six O'clock Charlie's next shot. The same round hit Charlie Mexico in the buttock. Culbertson helped check Charlie Mexico for damage. A medevac chopper was called by radio and air lifted the wounded man out.

Lieutenant Smith told Culbertson: "PFC Culbertson, you are an expert rifleman are you not? You will position yourself each evening beside my bunker in a camouflaged fighting hole and kill that Commie sniper next time he dares to shoot at the command post. Do you read me?" Culbert-son was wary of inexperienced young officers who might get him killed; he replied: "Sir, I'd be glad to take a shot at Six O'clock Charlie for you, but this M-14's got no scope and the stock is wet and swelled up to beat Hell. Sir, I don't know if I can hit the little bastard with one shot and he may disappear if I miss. I hate to miss, sir!" Despite Culbert-son's protests about the state of his weapon, he was ordered to report to the command bunker the next day at 1500.When he reported for the duty, he was told to dig in and return fire when Six O'clock Charlie fired at Lieu-tenant Smith.

Just at that moment, Casey and Willoughby walked past.

Lieutenant Smith asked them who they were. After they had told him, he asked them to help Culbertson take out Six O'clock Charlie.

The next day Casey studied the ground which Six O'clock Charlie was using to take shots at the command post bunker. He found a small group of rocks that jutted out from a slanting mound about 400 metres from the perimeter wire at two o'clock.

Six O'clock Charlie impressed Casey by his approach route to the group of rocks: "Smart little asshole can crawl up to his position while the dyin' sun blinds our eyes to the southwest around six o'clock. That's why the bastard is so punctual. He's got to come directly into his hole with the sunset or he'd be spotted."

There was something alse about Six O'clock Charlie that amused Casey. Despite the fact that some Marines had deliberately exposed themselves to the Viet Cong sniper out of bravado or boredom, he hadn't hit any of them. He could move like a phantom but he "couldn't hit old Maggie's drawers" (US Marine slang for a missed shot). The Marine snipers concluded that Six O'clock Charlie "can't hit nothing, but he might just get lucky!"

At about 1745, Ron Willoughby was in a tight sitting position scanning the fields with his rifle's scope. He wondered why Vaughn Nickell was "hidin' in the bottom of his bunker". Suddenly a shot rang out. Vaughn Nickell yelled at Willoughby, "The little rat bastard is shootin' at you, for Chrissake. Get down, man! There's only dead heroes."

The next shot was only inches over Nickell and Willoughby but Casey saw the muzzle flash way off on the hillside about a thousand metres distant. Only a lucky shot would hit a Marine at that range. It was too far even for Casey's plan to return fire. They would have to let him get closer. Willoughby spotted for Nickell as the Viet Cong sniper crawled towards them. Culbertson:

Willoughby caught the slightest glimmer of movement over the paddy, along a ditch where the Viet Cong was working his way closer to the Marine lines. He pointed out the direction to Vaughn with his hand, making a chopping motion toward the ditch. Vaughn soon picked up the movement, although at that extreme distance he couldn't see a weapon or the sniper's face, even though he was looking dead on. He let the Vietnamese come directly on as he flicked off the safety inside the trigger housing and started taking up the trigger slack. Vaughn guessed the shot was over a thousand meters, but he figured that if Charlie got up and ran, he would only make a much bigger target. The aim point was definitely a guesstimate about six feet over a center mass hold, as if the target had been dead on at 300 meters. The trigger broke cleanly and the rifle bucked, throwing the scope out of eye focus until the muzzle again found its aim point.

Dammit! Charlie was still there and crawling ahead undaunted. Willoughby had seen the round impact with his $7.5 \times 50$ power binoculars. The bullet had broken ground slightly left about one meter and another meter short and, ricocheting over the paddies, had splashed down a half mile farther down the valley. Ron spoke to Nickell as the M1-D came up into the shooter's shoulder for the second shot. "Your windage is a titch left, so come right a hair and hold about three feet higher or about two titches, whichever feels right. Okay, brother, let's kill this fucker."

After the snipers had joked about the fine adjustments to his aim that were necessary, Willoughby saw Nickell's second shot hit the Viet Cong sniper in the head. It had been one of the longest shots in the history of Vietnam sniping.

Later Casey warned Nickell: "You know there's more than one Six O'clock Charlie. Hell, every Marine outpost in Vietnam has some Viet Cong guerillas trying to get famous by wasting one of our asses." Casey continued to scan the valley behind the firebase. He let his vision focus for a moment on any feature that could provide cover and concealment for another Viet Cong sniper.

After half an hour, another shot rang out as a bullet whined and cracked over Casey and Willoughby's fighting hole. Casey scanned his front with his binoculars. A second shot came in. Then Casey picked out a small mound of earth and rocks about 400 metres to his left front. He brought his rifle up to his shoulder and let the barrel fall to its natural point of aim. He snugged his left arm into the hasty sling as he brought his left hand along the gunstock, steadying his aim. The scope came into focus and he waited for the enemy sniper to show himself. Vaughn Nickell was watching through his binoculars as Six O'clock Charlie number two exposed himself. He was shouldering his Moishin-Nagant sniper rifle: a weapon of Second World War vintage but deadly enough in capable hands.

The .30 calibre bullet from Casey's M1-D blew Six O'clock Charlie number two's head into "a violent red spray of blood and tissue that never ceased to amaze the Marine snipers".

By January 1967, Captain Jerry Doherty was an experienced company commander and was the CO of Hotel Company 2/5 Marines. He had personally led his Marines through the rice paddies of the An Hoa basin as they searched for the enemy units that harassed the civilian population if they even showed deference to the Americans. Colonel Airheart, CO of 2/5 Marines, decided to add Hotel Company to his operation against the Viet Cong in the Arizona territory. Arizona territory was an area between the converging Vu Gia and Thu Bon rivers, which the Viet Cong were using as a sanctuary.

Airheart told Doherty: "Jerry, I know your Marines have run the paddies hard the last few weeks. The brass have ordered a full scale attack on Go Noi island next week . . . Intelligence advises that the R-20th Main Force Regiment is occupying Go Noi island and launching harassing and interdiction operations against our patrols along the river . . . I feel I have no choice but to order Hotel Company to take the field again and spearhead the battalion into the attack."

Doherty protested that his company was not only "worn

pretty thin" but had lost their best platoon commander to a "freak explosive device" the previous week. Despite his protest, Doherty and the commander of Foxtrot Company, Captain George Burgett, left the briefing resigned to do their solemn duty.

On 24 January the three sniper teams attached to the operation set out. Their role was to screen the Marines' front as they went into the attack.

PFC Culbertson was learning how to be a point man on the job, like a real apprentice. He was learning from Hotel Company's chief point scout John Lafley. Lafley was part Sallish Indian and a master of the "approach march". Culbertson was walking "trace" or second scout position in the column. Lafley occasionally pointed out mounds of earth, depressions, thickets or cuts in the terrain that could conceal an enemy sniper team who would "fire up" into the column then disappear into their spider holes.

After marching for four hours, the company commanders ordered their platoon commanders to form their platoons into defensive perimeters for the night. They dug their foxholes and set up their machine guns with their interlocking fields of fire. In addition they sent out ambush teams to provide security along likely enemy approach routes. Willoughby and Nickell went with Culbertson's ambush team. The snipers were chosen for their ability to accurately call in close artillery support against large enemy formations. They were forbidden to engage any enemy formation of platoon strength or larger.

Nickell focused his binoculars on a group of farmers who looked like the local Viet Cong guerillas who guided ambush teams towards the Marine perimeters. The Marines brought up their rifles and flicked off their safety catches. Nickell told them: "Hold your fire, boys. That file of gooks is only farmers, they've got no weapons and they're two women in the group. If they don't come any closer, we've got to let 'em go."

The next day, the Marines left the Thu Bon river behind and headed into the glistening green mountains of the Arizona Territory. Willoughby and Nickell marched in the middle of the column, waiting for the column to come under fire. Then they would hear "Snipers up!" and it would be their duty to run through the incoming bullets to the point and take counter sniper meassures. John Lafley or another point scout would guide the snipers to a shallow depression or irrigation ditch from where the position and range of the hostile sniper could be identified. The point scout would take over fire control of the platoon, giving the snipers time to take aim and despatch the hostile sniper.

Late in the afternoon, the Hotel point scout saw some Viet Cong soldiers running through the treelines towards a distant village. They might have been shadowing the Marine column and going to report to their main force on the Marines' progress. Lieutenant Smith called: "Snipers up!"

Willoughby and Nickell ran up to the point, which was by a shallow mound already manned by a dozen riflemen. Through his glasses Nickell saw the Viet Cong flicking in and out of patches of sunlight which penetrated the through the forest canopy.Willoughby recognized that this was an opportunity to find their main force by following them, but after another hour's marching it was obvious that the enemy troops were playing a game of cat and mouse with them. As the nightime shadows grew, they were ordered to take up their defensive positions for the night. At night the snipers' M1-D rifles were almost useless because of their scopes. Nickell also had an M-14 which he could rely on at night.

If they were attacked, the snipers' priority was to pick off the enemy leaders and machine gunners. During the night they heard automatic rifle fire less than 100 metres from their company lines. Willoughby used the scope of his M1-D t o try to see what was going on. Some Viet Cong were firing into a bamboo thicket, and their silhouettes were hidden behind a herd of cattle. Vietnamese voices and green tracers broke through the cover of the night, but the only incident that directly affected the snipers' column was "up" at their Listening Post (LP). The LP was manned by Culbertson and Lafley. It was Culbertson who had been "fired up".

When Willoughby met them, Lafley said: "Naw, Okla-
homa will be all right. He just learned to keep his young ass
real still on that LP last night. It was probably VC guerrillas
that shot his butt up. NVA troopers would've likely killed
his sorry ass for sure. Shit this ain't nothing! Bad Boy Burns
didn't even hardly wake up when the shootin' started. Just
maybe today we'll hit the Viet Cong main force. Then you
boys gonna really see the fur fly. Yes, Siree!"

The area known as Arizona Territory was infamous
because it was "a beehive of enemy traps and mines and
a maze of tunnels that could hide a large battalion-size force
from enemy air power or shelter an ambushing blocking
force from American artillery". Colonel Airheart, CO of
2/5 Marines, was well aware that invading Arizona Territory was a risky business. There were twenty-four enemy
battalions active in the surrounding areas, but Airheart's
mission was to search out and destroy the Viet Cong. If the
VC and NVA forces would not attack his base at An Hoa, he
had to send his forces to attack theirs.

26 January 1967 was to be the final day of Operation
Tuscaloosa. If they did not sight the enemy that day
Operation Tuscaloosa would be considered a failure. By
0900 both companies of Marines had reached the northern
bank of the Son Thu Bon river. By radio, Colonel Airheart
ordered Captain Doherty to take both companies across the
river to the friendly southern bank. Doherty and Burgett
agreed on their plan. Foxtrot would cross the single stream
of the river 1,000 metres to Hotel's left flank, and would
then be in a position to cover Hotel, which would advance
by platoons across the open sandbar of Football island.

The three sniper teams were divided between the companies. Willoughby and Nickell went with Hotel Company
as team one. Jim Flynn and Dennis Toncar also accompanied Hotel Company as team two. The third team, Loren
Kleppe and Ulysses Black, went with Foxtrot Company.

Once Foxtrot Company had crossed, the sniper teams
could set up positions from which to cover Hotel Company
when it crossed. Culbertson:

As Foxtrot moved down the riverbank and into position, Willoughby waved to Loren Kleppe as he faded into the green column whose point scouts had turned south, facing the single blue channel of fast-moving water. Foxtrot would cross their water obstacle at the far left extreme of the football-shaped sandbar island. After fording the four-foot-deep stream, the grunts would fan out into skirmish lines and assault into the high riverbanks. Once all the troops had crossed, the snipers would set up positions to provide covering fire for Hotel as they crossed the middle stretch of the sandbar.

As Willoughby and Nickell strained their eyes on the Foxtrot point scouts now splashing chest deep through the stream, they heard the loud reports of rifle fire. The Leathernecks of Foxtrot had no way to backtrack or deviate the direction of their advance, and in classic Marine Corps fashion the grunts hit the deck and returned fire at an almost invisible dug-in enemy. More Marines forded the stream and became pinned down under the withering fire of the Viet Cong's automatic weapons. The point fire team was well beyond the water and had started inching up the flanking banks when all hell broke loose. The gunmetal-gray cold sky was filled with the terrifying shrieks of 82mm mortar rounds as they arched downward into Foxtrot's column. The Marines formed a loose perimeter and got down along the sandbanks, trying to escape the deadly salvoes of high explosive.

Culbertson thought that the North Vietnamese were the finest mortar men in the world. They had used the weapon for years against the Japanese and then against the French. As well as the deadly barrage of mortar rounds, the Marines were pinned down by automatic fire. Culbertson:

The mortar rounds slammed with fiery vengeance into the Marine lines, where frightened young troopers held their helmets tight to their heads as they wriggled their bodies ever deeper into the sand dunes. An errant missile crashed into the unlucky command post group and severely wounded the company commander, Captain George Burgett, in the legs. Burgett's radio operator was cut into a bloody sack of mush by the direct hit and died instantly. Another rifleman felt the hot shards of shrapnel tear into his body as he tried to shoulder his weapon and return fire. The riflemen on the front edge of the perimeter kept shooting into the maze of tree-lined riverbank that stood a full thirty feet above their position just across the stream.

Targets were hard to find, but Loren Kleppe zeroed in on the muzzle flash of an enemy machine gunner. Kleppe's M1-D bucked as his heavy 173-grain match bullets tore into the Viet Cong gunners, flinging them back into their gun pit in a spray of blood flecks. Big pieces of flesh were sliced off their facial bones like the meat a butcher cleaves off a carcass when the blade nicks into a thick chunk of bone. The rhythm of the VC rifle and machine-gun fire picked up a nauseating cadence as the Marines were strafed time and again by devastating plunging fire.

On the sand banks the Marines of Foxtrot were waiting for the Hotel platoons to come to their rescue. Kleppe and Black were fighting back from a shallow hole which they had dug two feet into the sandbank. The artillery fire from two 105mm guns at An Hoa wasn't doing much damage to the enemy beyond raising dust to choking level But, every time the artillery gunners reloaded, two Viet Cong snipers popped up looking for targets. Loren Kleppe was lying prone in his hole, waiting for the chance of a quick head shot. Culbertson:

He saw a brave enemy sniper crawl over the lip of his trench and sight into his PU scope, mounted on an antiquated but deadly Moishin-Nagant sniper rifle. This was what Kleppe had trained for in the hot marshes and arid hills around Chu Lai. Few Marines ever experienced head-to-head duels with an enemy sniper, and even fewer ever actually killed one. Vaughn Nickell and Tom Casey had killed two enemy snipers off Phu Loc 6 back in December, but they were protected in their bunkers with a good field of fire off the hill. This shot would take an uphill angle into the foliage that covered the bank, with only the head and shoulders of the Viet Cong sniper visible from Kleppe's position.

The Viet Cong sniper's rifle barked, and a Marine who lay wounded on the flat ground above the stream twitched in agony as another enemy bullet burst through his leg. While the Marine yelled for help, Kleppe realized that he had to make the shot or the sniper would waste his buddies one at a time. The Viet Cong were masters at creating chaos and panic in the kill zones of their ambushes. They much preferred to wound a Marine than kill him outright since, the more casualties a sniper produced, the more Marines were required to tend his wounds. The Viet Cong also did not fail to understand the psychological damage to troop morale near a kill zone, when men had to endure the anguished moans and helpless agony of their wounded comrades.

The sniper's rifle spat leaden death into the Marine ranks again, and another youngster cried out in pain and mortal fear. Loren Kleppe raised his rifle above the bunker's lip and sighted in on a dark shadow that lay facing his bleeding brothers. The smoke and debris that had filtered over the battlefield made a clear sighting impossible. The Viet Cong sharpshooter no doubt felt a degree of safety, with the Marines bloodied and confused by mortar rounds still tearing into the sand dunes as they lay stunned and weary. Loren took up the trigger slack, and the M1-D bucked hard against his shoulder.

It was only 100 metres' range but there were no more shots from the Viet Cong sniper. Captain Doherty had called down artillery support as soon as the enemy fire had pinned down Foxtrot Company. They had called for the spotting round from a 155mm belonging to the "Steel Curtain" at An Hoa (Steel Curtain was the artillery's call sign). Doherty had to take over the command of Foxtrot as well as looking after his own company and adjusting the artillery.

Captain Doherty gave a sitrep and asked his battalion commander for orders. Colonel Airheart was a Second World War Pacific veteran and he knew that unless Hotel Company's platoons were committed his Marines would bleed to death if they stayed where they were. He ordered Doherty to cross the river. The Hotel Company platoons should set up on the sandbar until the artillery could be adjusted onto the enemy position. Then they could assault it frontally.

Hotel Company's second platoon with Willoughby and Nickell set off towards the sandbank. Third platoon, including Culbertson, advanced on their left.

The Marines forded the chest-high water with their M-14 rifles above their heads. It was even harder for the snipers carrying the M1-Ds with their delicate scopes. As soon as the Marines reached the sandbar island, it was "assholes and elbows". Each man burrowed into the dunes with hands, helmets and entrenching tools. The Viet Cong were highly disciplined and had allowed the Marines to come within 50 metres of their position before they had opened fire with their AK-47 assault rifles on automatic. Then they began firing B-40 rockets at virtually point blank range. Willoughby fired shot after shot at the enemy muzzle flashes coming from their trench line. Nickel fired snapshots from his M-14 at the enemy bunkers. They knew that they had to protect third platoon from sharing the same fate as the second platoon.

Culbertson himself crawled along the valleys between the sand dunes, trying to give aid to his wounded buddies. His rifle was jammed by a round stuck in the chamber. The sling was cut from his rifle and his canteen shattered on his hip. The mangled gore from a Marine wounded in the buttocks hit him in the face. He had reached the point of praying that he would serve God and his fellow man if he was allowed to live when the Marine artillery began to hit the Viet Cong bunkers.

The Viet Cong had opened fire at 0915. By 1030 Doherty was able to tell the artillery to "fire for effect": full salvoes of a round each from the four-gun battery of 155mm. Doherty could finally rally his men into the attack.

The snipers had achieved a defensive miracle on the sandbar. Willoughby thought they would have been more effective providing long range covering fire from the northern bank's bunkers. However, he approved of Doherty's handling of the situation. Doherty was well supported by his NCOs. Gunnery Sergeant Roberto Gutierrez of Hotel Company began to get the men on their feet to form an assault line.

Culbertson jumped to his feet to join the assault line. His weapon was clogged with sand and he couldn't even force a round into the chamber so he advanced with his useless M-14 at his hip mouthing, "bang, bang, bang, bang."

Before they reached the enemy trenches they could see that the artillery had already killed many of the Viet Cong defenders, but a squad of wounded soldiers had remained to defend their bunkers and slow down the Marines' advance. They suddenly appeared and fired at point blank range.

Willoughby and Nickell were among the first to return fire with deadly effect. Lafley shot all three of the crew of a water-cooled Maxim machine gun as it was being wheeled into position to strafe the assaulting Marines. That Maxim machine gun was made in 1908.

When Willoughby finally got over the riverbank, he saw for himself the remains of the R-20th Man Force battalion. The bodies of the Viet Cong soldiers lay in piles except where they had been dragged into bunkers by ropes. The Viet Cong always tried to bury or conceal their dead after a battle to confuse the American body count statistics.

Afterwards, Culbertson described the Viet Cong position as "a masteful U-shaped ambush of startling proportions." The major problem confronting the Marines was the Viet Cong's mastery of their own terrain.

After a short halt, Doherty had to order his platoons into the attack to trap and finish the Viet Cong survivors. The remaining Viet Cong had fallen back to the main force's secondary positions at La Bac 1 and La Bac 2. Once again, Willoughby and Nickell responded to the call of "Snipers up''. The Marines of Foxtrot Company were approaching a Viet Cong kill zone covered by mortars, machine guns and riflemen in spider holes.

Captain James A. Graham was in command of Foxtrot Company in the place of the wounded Captain Burgett. Faced with ground covered by mortars and heavy machine guns, he decided to bring up his sniper teams. He told the teams of Kleppe and Flynn to get into positions where they could fire into the mortar bunker. Captain Graham expected the machine gun to open fire to neutralize the threat to the mortar team. When they exposed themselves by opening fire, Willoughby and Nickell should kill the machine gunners; then the Marines would go in with riflemen and M-79 grenadiers.

Kleppe and Black approached the mortar position from the left. The mortar coughed somewhere near Kleppe. He crept towards the sound. After ten minutes of stealthy progress he saw the dark outline of the mound that hid the Viet Cong mortarmen. Ulysses Black looked through his binoculars for the guarding rifleman. Finally he saw a bush move as a VC sniper crawled to a more forward position. Kleppe brought his rifle to bear and focused his scope on the still moving bush tied to the sniper's back. His bullet kicked the enemy sniper's body over on its side. Another Viet Cong came up for a look and was in turn hit by a snap shot.

Willoughby and Nickell lay 100 meters to Kleppe's right. After the two shots from Kleppe's M1-D, Willoughby and Nickell heard one of the Viet Cong's RPD light machine guns trying to flush out the Marine sniper team. They had a long crawl before they closed in on the Viet Cong machine gun, which was about 40 metres ahead. Willoughby was in a low crouch looking at the machine gunners with his naked eyes when a VC rifleman appeared from nowhere. He was camouflaged with a mass of foliage fastened to his backpack and armed with a rifle and bayonet which he was already holding at high port. Willoughby knew that he couldn't bring his heavy sniper rifle up in time, but a terrific blast of rifle fire came from behind him. Nickell had snapped off the shot by looking only along the front sight of his M-14. At thirty metres he had shot the Viet Cong through the chest and he was just another Dead Right There (DRT).

The mortar crew was now trapped without supporting arms so Captain Graham called in an air strike. Ten minutes later a pair of F-4 Phantom jets came in and bombed the mortar position. The remaining Viet Cong were killed where they made their last stand at La Bac 2.

Upriver at La Bac 1, Lafley led Culbertson and the remaining men of third platoon into the hedgreows of a rubber plantation on the high ground above the river. They found several enemy bunkers. They called in artillery to destroy the bunkers.

It was the Marine snipers' first pitched battle.

The next major operation for the Marine snipers was codenamed Independence. Sergeant Casey chose the team of Dennis Toncar and Fred Sanders to accompany Golf Company 2/5 marines.

On 1 February 1967, Toncar and Sanders boarded a CH-46 Sea Knight helicopter. The snipers and Golf Company were flown south over the Que Son mountains towards a valley where the Marines were landed and deployed without incident. They formed columns abreast and began to march through the light brush towards some shallow hills. The point unit came under fire and the Marines went to ground. Toncar and Sanders tried to locate the muzzle flashes of the enemy gunners. Just as they saw the dust kicking up from the enemy muzzle blasts, an accurate burst of fire killed the Marine point man and wounded two other members of the point team. The Viet Cong broke off their attack.

The Marines called in a medevac. After the chopper had lifted off, Golf Company followed a new point man further south into the Que Son valley.

Around midday another burst of 7.62mm Chinese 123–grain full metal jacketed bullets with steel cores killed the replacement point scout and hit two more Marines. Again Toncar and Sanders tried desperately to locate the enemy gunners. The Golf Company gunnery sergeant yelled at them: "You two snipers, get your weapons and take the point. We got to shoot our way out of here. There ain't enough fuckin' cover here to hide a damn rabbit."

The snipers were reluctant to take point because they might be engaged at close quarters. Sanders' scoped rifle was a poor close-quarters weapon. Sanders protested: "Gunny, I can't see shit through this here scope up close like that. We ain't taught to take the point! We're supposed to cover your troops when they move, or shoot somebody way off yonder!"

As the enemy fire stopped, the Golf Company gunnery sergeant said, "Well, dammit, if you two boys can't walk point or shoot that fuckin' rifle up close, what the hell are you snipers good for?" The gunnery sergeant's attitude to the snipers was common. If their troops got pinned down by enemy fire, most Marine combat leaders relied upon company artillery such as mortars and recoiless rifles, heavy artillery and air support.

Once again the Golf Company commander called in a medevac. Golf Company had reached the outskirts of a small village 500 metres south east of their last contact when the CO called Toncar and Sanders forward. Culbertson:

Toncar observed about a dozen small hooches and as many men grouped around a fire in the middle of a small clearing. One Vietnamese was holding a Chi-Com automatic rifle as he stood watch at the front of a hut. The others bullshitted and smoked long Vietnamese pipes. Another two Viet Cong porters strode past the gathered soldiers, hefting large bundles of rice or some other foodstuff over their shoulders.

The gunny got on the radio and made a Situation Report (SITREP) to battalion headquarters at An Hoa. The artillery battery at the 11th Marines Headquarters looked over their plotting boards and realized that the Golf Company patrol was at the far limit of the big guns' range – out to almost 17,000 meters. Finally realizing that his company was getting into some deep shit, the gunny ordered Sanders to take out the Viet Cong sentry. Two squads of Golf Company grunts edged forward, low-crawling with M-14 rifles cradled in their elbows.

Fred Sanders spread his legs into a comfortable prone position and pulled his left wrist back, tightening up the slack in his hasty sling. The M1-D was heavy but the weight steadied the shot. The side-mounted, 2.5 power scope came up into his eye, and the focus was bright as the crosshairs centered on the sentry's chest. Sanders had time, and watched his sights bore into the Viet Cong. The air filled his chest, and he slowly exhaled most of it until the rifle's sights fell back on the sentry, who looked bored and relaxed. The trigger slack took up until the two-stage pull stopped. Sanders squeezed ever so gently until the trigger broke, sending the heavy .30-06 match bullet smashing cleanly through the Viet Cong's sternum – exploding his heart as if it had been cleaved by an axe. The sentry was lifted off his feet and flung against the nearby hut, where he lay limp – DRT.

Never underestimate the Marine Corps' ability to achieve the proper degree of destruction when there are villages to be burned and Viet Cong to be violently dispatched.

As Fred Sanders took his sniper rifle down from his shoulder and gave a self-assured smile to his buddy Dennis Toncar, the two squads of Golf Company grunts opened fire with everything they had in the general direction of the unlucky Viet Cong village. M-14s blasted away, tearing the thatch in chunks from the walls of previously pristine huts. M-79s lobbed 40mm high explosive grenades by the dozen through the roofing and interiors of now burning hooches. A young Golf Company grunt stood stiffly aiming his M-72 LAAW [Light Anti-tank Assault Weapon] into the center of the ville's main street, where the prostrate bodies of Viet Cong who had not escaped into spider holes or tunnels under the huts still lay. The rocket-propelled warhead sped behind a stream of propellant gases into a large outbuilding, blowing the thatch and lodge poles high into the gray sky in a fiery orange ball of death. M-60 machine-gun crews traversed their weapons from one side of the village to the other. Their bullets lifted thatch and hundreds of wood splinters that brewed up into a storm of chaos spreading across the village.

The grunts finally got their fill of death and disaster, and their adrenal glands could finally rest for another tortured day. A perimeter was set up around the village, and the fallen Viet Cong were left lying where they had died. Some lucky few Viet Cong soldiers had escaped to the nearest tunnel complex, which would lead outside the village into the jungle – and safety. The Golf Company grunts figured that they would eventually run across the lucky bastards who escaped and finally put them out of their misery. Fred Sanders had just begun to relax, and he spoke quietly to Dennis Toncar about having lined up the Viet Cong sentry for the first kill of the engagement.

Just when the snipers were feeling useful, another Viet Cong machine gun opened up just above Toncar's head. Toncar replied with rapid fire shots into the Viet Cong positions. He had his M-14 on semi-atomatic, firing short burts of three to five rounds. Golf Company's CO called in a spotting round from his artillery support.

Their opponents must have been NVA-led or they would have broken off the engagement. They were staying close to the marines because it would be safer when the shelling started. In fact, the first shell exploded 200 metres over the enemy ambush position. Golf Company's CO called for a second spotting round 150 metres shorter; this burst 50 metres beyond the Viet Cong position. Golf Company's CO called Steel Curtain to drop 50 metres and "Fire HE for effect: danger close". He was optimistic that after the artillery had completed its fire mission they could send an immediate medevac.

Sanders sighted a standing Viet Cong in a camouflaged pith helmet and a dark green uniform with a pistol in a leather holster strapped across his chest. He was evidently a North Vietnamese or Chinese military advisor. Sanders fired. By the time his rifle had settled back and the scope had cleared the military advisor had disappeared, hit in the heart at 100 metres range.

The artillery support from An Hoa caught the Viet Cong in the open, where they were sitting up to shoot at the Marines. By the time the second pair of rounds impacted there was no more ambush site left. Many of the Viet Cong gunmen had been killed by the concussion; any Viet Cong who survived had hit their escape tunnels before the artillery shells had impacted.

Sergeant Tom Casey, with Ron Willoughby as his spotter, joined Echo Company 2/5 Marines on a patrol north into Arizona teritory. At nightfall they began to dig foxholes for the night. Their foxholes were closer together than back at An Hoa where they were behind their wire and mines. Casey and Willoughby began to share the four-hour watches until first light. Suddenly a Viet Cong sniper fired two shots past Sergeant Casey's foxhole. The sound of the bullets striking in the surrounding bush were identifiable as those of a rifle like a Moishin-Nagant scoped rifle. Casey thought the sniper was changing his position when the squad M79 grenadier came up alongside his shoulder. Casey pointed out a direction for the M79 grenadier, who followed Casey's instructions and fired a pattern. There were no more interruptions that night. In the morning they found a badly burned body in the direct line of the grenadier's fire.

On 4 February Echo Company formed a perimeter around a live Sidewinder missile that had been torn off an F-4 Phantom's weapons pylon during a napalm run. They were waiting for an Explosive Ordnance Disposal (EOD) team to arrive by helicopter when Casey noticed a group of Vietnamese running away from the Marines. Through his scope he could see that some of them were armed but they were mixed in with women and children. Casey had just lowered his rifle when a Marine near him triggered a booby trap. The Marine had stumbled across a trip wire stretched over a footpath. It was attached to a Chinese Communist grenade. The Marine was blown into the air with serious wounds on his legs and torso. Casey was hit in the legs by shrapnel from the blast. Willoughby held down his partner while the medical corpsman came over to check his condition.

Both wounded Marines were evacuated by medevac chopper to Da Nang. After a brief period of recuperation, Casey was returned to An Hoa on limited duty.

US forces had become so highly mobilized and reliant on heavy weapons that their standard tactics were "find, fix and destroy". Culbertson described the nature of the infantry's war in Vietnam:

But Vietnam was a jungle war where the enemy was almost impossible to "find-fix-destroy". The reality of warfare there was that no distinct battle lines were formed. This contributed to the difficulty *of* conducting purely conventional tactics. So Vietnam became one of the last great infantry wars where small units tracked each other down over the limitless jungled hillsides and mountains, meeting in brief but bloody firefights almost always broken off by the Viet Cong.

The United States Marine Corps had been the only US branch of the armed services to continue to emphasize excellence with small arms, including rifle marksmanship, machine gunnery, mortar training, and combat training with the Korean vintage 3.5-inch rocket launcher. Improved high-tech weapons like the LAAW rocket system and the new M-79 grenade launcher were now employed in the rifle platoon. The Marines were well-schooled in close-quarter fighting and the use of every small (portable) arm in the rifle company arsenal. Yet an expert analysis of the weaponry carried and used in jungle combat by young Marine infantrymen revealed little improvement from the arms used by the American G.I. or German Wehrmacht grenadier of World War II. The conditions, however, were decidedly different. There had never been a war where the battleground favored the indigenous military forces more than Vietnam favored the Viet Cong.

The VC could hide from the Marines underground in tunnel systems dating from pre-World War II conflicts against the Japanese. The Viet Cong could retreat after a losing battle into neutral Cambodia or Laos, escaping pursuit by the Marine battalions closing in for the kill. The VC could, of course, slip into and out of the clothing and role of a peaceful noncombatant villager.

The Gunnery sergeant who had trained Casey was brought out to help train more snipers. Culbertson described the war up to 1967:

During the first two years of the war, the Viet Cong had yet to win a decisive battle. Their battalions were incapable of overpowering the Marines fighting head-to-head in a conventional battle. The old guerrilla strategy of hitting the Americans quickly and withdrawing into the jungle, leaving a few Marines to bleed out and die would have to suffice until the better armed North Vietnamese divisions could pour across the South Vietnamese borders from their marshaling points along the Ho Chi Minh Trail. The Que Son Valley would eventually become the tactical operating Headquarters for the NVA 2nd Division; specifically, the veteran NVA 21st Regiment of crack infantry battalions, with their deadly anti-aircraft batteries, would contest the best the Marines could muster during the entire year of 1967. The series of hard-fought battles in the 5th Marines' TAOR was no doubt the most intense period of nonstop combat during the Vietnam War after the bloody battles of Operation Prairie on the Demilitarized Zone were concluded.

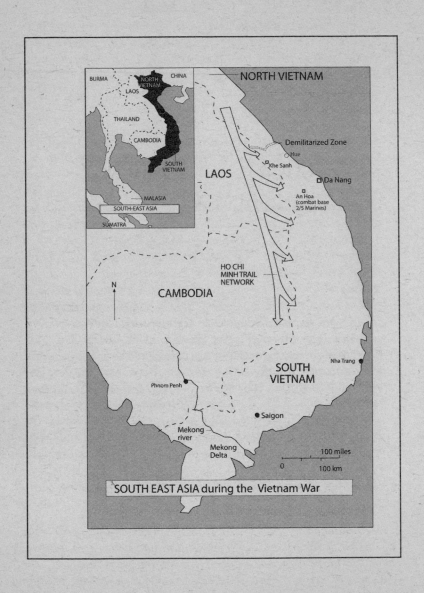

SOUTH EAST ASIA during the Vietnam War

# COUNTER INSURGENCY
# IN FALLUJAH (2003)

*During his fourteen months as an embedded writer with US forces in Iraq, Mike Tucker spent time in Fallujah.*

*On 9 November 2003 Tucker was flown to Fallujah, where he was attached to the first battalion, Five Hundred and Fifth Parachute Infantry Regiment (1/505), Eighty-Second Airborne Division. Their Forward Operating Base (FOB) was at Volturno near Fallujah. Coalition forces had reached Fallujah at the end of March 2003 but by mid April they had been pulled out. There was no ethnic group in Fallujah which welcomed the Coalition.*

*The Eighty-Second Airborne Division reached Fallujah on 28 April 2003. They were part of Task Force Gauntlet, which reached Fallujah, held it down for two weeks, then left. They were relieved by the Third Infantry Division (Third ID).*

*Most of the population of Fallujah had worked in some way for Saddam's regime. When his regime was toppled, their source of easy money was eliminated. The troops intended to shut down Fallujah were the Third Infantry Division (ID). They had been some of the troops who had advanced night and*

*day on Baghdad. Unlike the Eight-Second, the Third In-*
*fantry Division responded weakly to looting. Anti-Coalition*
*forces poured in.*

*Staff Sergeants Wettstein, Browning and Viburs worked in*
*psychological operations and aiding US Army military in-*
*telligence in Fallujah. They told Tucker that the basic attitude*
*of Iraqis in Fallujah was, "Where's my cut?" The idea of*
*doing the right thing did not apply because the culture in*
*Fallujah had always encouraged corruption. The imams had*
*incredible influence but they were stridently anti-Western.*
*Wettstein, Browning and Viburs respected Lieutenant Colonel*
*Drinkwine, the Commanding Officer of the Task Force 1*
*Panther. Drinkwine included them in operational planning*
*and listened to their advice and analyses. This had not been the*
*case when the Third Infantry Division had been in town. They*
*also felt that Drinkwine understood respect and how important*
*it is in theArab Bedouin culture of Iraq. This had helped him*
*in his dealings with the local sheikhs. Tucker also met Sergeant*
*Ruben Quinones. Sergeant Quinones had built up his own*
*intelligence network on the street in Fallujah. He did not use*
*paid sources but he and his intelligence team were on the street*
*every day raiding and patrolling. On 4 February 2004 he told*
*Tucker:*

If you go spreading money around, especially in Asian
cultures, people believe they can tell you anything that will
save face for them, first and foremost, and in some way
please you. Remember, the most important thing in Asia is
saving face. We are in southwest Asia. Will paid information be the intelligence you need to kill the enemy? No, it
will be the information that does two things: saves face for
the informant, and keeps the informant paid. And at that
point, the informant doesn't care about you saving face.
Because you already lost face, hugely – you already showed
you have a lame, money–is–all–important attitude toward
understanding the culture. What's the worst thing in Asia?
Losing face. Now you can see why the CIA, with its money-
buys-everything operating schematic, is so disrespected and

also, simply incompetent, when it comes to working the intelligence. It's easier to hand over money and sit in an air-conditioned office than it is to infiltrate a terrorist cell. It's also the worst way to gather human intelligence – to think you can buy intelligence. Especially in Asia. And once you lay those dollar bills in a source's hands, then he's played you: he's suckered you into keeping him on your payroll, and he knows that you don't know, or care about, the culture or the street.

Know this: the CIA, with all its money and technology, did not provide the primary intelligence that nailed Khamis Sirhan and Abu Shihab.

Khamis Sirhan and Abu Shihab were two key insurgent leaders captured in mid-January 2004 in western Iraq. Quinones continued:

We did that, with solid human Intel from sources in my network. How did we nail Uday and Qusay, Saddam, and practically every major raid in this country, successful raids, main target killed or captured? With solid human Intel and tip-offs in the street from Iraqi Arabs and Kurds, not paid informants. Same – same right here on the street in Fallujah. We're in a war here. All the Intel I get, I get because my network knows one thing: I am here to kill or capture anyone who is funding, supporting, leading, or fighting with Iraqi insurgents, Ba'athist loyalists, al-Quaeda, al-Ansar Islam, or any other anti-Coalition forces. The worst is Sheikh Gazi, by far. He buys the majority of the RPGs and IEDs, pays people to make the attacks, and pays people to build insurgent cells. He is evil and he is slick. He was in bed with Saddam for years. Make no mistake, he is very clever.

In November 2003 Tucker joined a raid into Fallujah. The target was the capture of Kurdia Tirki Ali Halif. This woman had been Chemical Ali's secretary and was reported to be building *fedayeen* cells. Chemical Ali (General Ali

Hassan al-Majid) had been the Baa'athist regional commander who had used weapons of mass destruction, including poison gas against the Kurds and Shi'ites after the First Gulf War. Chemical Ali's former secretary was referred to as Chemical Evil Fat Mama.

First platoon Alpha Company, 1/505, was the recconnaissance unit. They called themselves the Desert Yetis. On 15 November 2003 Tucker joined them for the first part of the mission. It was a starlit night as they drove through along a two-lane asphalt road; the curfew was being observed. Tucker noticed occasional trash fires smoking on empty concrete sidewalks and there was a strong smell of raw sewage. Dogs scattered or just froze as they approached.

Across a field they scanned a row of houses. Tucker was given a set of night vision goggles known as NODs (Night Observation Devices). Tucker:

The night became lime-green and alive through the lenses. By the third house down in the row, I could see a kid coming out of an open gate. I could see a cat prancing along a brick wall, the cat eyeing us as we eyed it, and the kid stepped back in the gate and left it open. Inside there was a Mercedes; it looked new, the finish gleamed in the daylight-bright glow of the Night Vision goggles.

The presence of the Mercedes suggested that their target was there so they headed back. The raid itself was on 18 November. Tucker:

Over a great hump in the desert we slammed down, dust clearing in front of us and mud huts and cinder-block houses lining a potholed road just right of us, convoy roaring down the road. Houses loomed west, stark in the starlight, massive in the night like boulders along a mountain trail deep in Karen highlands in Burma, two- and three-story concrete and stone houses like small fortresses within their sand-colored, walled compounds.

Hanley broke hard and we leaped out, Captain Huston leading the source west down a narrow, jagged lane, streams of sewage and refuse pooling near an alley corner some thirty meters ahead. Sergeant Major Lambert joined us and asked me, "You all right, Mr Tucker?" and I thanked him and told him I was fine, and he replied, "Solid, keep your head down buddy, stick with me." Huston moved on with the source, heading fast up the alley, the Iraqi keeping his head down, two kaffiyehs draped over his head. I could see Drinkwine, whom I called "Spartan Six", up ahead, his M-4 at the hip, rushing forward up the alley in the darkness.

First Sergeant Dunn, about six foot two and built like a middle linebacker, came up behind us as Captain Terence Caliguire's Alpha Company swept past, staying close to walls on both sides of the alley, hustling up, securing alleys, scoping rooftops, moving fast in the darkness.

First Sergeant Dunn said, "Come with me," and we hustled up through mud and dirt and sewage to the southern end of the alley, where it met a field. Right of us, some thirty meters immediately to our north, fire teams gathered along the wall, one team on each side of a wide, heavy, green steel gate, the gate we'd seen open on the Desert Yetis reconnaissance patrol.

A blast boomed in the night north of us, perhaps a mile away. Dunn nodded, a sidearm on his right hip and cradling his M-4.

"Charlie Company, no doubt. Just set off their raid. Going after the bastards that shot down the Chinook. Most affirm." As he spoke, four paratroopers and Captain Zawachewsky approached us, towing along a middle-aged man in a long white dishtasha.

They halted and First Sergeant Dunn talked with Captain Zawachewsky, their voices low in the darkness, raiders swarming up toward us, fire teams leaning forward now on the house just north of us. I waited with Staff Sergeant Tormale Grimes, a shrewd and tough raider whom I nicknamed "Shaft", and Detroit City, who had dismounted his heavy machine gun, the M240 Bravo 7.62-caliber machine gun.

Shaft carried an M-4 and he had it shouldered for quick action, flak loaded with thirteen clips, as we held fast by the corner. He took a knee and I did likewise, Detroit City covering the west and south for us, in the prone on his heavy machine gun.

"He knows where she is," said Captain Zawachewsky, pointing to the man in the white dishtasha.

Shaft scanned the night and rose off one knee and looked toward the house. First Sergeant Dunn said, "Stay with Captain Zawachewsky, stay with him."

I nodded to him as we all moved together, Staff Sergeant Jeremy Anderson leading the sappers on the assault, two sappers working on the gate. Anderson said quickly, "Battering ram, do it, Tommy, fuck it up!"

Specialist Thomson rushed hard at the gate, battering ram in his arms, slinging it forward all in one swift hard rush and the gate busted open and Alpha company rolled in hard, rifles shouldered, tactical lights on their rifles flashing in the night like fireflies in the Burmese jungle on a night with no moon, second-fire team rushing in, raiders shouting in the courtyard, "Move, get the door, do it!"

I fell in with the second-fire team and the captain bolted up, coming from behind me, and pointed to shadows along a wall and said, "Over here, get here now." I got in the shadows and he told me to wait. Zawachewsky held his rifle down slightly and moved forward with the assault team, shouting back over his shoulder, "Mr Tucker, move with second team," raising his rifle as he stepped into the house, his voice carrying from within the house. "Go, Morales, go go go!"

The second-fire team rushed in and I fell in behind a light machine gunner, raiders scoping the dark halls and rooms with their rifles shouldered, shouts of, "Clear, clear," and, "There's a kid in here, take it easy, just a kid," coming from within the dark house, lights flickering on in the early morning.

The odor of kerosene was strong in the hallway, para-troopers separating the men from the women and children. Velvet paintings, like those you'd see of Elvis in his Vegas years, hung from concrete walls. Horses in the paintings ran through the desert, nostrils flaring, carrying men with rifles and leather bandoliers strapped across their chests.

Men from Alpha company pulled a man from a rear room and came forward with him. The man wore a black leather jacket and on one sleeve was the Iraqi police identification badge. He kept his head down and was silent and they rushed him forward out to the courtyard. I could hear Napoli say, "Fuckin'-a, he had this halfway out from under the bed, fuckin' submachine gun," as I entered the room. Napoli stood by the side of a sagging mattress, a long wooden closet behind him, holding a Sterling wooden-stocked submachine gun in his left hand. Corcione checked it out as his men continued to clear the room, searching through closets and in small bedside tables for pistols, ammunition, rifles, det cord, plastic explosive, mobile phones – any of the common weapons of war that the Iraqi insurgency used to kill and maim and wound our warriors in Fallujah.

"Got AK clips," said Morales in a hurried tone as he grabbed AK-47 magazines from out of a dresser. "Live rounds, 7.62." Morales's wife, who was in Bayamon, Puerto Rico, was pregnant. I called Morales the "King of Puerto Rico". He was a dynamite light machine gunner, and like DJ Rush and Kentucky Rifle, you always felt better when Morales was on a raid with you.

Corcione nodded. "Throw them in here," he said, rip-ping a pillowcase off a pillow and handing it to Morales.

Morales, his light machine gun slung over his back, tossed ten AK clips and heaps of loose 7.62 rounds into the pillowcase, Staff Sergeant Corcione holding it open for him. Napoli was checking under the mattress again, making sure. Staff Sergeant Corcione scanned the room and said quickly, "Clear, are we all clear here?"

The raiders answered as one, shouting, "Clear!"

Corcione nodded and said, "Good, because there's one more room, let's go," and he led us to an adjoining room, the rich scent of fragrant perfume strong as we entered. There were silk dresses smothered in gems hanging in wooden closets, and perfume everywhere. Morales shouted, "More ammo, more clips, *hijo de la chingana*!" and Staff Sergeant Corcione grinned.

"Ain't no doubt, this house is all wrong. Chemical Evil Fat Mama fuckin' well ought to hang. Good job Morales," he said. He opened a closet and there were about twelve more AK clips stacked on shelves.

"Supply safe house for *fedayeen*, Mr Tucker," he said as he grabbed the clips and tossed them into the pillow-case. I nodded to him; no doubt, he was right. There was way too much ammunition and war supplies in this house for two or three *fedayeen*. Corcione leaned over and listened to his I-Com and he raised his eyebrows, grinning slightly.

"Solid. We're coming out," he said into his I-Com. He looked around as the raiders glanced up at him and asked, "Clear, are we clear?"

His raiders shouted, "Clear!" Carrying pillowcases full of AK-47 ammunition and clips, the Alpha company men rushed out of the room, flashing their tac lights in the darkened hallways. The scent of burning kerosene was strong now in the hallways, and the thick smoky scent hung heavy in the night air.

In the courtyard, Zawachewsky was talking with Caliguire. "Right here, we got her," Zawachewsky said, pointing just outside the gate, raiders at all compass points in the courtyard, a low metallic rumble coming from our trucks beyond the courtyard.

Chemical Evil Fat Mama was babbling in Arabic, great jowls napping on her fat sagging cheeks as two raiders tried to flex-cuff her, two other raiders watching over her, M-4s at the ready. Paratroopers were everywhere, rushing to their trucks, shining neither flashlights nor tac lights, sweat steaming off them in the zero dark cold.

At the same time as first platoon Alpha Company was capturing Chemical Evil Fat Mama, Charlie Company and the rest of Alpha Company were successfully raiding some fedayeen who had shot down a Chinook on 2 November. Seventeen US personnel had been killed. Tucker was invited to join a counter IED patrol on 19 November. Tucker:

> We rolled out the wire on the counter-IED patrol, zero dark thirty in Fallujah, 19 November 2003. It was four-thirty in the morning and the Desert Yetis led the way. Zero dark thirty is a term we used in Marine infantry to mean any wee dark hour of the morning, anywhere in the world, between midnight and dawn when it's dark and black and you are on a mission.
>
> Sappers rolled with us, mine detectors laid outboard in their trucks like oars in a skiff before it's launched to sea. We had gun trucks on point and trail – every truck on the patrol save our MK 19s had a machine gun mounted. The sappers rode with heavy machine guns mounted on their gun trucks, Private First Class Vincent Carter manning one 7.62 machine for the sappers and Private First Class Brown from Pasco, Washington, manning another, waving to the machine gunner on my truck as we rolled out the south gate.
>
> Lieutenant Matthew Leclair was in the TC seat, riding like the Guerrilla Fighter in Mosul on the passenger's side up front. Specialist Cook was driving; we were trail truck on the patrol and the men were scoping the darkness with their superb night vision devices. Quiet out the wire as we rolled far to the west and north down hardpacked dirt jeep trails through fields of harvested wheat and cotton. Donkeys roamed the fields on the outskirts of Fallujah in the wee dark hours.
>
> Patton was with us, in the back of the truck, and Doc, the platoon medic, and Specialist Jake Eller and Specialist Stephen Carmac, paratroopers all. I called Eller, "Jake the Snake", and Carmac, "Longstreet", after Confederate General James Longstreet. Jake the Snake and Longstreet

were both from North Carolina, though Longstreet liked to say of his buddy, "Southerners don't claim Jake the Snake. He's a rare breed. Definitely not from North Carolina," to which Jake the Snake would swiftly reply, "Don't listen to him. Longstreet is long on ammunition and short on brain matter. I am a son of the South, and I will surely profit in time, due to my Southerner's wisdom and natural grace and charm."

Eller said that once again in Fallujah as the sun rose over fields and irrigation canals east of us. Patton laughed and said, "Jake the Snake, the only grace and charm you'll ever find is standing in front of Graceland getting charmed out of your pocket money by some Memphis hustler!"

Carmac busted up laughing, eyes on, steady on his light machine gun. Eller rolled his eyes and said, "That's Patton. Lord. Patton! We got hit on 13 September, a date forever engraved in the memory of the Desert Yetis. Firefight lasted an hour and a half. Patton tells us, in the middle of all this, us trying to keep our heads down in the desert and praying we'd survive, 'Men, this is what it's all about! Remember this night. This is it, movement to contact, movement under fire. Kill the enemy!' And he's standing there, AK fire all around us, RPGs flying, and I said to him, 'Staff Sergeant Smith, my God, since when did you become Patton?' And he just looks at me and says, 'Jake, conserve your ammo.' So after that night, we all called him Patton."

Longstreet grinned and nodded to me and I asked him if Jake the Snake was bulljiving me or telling it straight. Carmac's eyes hardened as he scanned the long plowed rows in fields of harvested cotton and he nodded and said, "Truth. Jake the Snake was praying the 23rd Psalm as we rode into that firefight. He was speaking for everyone on that truck. That night, yes indeed, that's when we started calling Staff Sergeant 'Patton'."

Dawn warmed us and we swung southeast off a jeep trail onto hardball, headed toward the Dam Road, a busted-up, potholed road that runs southwest out of Fallujah past mud huts and cinder-block compounds. The road continued alongside a few massive, well-constructed concrete villas before passing through saw grass fields and swamps on the eastern banks of the Euphrates, date palm groves green along its eastern shores.

A car pulled out of a driveway some 50 meters behind us, and as it neared the road, six other cars pulled out with it, all spread out roughly 50 meters apart. I noted this to Patton. He said to Lieutenant Leclair, "El-Tee, we've got *fedayeen*. Seven on our six."

"Keep eyes on. Any weapons on the vehicles?" the lieutenant asked.

"I've got it, sir," Eller said, eyeing the seven vehicles trailing us. He scoped the vehicles with his M-4. They were all still about 50 meters apart. We sped up and hung a right near a junction of dirt roads and hardball and our convoy halted. Desert Yetis leaping out, shouldering their rifles and machine guns at quick action.

The seven cars, still equidistant, slowed down as we stopped and Carmac faced west, his light machine gun at the ready. One car slowed some 50 meters west of us. Eller shouldered his M-4 and came up alongside Carmac, and the car sped up, driving on, not following us any more. I counted the vehicles following it; all six drove on, still equidistant.

Everyone dismounted, paratroopers securing alley corners and scoping rooftops in the warming dawn, gulls swarming over heaps of smoking trash near the junction. The sappers carried mine detectors, sidearms, machine guns, rifles, and assault rucks. They swept the ground for IEDs, paratroopers securing their flanks, mangy dogs barking at us from nearby mud huts.

The sappers cleared the junction of IEDS and hustled back to their trucks, led by Staff Sergeant Jeremy Anderson and Staff Sergeant Snyder, both Afghan veterans. I called Anderson, the "Streetfighter", and Snyder, "New York Warrior". The Streetfighter was fearless on raids and backed his sappers 1,000 per cent. He was clever and stoic and his men respected him.

New York Warrior volunteered on 11 September 2001, for rescue crews at the World Trade Center. For three days he pulled rubble and steel and rock out of the ashes with the Lady in the Harbor watching over him. He'd been home on leave that September and he was riding in a car on Long Island when the news broke of the first plane striking the first tower. A year later, with the Streetfighter, he was in Afghanistan, going cave to cave, searching for al-Quaeda weapons caches and al-Quaeda terrorists.

I got back on Leclair's truck and rode with the Desert Yetis on the Dam Road, patrol slowing as two M113s joined us. The M113 is a wide-bodied, armored fighting vehicle that first saw action in the Vietnam War. A machine gunner stood up in the turret. The M113s were from Big Red One, and it was great to see them in the brightening morning. Iraqi insurgents had set off many IEDs in the "Boneyard" section of the Dam Road, where Big Red One rallied to us on that dawn, M113s rumbling slowly. Iraqi children raced out of mud huts and cinder-block houses to wave to us.

We halted in the Boneyard and the sappers rushed forward, on point, sweeping the dirt shoulders of the Dam Road with their mine detectors, Anderson and Snyder in the thick of it.

Grimes and Staff Sergeant Rodrick Hodges secured the sappers' flanks, flicking hand-and-arm signals to their men and to Anderson and Snyder, Hodges leading his squad on the eastern side of the Dam Road.

The sun was high and stellar-bright in hazy blue sky, and I asked Leclair if I could move up with the sappers. He nodded and said, as I hustled up the road, "Remember, our truck number is twenty-seven," pointing to the white-painted numbers on the dark-green side. I jogged up to combat sapper Private First Class Vincent Carter on left flank, some 5m eters east of Big Gus and the Woodsman.

Carter, whom I nicknamed "Ultimate Gunner", carried his light machine gun, wide black nylon strap slung over his back, sweat pouring down his face in the hot desert morning. Ultimate Gunner was the only sapper issued two machine guns, both the SAW 5.56 and the M240B 7.62 caliber. Carter was from Virginia Beach, Virginia, not far from the Cape Henry lighthouse my great grandfather had passed all his life as a boat pilot, guiding clipper ships and freighters up the Chesapeake to Baltimore. When I told him this, in the dust and heat of Fallujah on that morning. Carter grinned and said, "I know that lighthouse. We're both a long way from the Chesapeake, brother. Solid to see it again, for real." The desert sun was burning now in the Boneyard, a great herd of water buffalo moving slowly through marsh and saw grass three klicks (kilometres) south of us, near the Euphrates.

"Keep eyes on for wires and det cord, Mr Tucker, anything that might be for an IED, trash, plastic bags, anything," and I nodded and scanned the dusty rubble-strewn Boneyard, road curving slightly about one hundred meters ahead of us. Behind us, our counter-IED patrol convoy was inching forward, trucks at a crawl. Leclair talked on his radio to his squad leaders, one hand on his sidearm, Dean right by his side, his M-4 at the ready. Looking east, it was a concrete wasteland, with dilapidated shells of concrete buildings all around us and stumps of rusted I-beams jutting up from bare concrete foundations. Starlings and sparrows flitted about in what shade they could find in the Boneyard, chirping in shadows cast by concrete boulders. A thin haze of smoke drifted from the trash fires over all of us, and the scent was unpleasant, though not nearly as foul as the raw sewage in the streets of Mosul and Fallujah.

"Move, move!" Carter shouted, grabbing my right shoulder and heading east and we ran, hustling some 100 meters. Carter looked back and then glanced forward and pointed behind two boulders.

We dropped down behind the boulders, trash blowing around us. Directly west. Big Gus and the Woodsman were standing still, mine detectors held over the loose dirt and gravel on the left shoulder of Dam Road. Everyone on the patrol had taken cover – Leclair was behind a truck, listening to his handset, nodding. Dean checked their three o'clock, rifle shouldered. Patton covered their six, M.203 shouldered, on one knee, facing north, his flak jacket stocked full with 40mm grenades.

Samurai, Staff Sergeant Hodges, had his squad well deployed, set in behind boulders and walls, securing the eastern reaches of the Boneyard. Some two hundred meters west of us, Grimes's men were spread in a loose crescent, waving off children as they neared, the children unknowing of the danger, smiling and waving to Shaft and his men as they scanned the wide dusty field that reached to concrete houses and villas beyond.

Anderson and Snyder walked up quickly to Big Gus and the Woodsman and began digging at the dirt with their hands. There was an EOD specialist with them, a big, lean warrior carrying an M-4, flak stocked with scissors and knives and det cord and clips, fatigues dusty and grease-stained.

He leaned down and snatched a wire from the dirt and ran, threading the wire in his left hand and shouting, "Got wire! Come on." He pointed to a paratrooper nearby who was carrying a light machine gun and the machine gunner ran with him, following the wire into the Bone yard. Seeing my camera, the EOD specialist yelled, "No pictures, no pictures," and I held both arms up, keeping my hands away from my camera. He nodded and ran hard through the rubble, wire in his hand.

"IED, Mr Tucker! We've got one. C'mon, Big Gus and Brownie, get outta' there, sapper brothers," Carter said quickly. Ten Iraqi children ranging perhaps from four to eleven years old, were standing about thirty meters south-west of the IED, gathered in front of a mud hut, holding their hands to their foreheads, shielding the Fallujah sun from their young eyes. Carter explained to me that the battery charge on a camera, set off when the picture is taken, could detonate an IED.

Big Gus and the Woodsman stepped back as Anderson and Snyder disarmed and pulled out two huge artillery shells from the ground, dust swirling up out of the hole, the shells lashed together with baling wire.

They slowly and carefully pulled the wire off, M113s covering them, Leclair talking into his handset as Dean raised his M-4 and scanned houses just west off the Dam Road, Samurai and Shaft talking into their I-Coms, Patton checking Leclair's six and listening to his I-Com. Patton nodded slowly, M.203 at quick action, as he kept eyes on the trucks behind him and the road beyond.

"They're 155s. Daisy-chained. When they're wired together like that, daisy-chained. *Fedayeen* are evil. They would've killed those kids, too," Carter said, pointing to the children. I thanked him for finding us the good cover and he said, "No problem." Anderson and Snyder carried the 155mm artillery rounds away and set them in the back of one of the sapper's trucks.

The EOD specialist shouted, "Got a hole!" He stood, shaking the wire over a hole dug in behind boulders, roughly 250 meters east from where the *fedayeen* had buried the IED on the shoulder.

"Command detonated. Whoever set in that IED was going to sit in that hole and kill us himself. Punch the button and the wire would've sent the charge and blown us to hell and back. Woulda' killed those kids, too, Mr. Tucker, or at the very least, scarred them for life. The *fedayeen* don't have any regard for life. Ba'athist motherfuckers. They won't hesitate to kill Iraqi civilians if it means they can kill or maim us," Carter said as we rose up, patrolling south through the Boneyard, continuing the counter-IED patrol, echoing Thoman in Mosul.

They patrolled night and day throughout November 2003. On 25 November Charlie Company tried to capture a very active and dangerous *fedayeen* leader, Abu Shihab. They were fired on with Rocket Propelled Grenades. Abu Shihab evaded capture but was finally captured in a daylight raid seven weeks later. On 15 January 2004, first platoon Alpha

Company, the Desert Yetis, caught him with two other prominent *fedayeen* leaders in a shop in downtown Fallujah. The operation involved US Army Special Forces commandos Ghost, Phantom and Cool Hand Luke.

On 29 November 2003 Tucker was with a dismounted patrol from Tenth Mountain Division when it found a substantial arms cache. It was nearly four in the afternoon. They had humped five klicks in the desert. They found mortar pits lined with gravel and sandbags. They had white-painted aiming marks pointing in the direction of the Eighty-Second's base at Volturno. They recorded the position of each pit on their maps.

Further south they patrolled towards a sandstone cliff. The machine gunners carried their light machine guns from the hip, fire leaders scoped the far sands. The only way up the 40–metre-high cliff was a steep groove, cut by the wind and the rain from its western side. Sergeant Shaun Hall slung his M.203 over his back and climbed up hand over hand.

At the top he turned and helped Tucker over the edge. Tucker turned and helped the next man up. There were tombstones and mounds of dirt at the other end of the cliff, which looked like an ideal mortar firing position. They radioed back, reporting that there was nothing up there "but graves and shit". Another group, just north of them, had found four 155mm artillery rounds, packed with Semtex and TNT and a crate of 7.62mm ammunition. The artillery rounds were a *fedayeen* IED cache that could have killed fifteen men. The soldiers were ordered to secure the munitions in a truck.

They formed a perimeter around their position with their machine gunners lying prone. The barrels of their machine guns were flush on burlap laid over piles of sand. As their trucks rolled up the light infantrymen yelled: "Hua! Fuckin'-a, we got a cache."

They started moving the 155mm rounds to the trucks. There was a bulldozer and a white pick-up truck 100 yards south of their southern perimeter. A man got out of the pick-up truck. He was wearing a white and red cheched kaffiyeh and a long white dishtasha. He glared at them arms folded. They decided he was probably *fedayeen* but un-armed. He pulled out a mobile phone and dashed behind the bulldozer. A second pick-up truck raced up and slammed to a halt in clouds of dust. Four men got out. They talked excitedly to the first man.

With the soldiers' approval, Tucker pulled out his knife. It was a curved Ghurka kukri knife. He held it high as he walked up to the nearest machine gunner's position and shouted, *"Mala Mustapha Barzani, peshmerga, peshmerga, Kurdistan, Mala Mustapha Barzani!"*

The men got back in their pick-ups, made a U-turn and drove away. The machine gunners cheered. They all thought Tucker's gesture had been outstanding.

Two nights later US forces began a series of raids based on information supplied by sources on the streets. They captured a *fedayeen* leader and a Ba'athist leader and former General Darhan Al Mehemdi. Tucker was with Attack Company from 10th Mountain Division on a "dry" raid far to the north. After the success of the raids in Fallujah they were recalled to base.

The following morning Tucker spoke to Sergeant Eric Viburs. Viburs was a US Army Reservist who had been conducting psychological operations and aiding US Army military intelligence in Fallujah and Western Iraq. Viburs had arrived in Fallujah in June 2003 and stayed until March 2004.

Viburs seemed to be in a good mood. When Tucker asked him why, he replied:

You're damn right! Oh, yes, first time we ever had Iraqis coming up to us on the street in Fallujah and congratulating us, first time. This morning, by God and General Grant! We're out on patrol, all right. Making contacts, dropping off leaflets, doing our regular "hit the street and meet and greet whole nine yards groove" in Fallujah. Oh, yes! First time ever Iraqis of all ages coming up to us and saying, "You got that Ba'athist general last night, you got Darhan! Thank you, thank you. He was an evil man, all Ba'athist generals, you must capture them. Good, good, tell the Americans they did good. Thank you for capturing Darhan, thank you."

Man, this is beautiful. In my duty here, it's dicey, you have to read the tea leaves, you know? You have to learn how to listen to the wind. When Iraqis in Fallujah, a Ba'athist stronghold, are coming up to us right on the street, in front of their neighbors and in front of the sheikhs and imams, no hesitation, and thanking us for taking down a Ba'athist general, then we know we're making a difference here. Oh, hell, yes, I'm in a good mood, brother. Man, what happened today never happened before. It was beautiful. Caliguire's Commandos, hell yes!

## Raid on a weapons market   2 January 2004

Tucker was told that every unit in Fallujah had tried to raid the weapons market. They knew where it was, the raid had been planned but then they had decided not to risk it. Offically the weapons market was regarded as "extremely hostile". An officer told Tucker that they knew the weapons maket was a key link between the *fedayeen* and al-Qaeda and all anti-Coalition forces in Fallujah. There were *fedayeen* lookouts everywhere.

The initial assault was to be the key with three Special Forces operators, Phantom, Ghost and Cool Hand Luke on point with Lieutenant Cook and his second platoon paratroopers. Charlie Company was to set off an explosion using a line charge. It was supposed to be as if an IED had gone off and they were all reacting to it. It was to be diversion and deception. Alpha Company would be involved in what should appear to be a company-scale reconnaissance. Attack Company would be rolling south of the town, while Bravo Company would enter the town from the north, apparently doing a psy ops mission. The idea was that any *fedayeen* on mobile phones would see four different companies in four different parts of town, none of them near the weapons market.

Tucker was assigned to Bravo Company. They entered an apartment complex, where children gathered around them. They handed out candy and talked to the children. Iraqi men in leather jackets pulled out mobile phones. Bravo Company were ordered out. There were Kiowa Warriors in the the sky above them and they were expecting Charlie Company's explosion when it went off. The echo from the blast boomed from across the Euphrates.

Ahead of them, trucks were halting and paratroopers were jumping out. Iraqis were running into small shops and alleys as they made the raid. Iraqi men carrying wooden AK-47 stocks and pistol holsters were huddled against the walls. Paratroopers were already confiscating AK-47s and RKM machine-guns and began calling, "This lane sealed, this lane sealed."

Special Operator Ghost called out for assistance in opening a steel door and a sapper used his combat skilsaw to neutralize the lock. Behind the door was a shop loaded with AK-47s and RPG grenades. To the east of them they could hear AK-47 fire and smell chemical smoke: a terrible, acrid smell, so they wrapped bandanas around their faces.

Tucker could see one of the Special Operators speaking into his radio. Up the alley sappers were busting illegal weapons dealers left and right. The Special Operator nodded to him, and Tucker gave him a thumbs-up.

There were paratroopers everywhere. They were rushing down alleys and slamming open doors,. shouting, "More here, goddam, all kinds of AKs over here!" and "7.62, all kinds of 7.62."

They found blasting caps in pick-up trucks in the street outside. They cut their way into an illegal gunsmith's shop and even Special Operator Ghost was impressed by the contents. It was a small room filled with rifles of all makes and ages, including a Bren gun and a Lewis gun [a drum-fed light machine gun from the era before World War Two]. A bolt-action Lee Enfield .303 had been left in a

vice; it was in the process of being modified to fire automatically.

Special Operator Ghost said, "Motherlode, baby."

Tucker was allowed to join Alpha Company to see how
they were doing. They had already seized seven IEDS and
were piling up RPGs and cases of linked 7.62 ammunition. Special Operator Cool Hand Luke stood at the
entrance to what appeared to be a fabric shop. He said,
"Ten IEDs inside set to blow. Two different shops within
this shop: this is IED central for Fallujah. All set to blow,
blasting caps in place." Later he added that there were
metal shavings, bolts, razor blades and every piece of
metal you can think of that would fit inside a palm oil
can, all stuffed inside those IEDs." By then they had
found seventeen huge IEDs and taken down three IED
factories.

Grey-green smoke was drifting down an alley towards
them. With it came a crowd. When the crowd was thee
hundred metres away from them, Tucker saw the wooden
stock of an AK-47 raised by its barrel guards through the
smoke. He reported it and and then he saw another near the
front of the crowd. He asked if he could go with them and
help by using his Arabic. If they backed the crowd up into a
mosque they could, perhaps, keep them from using the
guns.

When they reached the east end of the mosque, they
could see a team from Attack Company, Tenth Mountain
Division, had sealed the west end. A man came out of a shop
adjoining the mosque. Tucker greeted him in Arabic. He
asked calmly, "Is there a problem here?"

Tucker replied, "Tell these men that if they are *fedayeen*,
we will kill them. The choice is theirs. There are at least two
AK-47s in that mosque."

The man translated for Tucker and a man with salt and
pepper hair answered, glaring back at him. "This man says
there are no weapons in the mosque, it is a holy place. There
are no *fedayeen* here. It is sacred. Iraqis would never put
weapons of war in a mosque."

Tucker asked the translator to ask him if he was a wise

man. He replied that he was as wise as the desert was hot. Tucker warned them that there were warriors at every corner ready to kill *fedayeen* but that they should stay inside the mosque if they were truly wise. The man glared and said nothing. He said something and the crowd behind him fell back.

The paratroopers and the men from Tenth Mountain Division began to pull out. They had seized:

17 IEDs
220 antipersonnel grenades
150 RPG grenades
55 heat seeking grenades for RPG rocket launchers
30 antipersonnel grenades for RPG rocket launchers
50 Lee Enfield .303 rifles modified for fully automatic
300 AK-47, 7.62 calibre assault rifles
ZU 23 12.7 calibre AAA gun
20 80mm rockets
1,000 12.7 calibre rounds
10,000 7.62 calibre linked rounds

The Eighty-Second Airborne Division was relieved in Fallujah by the First US Marine Division on 27 March 2004. Four days later, four US security contractors were killed in Fallujah. Their bodies were either mutilated or burned by a celebrating mob. When the First US Marine Division attempted to restore order, six Marines were killed and six wounded. Six hundred insurgents were killed and many residents fled. After they had cleared two-thirds of the city, the Marines tried to hand over the task of restoring order to an Iraqi force composed of former Iraqi soldiers.

The Marines withdrew and encircled Fallujah, which became a centre for dissidents until November 2004. In early November 2004 it took the first US Marine Division, the first US Cavalry Division, the first US Infantry Division, US Army Special Forces, US Navy Seabees, the Black Watch regiment of the British Army, Iraqi Army thirty-sixth commando battalion and Iraqi SWAT teams to assault and clear Fallujah.

# CUSTER'S LAST STAND (1970)

*Franklin D. Miller joined special forces Military Assistance Command Vietnam Studies & Observation Group (MACV SOG) from the first Cavalry Division in 1968. On 5 January 1970 Miller's special forces Recon Team (RT Vermont) was sent on a mission to locate a suspected enemy base in an area close to the borders of Cambodia, Laos and South Vietnam. On their way to the target they were to search for the wreck of an intelligence gathering aircraft which had been shot down the previous day. The crash site was estimated to be 3km from where they wanted the area they wanted to search.*

*RT Vermont boarded two "slicks" (UH-1D Hueys) at Kontum at about six-thirty in the morning of 5 January. They landed at Dak To. Dak To was the helicopter refuelling point and standby reaction centre for the mission. After inserting the team, the "slicks" would return to Dak To and the helicopters would wait there in case of an emergency or until it was necessary to extract the team after the mission had been completed. There would be nine helicopters on the ground in support of RT Vermont: two "slicks" and four Cobras from Kontum, two more Cobras from Dak To and a "Chase slick" which carried a special forces medic and full medical facilities.*

*The Standard Operating Procedure for an airborne inser-*
*tion involved a formation of seven helicopters. Two Cobras*
*flew escort just above and to the sides of the two slicks. During*
*insertion they circled and listened to their radios in case their*
*firepower was required. Another pair of Cobras followed*
*behind and flew in a holding pattern well behind the insertion*
*point. The "Chase slcik" flew further behind and much higher.*

*Another team had the duty of being a Quick Reaction Force*
*(QRF) in case the recon team ran into trouble. The QRF was*
*known as the "Bright Light" team.*

Miller's recon team consisted of three Americans: Green
(medic), Hobart (RTO) and Miller with four "Yards" –
Prep (zero one Yard or number-two), Hyuk (point man),
Gai (interpreter) and Yube (tail gunner). The code name
for the operation was "Cole Slaw".

Miller crashed down the last four feet to the ground.
Immediately afterwards he gave the waiting Cobras their
status and they set off. There was a Forward Air controller
(FOAC) flying at high altitude in an Air Force light aircraft,
code name " Covey". It monitored radio transmissions in
its Area of Operations (AO). Miller contacted "Covey" and
informed him that their situation was "green".

When they came near to the crash site Miller took
Hobart and Prep with him for a careful inspection of the
area. They could see where the tops of trees had been
sheared off by the approaching aircraft. The grass was so
high that they dared to start out across the open terrain.
About halfway to the actual wreck, the grass began to drop
away so they could see the remains of the aircraft.

What they saw made them freeze. They could see from
the remnants of the cockpit canopy that the pilot hadn't
ejected but was dead inside. But what had shocked them
was that thirty-five to forty enemy troops were surrounding
the plane. They were sitting in the thigh-deep grass around
the plane.

Miller fixed the plane's position and called in a Situation
Report (sitrep). Then he planned his next move. Their
main target was a few kilometres the other side of the

wrecked aircraft. Miller and his team would have to back track to get around the crash site undetected.

They were moving through dense brush next to a stream when he heard a shot 500 or 600 metres off in the distance. Hyuk was on point followed by Miller, Yube, Hobart, Prep, Green and Gai. Yube made a hand signal to everyone behind him, alerting them to possible danger. Unaware that the rest of the team had stopped, Hyuk and Miller continued to move forward, opening up a gap between them and the main body of the team.

Suddenly the entire jungle erupted and shuddered. Miller crouched and looked back in the direction of the rest of the team. He saw Prep stagger out of a cloud of grey explosive powder. He was badly injured in the lower jaw and had lost his rucksack and his weapon. Miller pushed Hyuk towards him and told him to take care of him. He detected movement with his peripheral vision, turned his head and saw part of an enemy squad coming around the tree that Hyuk had been standing under. Miller immediately opened fire from his crouching position. Hyuk wheeled and added his fire. Although both of them were in the open, they had responded so quickly that their attack knocked down the first four or five enemy soldiers before they were able to fire more than a couple of shots. The rest split.

Twenty-five or thirty North Vietnamese Army (NVA) soldiers jumped up from the hillside to Miller's left and rear. The NVA soldiers began assaulting the ambush site where the blast had occurred. They remained unaware of Miller and Hyuk on their flank. Miller:

Our initial bursts hit several NVA. I'm not sure how many, maybe six or seven. When you hit a large element out in the open, especially from the flank as we did, you can mess them up badly, even with just a few guys doing the shooting.

Not all of the people we hit were killed; some were wounded and fell out of our sight in the vegetation. But the key thing was that we were hitting people. We tried to concentrate on small groups of people as they ran down the dope. Every now and then I'd see one of my tracer rounds impact on someone, knocking him flat. I always loaded my magazines with two tracers near the bottom and two more rounds under them. That way I knew I was near the end of the rounds in that magazine when the tracer rounds flew.

It took a few moments for them to realize we were there. When they did discover our presence, they turned and tried to fire on us. However, they quickly realized that they were shooting through their own people. When they figured out that their position was very awkward, they performed a mass withdrawal.

There was still a slight haze in the air when the enemy disengaged. As Hyuk and I quickly headed down into the kill zone to inspect the damage, I saw people lying everywhere.

It looked like the bodies had been put through a meal grinder. Dead enemy troops were mixed in with the prone members of my team.

Prep, who staggered up the slope after the blast, still clung to life by a bare thread. Yube, the one who'd discovered the booby trap, was – unbelievably – still alive. He'd taken the brunt of the blast and had hundreds of holes over his entire body. Amazingly enough, not only was he still alive, but he was the least critically injured of the five who were caught in the explosion.

Hobart, Gai, and Green were all very seriously injured and not capable of moving under their own power. I turned to Hyuk and as calmly as I could said, "Let's get the fuck out of this area. We'll move everyone across the stream and get it between us and them. That way, if they come for us, we'll have some kind of barrier and open ground to help us deal with them."

Less than a minute had elapsed since the enemy withdrew. They wouldn't stay away long; of that I was positive. I was sure that any second they'd regroup and come slamming into us. Fighting down panic, I threw Gai's arm around my neck, grabbed Hobart by his web gear, and literally dragged them across the rocky streambed and through the water to the other side. Hyuk gathered up Yube and placed Green over his shoulder.

They moved the injured men across the stream then came back for Prep. Miller radioed back that they had a TAC E, a tactical emergency. This meant that they had been engaged by an enemy who was superior in size and likely to kick their ass. TAC E would put the chopper pilots at Dak To on stand by; pilots would go to their aircraft and Bright Light team members would start putting on their gear and moving over to the slicks.

They weren't in good shape for escape and evasion; only Hyuk and Miller were able to give first aid. Two of their guys had chest wounds but they couldn't even be given morphine because it would kill them. Prep died around midday.

The enemy had regrouped, spread out and was moving down the hill towards the ambush site. Miller and Hyuk were about to begin moving their wounded up the hill when they heard another big group of enemy soldiers coming down towards them.

The enemy group at the ambush site saw the blood and began shouting, "We hit them! We got some of them!" Then they found Prep's weapon and rucksack. They were jubilant until their platoon sergeant recalled them to their duty. He began to bring up a machine gun and sent out two soldiers in a flanking movement.

Miller watched them as they approached. He was trying to think how to get his men out of the trap. He was still trying to watch the progress of the two soldiers and the machine gun when one of the flanking soldiers saw the wounded group and opened fire. Miller:

It startled me when he started shooting. By now half of my attention was focused on the machine gun by the stream, That was the big hammer, and I was trying to decide how I was going to deal with it when — I knew it would be when and not if — we were discovered.

There was no more time to think.

Instincts took over.

Seconds after the enemy troop started firing I leaned back, raised myself up slightly to get a clear shot, and cranked off a single round. It caught him square in the shoulder and slammed him to the ground like a rag doll.

The soldier lying near the streambed saw me rise up and immediately took me under fire. As he was shooting at me, I was already pivoting in the direction of the machine gun. My primary hope was to somehow luck out and damage the weapon with a burst of rounds. However, it would be tough enough just to hit around it under the circumstances.

But when I turned I found the assistant gunner standing straight up, wondering what was going on. His mental lapse proved costly. I cut loose with a controlled automatic burst in his direction and managed to drop him. The gunner quickly shifted his sights and put some major smoke on me. I hit the ground in a hurry.

After the machine gun opened up, everyone on the hillside followed suit. Since I was the lone target they concentrated their fire on me. They threw rounds at me the likes of which I'd never experienced before. I was concealed in bushes and tall grass only; I didn't have any type of cover available – such as a tree or rock – to stop the rounds. They ripped through the vegetation all around my prone form, miraculously missing their mark.

Miller had the sole advantage that he was on higher ground than his attackers. He threw a gas grenade. CS gas was "nasty shit that troops on both sides don't want to deal with."

It made a big cloud which engulfed the ambush site. The enemy started to withdraw. Miller followed up with a White Phosphorus (WP) grenade. The White Phosphorus mixed with the CS gas to make a denser, heavier fog that lasted longer. Miller was able to get back to his team. Hyuk had continued to give first aid the whole time, and Yube and Hobart had recovered sufficiently to be able to move slowly. Miller grabbed Green, Hyuk picked up Gai and they began moving parallel to the stream.

It was slow progress and physically very demanding. After 100 metres they stopped to catch their breath. Miller got on the radio to call their HQ when heavy fire came from the bushes 20 metres on their left. Miller rolled over into a prone position and returned fire. Hyuk got off a sustained burst of automatic fire before he was killed by a round which hit him in the neck. Miller threw a frag (fragmentation grenade), which neutralized the attack.

At approximately 1 p.m. Miller called his HQ. He still reported his situation as a TAC E because they weren't surrounded yet. But his problem was how to move the wounded. Two of them could move by themselves but the other two could not move without assistance.

Miller looked for a good defensive position. He actually moved towards the advancing enemy, trying to anticipate avenues of approach and areas where they might gather for an assault. He found a suitable defensive position after about a minute. A couple of large rocks and some fallen timber provided the position with cover and it offered fair views of the probable avenues of approach. Half a minute later he saw the enemy point man step around a tree about 20 metres in front of him. Five or six others followed him. The last man was carrying the machine gun. The enemy were moving casually, as if they weren't expecting contact yet.

Miller knew that he had the element of surprise. He opened up immediately, putting down the machine gunner, then nailed the next guy. The group recovered from their shock and started hosing him down. Miller ducked low behind some fallen trees. The incoming rounds ricocheted off the rocks. He hit the point man; then a grenade landed close enough to swat him to the ground. He nearly blacked out, but most of the blast was absorbed by the trees. His head cleared just in time to see two enemy soldiers cutting around the rocks, searching for him. Miller was able to jerk his weapon up from the ground and fire at them. His movement attracted their attention but their reactions were too late.

Miller was able to fall back to his team. The four surviving members were covered in blood-drenched bandages, and Miller was aware that they were depending on him.

He called in a sitrep. The FOAC, Covey, had been monitoring his comms from overhead. He told him there was a bomb crater 200 metres to their east. He suggested that they should move to it so that they could be extracted. Miller agreed to try to move to it, and went to recconnoitre the crater. He reached the crater and signalled Covey by flashing a mirror, then started back towards his team.

Suddenly he found himself on the ground. He was trying to gather his wits when he vomited and realized that he was hurt. Blood was running out of his nose and down his chin. When he examined himself, he found that he had a hole in his chest and an exit wound in his back. Every breath he drew was accompanied by horrible sucking sounds. He managed to bandage the entry wound and dressed the exit wound with a piece cut from his poncho. He lost track of time while he was examining and dressing his wounds. He noticed three men approaching his position with a fourth lagging behind. Miller thought they reckoned he was dead. It wasn't until they came close enough to see him sitting up that they realized he was still alive.

He was able to fire two or three short bursts with his weapon from where it was slung around his waist. He hit two of them before they could fire a shot. The third turned and ran but was caught by a couple of rounds and went down.

Miller managed to get to his feet and reach the cover of the trees. When he got back to his team, Hobart said: "Man, are we fucked now."

Miller was seriously wounded but he was still the "most physically fit guy there". He began to carry his men to the bomb crater. Miller:

I can hardly begin to describe the genuine effort it took for me to carry, push, and drag everyone to that giant hole in the jungle. The entire episode remains blurred in my mind to this day; I really don't remember too many details. I do recall feeling incredibly tired – I wanted to go to sleep so badly. I remember concentrating on putting one foot in front of the other as one of the Yards hung limp at my side. Once I was on my hands and knees as I pulled someone along by his web gear. Crawl forward a few feet, pull hard, fight the pain. Crawl, pull. Crawl, pull.

In time I somehow managed to assist or flat-out transport each member of RT Vermont to the extraction point. Once we were all in the crater, I established some semblance of security. Hobart and Yube were capable of firing their weapons if push came to shove, so I positioned them where they could provide the most help in our defense.

We waited.

Shortly after taking up residence in the crater, we were assaulted by a sizable force. Rounds began to fly back and forth. Just as the battle was beginning to heat up, a new and unexpected variable entered the equation.

Dramatically, a Huey materialized out of thin air! It simply came out of nowhere and dropped down to within five meters or so of the crater's rim, where it hovered unsteadily. I looked skyward and spotted the door gunner shifting around behind the M-60, scanning the area. I didn't have a clue as to who was in the chopper or what operation they were running. All I knew was it didn't belong to my organization. But man, it was the first sign of friendlies I'd seen all day, and my emotions ran wild.

Too bad I didn't have any time to enjoy the moment.

Mere seconds after the Huey dropped in from out of the blue, the jungle surrounding the crater came alive in a frightening display of firepower. 7.62mm, mortar, and antitank rounds burst out of the light vegetation. All the destructive force was focused on one target: the chopper.

I didn't attempt to return any fire. It would have been useless and a waste of ammo. We were in a whirlwind of devastation, and the best course of action was to hug the ground and ride out the storm. I watched in awe as the drama unfolded.

The noise was deafening. Shit was flying everywhere. Scores of tracers ripped up through the trees, and rockets spewing smoke crisscrossed every which way. If even one of the anti-tank rounds had hit the chopper it would have been all over; as it was, none found the mark. However, the 7.62mm rounds found their target often. The Huey was being eaten up by the rifle and machine-gun fire. The door gunner was hit and hung limp over the M-60. The chopper's skin was pockmarked from hundreds of rounds. There must have been fifty or more enemy troops assaulting the Huey with but a single thought – bring that son of a bitch down!

All this activity occurred within ten to twenty seconds. How the chopper stayed in the air I'll never know. By all rights it should have been shot down. But stay aloft it did and, badly scarred from the effort, it beat a hasty – if somewhat erratic – retreat. Its departure sent a chill down my spine.

Now the enemy would focus his attention on us.

A lull ensued after the chopper left. No more 7.62mm, mortar, or anti-tank rounds were fired. There was movement all around us, but no hostilities were directed our way. I couldn't understand why they didn't attack immediately. They knew we were in the crater; surely they could have overwhelmed us with sheer numbers or simply lobbed a few mortars or frags on top of us. As strange as it may seem, I was irritated and concerned as to the reasons for the delay. I knew the asskick was coming. Finally, I concluded that they were toying with us.

Ten minutes later they mounted an assault, although it wasn't quite as strong as I had expected. They laid into us with a heavy barrage of fire as we met the challenge. Hobart, Yube, and I gave as good as we received, and we forced them to back off after a few minutes of frenzied action.

Miller decided it was time to take the offensive. It was now four o'clock and it would be dark in a few hours. He was beginning to run low on ammo. He was already using Green and Gai's basic loads and had used up all he had retrieved from Prep and Hyuk. He told Hobart and Yube to hang tight, he would come back in a few minutes. He dragged himself out of the crater and crawled to the edge of the jungle cover. He found an ambush position with a good rock for cover and plenty of vegetation for concealment, then prepared by taking up a good firing position covering the direction he thought the enemy would take. He got out his final frag, his last two CS grenades, his remaining two magazines and waited.

When there was about an hour of daylight left, he heard the sound of soldiers gathering for an assault in front of him.

They began advancing towards him. The terrain was forcing them into clusters. When they were 15 metres from his position he opened fire. They weren't expecting any contact forward of the crater, so he hit several with his opening rounds. The rest dropped but quickly recovered and kept him pinned down while they prepared and fired an anti-tank rocket which hit the rock he was hiding behind. Miller threw his frag just as the remaining troops were charging towards his position, and took out several of the attackers. He shot the survivors who hadn't turned and run. He threw the CS grenades and hauled his ass back to the crater.

He had just cleared the rim of the crater and got himself into a fighting posture when the enemy came through the cloud of gas. Miller, Hobart and Yube all began shooting. They finally stopped the charge when it was 10 metres from them.

Then Miller was hit in the arm. Yube and Hobart had been hit again and were stretched out on the ground. Miller thought he had lost the use of his hand until the sensation returned. It was almost seven o'clock and it was getting dark.

Miller heaved his last frag in the direction of the enemy. He and Hobart looked at each other with tears running down their faces. They thought that it was the end. Then Miller saw a Yard coming towards them. He thought he was "seeing things". It was the point man of a Hatchet Force. A Hatchet Force was a bigger relief effort than the seven-man Bright Light team; it was an entire platoon of Yards with American officers.

An American lieutenant reached the crater and said: "Motherfucker, this looks like Custer's Last Stand."

The Hatchet Force was able to establish a perimeter for long enough for them to be extracted. Miller was the last man to leave the ground. He was also the last one to receive surgical attention because he was still the least injured.

Miller, Yube and Hobart survived. Gai and Green died during surgery. While Miller was in hospital in Japan he wa told that he had been recommended for the Congressional Medal of Honour. As he began to recover he realized that he wanted to go back to Vietnam. He met an administrative orderly who fixed the paperwork and told the hospital that he had received orders to return to his unit. When he got back to his unit his buddies could scarcely believe it. He went back to doing missions.

A year later, in June 1971, he was summoned to Washington DC to receive his medal but he had become too valuable to be risked on dangerous missions.

By 1972 he could see the writing on the wall: the war was coming to an end and his way of life with it. In November 1972 he was sent back to the United States for some medical tests, because the authorities thought that he might desert to stay in Nam.

He was assigned to a Special Forces training unit. He met Elwood J.C. Kureth in Korea in 1988 and they agreed to work together on his memoirs. Miller died from cancer in 2000.

# RESCUED FROM A MOB (2005)

*On 20 September 2005* The Times *reported that two British
soldiers had been stopped in their car by an Iraqi police patrol
at a roadblock in the southern town of Basra. The two British
soldiers were acting undercover. The situation became a stand-
off which developed into a firefight. One Iraqi was killed and
the two soldiers were arrested by the Iraqi police. They were
taken to the al-Jameat police compound.*

The Times *reported:*

Special forces are understood to have been targeting a
number of well-known figures in the city.

Two of this undercover team were in an unmarked car,
reportedly wearing Arab robes and headdress.

Muhammad al-Abadi, an official in Basra, claimed last
night that the two were driving fast and aroused the suspicious of police who were manning a checkpoint on the edge
of the city.

"A policeman approached them and then one of these
guys fired at him. Then the police managed to capture
them," Mr al-Abadi said.

Despite requests from the British Army the Iraqi police refused to release the two soldiers. A British Army armoured patrol was sent to the police compound. Demonstrators ambushed the patrol, throwing stones and firebombs at their vehicles. *The Times* reported:

Sergeant George Long, 29, of the Staffordshire Regiment, yesterday described to *The Times* the moment he had to dive in flames from his Warrior armoured vehicle as a furious mob closed around it outside a Basra police station.

"My face was on fire. Petrol poured down behind me and into the back. Luckily I had goggles on. It was panic. You don't think about anything, you just want to put the flames out."

As the vehicle moved towards the al-Jameat station to help troops to rescue two servicemen seized by Iraqi police, the optical scopes through which the commander steers were smashed. Sergeant Long had to open his turret to guide the vehicle without crushing the mob or British troops. Then a petrol bomb lobbed through the turret hatch set him and his gunner alight.

"The petrol came down on both of us," he said. He plunged to the ground. "I just remember hitting the deck and rolling and rolling, trying to get the flames out, hearing soldiers shout 'stay down, stay down'." The flames were extinguished and he was pulled away by other troops.

Behind him his gunner fell in flames on to the Warrior's side. Badly injured with serious burns, he was evacuated and is in hospital in Britain.

From his nearby Warrior, the company commander, Major Andy Hadfield, saw what was happening. "I saw them come out as fireballs, and I felt sick. They were my soldiers," he said. "Then five minutes later, I heard Sergeant Long back on the radio. He said he was back in the vehicle but needed a new gunner as the last one was a casualty."

In the late afternoon, the soldiers briefly withdrew and were fired at with rockets and small arms. But they deployed to al-Jameat again after a six-man negotiation team who had tried to get the release of the first two prisoners was surrounded by the mob. It was only then that Major Hadfield realized that Sergeant Long's burns were more than superficial.

"He is a modest man and a professional," the major said. "It was nine hours before I discovered that he had actually been burned badly around his waist and back. Nine hours in which he had chosen to get back into his Warrior and continue. That is some example."

Official sources in London tried to play down Monday's clashes, suggesting only 150 rioters were involved. But in Basra the story that emerged from officers and men was of a mob up to 1,000 strong.

A second attempt succeeded in freeing the two soldiers. *The Times* reported:

When army commanders witnessed a mob converging on Basra's main prison threatening revenge on two British soldiers imprisoned inside, they dared not leave the men in Iraqi police custody overnight.

A rescue mission was hastily put together to free the undercover soldiers without causing injury to the local police inside.

Armoured vehicles had already sealed off the roads leading to the police headquarters to keep away protesters and prevent local reinforcements reaching their Iraqi colleagues locked inside.

After a day of worsening violence that reportedly left two Iraqis dead, three British soldiers seriously injured with burns and dozens of local demonstrators hurt, senior commanders realized they had to get back their men.

One military source said last night: "We believed that we had no other option". He added: "The safety of our two soldiers was our priority. The ferocity of the earlier clashes showed how determined some iocal groups were to get their hands on these two men."

Senior officers are sure the mob was being orchestrated by insurgent leaders in Basra who were demanding the release of three influential figures from their militia.

The concern was that a vigilante mob would try to overcome the police guarding the Britons and seize the two prisoners who could have been held as hostages to exchange for their imprisoned leaders. Basra's police chief has reportedly claimed that his own force has been infiltrated by militiamen.

While a rescue was being plotted, senior officers were also in negotiations with local police to hand over the two Britons, reminding the Iraqis they had no legal right to hold onto the soldiers.

Last night there was some dispute as to whether the soldiers were handed over or rescued.

The show of force by British troops would have allowed the Iraqis to save face by claiming they had no option but to release their captives.

The Ministry of Defence claimed last night that a wall of the prison was knocked down "by accident" in a manoeuvre by the armoured unit, though the governor of Basra described the Army's behaviour as "barbaric".

"A British force of more than 10 tanks backed by helicopters attacked the central jail and destroyed it. This is an irresponsible act," Mohammed al-Waili said.

While he and other officials said that the British raid made use of tanks, it was not clear whether the vehicles were Challenger 2 main battle tanks or Warrior infantry fighting vehicles. Both are used by British forces in Iraq.

The British would have realized that extricating their own men would also mean freeing other prisoners.

Local reports suggest that the British rescue force made no attempt to prevent the escape of the other captives.

Commanders will realize that last night's raid will only inflame tensions in the area. Troops going out on patrol had been warned to expect more trouble in Iraq's second city after three days of skirmishes.

Army convoys were given additional protection and all

but the most necessary patrols in the centre of Basra were cancelled.

This order did not include undercover operations by special forces, which have been intensifying their hunt for terrorist leaders.

A British commander, Brigadier John Lorimer, of the 12th Mechanised Brigade, had given warning that if local police were prevented from "bringing criminals to justice" then the Army would do so.

Special forces are understood to have been targeting a number of well-known figures in the city.

Two of this undercover team were in an unmarked car, reportedly wearing Arab robes and headdress.

Muhammad al-Abadi, an official in Basra, claimed last night that the two were driving fast and aroused the suspicious of police who were manning a checkpoint on the edge of the city.

"A policeman approached them and then one of these guys fired at him. Then the police managed to capture them," Mr al-Abadi said.

*The Times* reported:

British forces smashed their way into Basra jail last night to free two soldiers seized by Iraqi police earlier in the day. After the doors to the jail were breached, troops stormed inside to find and rescue their colleagues. The Ministry of Defence confirmed that the men had been freed, but would not comment on reports that they were undercover commandos.

Army commanders are believed to have taken the decision to use force after deciding that they could not leave the pair in the prison overnight. Agitators reportedly had been driving through the city using loudspeakers to demand that the soldiers be kept in detention.

The dramatic show of strength also allowed about 150 Iraqi prisoners to escape, an Iraqi defence ministry source said.

The move ended a stand-off that began after a gunfight with police in which two Iraqis were allegedly killed. In a challenge to British authority in Iraq, the special forces soldiers, who were in plain clothes, were taken prisoner.

*The Times* described the second attempt:

Before the prison was attacked nearby roads were sealed and reinforcements surrounded the police station. "We are not leaving without our men, said a British commander. The former Iraq commander, Tim Collins, said it was "not a good turn of events", but added that he believed the events did not represent a breakdown of law and order in Basra.

British diplomats had demanded the release of the men, reminding the Iraqi authorities that British troops in Iraq were answerable only to British military justice. But the Government in Baghdad had appeared unable to impose its will on the authorities in Basra.

More than 8,000 British troops are deployed to maintain order and to train the very police that were holding the two soldiers prisoner. The Coalition's entire exit strategy depends on Iraqi security forces being able to take over.

Last Saturday British soldiers detained a commander of al-Sadr's militia over the recent bomb attacks on British troops. Shia demonstrators and militiamen have subsequently been been staging shows of force in Basra, orchestrating demonstrations and roadblocks.

That heightened tension may have triggered yesterday's gunfight. It appears that the two soldiers, who were dressed in Arab clothing and driving a civilian car, refused to stop at an Iraqi police checkpoint, fearing that it might be manned by disguised insurgents.

Shots were exchanged as the police moved to arrest the soldiers. Iraqi authorities later released photographs of the men sitting handcuffed, with bandaged heads, in a police cell.

*The Times* continued:

The violence that erupted on the streets of Basra yesterday was the result of a simmering struggle between British forces and the increasingly powerful Shia Muslim militias active in southern Iraq.

Attention has been focused on the Sunni Muslim insurgency against US-led forces further north, yet the British have been facing a sharp rise in attacks from an increasingly sophisticated and deadly foe.

The clashes and the arrest of two undercover soldiers was almost certainly triggered by the arrest at the weekend of Sheikh Ahmed al-Fartusi, the leader of the Mahdi Army, a banned militia loyal to Moqtada al-Sadr. He was seized by British troops in a raid that also netted his brother and another colleague.

"The operation is the result of an ongoing multinational force investigation that identified individuals believed to be responsible for organizing terrorist attacks against multinational forces," said a statement released by the British military on Sunday after the deaths of six British soldiers and two security guards over the past two months.

Al-Sadr's supporters are known to dominate the local police and can mobilize gunmen or mass protests at short notice, as they did regularly during an uprising last year that swept across southern Iraq.

British officials are convinced that Iran is implicated in the upsurge in violence and suspect it may be connected to Britain's hardening position against Tehran's nuclear programme. Britain has been working closely with Iran over the past two years to reach a compromise. But with the victory last month of the hawkish President Ahmadinejad, Iran has hardened its position.

Britain is now actively lobbying to have Tehran referred to the UN Security Council, where it could face sanctions.

Iran's policy in Iraq is co-ordinated by the Supreme National Security Council – the body responsible for running its atomic industry. "The Iranians are careful not to be caught," a British official said. "But they like to stoke up the temperature in Iraq when it suits them."

Apart from the activities of al-Sadr's supporters, military intelligence has concluded that Iran has been supporting a local terror group run by Abu Mustafa al-Sheibani, who is blamed for the murder of at least 11 British soldiers.

In a secret report, military intelligence warned commanders that attacks on British forces were being deliberately intensified, with the use of a new bomb, developed in Iran, that can penetrate the thickest armoured protection.

Al-Sheibani's group is said to have an estimated 280 fighters, divided into 17 bomb-making teams.

One of al-Sheibani's bombs, a passive infra-red device, is blamed for the deaths of Second Lieutenant Richard Shearer, 26, Private Leon Spicer, 26, and Private Phillip Hewett, 21, of the Staffordshire Regiment, in the Risaala neighbourhood of central al-Amarah, near the Iranian border in July.

A similar roadside device was used six weeks ago against a British embassy convoy in Basra that killed two British bodyguards.

The report, drawn up by British and US experts, said that al-Sheibani's group was being investigated for its role in the murders of six Royal Military policemen in June 2003 by a mob in Majar al-Kabir.

On 21 September 2005 *The Times* reported that a senior military source had told the newspaper that:"The intelligence we had received left us in no doubt that these men were going to be killed."

The British feared that their captured soldiers were going to be executed by Shia militamen. Further details of the rescue were published:

An SAS team used the noise of armoured vehicles bulldozing their way through a nearby police compound to mask the raid that freed their comrades.

The rescuers, from the same squad as the captives, blew out the doors and windows of the smart suburban villa with plastic explosive and hurled stun grenades at the militiamen guarding the two undercover soldiers.

A short, intense burst of automatic gunfire was heard before the men were freed and their captors were seen being dragged away, hoods over their heads and their hands tied behind their backs.

Neighbours said the entire operation took only a couple of minutes while attention was focused a hundred yards away on the army's invasion of the main al-Jameat police compound.

Army commanders denied being heavy-handed, insisting that they had no option but to stage a rescue mission once they had learnt that the soldiers had been handed over to extremists.

Brigadier John Lorimer, who commanded the operation, said:

"I had good reason to believe the lives of the two soldiers were at risk."

The soldiers had been beaten and rogue policemen had been touring the area with loudhailers urging demonstrators on to the streets to protest that the "British saboteurs" had been planning explosions in the city which would be blamed on followers of Moqtada al-Sadr, the Shia cleric.

The Iraqis displayed photographs of the explosives, weaponry and several bags of equipment allegedly found in the boot of the men's unmarked car when they had been stopped at a checkpoint. There were also wigs, Arab headdress and sophisticated communications equipment.

The two soldiers are believed to have been investigating a corrupt police unit in Basra who were colluding with Shia militia leaders. Some of the men who later interrogated them are believed to be part of this same unit.

The mob which quickly gathered outside the detention centre were shouting for the Britons to be hanged as spies.

Hours of negotiations between army officers and local

dignitaries were getting nowhere, and after armoured vehicles were firebombed by a mob and three soldiers injured
the order was given at 9 p.m. for Warrior armoured personnel carriers to smash their way into the compound.

A policemen said that he saw two walls knocked down as
the Warriors crushed parked cars and demolished a line of
prefabricated huts used as offices and sleeping quarters.
Abbas Hassan, another officer, said: "Four tanks invaded
the area. A tank cannon struck a room where a policeman
was praying."

The British search parties had to pick their way over
splintered furniture, metal-bed frames and air-conditioning
units.

Brigadier Lorimer would later call it "minor damage".
Muhammad al-Waili, the Governor of Basra province,
claimed it was "barbaric, savage and irresponsible".

Troops burst into every room as senior officers explained
they had to ensure the missing Britons were not being
hidden among the sprawl of buildings. If not, then they
had to force the police to reveal where they had been taken.
A military source said:

"We knew they couldn't have gone far because of our
cordon but we were sure time was running out."

One of the Iraqi prisoners who took advantage of the
chaos to escape said that he had briefly shared a cell with the
Britons. The man described how he watched as the pair
were hauled away by guards who ordered inmates to strip
off their Arab robes so they could disguise the men.

The suspicion was the militiamen would try to smuggle
their captives out of the protective cordon and use them as
hostages in exchange for their leaders arrested by British
troops on Sunday. The turning point came just before 7.30
p.m. with the report that the Britons had been moved and
officers manning the protective cordon thrown around the
Hay al-Khalij district spotting a number of known agitators.

These were the same men who had orchestrated the
earlier petrol bomb attacks on troops as they tried to pull

back to neighbouring streets of Hayaniyah, a stronghold of the outlawed al-Mahdi Army. They were seen leading a gang of protestors converging for a second attack on troops from 12 Mechanised Brigade who were guarding the police compound.

Brigadier Lorimer later demanded that the Iraqis explain why the soldiers were not immediately handed over to Coalition forces as required by the agreement regulating the British presence in Iraq.

"This is unacceptable and we won't hesitate to take action against those involved in planning and conducting attacks against Coalition forces," he said.

In October 2005 the British Government agreed to pay compensation for the damage caused while rescuing the men.

# THE TET OFFENSIVE (1968)

*Richard Burns was a Pathfinder in the One Hundred and First Airborne division. At the beginning of January 1968 his detachment had only been in Vietnam for a month. They were stationed on the airbase at Bien Hoa north of Saigon.*

*During 1967 the US forces could claim that they were winning the struggle against the Viet Cong but early in 1968 it did not look as if the Viet Cong had been defeated. Burns:*

As the end of January neared, the Tet holidays approached. Tet is the Vietnamese lunar New Year, a sacred holiday during which for several days the Vietnamese people participate in traditional celebrations, hold street festivals, and worship revered ancestors at family altars. This time the Communists decreed a truce, claiming it would last from 27 January to 3 February 1968.

A few days before the Tet cease-fire, rumors started circulating that the enemy was going to launch a major attack on a number of rear-area installations, including Bien Hoa. Intelligence reports had supported the assumption all along. But the South Vietnamese leaders thought it inconceivable. Surely the Communists would not attack on such a hallowed occasion, especially since it was the North Vietnamese themselves who called for the cease-fire agreement.

The American military knew that the Communists had a long record of breaking agreements. As far as the North Vietnamese were concerned, a war was in progress. Their only goal was to win, and by any means. Therefore, the US military wasn't taking any chances, including the 101st Airborne Division. Every Screaming Eagle was put on alert, and infantrymen from the 502nd Infantry relocated to our compound at Bien Hoa to help strengthen the perimeter.

Flak jackets and steel pots became everyday wear. We kept extra batteries and ammunition on hand and drilled rushing to our assigned bunkers. Chopper crews practiced getting gunships armed and into the air quickly. More fighting positions were created and older ones fortified.

Most of the guys I talked with hoped the Communists would attack in large numbers so we could fight them outright for a change, without having to search the jungle and engage them on their terms.

At three in the morning on 31 January 1968, three days after the beginning of the Tet holidays, mortar and rocket fire began pouring into our compound. It sounded like the Fourth of July except louder. The Communist 122mm rocket was particularly menacing. It weighed 112 pounds and had a range of ten miles. Carrying an immense warhead of 42 pounds, each one sounded like a low jet fighter ripping through the sky overhead. It made a thunderous explosion, which shook the ground. Although extremely inaccurate, it scattered huge chunks of jagged metal, which tore through anyone and anything in its kill radius.

Rushing into the bunkers, we stumbled and fell on top of one another like the Keystone Kops. Explosions continued, jolting the ground around us. The bunker was a four-foot-deep, four-foot-wide trench, protected by a steel culvert and a few layers of sandbags. It probably would not have withstood a direct hit, especially from one of the rockets.

Within a short while, Lieutenant Wilberding came by

and informed us that a ground attack was highly probable. He told us to proceed to the helicopter revetments and protect the aircraft until the flight crews got the choppers into the air. He, Sergeant Guerra, and a few others remained behind to coordinate additional support. [Revetments were parking sites for helicopters. Each such site was surrounded by barrels filled with sand to protect the aircraft from shrapnel and other projectiles.]

In addition to our M-16 rifles, we grabbed two radios and plenty of ammo, then rushed to the revetments. Although it was still dark, the incoming explosions illuminated the night sky, allowing us to find our way easily. Once at the revetments, our group spread out in two-man teams and took up positions behind the sand-filled barrels.

We could hear sporadic gunfire in the distance, and every once in a while a bullet zipped overhead or slapped into one of the barrels protecting us. It was a frustrating situation, because we didn't know the enemy's exact location and friendly units were scattered around us. Consequently, we couldn't return fire for fear of hitting fellow Americans. Anyway, our primary concern was a possible assault by enemy sappers.

Sappers were elite enemy soldiers highly skilled in the art of infiltration. They could penetrate just about any perimeter given the right circumstances and a little luck. Generally they were fully clothed and armed like other NVA soldiers. Sometimes, however, they simply wore a scanty loincloth with a type of grease covering their bodies. That made it easier for them to slither through barbed wire, trip wires, and other obstacles.

Normally, sappers toted explosives attached to their bodies, usually a satchel charge that they could easily throw into a bunker or building, or beneath an aircraft. Since they were not expected to survive or to return from an attack, it was not uncommon for them to blow themselves up along with the intended target, if necessary, to ensure its destruction. The probability of their successful penetration increased when they were assaulting under the protection of a mortar or rocket attack.

In short time, helicopter crews showed up and manned their assigned choppers. Fortunately, none of the choppers appeared to have been seriously damaged by any of the incoming rockets or small-arms fire. While the gunships relocated to load their armament, some of the utility helicopters received orders to immediately transport an infantry platoon of Screaming Eagles to the US embassy in Saigon, which was under attack. Lieutenant Wilberding radioed us that he and another Pathfinder already at his location would coordinate the pickup zone of the platoon.

Suddenly, intense small-arms fire broke out all along the installation's perimeter. By the sound of it, one hell of an attack was under way. Wilberding's voice blared over the radio. He informed us that the enemy was assaulting the perimeter in large numbers. Our group was directed to leave the revetments and immediately proceed to the perimeter to find any position that needed additional reinforcement. By the sound of the gunfire, we had to get there fast.

Hurrying to a nearby road, we hitched a ride on a truck delivering supplies and ammunition along the perimeter. When we arrived at the perimeter, we discovered a place with a forty-meter gap between fighting positions. As the truck screeched to a stop, a few rounds zinged by. The driver yelled for us to get off. Quickly jumping from the bed of the truck, we all crouched low off the side of the road. Hastily, the vehicle sped off, the driver obviously happy to be away from the scene.

The site we picked contained two deteriorating sandbag walls about ten feet long and four feet high for use as cover. Larry Foracker, Ron Reynolds, Joe Bolick, and I bolted behind one stack of sandbags while the rest of the detachment members dashed behind the other. The position had a clear view to our left front, which encompassed a large open area with shrubbery, rolling hills, and ditches. The right front overlooked the Bien Hoa Air Base and its runway in the distance.

Instantly, bullets cracked all around us, some slamming into the sandbags shielding us.

Larry was on my left, Ron and Joe to my right.

Breathing heavily, Larry gasped, "Damn, man, that was close!"

Ron slowly raised his head to peek above the sandbags. "Maybe I can see where it's coming from."

Sand splattered in his eyes and on his face as bullets impacted into the sandbags. He quickly dropped to the ground. "Goddamn! Someone has us zeroed in."

Watching Ron wipe the sand from his eyes with his sleeve was so humorous we all started laughing.

I turned to Larry. "Hey, Larry! Poke your head up there and tell us if you can see anything, will you?"

"You're crazy, man. This shit's for real. My mother will be real upset if I get killed." I would have given anything to have a photo of his face; his expression prompted us to laugh all the harder.

It was Joe's turn. "Richie, weren't you the one bitching about having to wear a steel pot and flak jacket?"

I shook my head. "Yeah! But not now, brother. You won't hear me complain about wearing this stuff again."

Bullets continued zinging overhead and slapping into the sandbags. Afraid to aim our weapons for fear of exposing our heads and getting them blown off, we sat huddled together, paralyzed. Glancing over at the other position, I saw our fellow Pathfinders trapped in the same predicament.

Finally, out of frustration, Ron cried, "We've got to do something! We just can't sit here like this."

Larry agreed. "He's right! For all we know an entire company could be charging across that field at us right now and we can't even look up to see them."

That scary thought was emphasized further when someone on the perimeter cried out, "Fix bayonets!"

That did it! As if Ron and I read each other's mind, we switched our weapons to automatic and lifted them above the top of the wall, exposing just our hands. We sprayed the area to our front once, then repeated the procedure. Within seconds the rest of the detachment followed suit, saturating the area with bullets.

They stopped shooting just as a jeep came to a halt behind them. Two more members of their detachment got out. They had brought an M-60 machine gun and ammo. One of the new arrivals straightened up for a moment to catch his breath. He immediately had to dive for cover as bullets ripped through the air around him. The others laughed at him until they heard explosions within the air force compound. They presumed that it was enemy mortar fire. They were astonished to see fifteen to twenty armed figures in brown uniforms rushing onto the runway. One of them tossed something at a jet parked on the runway. It exploded in a ball of fire.

Later they heard that a sapper unit of approximately two hundred enemy soldiers had broken through the perimeter where it was held by the Army of the Republic of Vietnam (ARVN). During the holiday half of the South Vietnamese soldiers were away on leave visiting their families.

The sapper unit was only 300 yards from their position. It was caught in the open. Burns and his fellow pathfinders opened fire. When they stopped shooting to assess the situation only a few of the sappers were still on their feet. The pathfinders had not yet set up their M-60. One of the pathfinders took over the gun and fired it continuously instead of the short bursts infantrymen were trained to fire. Eventually they all screamed at him to cease fire because there was a danger of hitting their own men. They had to twist the ammunition belt to force the gunner to stop firing.

Most of the sappers had been killed. Those within the perimeter were trapped but some of them remained concealed and continued to take potshots from concealed positions.

Burns spotted a concealed enemy soldier. He rested his rifle on a sandbag and waited for the enemy to expose himself. When he had the enemy's torso aligned between his front and rear sights he squeezed the trigger. He couldn't quite believe he had made a certain kill.

At about eight in the morning there was a huge explosion about ten miles away. Burns was awestruck by a massive, dark cloud mushroom that had risen high up into the atmosphere some ten miles away.

They speculated as to whether it was an atomic bomb until they heard a radio report that sappers had blown up the ammunition dump at Long Binh, one of the biggest in all of Vietnam.

Franklin Miller was serving with US Special Forces at the time of the Tet Offensive. While he was recovering from a wound Miller was sent to a military outpost at Nieh An. He was spending the night with a girlfriend in a nearby village when he heard the sound of distant artillery. He was aware that it had continued all night but he was enjoying himself so he didn't think about it.

The next morning he collected his gear and weapons. As he left the house he could tell from the atmosphere that things were not normal. After he had walked a short way, some villagers told him that his outpost was under attack.

He paid a passing Vietnamese to give him a lift on his little 90cc motorcycle. When he reached the outpost's gate there were dead bodies everywhere, twisted in the barbed wire. Most of the troops in the outpost were South Vietnamese with about eight Americans. They were reluctant to let him in, as they had been hit about twenty minutes before and were expecting another attack. Miller entered the command bunker, where they were glad to see him "cause you know what the hell's goin' on."

Almost immediately they heard automatic weapons fire. Through a window in the bunker Miller saw NVA emerging from the village which he had just ridden through on the motorcycle. He jumped towards the radio and called down some 155mm artillery fire on the NVA troops. The airbursts from the 155mm artillery shredded the village after eight rounds. Miller and a lieutenant moved to a .50 machine gun position on top of the outpost's main bunker. They came under 120mm mortar fire. "They really blew the shit out of the camp." A round hit the fresh food conex (container). The lieutenant was hit by "a big piece of frag" and " in a matter of seconds he was dead". An entire section of their perimeter wire had been destroyed. Miller:

> We didn't know it was going to be the big event of the year but we were sure the shit was about to hit the fan big-time because of the intensity with which the enemy assaulted us.

A smaller camp nearby was overrun and a mechanized infantry platoon came to relieve Miller's outpost. The second night they were there Miller was up on the .50 when there was a white flash from a rice paddy and a clang as red-hot sparks exploded from the front of one of the APCs. A sapper had crawled right up on one of the mechanized infantry vehicles and hit it with an anti-tank round.

Immediately seven or eight of the Armoured Personnel Carriers (APCs) opened fire with their .50s. Miller realized: "They were firing down in the dirt in front of them. They were being overrun!"

The NVA actually captured one of the APCs and turned its machine gun on the US infantry vehicles for a few seconds. Miller called down some artillery fire. After that the remaining NVA broke off the assault and retreated across the rice paddies into the jungle.

More armoured vehicles from the mechanized infantry unit arrived later that day. That night the mechanized infantry unit ran into a substantial enemy force. They saw thousands of tracers arcing above the tops of the trees. A Spooky – a C-47 aircraft armed with three 7.62 mini-guns – turned up to support the mechanized infantry unit. The mini-guns each fired six barrels at a rate of six thousand rounds per minute. The NVA stood up to it and actually drove it off.

At two in the morning the mechanized infantry unit came back into their area. It had been decimated. Only four of the eleven vehicles that had left came back and one of them had to be towed. Apparently they had encountered a "heavy-duty enemy battalion on the move." They found "about 120 enemy dead scattered all over the battlefield."

Although the US and South Vietnamese only lost 6,000 men while the North Vietnamese lost 50,000, this unconventional operation had a significant effect on the outcome of the war.

In the opinion of Marine Corps sniper John Culbertson: "After Tet in early 1968, the Viet Cong were broken, and the North Vietnamese Army refused to stand and fight like their predecessors in 1967."

But the Tet Offensive was a turning point. For the first time the North Vietnamese had taken the war from its rural base into supposedly impregnable areas of South Vietnam. They attacked targets in urban areas including the US embassy in Saigon, the Headquarters of both the US and South Vietnamese armies and the main Saigon radio station. According to US secretary of state, Henry Kissinger: "Henceforth, no matter how effective our action, the prevalent strategy could no longer achieve its objectives within a period or within force levels politically acceptable to the American people."

TV pictures played a significant role. Stanley Karnow described what millions of Americans saw: "Dead bodies lay amid the rubble and rattle of automatic gunfire as dazed American soldiers and civilians ran back and forth, trying to flush out the assailants. Americans at home saw the carnage wrought by the offensive."

The North Vietnamese General Giap pointed out after the war: "For us, you know, there is no such thing as a single strategy. Ours is always a synthesis, simultaneously military, political and diplomatic – which is why quite clearly, the Tet Offensive had multiple objectives."

A 1968 CIA report concluded: The intensity, coordination and timing of the attacks were not fully anticipated. The report added: another major unexpected point was the ability of the Viet Cong to hit so many targets simultaneously.

US President Lyndon Johnson's popularity ratings plummeted. Stanley Karnow commented: "But then came Tet – and his ratings plummeted – as if Vietnam were a burning fuse that had suddenly ignited an explosion of dissent."

Johnson decided not to apply for re-election. He also announced that, in future, air strikes would be confined to below the twelfth parallel. He authorized the opening of negotiations with the North Vietnamese.

# TASK FORCE VIKING (2003)

On 20 March 2003 US Special Forces entered northern Iraq. Task Force Viking consisted of nine A teams, each of twelve Green Berets. Each A team was accompanied by an Air Force combat controller. Their mission was to link up with the Kurdish guerillas known as Peshmerga. The Peshmerga were indigenous to the area and were united in their opposition to Saddam Hussein's regime. Once they had linked up with the Peshmerga who held the high ground they would be able to call in Close Air Support (CAS) to deal with any reaction from Saddam's forces.

By 23 March the Special Forces operational detachments were on the hilltops of north western Iraq with their Peshmerga allies. On 24 March Operational Detachment Alpha (ODA) 056 began calling in CAS from an Observation Position (OP) known as hill 725. In response two F/A-18 Hornets dropped two 500-pound bombs on enemy positions on a ridgeline overlooking the northwest Irbil airfield. Eight Iraqis were killed and sixteen wounded.

Weather conditions were unfavourable but by 1 April, similar operations enabled them to report: "what appears to be a withdrawal by the Iraqis from positions 5 kms south OP 725, sent SALUTE to higher, requested CAS, 'NO CAS' and then watched 500 Iraqi soldiers load 6 buses and safely depart area heading south towards Mosul."

The Iraqi military had never been able to get very far into Kurdish territory. Just north of Kirkuk there was a ridge-line, which was the limit of the territory controlled by the Iraqi military. The Green Berets of Third Special Forces Group (SFG) (A) dealt with the Iraqi forces in their front. With CAS they cleared them out even where they tried to hold their ground. The Peshmerga were convinced of their effectiveness and took them on to the next objective, the town of Chamchamal. This would be a stepping-stone towards the Special Forces' ultimate objectives: the liberation of the two northern cities of Kirkuk and Mosul. When they had been liberated they could be used to resupply and reinforce coalition army units around Baghdad, once the forces on the ground had begun to advance northwards from Kuwait and Saudi Arabia.

3rd SFG (A) was assigned to the liberation of Kirkuk. 10th SFG (A)'s goal was the liberation of Mosul. Chamchamal was on a main road, twenty-five miles east of Kirkuk. It was on the border of the areas controlled by the Kurds and those controlled by Saddam's forces. The edge of these two areas was known as the green line. It ran through Chamchamal, which had once been a town with fifty thousand inhabitants. It was then deserted. An Iraqi battalion was dug in on a ridge west of the deserted town. In front of the ridge was a "no man's land": 1,500 metres of flat ground which had been sown with land mines. The Peshmerga and the Iraqis had set up vehicle checkpoints on their sides. Several hundred Kurdish fighters were actually in the town, and the Iraqis shelled it every day between 1700 and 1800 hours.

The Kurdish fighters in the town were wary of the Green Berets. In their turn, the Green Berets were wary of the inhabitants of the town. One of the special operators said:

You could never really trust who was who in that town. The town's population was all made up of male soldiers, so that there was always a chance that one of the denizens was an Iraqi agent. If the word got out that there were American soldiers present in the town, it could spark an offensive by the Iraqi army. Tensions ran extremely high.

At night members of ODA 083, dressed like Peshmerga, were led up onto the rooftops where they could spot the Iraqi positions on the ridgeline. During the day they targeted every Iraqi position. They were close enough to see them with the naked eye. They had brought satellite imagery with them so the job was much easier than it would have been using only a map. They were anxious to avoid bringing down friendly fire on their new allies.

Anything that wasn't apparent from the satellite imagery was provided by Human Intelligence (HUMINT). The HUMINT was provided by the Kurds. They not only knew exactly where and what each Iraqi position was but they could lead the Special Forces safely to their destination. Whereas previously the Kurds could not put their knowledge to good use, the Green Berets brought with them the power to take out any permanently fixed target. The Kurds were motivated by the brutality that had been inflicted on them by Saddam and his regime.

One Green Beret said:"I did not meet a single Kurdish male between the age of fifteen and sixty that had not either been in prison or tortured, at one point or another, or had a brother or father killed."

The first day on the rooftop had been spent targetting. By the end of the second day they had begun to call in aircraft which dropped precision-guided bombs. The rooftop was less than 1,200 metres from where the bombs would land.

The targets of highest priority were taken out first. B52 heavy bombers flew overhead at 45,000 feet. From the ground they were nearly invisible to the naked eye; only a thin white con trail could be seen. Each bomber dropped twelve Joint Direct Attack Munitions (JDAM), which were conventional bombs with guidance units attached to their fins. Each Green Beret detachment operated in split teams, with four to six men on each shift. That way the CAS missions were called in without any break.

As their positions were destroyed by the pinpoint accuracy of the bombing the Iraqis retreated over the ridgeline towards Kirkuk. Once the nearest threat was over the ridgeline, Chamchamal became the FOB and the Third SFG ODAs advanced towards Kirkuk itself. Thousands of Peshmerga advanced with them. The Iraqis were so thin on the ground that there were no real targets for CAS left. One special operator said: "It was like, we bombed them, we bombed them and we bombed them . . . the ones who were left were not giving up so we knew it was time for a ground assault."

Once a target was destroyed, the Standard Operating Practice (SOP) was to clear the objective before moving onwards, but before the special forces and the Peshmerga got there any Iraqis who had not been killed by the bombing had already retreated. Only when there was nowhere else to go did the die-hards remain.

When ground assaults were necessary, the special forces had to organize the Peshmerga into ordered assaults with fire support. This was vital because of the danger of friendly fire both from the normally wild Peshmerga and also if any hostile bunkers needed to be taken out by CAS.

The attackers had to be organized into two assault lines and a fire support position. Each assault line or team was 150 to 200 men strong. Mortar teams were organized to give them fire support; the mortars were augmented by vehicle-mounted MK-19 automatic grenade launchers. These weapons "really spooked" the defenders, who either ran or stayed in their bunkers until they were destroyed by CAS.

Kirkuk fell quickly. At that time, it was basically a military supply depot. Everything was abandoned, including hundreds of T-55 and T-72 Russian tanks and thousands of uniforms. Many of them had just been left by soldiers melting into the civilian population. It was a form of osmosis which would feed the insurgency later.

# THE ONE-HOUR RESCUE (1987)

In October 1987 there was a riot at Peterhead maximum security prison in Scotland. A group of long term prisoners on D wing rioted and all but destroyed the building. They took one of the warders hostage.

Most of the rioting prisoners gave themselves up to the prison authorities but a group led by three ringleaders refused to give in and threatened to kill their hostage. He was a fifty-six-year-old warder, named Jackie Stuart, who only had one kidney and needed medical care and drugs to stabilize his condition.

The three ringleaders were men with little left to lose. Malcolm Leggat was a twenty-four-year-old who was serving life for murder; Douglas Matthewson was a thirty-year-old who was also serving life for murder; and Sammy Ralston was a twenty-five-year-old who was a convicted armed robber.

The ringleaders and the remaining rioters barricaded themselves into an area beneath the roof of D Wing. They made a hole through the slates of the roof and pushed the warder through the hole. They put a noose around his neck and threatened to set him on fire. They yelled their threats to

*the prison authorities and police who were watching from
below.*

*All this was taking place before the media. Jackie Stuart
was filmed with his arms outstretched, pleading for help. His
captors laughed at him and threatened to throw him off the
roof, 70 feet down into the yard.*

*The Prime Minister, Margaret Thatcher, was watching on
television. She telephoned the Secretary of State for Scotland.
Twenty-four hours later they were still debating whether or not
to send in the SAS.*

In October 1987 Peter Ratcliffe was D squadron sergeant
major. The SAS had a Special Projects (SP) team on
permanent standby as their Counter-Terrorist unit. Each
squadron took it in turn to provide the SP teams; at that
time it was D squadron's turn for SP duty. The squadron
on SP duty was divided into two teams of twenty men each,
known as Red and Blue teams. Red team was standing by in
case it was needed.

From its base in Hereford, Red team drove to RAF
Lyneham, accompanied by a police escort. At RAF Lyneham they were loaded onto a C-130 Hercules aircraft which
flew them to Aberdeen. They landed in the very early hours
of the morning and another police escort guided them to the
maximum security prison at Peterhead.

They left their vehicles out of sight to avoid the media
and picked their way along a fence that ran alongside the
warders' houses. They reached the back entrance of the
prison without being seen. All their equipment had to be
carried into the prison by this route in green canvas hol-
dalls. Each holdall contained a gas mask, black leather
gloves, fireproof black overalls, black rubber-soled boots,
a 9mm Browning High Power automatic pistol, a Heckler &
Koch 9mm sub-machine gun, body-armour, belt kit, ammunition, riot baton and personal radio. Additional equipment was taken into the building, including explosive
charges, stun grenades, extra ammunition and ladders.

Red team was briefed in the prison gymnasium. Their
CO had a map of the prison laid out and detailed drawings

of the roof and each level of D wing were put up on a blackboard. The plan involved entry and approach at four points, involving sixteen SAS men. The prisoners had taken over three floors of D wing and the hostage was being held in a cell beneath the roof which had been barricaded off.

Four members of Red team had to climb out of a skylight in a different part of the prison. Then they had to make their way, at night, along a parapet above a 70–foot drop. The parapet was so narrow, they had to proceed in single file. They also had to try to to avoid being seen by prisoners who were locked up in another wing across the yard. It had rained and the parapet had become slippery.

When the officer in command gave the word, by radio, the men on the roof were to ease themselves down through the hole in the slates and then crash through the ceiling of the room where it was thought the hostage was being held. Simultaneously, shaped explosive charges would be detonated to blow off the hinges of the three metal doors of D Wing. Then the other three SAS teams would charge in.

In the gymnasium they put on their fireproof black overalls, black, rubber soled boots, body-armour and gas masks. They were going in with batons, stun grenades and canisters of CS gas and were going to try to make "hard arrests" . This meant no firearms were to be drawn unless absolutely necessary. They were relying on the stun grenades and CS gas to do most of the work of subduing the prisoners.

The four teams got into position silently. As they made their way along the slippery parapet, they were seen. The prisoners in the block opposite began to shout warnings and bang their pisspots on the bars of their cells to alert the hostage-takers.

But everything was in place and the officer in command was able to give the go-ahead over the radio. At exactly 5 a.m. the SAS went in. Peter Ratcliffe:

And in we went. The prisoners didn't know what had hit them. The moment the stun grenades exploded and the CS-gas pellets released their fumes, the fabled hard men of Peterhead were no longer in the game. Indeed, they had never had a prayer from the moment we were called in.

It was all over within three minutes. Reeling around, stunned by the bangs and choking on the gas, they were grabbed from the room they'd barricaded in D Wing and dragged down the iron stairs from one landing to the next. Other SAS guys in black overalls and gas masks gently led the prison officer to safety.

I had been tasked along with a guy called Johnny, an Ulsterman, to go through the door on the first-floor landing. When the simultaneous explosive charges blew the hinges off the door, I charged in. It was extremely difficult to see anything, owing to the gas and the amount of smoke from the flash-bang grenades. The rioters had wrecked or ransacked everything in sight, hurling the debris on to the walkways outside the cells, which further impeded our progress. Johnny and I cleared each cell, but there were no rioters on this floor. Then, over the radio, the OC reported that the hostage had been rescued and the rioters seized.

I was still on the first floor with Johnny when our guys brought Mr Stuart down the stairs to our landing. He was wearing a donkey jacket with orange flashes on the sleeves, and was utterly bewildered. He had been sitting at a table in the cell beneath the roof when our guys burst in, and it was obvious that he didn't know what was happening to him.

Other teams cleared any remaining resistance from the landings. Apart from a thundering great racket from the rest of the prisoners in the other wings, who were locked in their cells and rioting, it was all over bar the shouting. The prison warders, the same warders who had been unable to cope with the rioting convicts, suddenly became very brave. They had entered the wing after we'd freed the hostage, and I watched as they dragged the ringleaders down the metal stairs.

Ratcliffe had a brief exchange with his commanding officer.

He told his men to change out of their kit, pack up and start moving out, as they needed to leave before dawn came up. This would ensure that they avoided the attention of the media. They slipped out quietly the way they had come. The entire operation had taken less than one hour from their arrival to their departure.

# SCUD HUNTING IN IRAQ (1991)

*On 2 August 1990 Iraqi troops invaded Kuwait. On 6 August the United Nations Security Council adopted Resolution 661, which called for the restoration of the legitimate government of Kuwait. The United States and Great Britain immediately sent aircraft to Saudi Arabia to deter any further Iraqi aggression.*

*On 29 November 1990 the United Nations passed Resolution 678. This Resolution ordered all Iraqi troops to withdraw from Kuwait by 15 January 1991. An international Coalition was formed, whose forces would defend any other states attacked by Iraq. The UN Resolution authorized the Coalition's forces to use "all necessary means" to expel the Iraqis from Kuwait if they would not withdraw peacefully.*

United States General Norman H. Schwarzkopf was the commander of the Coalition forces. At first he did not think that Special Forces had any part to play in the conflict. He was quoted as saying: "What the hell can a Goddammed Special Forces unit do that a Stealth Bomber or an F16 can't do a darned sight better?"

On 18 January 1991 the Iraqis began a series of missile

attacks. The Iraqis had modified versions of a Soviet medium range ballistic Surface to Surface Missile (SSM). Its NATO codename had been "Scud". The Iraqis had reduced the payload and increased the burn rate of the fuel carried by their Scuds, so they were less accurate and less reliable than the original form of the missile. In 1988 the Iraqis had launched over 200 Scud missiles during their war with their neighbour Iran. During the early 1980s they had received over 800 Scuds from the Soviets.

The modifications which the Iraqis had made to their Scud missiles did not make them more effective or more destructive weapons, but made them quicker to launch and therefore harder to detect. They had proved this in their war with Iran. They had four or five fixed launch sites and an unknown number of mobile launchers. The Iraqi Scud missiles were capable of carrying a 2,000-pound conventional warhead at just under 4,000 miles per hour, with a range of between 100 and 180 miles.

They began by aiming their "Scud" SSMs at the Coalition airbase at Dhahran. The Scuds were shot down by MIM-104 Patriot Surface to Air missiles (SAM).

The Scuds were easily destroyed by the radar guided Patriot SAM launched into their path, and did not form a direct threat to the Coalition's forces. But because of the mobility of their Transporter-Erector-Launcher (TEL) units, they posed a threat to the Coalition itself. The Iraqis were able to move their TELs into Western Iraq where they were within range of Israel. They fired seven SSMs at targets in Israel; three landed in Tel Aviv, two landed in Haifa and two others landed in open country.

On 19 January two more hit Tel Aviv and seventeen people were wounded. If the Israelis retaliated directly against Iraq, the Coalition could lose many of its Arab members. Syria and Egypt were the most likely to withdraw. It was a very anxious time for the Coalition while the Israelis decided how they would respond.

On 20 January, Patriot Missile systems were deployed to protect Israel from further attack. The Coalition sent F15 Strike Eagle aircraft into southern and western Iraq to try to locate and destroy the Scuds and their TELs. However, the air sorties failed to find the launchers. General Schwarzkopf was forced to concede that aircraft could not deal with the problem by themselves. General Sir Peter de la Billiere was the Commander of the British Forces in the first Gulf War; he saw the situation would require Special Forces, and expected that General Schwarzkopf would order Special Forces to help to counter the threat from the Scud missiles.

In fact General Sir Peter de la Billiere actually anticipated the order. He had been OC of 22 SAS himself. Thirty-six hours earlier, he had given four half-squadron teams from A and D squadrons the task of locating the remaining Scud missiles and cutting their communications with both static and mobile launch sites.

Each half-squadron team was given an area of responsibility within a region of Iraq. They usually operated at night and laid up during daylight hours.

A recce unit for an Iraqi artillery brigade discovered an SAS Lying Up Position (LUP) by accident. They presumed that the SAS were friendly forces and stopped their Russian built Gaz-69 truck near the SAS position. An Iraqi officer carrying a map case got out of the Gaz-69 truck. He walked towards the SAS soldiers. He did not realize his mistake until he was quite close, when he pulled out a pistol. There was a firefight. All except one of the Iraqis were killed. The surviving Iraqi was taken prisoner and flown back to Saudi Arabia with the maps and information from his vehicle. The information enabled the Coalition to identify further valuable targets that had not been detected from the air.

The experience of an SAS staff sergeant confirmed that "eyes on the ground" could trace the Scuds. He described:

Scuds were usually launched at night and gave a huge signature, a great big ball of light. You could see the fireball at the base of the motor from thirty miles away across flat open desert, and that gave us an indication of where to look. The launcher would be moved immediately after firing, but if you looked at the layout of the roads and interpreted it intelligently you could generally pick up where the launcher was going to be.

By midnight on 20 January all four SAS half-squadron teams were heading for the Iraqi border. They were to cross 25 miles into Iraq and hold there while the Coalition waited for the Israeli response.

On 21 January the Israelis agreed not to do anything "for the time being".

Three out of the four half-squadron teams crossed successfully. The fourth half-squadron team was held up by a berm on the border itself. A berm is a manmade bank or dune made from sand or earth, usually formed by bulldozers, which stands from six to sixteen feet high. They often have a ditch facing the unfriendly territory. The berm on the Iraqi/Saudi Arabian border extended continuously for miles.

The SAS teams were given other high priority missions while they were behind Iraqi lines. The military planners in Riyadh needed to know if the ground in Iraq could support the weight of tanks and heavy vehicles. They needed soil samples before any major ground operations could begin, and the job of collecting these samples was given to the SAS teams. The results were very useful to the Coalition. The missions also revealed that the Iraqis' weakness was their communications network, which relied upon buried fibre optic cables. These were, by their nature, almost impossible to detect from the air but vulnerable from the ground.

The SAS had two tactics which worked against the buried fibre optic cables. Once they found a cable they could blow it up with charges placed by hand. Then they could leave booby traps for the Iraqi repair teams. This slowed down the time it took for the Iraqis to get their comms system working again. The delay was vital because the longer the Iraqis were kept in the dark the easier it would be for the Coalition's forces to operate.

An SAS operation against a communications tower revealed that the Iraqis had very little idea that the SAS were conducting mobile operations so far within their territory. When the SAS attacked the tower they were surprised by how little resistance they met. They attacked at night with their heavily armed vehicles and destroyed the tower and its support equipment. Afterwards, they found out that the Iraqi soldiers had formed the impression that they were under an air attack and had taken shelter in their underground bunkers.

The SAS used three stratagems against the Scud threat. Firstly, they deployed road watch patrols to report on Scud movements. Secondly, the mobile patrols would be used to attack the convoys of TELs and their support vehicles. Thirdly, the SAS would intensify their operations against the Iraqis underground communications network.

Three more eight-man patrols from B squadron, 22 SAS, were sent to observe the Main Supply Routes (MSRs) 200 miles west of Baghdad. Two of them decided not to take vehicles. When one of them, Bravo Three Zero, landed, the patrol leader jumped out of the helicopter to look at the terrain. Bravo Two Zero and Bravo Three Zero were the patrols that had decided not to take vehicles. Bravo Three Zero had landed on a flat featureless gravel plain and the patrol leader decided that it would be impossible to remain undetected. He ordered the helicopter to try a second landing site. They tried again a few miles away but at this second location the patrol leader came to the same conclusion. When they returned to their Forward Operating Base (FOB), at Al Jouf, he reported that there was nowhere to hide.

At 0830 on 23 January one of the half-squadron teams, Alpha One Zero, still had not crossed the border. The Regimental Sergeant Major of 22 SAS, Peter Ratcliffe, was sent to talk to the officer in command (OC) of Alpha One Zero. Their rendezvous was delayed because the Chinook helicopter which was due to take him to the rendezvous had a hydraulic failure.

In the meanwhile another officer met up with Alpha One Zero and got them across the border. They found a Lying

Up Position (LUP) in enemy territory. Then Alpha One Zero sent a message to FOB, reporting that they had made contact with the enemy 50km inside Iraq. They had killed three Iraqis and captured another with their vehicle, a Russian-built jeep.

At FOB they expected Alpha One Zero to move north towards their designated Area of Operations (AO). Instead, they received a second message saying that Alpha One Zero was moving south towards the border for rendezvous, resupply and to hand over their prisoner. Peter Ratcliffe was given a letter authorizing him to take over the command of Alpha One Zero if he felt that it was necessary "to ensure that the unit was operating to its maximum efficiency".

The temperature was below zero when Ratcliffe landed. He handed the letter authorizing him to take over the command of Alpha One Zero to its commanding officer, who accepted that he had been replaced and boarded the helicopter with the prisoner. Ratcliffe immediately ordered Alpha One Zero to head north east 50km to their next LUP. Their convoy consisted of eight Land Rover 110s, three motorbikes and an unarmed Unimog support vehicle.

The motorbikes were used to check out the ground ahead and to pass messages between the vehicles during times when radio silence was necessary. They threw up much less dust than the 110s.

The Land Rover 110s had all their lights painted out and no windscreen, doors or roof. The spare wheel was carried flat on top of the bonnet. They carried sand channels lashed to the vehicles' sides and winches at the front for dragging vehicles or people out of difficulty. One of the few things they had in common with the civilian equivalent, the Range Rover, was their coil-spring suspension. Driving across the Iraqi desert was extremely bumpy, noisy and slow, so they only covered between ten to twenty kilometres an hour. Without a windscreen it was cold and uncomfortable because they were facing into an icy wind interspersed with long periods of sleet.

The Land Rover 110s each carried three men and weighed about three tons. They were armed with a 7.62mm general purpose machine gun (GPMG) mounted on the bonnet. They also had a Browning M2 0.5 inch calibre heavy machine gun, mounted so that it was rear-facing, as well as an 81mm mortar and a MK 19 grenade launcher.

Ratcliffe's Land Rover 110 was equipped with a Milan anti-tank missile launcher. The Milan was a wire-guided weapon that was mounted on the top roll bar and had a range of 2km. It was effective against prepared defences as well as armoured vehicles.

On top of the Milan, a device known as Milan Infra Red Adaptor (MIRA) was mounted. This was a thermal imaging device which could see people and vehicles in poor visibility several kilometres away.

Each man had an M16 as his personal weapon.

They reached the LUP an hour before dawn. The Land Rovers were formed in pairs in a ring around the Unimog. Each pair posted a sentry further out. He communicated with his pair of vehicles by using a string or wire. If all else failed he would have to crawl back. A sentry's stag (spell of duty) lasted two hours.

The next day they pushed hard to cover 160km to their next LUP, where they met up with Alpha Three Zero. Alpha One Zero's AO was to be on MSR3, the road from Amman, in Jordan, to Baghdad.

Ratcliffe decided that the risk of being spotted by Iraqi aircraft was virtually nonexistent. Consequently they did not need to use camouflage nets when they laid up and they could risk moving in daylight. They spread out Union Jacks weighed down with stones so that they would be not only visible but identifiable from the air.

After eleven hours' driving, at 0400 on 30 January they reached the area of their rendezvous with Alpha Three Zero. They had only averaged 15kph because of the terrain. They sighted three men from Alpha Three Zero through their thermal imaging device; Ratcliffe edged closer then went forward himself to confirm the contact.

By 31 January they had reached a new LUP, 200km

inside Iraq. The next night they pushed on another 50km. They had arrived in the centre of their designated AO. By radio they were given a "specific mission outside their main task".

Their mission was to make a reconnaissance of Mudaysis airfield, a large Iraqi fighter base 20km west of the MSR. They had to go round a Bedouin encampment and passed several other encampments during the night. They passed so close that people waved to them; they waved back.

By 0200 on 2 February they were on top of a slope above Mudaysis airfield and set up their LUP 3km from the airfield. Ratcliffe sent two men to a Forward Observation Post (FOP), who observed very little activity during the day. They sent in a Situation Report (sitrep).

The next night they were heading back towards MSR3 when they struck a road heading north–south. They decided to use the road for a few kilometres. While they were travelling on it, they noticed an unusual manhole cover, sealed with metal bars and a padlock. They discovered a second manhole cover 200 metres down the road. This confirmed their suspicions that the manhole covers concealed fibre optic command and control cables, which probably connected the airfield to Baghdad. They fixed the location for future reference and withdrew.

By this stage of the war there was virtually no Iraqi ground activity during the day. Their LUP that evening was on a wide plain. Ratcliffe reassured his men that they were actually safer not using camouflage nets because Coalition aircraft would be less likely to mistake them for a hostile unit. If any Iraqi armour appeared they would have time to call up Air Support.

Over the radio he got permission to cut the fibre optic command and control cable which they had found earlier in the day.

Ratcliffe had to split his force because it would be foolish to risk compromising the entire patrol for a small demolition task. He took two Land Rovers, one motorcycle and their crews. He sent the rest to find an LUP which could serve as a rendezvous for a helicopter resupply which was due the following night.

When they opened the manhole covers, they found three fibre optic cables and another type of cable. They placed explosive charges with a thirty-minute delay.

They had just finished placing the second explosive charge when they noticed three sets of headlights coming towards them. Ratcliffe was considering his options when the oncoming vehicles stopped.

Within a couple of minutes the vehicles came on again at the same steady pace as before. One of Ratcliffe's men said that he thought they were checking the manhole covers because the other cable must have been a "trembler" which had tripped an alarm system. Ratcliffe decided to use the road to escape. Between the road and where they had left their vehicles there was a small berm. The first Land Rover got over it without a problem but the second one stalled. They had to pull it off backwards before trying again. The enemy vehicles were only 600 metres away when they succeeded in getting onto the road.

Ratcliffe reckoned that the headlights of the enemy vehicles would badly affect their night vision. Consequently they would need to be within 100 metres before they saw the SAS vehicles. The noise of their own engines would prevent them from hearing the SAS vehicles.

They had increased the distance between them and the Iraqis to a kilometre when Ratcliffe signalled to the other vehicles to turn off the road into the desert. They had stopped for a break when the the first set of charges blew. The headlights of the Iraqi vehicles suddenly stabbed out in all directions. Five minutes later the second set of charges went off.

Before they met up with the rest of Alpha One Zero, they spotted some enemy activity, which they reported to Al Jouf. They only had two hours before the helicopter was due for the resupply. On the way, one of their Land Rovers accidentally drove into a ravine. Its three occupants were saved by the roll bar, but their weapons, equipment and rations were thrown all over the bottom of the ravine. It took them an hour and a half to winch it upright and they had to hook it up to the Unimog to drag it out of the ravine. They checked it over and it started first time. Finally, they reached the location of the resupply.

They were given orders to find a disused airstrip that C-130s could land on for resupply on a series of moonless nights that were due 14–20 February. Helicopters could not operate without moonlight, whereas the C-130s could. They found a suitable disused airstrip on 4 February. After they had reported its location they took up an OP near the MSR.

On 6 February they were in a position close to MSR3 when they were ordered to penetrate and destroy a micro-wave Scud control station known as Victor Two. They had to complete their mission by 0600 on 8 February. Their target was situated right by the MSR in a key staging area used by civilian convoys. The key equipment was some switching gear and fibre optic cables which were contained in a fortified underground bunker They were told that it was defended by a force of about thirty soldiers.

Ratcliffe got a SATCOM (voice) radio link to Al Jouf so that he could ask for more details. He was told that the main target was in a bunker about 40 metres square. It was surrounded by an 8-foot-high wall. The wall was made of pre-fabricated concrete slabs slotted into concrete posts, and there was a chain link fence between the wall and the bunker. The vital switching gear was in one of three under-ground chambers inside the bunker. A 250-foot-high mast behind the bunker was to be the secondary target.

The target was only 35km from their LUP. Ratcliffe decided to do a reconnaissance that night. A motorway lay across their route, which had been under construction and was now almost complete. It was due to replace the MSR. The difficulty of getting their vehicles across the motorway barriers and storm drains added to the dangers they already faced.

Ratcliffe's plan of attack on the control station was to send in a demolition team, while the rest of the unit would

provide supporting fire and additional back up. The demolition team would get through the wall and fence by
blowing holes in them with instantaneous shaped charges.
As soon as they had blown the walls open they would rush
in and head straight down the steps. If there were any doors
blocking their way they would remove them with similar
charges, then place charges with two minute fuses in each of
the three underground chambers. Then the demolition
team would dash back to the main group.

Ratcliffe assigned nine men to be the demolition team:
three demolitionists, each with two assistants who would
help carry the gear and give them covering fire. Ratcliffe
himself would be one of the assistants. He outlined his plan
to his senior NCOs and the two officers who were members
of the unit:

> The attacking unit will cross the east–west road directly in
> front of the target building. The main fire support group –
> at least half of our total force – will be positioned south west
> of the junction where the north–south road meets the first
> one. The rest of the men will be given their positions nearer
> the time – when, I hope, we know a bit more.

He sent a section to make a reconnaissance of the motorway
and find a decent crossing point. The reconnaissance party
came back with a plan for crossing the motorway. They had
found a gap in the crash barriers on the central reservation,
which left the problem of crossing the big central storm
drain. They reckoned that if they piled their sand bags in
the middle of the drain, they could bridge it using their
sand channels. After they had done this they would move to
within 1km of the target to do a Close Target Recce (CTR).

Ratcliffe told his men to check their weapons, spare
ammunition and vehicles. They would leave everything
else in or alongside the Unimog. This would be booby-
trapped but otherwise left undefended under a camouflage
net at the LUP. He radioed FOB to inform them of his
intentions and to advise them not to expect any further
radio contact until after they had completed the operation.

At 1730 their convoy of eight Land Rovers and all three motorbikes pulled out of the LUP.

When they reached the motorway, they found the place where they planned to cross. They packed their sandbags into place in the storm drain, unhooked their metal sand channels and laid them in place. They slowly drove across to the north side, where Ratcliffe ordered his men to leave it all in place so they could beat a hasty retreat if necessary.

They carried on towards their target. They stopped 1,000 metres short of the installation. From there Ratcliffe took his three demolition men and one other trooper forward on foot for the CTR. The other man was supposed to be an expert with a "spyglass" or compact thermal imaging device.

They stopped about 30 metres west of the north-south roadway, which connected the town of Nukhayb with the MSR. To their left was a berm about 10 feet high. Ratcliffe had hoped to make the attack before the moon came up but it was already well over the horizon and rising. It was less than a quarter full but there was a fair amount of light. Ratcliffe was bare-headed but the rest of his CTR team were wearing helmets.

The expert with the spyglass was wearing a flak jacket, full belt kit and pouches with bandoliers of extra ammunition. The rest of the team wore ordinary desert gear with their sleeves rolled down, standard belt kit and weapons. There was no time to change. Ratcliffe pointed north to where they could see the mast, and told the man with the spyglass to lead.

The man with the spyglass had only gone about 50 metres when he stopped. Ratcliffe asked him what was wrong. He was told there was a bunker about 50 metres ahead of them but he didn't think it was manned. Ratcliffe kicked the man on the ankle and told him to get on his feet and to keep moving.

When they were 100 metres further forward, they could see the target building. They could also see pinpricks of light beyond it, covering an area the size of a small town.

Just beyond the MSR the relay block and the steel mast were clearly visible in the moonlight; to the right of them there was a large enemy bunker made of sandbags and timber. They could see lights through the slits in its sides, and it was clearly manned by a considerable number of men.

As they watched, a large, brightly lit vehicle drove along the MSR from the east and turned down the north-south road. It was a passenger coach with all its interior lights on. Ratcliffe learned afterwards that the Iraqis were using this type of vehicle to transport Scud missiles. The driver was, presumably, trying to give the impression that it was not being used for military purposes.

Once the vehicle had passed they moved forward again. They saw another bunker to their left, though the spyglass man refused to look to see if it was manned. Ratcliffe crawled forward himself. It was unmanned. He lost patience with the spyglass man and signalled to another of his CTR team to come forward and take the spyglass man back. Then he was to tell the others that he wanted all the vehicles and the rest of the men to assemble there in half an hour.

Ratcliffe led the other two men to the bunker. From there they could see not only the main target but some kind of encampment half a kilometre further north. It was clearly military and it was clearly manned. He told the two men to move forward to see what else they could discover. In the meanwhile he worked on his final plan.

He decided to eliminate the manned bunker to the right of the main target building. The best weapon they had for this was the Milan system, where the operator only had to keep the target in his sights after launch. The minimum safe range was 400 metres, so the vehicle carrying the weapon could be fired from where Ratcliffe was watching. He went outside to look at the target through his night glasses.

The two men who had moved forward came back to report. They had seen another bunker like the manned one on the right. This one was about 50 metres west of the road junction on the far side of the MSR.

Ratcliffe planned to eliminate this bunker with a LAW 80. This was a single shot, rocket-propelled Light Anti-tank Weapon (LAW). The two men who had moved forward also told him that there were some military-type trucks parked on the other side of the MSR right in front of the target building.

When the rest of the men and the vehicles had assembled exactly where Ratcliffe wanted them to be he briefed them:

> There are two vehicles parked across from the target. I want four men to go forward and cover those and another two to go to the same spot with a LAW 80 to take out the enemy bunker beyond the end of the berm on our left. I also want a Land Rover fitted with a Milan to be positioned just on the road over there [a spot 30 metres to their right] to take out the main bunker on the right of the target.

He told four of them and those not given a specific task to wait there as a reserve. Everyone else except for the Milan vehicle and crew was to go forward and set up a fire support position at the end of the berm to the left of the road. He told them to keep as quiet as they could for as long as possible. Ideally they should not need to take out the bunkers until the charges went off.

Ratcliffe led his demolition team off to the left. They made use of the available shadow cover. Three of their Land Rovers followed them as they moved up to a position 200 metres from the target building.

They could see the wall around it and the steel mast. The wall appeared grey in colour, apart from a section that was a few metres wide and looked different. Ratcliffe:

> The six men who had moved forward with us – one of them with a LAW80 – had already broken away and crossed the road to come up on the two trucks. To the right and less than 50 metres beyond them was the large bunker, where I could easily make out the enemy coming and going. Even though it was late there seemed to be quite a lot of activity.

About 150 metres to our left the other bunker was now clearly visible. It too was brightly lit inside and had enemy personnel moving about. There were other, smaller buildings behind the left-hand bunker, and about a hundred metres beyond the target was the large military encampment that we had spotted during the recce.

They had been told that there would only be thirty soldiers guarding the installation. They could see many more than that. They crept forward, crossed the MSR and past the right-hand bunker. A minute later they reached the wall. They reached the section of wall that looked different; it was covered with plastic sheeting. When they pulled the sheeting back they discovered that the wall had already been breached. There was "a bloody great hole" there. So they went through the gap. Ratcliffe:

Within thirty seconds all six of us were through the gap and had pushed the plastic sheeting back in place. Inside, there was total chaos. The place had obviously suffered a direct hit from an Allied bomb or missile. In places the fence was twisted and flattened, and in others completely torn from its cement base. Of the main bunker there was almost nothing left. There were buckled steel girders and shattered concrete everywhere. Some of the wreckage was so precariously balanced that it looked likely to crash down at any moment.

I took a look around for an entrance to the three underground rooms, but the stairway and the rooms had been completely buried beneath the rubble. The whole site was extremely hazardous, and I realized that one or more of us could get badly injured simply walking in the ruins, especially since the moonlight on the wreckage left large areas in deep shadow. It was perfectly certain, too, that there wasn't any switching gear left for us to destroy.

Ratcliffe decided they should try to destroy the secondary target, the mast. They placed their explosive charges around three of its four legs. They were beginning to leave the site when "all hell broke loose". Ratcliffe:

At which point our good fortune took a nosedive. We were through the tangled fence and close to the gap in the wall when all hell broke loose. There were several single shots followed by a burst of automatic fire, then the enormous whoosh of a Milan going in and, seconds later, a huge explosion as the missile struck home. Then everyone seemed to let rip together. Rounds were zipping overhead and we could hear them smacking into the other side of the wall.

There were bullets flying everywhere, riddling the sheeting covering the gap while, above, tracers created amazing patterned arches. We were safe enough on our side of the wall, but not for long. Behind us, no more than ten metres away, was over 100 pounds of high-explosive getting ready to blow in less than ninety seconds.

"What do you reckon, Mugger?" I asked. [Mugger was one of the demolition men.]

"We haven't got much racking choice, have we?" he replied.

I grinned at him. "No. I suppose not. So let's go." And with that I ducked round the plastic sheet and into the open area on the other side. The other four were all lying by the wall outside.

"Line abreast and back to the jumping-off point," I yelled. "And let's move it. It's all going to blow in a few seconds."

Surging forward, we spread out like the three-quarter line in a rugby game and belted towards the dark, looming mass of the north end of the berm. Though I swear that not even the finest line-up ever made it from one end of a rugby pitch to the other at the speed we travelled that night. Of course, we were all as fit as professional athletes, and given the amount of adrenalin fizzing around in our muscles we'd have been good for a few world records – if anyone could have spared the time to clock us.

We were halfway between the wall and the jumping-off

point when the first explosive charge blew, followed seconds later by another boom and, almost immediately afterwards, by a third.

None of us stopped to watch the effects, however, for there were bullets whistling all around us. As I ran I looked to the left. The bunker there was gushing flames and smoke from its gun slits and entrance, which meant the Milan had done its job.

The bunker on the other side was still intact, and there seemed to be a lot of the enemy fire coming from that direction. But Pat and his team on the 110s had the heavy machine-guns in action, while some of the guys with him had brought their grenade launchers to bear and were peppering the bunker with high-velocity fragmenting metal. As a result, most of the enemy fire was wild, since they were reluctant to face the streams of 0.5-inch rounds and 40mm grenades.

We ran to within a few metres of the Land Rovers' position, and I yelled to the fire-support team that we were all through and evacuating the area. On we dashed. Suddenly we were at the north-south road and I could see dark shapes over to our right where the enemy trucks were parked. Our guys there were firing on groups of Iraqi troops who were taking cover at the sides of the ruined bunker and in a few small huts, or crouching behind low humps of sand and rock.

The enemy soldiers appeared to be using automatic rifles and light machine-guns, as well as standard magazine rifles – and there seemed to be a lot of them. My immediate impression, however, was that none of them was capable of shooting very straight. Not that it mattered. You could just as easily die from a lucky shot as from the perfect aim of a sniper.

Among the SAS men near the trucks I thought I could make out Major Peter in the group closest to us. I yelled, "Cease fire and retire with us back to the vehicles," meaning the four 110s we had left behind near the abandoned L-shaped bunker. We continued to run up the slight slope, parallel with the berm. When we reached them the wagons were all intact, including the one that had fired the Milan, which had rejoined the other three after taking out the bunker. Tracer and bullets were still flying everywhere, and back towards the target we could hear the roar of the Brownings, the lighter rattle of the GPMGs and the thump of the grenade launchers as Pat and his fire-support group continued to lay down a stream of heavy and accurate fire.

Major Peter was one of the officers serving with the unit and had been one of the men sent to cover the parked trucks. Ten minutes after Ratcliffe and his party had entered the site, Major Peter saw a military driver open the cab door of his truck. He obviously saw them because he reached for his rifle, which was propped up on the seat beside him. Major Peter shot him. Seconds later, the enemy troop in the right hand bunker opened fire. Then the Milan fired at the bunker.

The driver of the second vehicle climbed out of his cab on the opposite side of his truck from the attackers. He saw the SAS trooper aiming his LAW at the left-hand bunker, leapt on his back and began trying to strangle him. One of Major Peter's group rushed forward and clubbed him with his rifle butt.

Unfortunately the left-hand bunker was still undamaged. By the time its operator had set it up again, Ratcliffe and his party were running across his line of fire. Ratcliffe yelled at them to retire.

When they reached the vehicles, Ratcliffe glanced up at the top of the berm. He saw some figures up there in dark uniforms, not the normal olive drab of the Iraqi military. Ratcliffe was told they were just truck drivers. He relaxed. When he looked at them again they had disappeared.

A few minutes later they came under intense fire, but it was sprayed rather than aimed. They returned fire. Without waiting for orders they began to withdraw.

One of the last vehicles to leave fishtailed as it began to move away. Its front wing struck Ratcliffe on the thigh. He was knocked off his feet and dropped his M16. Halfwinded, he scrambled aboard the last of the Land Rovers as enemy bullets pinged into its side.

They could still hear firing as they bounced and bumped southwards. The fire support group were still engaged. About 1 kilometre down the road Ratcliffe signalled to the other vehicles to stop. There were no casualties and no one was missing. They waited another ten minutes befrore the fire support group rolled up in their vehicles. The steel mast still seemed to be standing. Ratcliffe was disappointed but Mugger told him it could go at any moment.

They reached their LUP just after first light. They were just about to report by radio when one of the demolition men told him that the mast was down, and Racliffe was able to report to Al Jouf that they thought that they had brought the mast down. He was told that an A-10 aircraft would be sent to make a run over Victor Two to check it out.

At sunset on 9 February they left that LUP, heading south. They needed fresh supplies. Instead of using the abandoned airstrip, they were to rendezvous with a supply convoy 150km inside enemy territory. Their job was to find a location within the convoy's range that would accomodate one hundred and fifty men and their vehicles. Then they had to make sure that it was secure.

It took them two days to find a suitable location. Wadi Tubal was a wadi within a wadi. The entrance zigzagged, which made it almost impossible to for anyone to see into it without actually entering it. The sides were high and steep, and a steep bank across the far end sealed it off like a blind alley. It was a good defensive position with space inside for at least seventy vehicles. Ratcliffe sent his motor cycles to make patrols to intercept and guide the other units in.

The first half squadron unit, Delta One Zero, arrived on the evening of 11 February. On 12 February Ratcliffe was ordered to take Alpha One Zero to relieve the other half of D squadron, Delta Three Zero. They were able to scrounge supplies from Delta One Zero. Ratcliffe's half squadron was most in need of rations and water. They pulled out just as the dust cloud from the supply convoy was sighted. The supply convoy consisted of ten 4-ton trucks escorted by six

Land Rover 110s, with crews from B and HQ squadrons.

They reached their AO, which was near the main supply route from Amman to Baghdad, then established an LUP about 1km south of the MSR and well to the west of Victor Two. Ratcliffe himself went forward to set up an OP overlooking the highway. They observed every variety of truck from cattle vehicles to articulated lorries. The flow of traffic was mainly from west to east; at that time Jordan was Saddam's only ally.

The second day was virtually the same. That evening, they were ordered to return to Wadi Tubal as they were out of water and rations. As soon as their needs had been met, Ratcliffe thought of a way that Wadi Tubal would become a part of the regimental history of 22 SAS. He called for a Sergeants' Mess meeting. There were at least thirty sergeants in the wadi.

So at 1200 hours on 16 February 1991, thirty-five members of the Sergeants' mess held a regular Sergeants' Mess meeting with minutes and proposals. Ratcliffe was determined to show that the regiment still had style. Later, General de la Billiere and General Schwarzkopf both signed the minutes of their mess meeting. General Schwarzkopf said that he was proud to do so.

Unfortunately, Alpha One Zero having found and secured the site, were the last to actually receive their supplies. They got news of the other half-squadron units. One of the D squadron units had caught a complete Scud convoy on site and had laser defined it for an air strike. The US pilots made a series of direct hits, which turned its liquid fuel into napalm, vaporizing the attendant troops and vehicles. The other half of D squadron had been ambushed and involved in in a major firefight with casualties on both sides.

Alpha One Zero was assigned to another patrol area. This time they were sent north west to an area near the Jordanian border. It was a tract of wilderness bordered by three main roads, known as the "Iron Triangle". To reach it, they had to cross the newly built motorway where they had used their sandbags and sand channels to cross before. They found a newly built bridge over the new motorway. Ratcliffe decided not to report the bridge until after they had returned over it.

Once they reached the "Iron Triangle", Ratcliffe realized that they needed to patrol in daylight to find any Scud launchers in the area. The wadis were shallow but they were so wide that they could not cover enough ground by night. They saw one possible missile site, and it took them less than three days to clear the area. They recrossed their motorway bridge safely, reported the possible missile site and were given another area to patrol.

On 23 February they finally received orders to return to FOB at Al Jouf. They could pick up BBC World Service broadcasts on their radios, and from these they knew that the main land offensive had begun that day.

On 24 February they tied Union Jacks to the radio aerials on their vehicles. The regiment sent a special reception committee to ensure they crossed the border safely. This was necessary because the Saudi troops at the border regarded them with considerable suspicion.

After travelling thousands of miles in enemy territory, the Unimog picked up a puncture within minutes of crossing into friendly territory.

One of the other SAS half-squadron teams had spotted a camouflaged Scud site within days of crossing into Iraq. They called in an air strike which completely destroyed the site.

The SAS concentrated their patrols around Wadi Amij near the town of Ar Rutbah. On 3 February a half-squadron team from D squadron spotted a convoy of fourteen vehicles. The commander called in an air strike and then watched as US F-15s and A-10s hit it with rockets, bombs and cannon fire. Despite the success of the attack, several vehicles and their crews remained intact. The SAS tried to finish the job with their heavy machine-guns and Milan anti-tank missiles. The Iraqi soldiers found cover and returned fire, and the SAS had to call in another air strike to finish them off.

One of the SAS half-squadron teams was heading back to

base when they discovered an Iraqi convoy ahead of them. They closed to within 600 metres of the convoy and saw that it was a mobile Scud launcher with its support vehicles. The Iraqis were in the process of camouflaging their vehicles and had not posted any sentries. The SAS quickly got into their attack formation and opened fire with their Milan missiles. All the Scud vehicles were hit and destroyed. The Iraqis were unable to return fire because of the thick, acrid smoke from their burning vehicles.

Another SAS half-squadron team spotted a Scud site that was protected by Iraqi troops in strong defensive positions. The SAS commander called in an air strike, and USAF F-15s attacked the site with cluster bombs and laser-guided munitions. A few hours later the SAS commander was told that an air recce had discovered that some of the launchers and their missiles had remained intact and were still capable of operation. He was ordered to attack the site with his half-squadron team. He agreed but requested reinforcements. A small team was flown in by helicopter and a plan was formed.

The SAS commander wanted to lure some of the Iraqis out of their strong defensive positions so he ordered his men to place explosive charges about 1km away from the Iraqi encampment. At dawn the next day they set off the charges. To the Iraqis' credit they were not drawn out by the SAS ruse. They stayed in their positions but began to fire wildly at any position where a vehicle or soldier could hide. Of course, they didn't hit anything.

The SAS formed up their vehicles on a nearby ridge. They made a crescent formation with the Milan vehicles on the outside and the vehicles armed with machine guns in the centre. When they opened fire, the machine guns concentrated on the Iraqi soldiers defending the position, while the Milan missiles picked off the Scud launchers. As soon as they were confident that every target of value had been destroyed they withdrew.

The operations against the Scuds were so intensive that the Iraqis withdrew their remaining mobile launchers deeper into Iraq where they could no longer reach Israel. They could still fire them at Saudi Arabia and continued to do so right up to the cessation of hostilities.

Ultimately the success of the Scud hunting missions may be judged by the fact that Israel did not take direct action against Iraq and the Coalition remained intact.

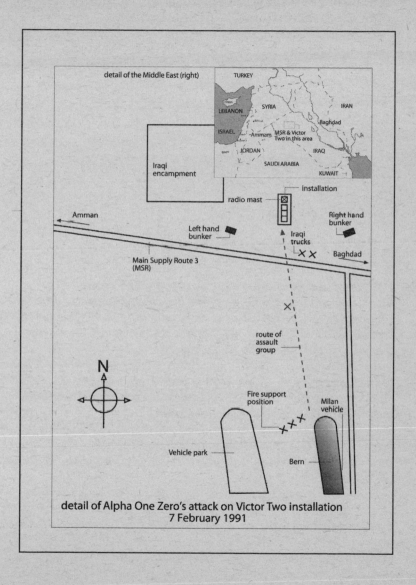

detail of the Middle East (right)

TURKEY

SYRIA

LEBANON

ISRAEL

JORDAN

Ammam

Baghdad

IRAN

MSR & Victor
Two in this area

SAUDI ARABIA

IRAQ

KUWAIT

Iraqi
encampment

installation

radio mast

Amman

Left hand
bunker

Right hand
bunker

Iraqi
trucks

X X

Baghdad

Main Supply Route 3
(MSR)

X

route of
assault
group

N

Fire support
position

Milan
vehicle

X X X

Vehicle park

Bern

detail of Alpha One Zero's attack on Victor Two installation
7 February 1991

# HUNTING SADDAM (2003)

*Saddam Hussein was born on 28 April 1937 in the village of Owja near the town of Tikrit. His tribal and extended family connections were established in the area; as is shown in his full name: Saddam Hussein al-Tikriti. He lived there until he moved to Baghdad when he was nineteen.*

*In Baghdad he joined the Ba'ath Socialist party. The Ba'ath party was of an ethnic pro-Arab nature. In 1959 Saddam took part in a Ba'ath party attempt to overthrow the Prime Minister, Abdul Karim Qassim.*

*After the failure of the plot Saddam hid in the Tikrit area before he fled to Syria. He moved to Egypt to study law. Three years later the Ba'ath party made a successful coup d'état which overthrew Qassim.*

*Saddam returned to Iraq. But he had to make a run for it again the following year. Abdal-Salam Muhammad Arif, Qassim's former partner, deposed and suppressed the Ba'ath party.*

*Saddam's attempt to flee was unsuccessful. After several months on the run he was caught and imprisoned for two years.*

*In July 1968 the Ba'ath party came to power as the result of a successful coup d'etat. Saddam's cousin General Ahmed*

*Hasan al Bakhr became President. Saddam became vice-president and head of the secret police, the Special Security Service.*

*Under the regime led by the Ba'ath party any opposition and various minorities were ruthlessly suppressed. This oppression began almost immediately that the Ba'ath party came to power. The Shia Marsh Arabs in the south and the Kurds in the north were the first victims of the Ba'ath party's policy.*

In July 1979 al Bakhr resigned and Saddam became President. He banned the only remaining political party which could oppose the Ba'athists, the Da'awa party. In September 1980 Saddam declared war on Iraq's neighbour, Iran. The cause was a border dispute over the ownership of the Shat al-Arab waterway. The war continued for eight years and finally ended in 1988. Towards the end of the war Saddam chose to use chemical weapons both against the Iranians and Kurdish insurgents in the north. Casualties during the Iran–Iraq war have been estimated at between one and one and a half million people.

On 2 August 1990 Saddam invaded his neighbour Kuwait. Both the United States of America and the United Nations tried to reason with him but he would not withdraw. On 17 January 1991 the first Gulf War began with a massive aerial bombardment. Five weeks later the ground invasion began. Within 72 hours Kuwait had been liberated.

On 3 March 1991 Iraq signed a ceasefire agreement. The conditions included the destruction of all Iraqi weapons of mass destruction and the cessation of the persecution of ethnic minorities, opposition groups and the return of all prisoners of war. Saddam agreed to these conditions but quickly suppressed a Kurdish revolt in the north and a Shia rebellion in the south.

The United Nations responded to these acts by imposing No-Fly Zones in the north and south of Iraq. The United Nations subsequently imposed economic and military sanctions on Iraq because Saddam had not kept any of the promises made in the ceasefire agreement of 3 March 1991.

Twelve years later, the United Nations passed UN Security Council Resolution 1441. This stated that Saddam had been in material breach of every agreement he had made in 1991. President George Bush of the United States decided to act. He formed a coalition of allies who were willing to support an invasion of Iraq to depose Saddam. The Coalition included the United States, Great Britain, Australia, Poland, Kuwait, Saudi Arabia, Oman, Qatar, Bahrain, United Arab Emirates and the Patriotic Union of Kurdistan (PUK). On 19 March 2003 the Coalition began bombing targets in Iraq.

Saddam's palace in Baghdad was one of the first targets. From that time Saddam Hussein himself was not seen for 254 days. Two videos of him were shown on Iraqi television on 4 April.

On 20 March US Special Forces entered northern Iraq to link up with PUK guerillas.

On 1 May President George W. Bush declared that the war was over. L. Paul Bremer III was appointed Head of a Coalition Provisional Authority, and a 25-million-dollar reward was offered for the capture of Saddam Hussein.

When the Coalition forces had finally reached Saddam's palace in Baghdad, it had been looted but Saddam himself was not there. The Iraqi army had never formally surrendered. Its soldiers were never formally processed anywhere. They had simply melted away back to their cities, towns and villages.

The Coalition's aim was the removal of Saddam's regime. The leading members of that regime became the Coalition's most Highly Valued Targets (HVTs). Saddam Hussein himself was HVT number 1. His sons Uday and Qusay were HVT numbers 2 & 3. HVT number 4 was Saddam's press secretary and cousin Abid Hamid Mahmud Al-Tikriti.

Information gathered from raids and pressure on detainees led to HVT number 4's capture at the Hadooshi farm on 17 June. 8,303,000 in US dollars and the equivalent of one million dollars in Iraqi currency were also seized.

The Hundred and First Airborne Division was holding down the area around Mosul. On 29 June 2003 they received a tip about the whereabouts of Saddam's sons, Uday and Qusay. They were reported to be holed up in a house in the Falah district of Mosul. The owner of the house was an Iraqi building contractor who told the Hundred and First Airborne Division. At first they didn't believe him. There was a fifteen-million-dollar bounty on each of their heads, so claims to have seen them were relatively common. Uday and Qusay remained there for three weeks.

The information was reported to Task Force (TF) 20, the special operations group hunting Saddam and his two sons, and on 22 July a cordon was placed around the building. An assault force from Task Force 20 was standing by, waiting for the moment to storm the building. The Second Brigade of the Hundred and First Airborne Division took up fire support positions. An interpreter with a bullhorn was used to contact the wanted men.

Task Force 20's assault force was working its way into the building when it came under fire from assault rifles or light machine guns from the first and second floors. They retired to the bottom of the stairs and then to the outside of the house where grenades were dropped on them from one of the balconies. Three Special Forces operators and a paratrooper were hit.

The Second Brigade provided covering fire from vehicle mounted fifty-calibre machine guns so that the men of Task Force 20 could try again, but return fire from inside the house kept them at bay. The special operators found that the defenders had a strong position at the top of the staircase.

Second Brigade brought heavier weapons to bear. Light anti-tank weapons and 40mm grenades failed to suppress the return fire. Colonel Joe Anderson, CO of Second Brigade, called in two Kiowa Warrior helicopters, military versions of the Bell Jet Ranger helicopter, armed with rockets and machine guns. They fired four 2.75 inch rockets and their belt fed .50 cal machine guns. The rockets missed.

Another attempt by Task Force 20 was held up by return fire. Colonel Anderson ordered Tube-launched Optically-tracked Wire-guided (TOW) missiles to be used. Eighteen were fired at the house. Colonel Anderson said that the goal was "a combination of shocking them if they were still alive and damaging the building structurally so that it was unfeasible to fight in."

When the men of Task Force 20 entered the remains of the building there was no movement at all. The dead bodies of three men and a fourteen-year-old boy were found in the strongpoint and on the staircase. Two of the men were identified by their DNA and dental records as Uday and Qusay. The fourteen-year-old boy was Qusay's son.

Saddam's birthplace was near the town of Tikrit, beside the Tigris river, northwest of Baghdad. The town has a population of 75,000. The area around Tikrit was where Saddam also had his extended family and tribal connections. He had hidden in the area when he was being hunted in 1959. At that time Saddam was wanted for being involved an attempt to assassinate the Prime Minister, Abdul Karim Qassim.

The US Fourth Infantry Division took over the area from the Hundred and First Airborne Division. First Brigade, Fourth Infantry Division was commanded by Colonel James Hickey. Lieutenant Colonel Steve Russell was Commanding Officer (CO) of the First Battalion, Twenty-second infantry (1–22) of the First Brigade, Fourth Infantry Division. Russell kept a journal from 20 June until Christmas 2003.

Major John S. "Stan" Murphy was the Intelligence officer (S-2) of the First Brigade, Fourth Infantry Division. He was sure that Saddam Hussein would remain in the area around Tikrit, because he had hidden there before. Major Stan Murphy's intelligence team combined with special operations forces and interagency colleagues. Their job was to follow the trail to Saddam Hussein.

Two million US dollars' worth of jewellery belonging to Sajida Khairallah Telfah – Saddam's wife and the mother

of Uday and Qusay – were found in a raid on a farm near
Tikrit. The success of the operation was ensured by the
quick action of First Lieutenant Chris Morris, OC recon
platoon, 1–22. The plan of the operation had involved
additional forces but Lieutenant Morris didn't wait for
them and captured the farm with his scouts. Captain Mark
Stouffer's A Company, 1–22 captured a senior member of
the Iraqi Republican Guard who had been one of Saddam's
bodyguards.

Saddam had been born in the village of Owja which is less
than twelve miles from Tikrit. On 26 August an informant
revealed that there were weapons and self-proclaimed *fedayeen* at a farm south west of Owja. (*Fedayeen* means "men
of sacrifice".) Fourth Infantry Division began to call Saddam Hussein "Elvis" because there were so many stories of
sightings of him.

A Task Force was formed from Special Forces and teams
from Fourth Infantry Division, designated Task Force 121.
It operated using intel gathered by Major Murphy's team,
which was gradually finding pieces of information. These
pieces of information began to form a trail that would lead
to Saddam Hussein. A raid in June 2003 captured Abid
Hamid Al-Tikriti (HVT 4).

Early in July 2003 Murphy's team began to assemble a list
of Saddam Hussein's "enablers" – a group of errand boys,
cooks and "yes men" drawn from five or six trusted families.
They formed a diagram based on family ties and tribal lines.
Then these were linked with anti-Coalition activity.

Each raid or capture brought more information. Interviews with detainees added more to the picture. Murphy's
team liased with intelligence units from other brigades and
divisions, special forces and other agencies. Any tidbits of
information about Tikrit families were incorporated into
the picture.

Major General Ray Odierno, CO Fourth Infantry Division, said:

We realized early on in the summer . . . the people we had
to get to were the mid-level individuals, his bodyguards.

We tried to work through family and tribal ties that might
have been close to Saddam Hussein.

Over the last ten days or so, we brought in about five to
ten members of these families . . . and finally we got the
ultimate information from one of these individuals.

Between July and December 2003 the Task Force made
twelve unsuccessful raids to capture Saddam Hussein.
They mounted 600 other operations against targets on
the linked diagram. All the intel led back to five extended
families from several villages within a twelve-mile radius of
Tikrit. The five extended families came from Abu Ajeel, Al
Alam, Al Owja and Ad Dawr.

Their search narrowed down to a key figure they called
"the Fatman" or "the Source". "The Source" had been a
senior officer in Saddam Hussein's secret police and was
one of Saddam Hussein's "enablers". On 12 December he
was captured by Special Forces in a raid in Baghdad. On 13
December he was brought, under guard, to First Brigade,
Fourth Infantry Division Headquarters. From his interrogation they extracted a trickle of information. By 1530
Colonel Hickey was able to tell Major General Odierno that
the Task Force was going to make another raid that night.
Colonel Hickey also told Russell to prepare his battalion for
any contingency and to have a force ready for use at a
moment's notice.

At 1700 "The Source" had told them that Saddam
Hussein was hidden in an underground facility in a farmhouse at Ad Dawr, 5km from Owja.

The raiding force included 600 personnel from First
Brigade, Fourth Infantry Division. These were 4-42 Field
Artillery Battalion, G Troop, Tenth Cavalry Regiment and
elements from Fourth Aviation Regiment and A troop,
First Battalion, Tenth Cavalry Regiment. These forces
would isolate and secure the area. They were strong enough
to deal with any counter measures. Meanwhile, Special
Operations Forces would go in after Saddam.

There were two possible locations. These were codenamed Wolverine 1 and Wolverine 2. There was no high-

tech hardware used in planning the operation and by 1800 the forces were in position east of Tikrit. Lieutenant Colonel Steve Russell described what happened: "The electricity in the entire area suddenly went out. There was complete darkness, and at precisely 2000 hours, the raid began exactly as planned."

Both objectives were cleared within minutes. Special Operations troops picked up one detainee on Wolverine 1, but no Saddam. Wolverine 2 was empty. Within a five-kilometre radius of Wolverine 1 and Wolverine 2, Hickey's forces tightened their cordon. The Special Operators moved in on a small mud hut in a palm grove just north of Wolverine 1. Saffeels and Bocanegra were members of Major Murphy's intel team. Russell:

Through their night vision goggles and thermal sights, soldiers of the 4th ID could see Special Operators moving soundlessly through the dark night to the target. Occasionally, the red beams of laser-aiming lights would reflect off trees and leaves, but it was deathly silent, save for the distant hum of OH-58 Little Birds and other Special Operations aircraft waiting for extraction, reinforcement, or attack. From his position, Saffeels could hear noises in the darkness. He and his fellow soldiers grew "a little jumpy", waiting for Saddam's forces. For Bocanegra the scene and all the activity became more intense. The assault force started clearing through the palm groves and came upon a little mud-hut structure with a courtyard. In that courtyard they heard a noise.

At 2010, with Hickey's troops sealing off the area, Special Operations forces burst into the hut, a simple construction behind a fence of dried palm leaves. It had been an orange picker's hut with one room and an open kitchen. They immediately seized one man trying to escape and another man in the hut. As it turned out, one was Saddam's cook; the other was the cook's brother and owner of the property.

Inside, they found that the hut consisted of one room with two beds and a refrigerator containing a can of lemonade, a packet of hot dogs, a can of "Happy Brand" tuna, an opened box of Belgian chocolates, and a tube of ointment. A poster of Noah's Ark hung on the mud-brick wall. There were also two AK-47 assault rifles, various packages of new clothes, and a green footlocker containing $750,000 in American hundred-dollar bills. More telling: an orange-and-white Toyota Corolla taxi was parked outside. Rumors that Saddam had hidden in taxis and even masqueraded as a taxi driver appeared to be true.

Saddam was nowhere to be seen. It looked like yet another dry hole when, suddenly, one of the detainees broke away from the Special Operators and ran, telling them Saddam was hiding elsewhere and he would lead them to him. His sudden desire to cooperate and zeal to get them out of there further convinced the operators they were close.

At the command vehicle, CW2 Gray stood next to Colonel Hickey, listening to the radio reports from the Special Operation forces. Those two individuals were exactly who the source stated would be at the farm. Things were going well.

Reports continued to come in that Special Operations forces were still searching the area but had not found the tunnels that the source had said Saddam would be hiding in. Hickey calmly told them to take their time. Task Force Raider owned that portion of Iraq. He'd hold the cordon all night if necessary.

Another ten minutes went by. Still nothing.

Outside the hut, the two dozen or so Special Operators were preparing to move off and expand their search. Something caught an operator's attention in the darkness of the moonless night, through the unearthly glow of his night vision goggles. The ground just didn't look quite right. The sensation of an odd landscape was nothing unusual under the glow of a night vision device, but it just didn't feel right, either.

The closer the operator looked, the more it appeared to be out of place. The bricks and dirt were spread about too uniformly, as if someone were trying to conceal something.

A thread of fabric protruded just slightly under the dirt. Strange.

At 2030 hours, the operators brushed away the debris, revealing a Styrofoam plug. True to his training, one of the Special Operators pulled the pin on a hand grenade while his colleagues prepared to remove the plug so he could drop it in. The remaining twenty or so soldiers prepared to fire their weapons, if engaged. The plug revealed a hole; the hole revealed a ratty-looking bearded man. The man raised his hands and announced: "I am Saddam Hussein. I am the President of Iraq, and I am willing to negotiate."

The Task Force 121 commando covering the hole calmly replied: "President Bush sends his regards."

Hickey's radio broke the silence as the Special Operator reported simply, "Sir, we may have the jackpot."

Hickey waited breathlessly.

Back on the objective, several Special Operators yanked the dishevelled, disoriented man to the surface, unavoidably scratching his head in the tight confines of the hole.

The operators quickly removed the 9mm pistol from his belt and checked him for the markings and other features that would preliminarily confirm they had their man. They began to prepare him for transportation with the standard, empty sandbag over his head and flex-cuffs on his hands. As they attempted to secure him, Saddam resisted – trying to shrug off the operators, acting belligerent, and even spitting in one soldier's face. In return, he was treated "just like any other prisoner", and forcefully subdued to the ground, where several operators held him down while others trussed him up.

At Hickey's command vehicle, everyone waited in painful silence. The word finally came. Although it was only minutes behind the first call, it had seemed like weeks. "Sir, we've got him. Jackpot." Hickey replied simply and unemotionally, "That's great."

Within minutes Saddam was strapped into a Special Operations Little Bird and spirited out of the immediate area. There was a quick stop at FOB Iron Horse for a

transload onto a larger Black Hawk helicopter for the flight
to the Baghdad Airport prison that once boasted his name.
As he moved through FOB Iron Horse, Saddam passed
through a cordon of Special Operations forces. It was the
only time they would see their prize, and the only recognition of their accomplishment these shadow warriors would
ever receive. Hickey was not so lucky. It happened so fast
that by the time Hickey's command vehicle arrived, Saddam was gone.

In the Raider TOC (Tactical Operations Center), Murphy had heard the objectives were clear with only two
detainees and felt the letdown of failure. As he'd feared,
they'd waited too long and came away empty-handed once
again. He got up and was about to head over to the phone
bank to call home when a single codeword broke the
building silence: "Jackpot."

In Baghdad Saddam was treated like any other prisoner. He
was stripped and searched. Some of his former aides who
were in detention were brought to verify his identity. He
was dishevelled but defiant. When he was asked why he had
killed so many people he refused to apologize but did not
deny the allegations.

The next day, at 1515 Baghdad time, the Head of the
Coalition Provisional Authority, L. Paul Bremer III declared: "Ladies and gentlemen, we got him."

A Baghdad shopkeeper expressed disdain that he had
been taken alive: "He talked only of fighting to the end and
of death for Iraq. His wife told us that he slept with a bomb
strapped to his chest so that he would not be taken alive.
But he did not fire a single shot."

# KOSOVO (1999–2000)

*In 1999 NATO and the UN embarked on a campaign of bombing followed by occupation in Kosovo. They had learnt from their experience in Somalia, Rwanda and Bosnia that the limited authority of a UN security council mandate was a recipe for lack of military progress. The Kosovo intervention worked. It was a turning point in terms of military intervention. It was also a turning point in the changing nature of special operations.*

*Kosovo was a province of Serbia and Montenegro. The majority of Kosovo's population of two million was ethnic Albanian. Since 1990 they had been trying to gain independence from Serbia.*

*The purpose of NATO and the UN's intervention was to protect the Albanian population of Kosovo from Serbian soldiers and paramilitaries.*

In Kosovo, fighting between Serbs and Albanians had broken out in 1998. Lightly armed bands from the Kosovo Liberation Army (KLA) fought against heavily armed Serb forces. Sometimes it was Serb village against Albanian village, or it could be a KLA ambush on a Serb military convoy.

The Serb Interior Ministry Police, Ministarstvo Unu-
trasnijh Poslova, (MUP) used wheeled armoured Personnel
Carriers (APCs). The KLA learnt that the best way to
disable these vehicles was to fire an RPG-7 anti-tank rocket
through a tiny triangular window beside the driver's seat.
Although the window was only 30 × 20 cm, when they left,
the Serbs left behind several APCs destroyed in just such a
way.

The Serbs reacted to these ambushes with reprisals
against villages known to harbour KLA fighters. The
situation worsened until another scene of Serb paramilitary
madness looked likely.

Plans were laid to send special forces into Kosovo to liase
with the KLA and act as "eyes and ears". Their job was to
assess the intentions of the KLA and to restrain them from
committing atrocities themselves. They were also intended
to find out who was funding the KLA and supplying them
with weapons.

On 23 September 1998, the UN Security Council passed
Security Council Resolution 1199. This called for an immediate end to actions by security forces against civilians.
Around the Drenica valley two Serbian special operations
and counter-insurgency units took no notice.

Some of the members of these units were former convicts
who had been serving sentences for violent crimes. They
were offered annulment of their sentences for helping with
the ethnic cleansing of Kosovo.

An international organization provided an opportunity
for the secret insertion of special forces into Kosovo. The
Organization for Co-operation and Security in Europe was
normally involved in training and helping the democratic
process, holding fair elections. It had a mission in Kosovo:
the Kosovo Democratic Observation Mission (KDOM).

At the time of the Drenica valley massacres KDOM
became the Kosovo Verification Mission (KVM), which
allowed Special Forces troopers to be sent to Albania. They
were able to cross the border and link up with the KLA.

In January 1999 forty-five Albanians were shot by the
Serb MUP in the village of Racak near the capital of the

province Pristina. Massive international condemnation followed but negotiations were not achieving anything positive. NATO began to act without a UN Security Council Resolution.

On 24 March 1999, 78 days of airstrikes began. Thousands of targets in Kosovo and Serbia were attacked. By the time the bombing campaign was nearly over special forces teams from Great Britain, France, USA, Canada and Germany were operating inside Kosovo. One of these teams was responsible for securing some bridges and tunnels that NATO's Kosovo force (KFOR) needed to seize, through the Kacanik gorge were on the single main road to Pristina.

The British part of KFOR was to lead the way into Kosovo on 12 June.

On 11 June the Russians decided that they, too, would act independently in Kosovo. On 10 June NATO intelligence received a report that the Russians were moving over 2,000 airborne troops by road and air to Kosovo. The Russian troops had been in Bosnia to monitor and oversee the Daytona Peace accords. They were now heading for Slatina airport; the only functional airstrip in Kosovo. The British commander of the whole NATO force and the NATO contingent was Lieutenant-General Michael Jackson. He planned to send an SAS troop and the Pathfinder Platoon of Fifth Airborne Brigade.

The Pathfinder Platoon was the lead reconnaissance unit of Fifth Airborne Brigade. The unit had its origins during the Second World War when its role had been to mark the drop zones before an airborne landing. Pathfinder Platoon consisted of forty men, equipped with armed Land Rover 110s. The plan was for them to drive straight to Pristina, picking up some SAS men as they passed through the Kacanik gorge.

On the night of 11–12 June 1999 a C-130 Hercules aircraft crashed while attempting to take off from an unlit airstrip on the Albanian border with Kosovo. It was carrying an SAS troop and their vehicles – three fully armed Land Rover V8 110s. They were possibly intended to help seize Slatina airport.

The Russians reached Slatina airport first. When the Pathfinder Platoon arrived they found 200 Russian paratroopers with their APCs blocking the entrance to the airport. The British held the centre of Kosovo. The Russians held on to the airport. They were not there under either UN or NATO control and were still there early in 2003.

The bombing campaign stopped on 8 June 1999 and the Serbs agreed to negotiate. After three days of talks a Military Technical Agreement (MTA) was signed. 35,000 regular troops would join the special forces in Kosovo, and the Serb armed forces would leave. Kosovo would become a UN-administered protectorate with NATO providing security.

Between 11–14 June the NATO forces rolled in from Albania and Macedonia. The Parachute Regiment quickly asserted its authority in Pristina. A drunken Serb policeman brandished his gun and yelled at a patrol from the First battalion; he was cautioned several times and told to drop his weapon. When he failed to reply he was shot and blown backwards into a shop window.

On the Macedonian border crossing at Blace a patrol of Ghurkas stopped a bus full of Serb Interior Ministry Police (MUP). They demanded that they give up their weapons. It was extremely hot and many of the Serbs were drunk. They told the Gurkha officer that they were not accustomed to being disarmed by a group of "monkeys". The Gurkhas told the policemen that they were prepared to kill them all with either their assault rifles or, preferably, their kukri knives. They gave them one minute to comply. All of them did.

On Sunday 13 June a German armoured brigade, accompanied by a battalion of paratroopers, reached the southern city of Prizren. The city was in a state of ferment. Albanians who had remained hidden came out to greet the Germans with flowers. Some of the German paratroopers had up to five ammunition clips fixed back to back on their Heckler & Koch 368 Assault rifles. They walked alongside their armoured vehicles with gladioli protruding from their body armour.

By 6 p.m. a large crowd of Albanians was hanging around the edges of an immense convoy of Serb cars, tractors and lorries. They were packed up ready to begin the journey north back to Serbia. Each car had grandparents and grandchildren on the back seat. The mother sat in front next to the father who drove. The roofs of the cars were loaded with their electrical goods such as washing machines and refrigerators.

The German soldiers edged along the Serb convoy, discouraging Albanians from getting too close. They even prised stones out of Albanian hands.

A small, yellow Zastava saloon car came out of a turning opposite the Hotel Theranda in the centre of Prizren. As it drew level with the hotel and the German soldiers standing outside it, one of the two men inside leaned out of the window and opened fire with a Bulgarian-made Kalashnikov. He fired a whole magazine; then he realized that he was leaning too far out of the window to be able to change magazines quickly. By then he had scattered the crowd and hit one German soldier, who was spun round by the impact. Then the Germans opened fire. Three paratroopers were the first to react with high-speed bursts. An NCO fired his 9mm pistol from the top of an armoured car. Then turret-mounted 7.62 mm machine guns joined in.

The injured German soldier was taken away on a stretcher. An Albanian teenager helped to carry him into the back of an armoured vehicle. It was the first time German troops had opened fire since the Second World War.

Kosovo had been liberated. The UN turned the former KLA into the Kosovo Protection Corps (KPC), funded by the EU, US and UN. By late 1999 they were clearing ice off streets and training as firemen. An international official described them as "a pefectly average terrorist organization masquerading as a not very good fire brigade". Most of their members melted back into the armed Albanian clan fraternity they had come from.

A 5km-wide buffer zone was formed between Serbia and

Kosovo. Known as the Ground Safety Zone (GSW), its role was to form a barrier between the international forces and the Serbs. Special forces teams were deployed in the snowy scrub and oak forests of the GSW. Lying up in observation posts, they were reported to patrol into Serbia itself.

By mid February 2000, UN policemen were making allegations that French troops serving with KFOR had stood by or withdrawn while a mob of Serbs had hunted down ethnic Albanians in the town of Mitrovica – a mining town which was ethnically divided between a Serb majority in the northern half of the town and an Albanian majority in the southern half of the town. The dividing line was the Ibar river. Mitrovica was being used as the HQ of a multi-national brigade Area which included Danish soldiers and Italian military police (*carbinieri*) as well as 4,600 French troops.

On 3 February a detachment of mainly American UN policemen were on duty. Revenge attacks on the Serbs who had chosen to remain in Kosovo had become so intense that the remaining Serbs had to live in enclaves protected by NATO troops. A large white coach marked with a blue UNHCR logo was hit by an RPG-7 rocket on a road in northern Kosovo. The warhead failed to explode because it lodged in the abdominal tissue of an elderly Serb.

The isolated Serb community in Mitrovica was the first to react. A 47–year-old Albanian, Gani Gjaka, related that he was with ten other people in his flat in north Mitrovica when seven or eight Serbs started shooting and throwing grenades through the door. His wife was killed in the attack. He telephoned the UN police and French NATO troops. Four and a half hours later seven UN policemen arrived. They reported that the French had refused to help the Albanians.

J. D. Luckie was a UN police investigator who was on attachment from Midland, Texas. He was an experienced policeman and a veteran of Vietnam, but he said that 3 February 2000 was the worst night of his life. He carried a pregnant Albanian woman down the stairs from her flat after she had been shot. Then he struggled through crowds of Serbs with only his sidearm to defend them. He reached the far side where some French soldiers were watching what was happening. The French soldiers just walked back to their armoured vehicles.

Logs record that there were numerous other incidents in which the French troops either ignored requests for help or withdrew. Radio traffic that night confirmed that the UN policemen lacked sufficient weapons, vehicles or radios to deal with the situation. They had received no help from the French.

By this time a German General, Klaus Reinhardt, was in command of KFOR. He wanted the French out of Mitrovica. They were doing nothing about a gang of Serb paramilitaries who hung around the northern end of Mitrovica bridge, drinking and not even bothering to conceal their weapons. NATO and UN regulations made it illegal for civilians to carry weapons but the French would not do anything about them. In fact, French soldiers were observed drinking with the Serb paramilitaries in other parts of the town.

The problems in Mitrovica became worse in mid-February when it became apparent that Albanians were also involved in the violence there. The French shot dead a number of alleged Albanian gunmen in the north of the town. They appeared to be former KLA men who had slipped into the town to incite violence. One of the dead men was identified as Avni Haradinaj. Twelve months before he had been a KLA rebel, armed, trained and supported by NATO. He was the first KLA fighter to be killed by his former allies.

General Reinhardt said: "When NATO came to Kosovo we were only supposed to fight the Yugoslav army if they came back uninvited. Now we're finding we have to fight the Albanians."

Reinhardt told the French and NATO that he was considering sending in a British taskforce to pacify the town. The French Ministry of Defence objected to any other nation interfering in their zone of control. They began to hint that they might withdraw their forces from Kosovo.

The situation in Mitrovica continued to deteriorate. By 18 February twelve Serbs and Albanians had been killed and more than fifty people wounded, including thirteen French soldiers. Homes had been looted; properties and cars had been burnt. So many had fled to areas which were safer for them that the town was much less ethnically mixed. It appeared that former KLA fighters were smuggling arms into the northern part of the town to hit French troops and increase the pressure on Serb extremists there.

At that time KFOR included troops from thirty-two different countries. A number of smaller countries had begun to contribute troops, but the majority of them came to Kosovo on the understanding that they would not be sent to Mitrovica.

In late February, the second battalion of the Green Jackets began to rotate single companies in and out of Mitrovica. They were prepared for a lightning deployment into the northern part of the town if it became necessary. They needed more reconnaissance there so SAS patrols were sent in, pretending to be aid workers. Four-man patrols drove around northern Mitrovica in a white Land Rover. For a day and a half they observed and noted both the French positions and apartment blocks occupied by hardline Serbs.

But before the British could make their deployment the Americans tried to conduct a large-scale weapons search. In March 2000, Operation Ibar was supposed to take five days and show the Serbs who was master. Men from Eighty-Second Airborne attempted to build a barbed-wire roadblock across one of the main streets. A local politician arrived with the gang from the bridge and told them that they couldn't do it. The Americans backed down and began their weapons search at a nearby apartment block.

When the Americans emerged from apartment block the gang from the bridge were waiting. One of them hurled a snowball with a stone inside at a young paratrooper. It hit him on the cheekbone just below the rim of his helmet. Other Serbs began throwing snowballs at the Americans, who brought their guns to bear. The young paratrooper who had been hit identified the man who had thrown it to his sergeant. The sergeant went up to him and squirted pepper spray into his face, and the man fell to the ground with what appeared to be blood on his face.

After a moment of silence the hail of snowballs became rocks and anything the Serbs could prise loose from the ice and snow. An hour later the Americans were back in their vehicles, driving back towards the southern part of town. A screaming mob of Serbs hurled things at the American vehicles as they passed.

The British never made their deployment and the SAS returned to their barracks in Pristina. British foot patrols of regular infantry brought three decades of experience in Northern Ireland to bear. Wherever they went they dominated the surrounding area using their effective patrolling "zone" technique.

Another situation was developing on the boundary with Serbia. A small Albanian group which called itself the Liberation Army of Presevo, Medvedjav and Bujanovac had sprung up in a part of southern Serbia known as the Presevo valley. The valley was in the Ground Safety Zone (GSW). The Liberation Army of Presevo was receiving weapons and logistical support from within Kosovo. In fact it was the Kosovo Protection Corps (KPC) which was supplying the Liberation Army of Presevo, Medvedjav and Bujanovac.

By 2001 the Serbian government had changed. NATO mounted further special operations in the area. These were intended to preserve the peace in Macedonia and Serbia. This time the threat was coming from ethnic Albanian rebels.

# AMBUSHED (1967)

*Franklin D. Miller was still with Recon Platoon, Head-
quarters Company, First Cavalry Division in the fall of
1967. He had become a patrol leader and he had been
promoted to the grade of specialist four. Recon Platoon
was operating in the Bong Son, an area in south central
Vietnam. He was given a mission to find a suitable location
for an ambush. Miller:*

We spent the day looking for an area that showed signs
of heavy enemy traffic, day or night. The entire platoon as
a group started out that morning in search of such a
location, but we couldn't find an ideal spot. At about
two o'clock in the afternoon we halted and established a
patrol base.

One hour later I took my patrol element with me and we
headed toward the west. After traveling about one kilo-
meter we came across what I considered to be a reasonable
ambush site. A trail came out of the jungle and skirted a
large open field for a good distance before turning back
into the bush. The worn condition of the path indicated
frequent use. I figured if we caught them on this trail and

they tried to withdraw, they'd have to go across the open field, which would make them easy targets.

After finding the ambush site we headed back to the patrol base and hung out with the rest of the platoon until the early evening, around six o'clock. At that time my patrol element and I packed up our gear and moved out to establish the ambush.

Turnabout is fair play, I guess, and on the way to the site we were ambushed.

We were less than 50 meters from our destination when my point man was shot through the leg, shattering his femur. I was right behind him in the order of march. Almost simultaneously I heard a scream to my rear as the guy directly behind me was shot in the stomach.

By now everyone had dropped in place to return fire. The enemy was about 15 to 20 meters to our left front. I started cranking off rounds when I heard and felt a tiny thump next to me. I looked over in the direction of the thump, and there lying on the ground beside me was a grenade!

I can't begin to describe the violent electrical jolt that assaulted my spine when I spotted that frag. Without wasted thought or motion I reached out, grabbed the grenade, and threw it back at them.

As soon as it went off, I jumped up and ran toward the spot where it exploded. It was always my belief that the best way to defeat an ambush was to attack it in the early stages if you had the opportunity. I figured I had the opportunity at that point.

As I ran toward the blast area I suddenly discovered that I was inside the enemy ambush! Out of the corners of my eyes I could see enemy soldiers on both sides of me lying in the bush, firing at my patrol. Obviously they weren't aware that I was there. Apparently the grenade blast acted as a perfect cover. Fortunately, my people saw me rush the ambush so they adjusted their fire away from my position.

I only stood there for a second or two before I swung my weapon to the left and cut loose with several short bursts. I immediately hit and killed two of the enemy lying on the ground. A third enemy soldier scrambled to his feet and started to run. I hit him in the back and put him down as well.

As soon as he went down I turned to my right to engage the other enemy troops. They were gone. I guess they got frightened by all the commotion and headed for tall timber, which was a good thing because they could have easily greased me when I had my back to them.

We obviously had to abandon our ambush plans and quickly evacuate the two casualties to the patrol base. Since the enemy had discovered us it was necessary for Recon Platoon to vacate the AO; we expected to catch hell anytime from the sure-to-come, numerically superior enemy forces. I radioed the patrol base and apprised them of the situation. I also called in the choppers.

My point man lived. The other wounded member of my element died before we reached the patrol base. The choppers arrived shortly after we joined the rest of the platoon, and we were extracted without further enemy contact.

For my actions during the ambush I received the Bronze Star with V device.

# MACEDONIA AND SERBIA (2001)

*In 2001 Kosovo was still technically a part of Serbia so the dividing line between Kosovo and Serbia was a boundary, not a border.*

*In 2001, X-Ray Company of the Royal Marines 45 Commando were patrolling along Kosovo's eastern boundary with Serbia. They were tracking ethnic Albanian rebels; 100 metres from the boundary one of the corporals saw a piece of white sacking hidden beneath some cover of sticks and leaves. Sergeant Andy Goodall described what they found underneath:*

This is the kit that would be used by a small fighting group, probably left behind as they crossed the boundary: RPG-7 rocket launcher, two Kalashnikovs, RPK light machine gun. Warsaw Pact, some Chinese stuff. Grenades, first aid kits, ammunition.

The find also included a 7.62mm Dragunov sniper rifle.

The Royal Marines had spent five months of their tour of duty in Kosovo patrolling the streets of the capital, Pristina. Out on the boundary they were making long-range flexible patrols, establishing checkpoints and carrying out observation duties. From their observation posts they watched an Albanian rebel training camp. Their job was to prevent the Albanians from getting their men and equipment across the boundary into Serbia.

The regime led by Slobodan Milosevic was overthrown in October 2000. Afterwards the West and NATO wanted better relations with Serbia. The Albanian rebels of the Liberation Army of Presevo, Medvedjav and Bujanovac became a problem shared by NATO and the Serbian government. Unfortunately they were active inside the Ground Safety Zone (GSW). This was a 5km-wide demilitarized zone on the Serbian side of the boundary; it had been designated in the Military Technical Agreement (MTA) under which the Serbs had agreed to withdraw from Kosovo.

Only lightly armed Serb police could enter the GSW. NATO was not allowed to intervene unless the MTA was severely violated.

On 16 February 2001 NATO's attempts to crack down on Albanian extremism took a severe blow. Eleven Serbs were killed and forty-five were wounded or missing after a massive explosive device blew up a coach carrying fifty-seven Kosovan Serbs returning to the province after a trip to Serbia. The attack happened near the town of Podujevo in the north east of Kosovo. The coach had been part of a convoy of five buses containing two hundred Serbs, and had been escorted by five Swedish armoured vehicles They were under British command and the attack had taken place in a British Brigade Area.

Within an hour of the attack Serbs living in heavily guarded enclaves within Kosovo began to form crowds and attack any Albanians they could reach. In the Serb enclave of Caglavica, south of Pristina, Serbs blocked the road south to Macedonia; they dragged Albanians from their cars and beat them.

On 19 March 2001 3,000 British and Norwegian troops arrested twenty-two Albanian men suspected of involvement in the bus attack on 16 February. The operation was spearheaded by thirty men from G Squadron 22 SAS. G

Squadron was Special Projects squadron at that time, commanded by Major Ivo Streeter. The arrest operation took twenty-seven hours. The SAS had been requested because the suspects were believed to be armed. The SAS men burst into the houses early in the morning while most of the suspects were asleep. There was no resistance as the suspects had been taken by surprise. They were plasticuffed and taken away for interrogation

Soldiers from the First Battalion of the Duke of Wellington's Regiment, the Second Royal Tank Regiment and Norwegian infantry units were also involved in securing the area. The First Battalion of the Duke of Wellington's Regiment had replaced 45 Royal Marine Commando at the end of February. During its service in Kosovo the Duke of Wellington's Regiment was regarded as an exemplary British infantry regiment.

By the spring of 2001 the hardline former KLA rebels were becoming isolated from the international community. Albanian rebels began attacking police stations and isolated targets in the Former Yugoslav Republic (FYRO) Of Macedonia, calling themselves the National Liberation Army (NLA).

By May the Macedonian army was firing 122mm artillery shells into villages held by the KLA. There was an old adage "when the snows thaw, the Balkans go to war".

As the fighting grew heavier, NATO was aware that arms were reaching the rebels in Macedonia from Kosovo. The FYRO Macedonian army was well supplied with heavy equipment, artillery, armoured vehicles and helicopter gunships but the rebels were more experienced and well dug in on the high ground. FYRO Macedonia had been largely uninvolved in the strife since the breakup of Yugoslavia. It had asserted its independence in 1991.

Back in March an SAS officer had been observing the border from an OP in a hide 150m above the mountainous Kosovo–Macedonian border. For twenty-seven days he and a group of three other SAS men took turns to observe the comings and goings on the border. They saw Americans, Albanians, Macedonians and Military Professional

Resources International (MPRI) personnel. MPRI was supposed to be training the Macedonians but the British suspected that they were the agents of any policy the Pentagon wanted to be able to deny.

NLA rebels reached the small town of Aracinovo on 8 June. They were only 8km from the capital Skopje, just outside its suburbs. The Slav townfolk had fled. Macedonian forces set up a roadblock at the far end of Aracinovo. They blasted rebel positions with rockets fired from their Mi-24 helicopter gunships and artillery and tanks. After four days of fighting, a ceasefire was arranged.

The Americans went in with units of the Eighty-Second Airborne Division. They lifted out 300–400 NLA fighters in air-conditioned coaches escorted by armed humvees; the NLA fighters were disembarked several kilometres away on the outskirts of the village of Umin Dol.

The Macedonians expressed their outrage in furious demonstrations outside the parliament building in Skopje. Foreigners, including TV crews, were abused and even attacked, although the majority of Macedonian Slav citizens remained peaceful. The country had enjoyed a decade of peace and prosperity. Experts described their security forces as "badly trained, badly equipped and badly led". This was, perhaps, why the Albanian rebels had been able to achieve what they had.

NATO peacekeepers were still trying to prevent the flow of weapons and equipment across the border.

In July 2001 soldiers from the First Battalion of the Duke of Wellington's Regiment set up a series of positions to interdict rebels trying to cross the border. They noticed that the rebels were using small hand mirrors to signal back down the mountains to their colleagues to indicate that a particular route was safe. The men from the Duke of Wellington's Regiment were so effective that the Albanians took to crossing in the areas further east. The forested areas outside the Kosovan town of Strpce were manned by German and Ukrainian troops.

Between July and August 2001 the violence escalated.

The EU tried to set up peace talks that would lead to a peace deal they hoped would grant greater political and constitutional rights to Macedonia's 600,000 Albanian minority. Once that was achieved, NATO would arrive. A 3,500–strong multinational NATO mission would deploy to collect the rebels' weapons under a voluntary disarmament scheme.

From 14 August an advance party arrived at Petrovec airport. The advance party was a multinational force of more than 500 troops. Their job was to assess whether the fragile ceasefire was stable enough to allow a further 3,000 troops to deploy to collect the rebels' weapons. The Albanian rebel leader, Ali Ahmeti, had stated that his 2,500 men would hand over their arms to NATO forces.

Thirty British paratroopers from the pathfinder platoon of 16 Air Assault Brigade were part of the multinational force. They were specialists in long-range reconnaissance and patrols and were accompanied by several four-man patrols from 22 SAS. They set out in their Land Rover 110s to scout routes into rebel-held areas in northern Macedonia.

On 21 August a four-man Parachute Regiment reconnaissance team laid out turquoise and fluorescent pink marker strips on a tiny football pitch in the village of Sipkovice, high up in the mountains of western Macedonia. A few minutes later the reconnaissance team guided in two Army Lynx helicopters. Three British NATO officers and a negotiator disembarked and were joined by a group of Albanian rebel leaders. After their negotiations, Ali Ahmeti said optimistically: "Perhaps discrimination against Albanians has come to an end."

The next day, in Brussels, NATO approved the plan. It was to be called "Operation Essential Harvest". The following day the Macedonian parliament approved the peace deal. On 26 August 3,000 NATO troops, including British Paratroopers and French Foreign Legionnaires, began to deploy for Operation Essential Harvest. Between 27 August and 27 September it collected 3,000 weapons. They were mostly old Kalashnikovs and machine guns but included a few ground to air missile systems.

# SPECIAL FORCES V.
# SPECIAL FORCES (1973)

*Just before the Jewish festival of Yom Kippur in 1973, Israeli Intelligence reported large concentrations of Syrian army units on their border with Israel.*

*Yom Kippur (Day of Atonement) was the most solemn date in the Jewish calendar. Not even cars moved on that day. The Israeli Defence Forces (IDF) were at level three alert. IDF Reservists were called up at the next level. The Israeli Air Force had virtually won the Six-Day War in 1967 by means of a pre-emptive strike. But this time the Israeli goverrnment felt that they should wait until they were attacked.*

*At 14.00 on 6 October 1973 the Egyptians and Syrians attacked along the entire length of the front.*

*Moshe "Muki" Betser was a senior staff officer of Sayeret Maktal, an Israeli special forces unit. Because they were special forces they were not at first involved. Betser and his CO decided to take Sayeret Maktal to the front, so they commandeered some armoured personnel carriers (APCs) and headed for the Golan plateau.*

*On the Golan, hundreds of Syrian tanks were threaten-*
*ing to overwhelm the Israelis. Tank battles raged all over*
*the Golan, and IDF's tanks were outnumbered ten to one.*
*Without their reservists, One Hundred and Eighty-eighth*
*Armoured Brigade held off 600 Syrian tanks with only 57*
*of their own. They lost 90 per cent of their strength. IDF's*
*Seventh Armoured brigade began with only seventy tanks.*
*They were decimated.*

*Reservists were slow in arriving because of chaos on the*
*roads. The Israeli Air Force was unable to provide effective*
*aerial reconnaissance because the Arab forces denied them air*
*superiority. The Arabs had the advantage because of their*
*anti-aircraft defences. The Soviets had supplied them with*
*SAM-6 weapons. Deprived of aerial photos, the Israelis were*
*blind.*

Betser and Sayeret Maktal were waiting for the chance to go
tank-hunting when they heard the sound of helicopters.
Betser was inspecting a post hit by a Syrian artillery shell at
the Israeli camp at Najah when a radio call came in from the
northern edge of the camp: "Helicopters coming in from
the northeast."

Betser saw three helicopters crossing the horizon from
east to west and descending into a field about 2km north of
the camp. He radioed his CO. They both knew that they
had to reach the helicopters before their enemies deployed;
his unit preferred attack to defence. He ordered all his unit
commanders to get their men onto the APCs and they drove
out of town, heading north. They had about one hundred
fighters and Betser reckoned that there must be about fifty
Syrians on the helicopters.

They halted about 300 metres from where the Syrian
forces had landed, and moved into "classic assault force
deployment". Betser:

We raced forward, producing as much firepower as possible, using it as cover while we advanced from boulder to
boulder. Assault is the essence of the IDF combat doctrine,
and we needed constant fire and movement forward to

avoid pinning us down.

Just as we reached the halfway point up the hill, about twenty meters from the top, their fire began hitting us. We shot back, continuing our attack, running and shooting, running and shooting, without stopping for any cover, all of us knowing exactly what to do. Hand grenades began flying through the air.

"Grenade!" I heard someone shout. Three hand grenades tumbled through the air over my head. I threw myself to the ground to take cover. Back on my feet before the dirt finished hitting the ground, I continued my advance, pausing only to reload my Kalashnikov.

Nearly at the top, we began throwing our grenades. More than a dozen flew into the air at the Syrians. The explosions clapped thunderously, putting an end to all the shooting, leaving us in control of the hill. Around us twenty-five Syrian commandos in brand-new camouflage uniforms lay dead. We grabbed vantage points all around the hill, scanning the area for more Syrian commandos.

My force lay to the east of Yonni's on the hill. We communicated by radio, yet close enough to hear each other's shouts. We knew we conquered the hill, but the morning mist, and the ragged terrain of the brush, boulders, natural ditches and old tank trenches below us, were perfect camouflage for the enemy in hiding. Every once in a while, one of our boys shot at something moving suspiciously in front of us.

The mists evaporated in the morning sun. Looking east I saw a helmeted head rise and then quickly duck out of sight about 30 meters ahead of me. I recognized the depression in the terrain as an old tank trench. "Yonni! Enemy in the tank trench! Cover me! I'm attacking!" I shouted, and at the same time signaled my force to follow my assault. But as we rose to attack, I saw Yonni, followed by about ten fighters, already heading toward the enemy position, firing as they moved.

I quickly ordered my force to change tactics, and provide covering fire to keep the Syrians' heads down while Yonni and his soldiers ran toward the trench. We improved our positions as we continued firing, heading toward the tank trench.

A sharp cry burst out of Gidon Avidov, a young officer from Nahalal, a few meters away from me. He looked down at his belly and collapsed.

"Medic," I called out. Two soldiers grabbed Gidon and pulled him to cover. Yonni and his forces reached the trench, shooting down into it. I ran the last ten metres followed by a dozen of my men, adding our gunfire to the trench.

Enemy soldiers, all dead, lay piled together where our fire drove them into a corner of the tank trench. But did we get them all? Yonni and I wondered. We took cover amidst the boulders and brush, surveying the scene ahead. Again we lay on the ground in the silence that followed so much noise, listening for the presence of any survivors trying to move in the terrain. Occasionally, the crack of a rifle fired by a soldier thinking he spotted something move ahead, broke the silence.

Finally, a Syrian rose from behind a boulder ahead of us, hands over his head. "Don't shoot!" he shouted in English.

We approached carefully. He wore the insignia of a Syrian officer, and he limped forward, his camouflage fatigues dripping blood from a wound in his leg.

"Don't move," someone shouted in Arabic at him.

The Syrian stopped. "You've killed them all," he said sorrowfully as we approached carefully, making sure he was alone.

"How many?" Yonni asked.

"We came with forty-two soldiers," the Syrian admitted.

Yonni and I had our men count the bodies, first the ten we found in the trench and then added the thirty-one on the hill. When we added the prisoner — their commanding officer, a major — it came to forty-two.

Gidon Avidov later died in the hospital. Baruch Tsur, a reservist from Moshav Hatzeva, died in the field, despite the medic's efforts. A few other soldiers suffered light wounds.

The captured major told them they had wiped out the most elite commando force in the Syrian army. The Syrians had fought stubbornly but had not had a chance.

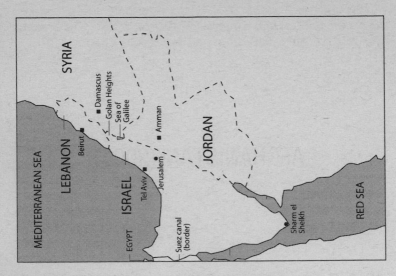

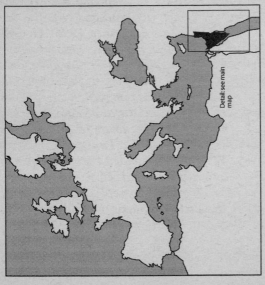

ISRAEL in 1973

# AFGHANISTAN (2001)

*After the attacks on New York on 11 September 2001, the evidence against Osama bin Laden accumulated rapidly. He was known to have been in Afghanistan since 1996. His al-Qaeda organization was based there, running terrorist training camps in a loose alliance with the dominant Taliban regime.*

*The Taliban regime controlled most of Afghanistan but there was strong resistance to them from alliances in both the north and the east. It would be a natural alliance between the United States of America and the northern and eastern alliances to expel both al-Qaeda and the Taliban.*

*US President George W. Bush demanded that the Taliban should give up al-Qaeda's leaders and close the terrorist training camps. The Taliban refused to reply but they made statements through their Pakistan embassy that this would be an insult to Islam. President Bush rejected the Taliban's response as insincere.*

*On 18 September 2001 the UN Security Council issued a resolution directed towards the Taliban, demanding that they hand over the terrorist Osama bin Laden and close all terrorist training camps immediately and unconditionally. US and British Special Forces clandestinely infiltrated Afghanistan to make contact with the Northern Alliance to help organize their forces to overthrow the Taliban.*

On 7 October 2001 the United States began Operation Enduring Freedom with air strikes against Taliban forces and al-Qaeda. The bombing attacks were carried out at high level but they were laser-guided onto their targets by US Special Forces Operational Detachment Delta (SFOD-D) teams. At first, the strikes concentrated on the area in and around the cities of Kabul, Jalalabad, and Kandahar. Within a few days, most al-Qaeda training sites had been severely damaged and the Taliban's air defenses had been destroyed. The campaign then focused on communications and "command and control".

On 20 October 2001 more than 200 US Army Rangers from Seventy-fifth Airborne Rangers parachuted on to a desert airstrip 96km south west of Kandahar. As they moved through buildings on the edge of the airstrip they came under hostile fire from al-Qaeda or Taliban fighters (AQT). At the same time operators from SFOD-D carried out a raid on a compound just outside Kandahar. There was a firefight with a number of Taliban fighters in which at least twelve Delta Force operators were injured.

During the last week of October 2001 the men of A and G squadrons of 22 SAS travelled to Pakistan via Oman and then into northern Afghanistan. The US command gave British Special Forces a mission in Helmand Province, codenamed Operation Trent. The plan was to deploy A and G squadrons of 22 SAS in mobile columns of Land Rovers. Operation Trent began by deploying their reconnaissance team by High Altitude, Low Opening (HALO) parachute drop. An eight man patrol from the Air Troop of G Squadron of 22 SAS jumped from the tailgate of a C-130 Hercules aircraft at 6,110m.

In the aircraft they breathed oxygen from a system mounted at the rear of the aircraft. When they jumped, each man switched to his individual supply, which came from small bottles mounted on their chest harness. They wore helmets and goggles as they fell through the sub-zero temperature night air, and had to use their gloved hands to prevent their goggles from icing. This required considerable skill to prevent themselves from becoming unstable. In freefall, a small hand movement can drastically affect the body's attitude, which can result in the freefaller tumbling out of control.

At 1,220m their parachutes opened automatically. They descended to the ground under their tactical assault parachutes. Their rucksacks and equipment had been attached to their legs but were released once their parachutes had opened so that they were suspended from the parachute harness. The equipment hit the ground just before the men did.

They all landed safely and began to prepare for the Hercules aircraft, which would bring the rest of A and G squadrons the following night. Six Hercules landed on the south west corner of a large sandy plain just before dawn. The men left the aircraft in their vehicles, then drove down the tailgates of the Hercules and immediately took up defensive positions around the improvized airstrip.

Operation Trent's target was a 190km drive away. It was a system of houses, compounds, trenches and caves at the foot of a mountain that was 1,800m high. It was being used as a headquarters and staging post for getting AQT forces, drugs and equipment across the border into Pakistan, and also as an opium factory. Consequently they had little or no idea how many men they would be attacking.

Their first difficulty was the very fine dust which made driving visibility very poor. Time was limited and they had to reach the target in time to form up for their assault. The actual attack would be made on foot by A Squadron while G Squadron provided covering fire from their Land Rovers. G Squadron would also form a mortar line. If necessary, they would send in additional men if the attack got pinned down.

After ten hours of driving, it was dark again as the leading troop took up their positions below the mountain. To their right the other A Squadron troops formed up; to the leading troop's left were the Land Rovers of G Squadron.

The 140 men of the attacking force lay in wait during the first hour of the early morning. It was time for a final weapons check. The fine grey dust was like talcum powder and could permeate anything which moved. Their magazine apertures and moving parts needed to be kept clean and dry, and their ammunition needed to be lightly oiled and kept free of windblown dust. Most of the men were carrying as much ammunition as possible as well as their medical and signalling kits, water, spare socks, main personal weapon, sidearm, knife, compass, distress flares and webbing. They left their Bergen rucksacks in their Land Rovers.

Just after 7.00 a.m. A squadron observed the enemy moving in and out of the trenches. The approach to the enemy position was not steep but it was hot, dusty and the ground was rocky. After forty minutes the main body of A Squadron formed a semicircle in front of and below the first trenches. They were ordered to open fire and begin their assault. AQT fighters could be seen popping up into the open, spraying fire from their Kalashnikovs and loosing off RPG-7 rockets. Other AQT fighters could be seen in support positions further up.

The main assault was in the shape of a pair of bull's horns which encircled the AQT position. With fire support from G Squadron at least twelve SAS troopers managed to penetrate the entrances to the trenches and caves. They killed at least six AQT fighters who were armed with Kalashnikovs. An SAS trooper was wounded, but two SAS men made a dash forward to reach the wounded man and managed to get all three of them out of danger.

In their assault on the al-Qaeda and Taliban (AQT) position in Helmand Province, before the action at Tora Bora, the SAS teams were used as a company of light infantry. In effect, they were Special Forces soldiers being used as highly trained infantry. Their ability at fire and maneuvre enabled them to outfight their Taliban and al-Qaeda opponents.

As fighting continued in the trenches, more AQT fighters came out into the open, where they came under fire from some of the SAS men who had found cover in front of the entrances to the trenches and caves. The amount of fire being exchanged was extraordinary. One SAS officer was hit by two rounds on the ceramic plates of his body armour. A third bullet hit the waterbottle on his belt kit.

They found that the trenches were not very deep and the caves were little more than bunkers dug into the slopes of the mountain. The SAS men had to use the Maglite torches under the barrels of their rifles. In the first cave, the first thing they illuminated was three AQT fighters still asleep. The fighters were shot while they were still fumbling for their weapons.

Outside, AQT fighters were closing in on the SAS men in the caves and trenches. SAS snipers in positions above and to the side engaged the approaching AQT reinforcements. Both sides were too close to each other for Air Support. The AQT carried on fighting, shooting and attacking until they were shot or stabbed to death or blown to pieces. After two hours the trenches had been cleared. The action turned to the approaching AQT; they were now the ones in a semi-circle and the SAS were facing outwards.

Two hours later it was over.

It was not until the next stage of the campaign began that the US and their allies began to see results. The Taliban had managed to hold a line against the northern alliance until their vehicles were hit by Hornet fighter bombers and their front lines were hit by 15,000-pound daisy cutter bombs, and by AC-130 gunships. Taliban fighters had little or no idea how to react to US firepower, standing on bare ridges where Special Forces could easily spot them and call in air attacks.

Eventually some Taliban fighters began to change sides.

By 2 November, the Taliban's frontal positions had been decimated. For the first time it seemed possible that the Northern Alliance could take Kabul. Many Afghan Taliban troops had terrible morale, and were regarded as untrustworthy. The Taliban regime had become so unstable that foreign fighters from al-Qaeda began to take over security in Afghan cities.

On 5 November 2001 Unmanned Aerial Vehicles (UAV)

scouted the hills and valleys of Afghanistan's southern border with Pakistan. They were being controlled from the ground by US Air Force and Central Intelligence Agency (CIA) operators. As they circled they fed video images back in real time, filmed through night vision lenses. They were looking for the tell-tale images given by the heat signatures of convoys of vehicles or large groups of people grouped around cooking fires.

On 9 November, Northern Alliance forces advancing from the south and west seized the main military base and airport of Mazar-i-Sharif.

On the night of 12 November Taliban forces fled from the capital city of Kabul. On 13 November the Northern Alliance forces arrived. After a fifteen-minute gun battle they killed the few foreign al-Qaeda fighters who had remained.

The al-Qaeda forces, almost certainly with Osama bin Laden himself, regrouped and began to concentrate their forces in a cave complex at Tora Bora, 30 miles (50km) southeast of Jalalabad, near the border with Pakistan.

It was at this time that a convoy of more than 100 four-wheel-drive vehicles drove into the Afghan village of Garikhil, near Tora Bora. The convoy brought 400 AK-47 assault rifles as a gift from Osama Bin Laden to the local tribal elders. The locals were highly skilled at smuggling anything across the border into Pakistan, despite surveillance by Coalition Special Forces, US aircraft, UAVs and every combination of thermal imaging equipment.

Tora Bora means "black dust". It is a small hamlet which gives its name to a complex of mountain slopes, ravines, ridges and valleys. They are crisscrossed with stony, un-metalled roads, donkey paths and tracks. There are sweeping masses of moraine and vast rockfalls, and the sides of the valleys and the mountains are pierced by caves. Some are vast caverns, others are tiny scrapes. It was in this area that the Afghan *mujahideen* resistance to the Soviet invaders of the 1980s had been so effective.

Tora Bora looked as though it might be Osama Bin Laden's last stand. The Americans concentrated on the

Tora Bora cave complex. Special Forces and CIA paid and organized over 2,000 local tribal militiamen. They gathered for an attack as heavy bombing of suspected al-Qaeda positions continued.

On 2 December, a group of 20 US commandos was inserted by helicopter to support the operation. On 5 December, Afghan militia wrested control of the low ground below the mountain caves from al-Qaeda fighters and set up tank positions to bombard enemy forces. The al-Qaeda fighters, who were mostly Arab, withdrew with their mortars, rocket launchers, and assault rifles to fortified positions on higher ground and dug in for the battle.

The Anti-Taliban tribal militia continued their steady advance through the difficult terrain. They were supported by highly effective air strikes which were guided in by US Special Forces. Facing defeat and reluctant to fight fellow Muslims, the al-Qaeda forces agreed to a truce to give them time to surrender their weapons. This may have been a ruse to allow important al-Qaeda figures, including Osama bin Laden, to escape.

On 11 December a Pakistani taskforce occupied the village of Tirah on the other side of the Afghan–Pakistani border. The first wave came from a unit known as the Khyber Rifles. Captain Ullah Khan of the Khyber Rifles described:

We gathered the tribal maliks and made it clear that our mission was to cordon off the territory as it was being used by al-Qaeda militants as an escape route into Pakistan. The villagers could hear the American B-52s bombing in the nearby Tora Bora range, where Osama bin Laden was thought to be in hiding. We told the headmen in no uncertain terms that if they didn't want some of the same, they would let our troops enter their land unopposed.

The Khyber Rifles' operation had two objectives. As well as cutting off the al-Qaeda escape route, they were making a strike against the drugs trade which was highly active in the area. The local clans' involvement ranged from poppy growing and refining heroin to smuggling the final products over the border to Afghanistan. From Afghanistan the drugs would be taken on to Western markets.

Over the next few weeks the Khyber Rifles rounded up a number of at-Qaeda militants and sealed off their escape route. The Khyber Rifles then set to work to improve the local tribesmen's facilities. They made hospital and school facilities available. They also connected villages to the national power grid and laid down a track suitable for motor vehicles to the market town of Landi Kotal. This would reduce the journey from eight to three hours. These facilities were intended to be an incentive for more legitimate activities than had been normal on the north west frontier, where smuggling and illegal border crossings were traditional activities for the local tribesmen.

The Khyber Rifles were a militia unit formed from local tribesmen. The unit had been originally formed by the British in 1878, when they were needed to protect a British expeditionary force making its way through the Khyber Pass. Their local knowledge and skills prevented the expeditionary force from being ambushed and destroyed as an earlier force had been in 1842.

When Pakistan gained its independence, in 1947, the original unit's descendants were immediately signed up as the Khyber Rifles. The unit's role was, once again, to seal the border and eradicate drugs traffic.

In 2001 the Khyber Rifles' local knowledge and skills once again proved invaluable on their home ground. By 2001 they were light infantry armed with light automatic weapons and mortars. The unit receives applications from hundreds of young tribesmen, and successful applicants are selected according to a tribal quota system.

On 12 December, the fighting at Tora Bora flared again, probably initiated by a rear guard buying time for the main force's escape through the White Mountains into the tribal areas of Pakistan. Once again Afghan tribal forces, backed by US special operations troops and air support, pressed ahead against fortified al-Qaeda positions in caves and bunkers scattered throughout the mountainous region.

Reporter Josh Tyrangiel described US special forces moving into position:

> The 12 bearded soldiers making their way up a pass in the White Mountains of Tora Bora were decked out in flat-topped Afghan caps and flowing shalwar kameezes. From a distance only one detail gave them away as Americans. Afghan alliance fighters – dedicated but largely untrained – walk upright, making themselves easy targets for enemy fire. The Americans were shimmying up the hill on their bellies. Late last week American special operations forces quietly made their way to Tora Bora, to the very front of the front lines . . .

On 11 December 2001 Matthew Forney reported how the caves were finally captured:

> Crazy led the charge on the caves. The six-foot-tall *mujahidin* fighter who chose his own nickname is famed in Jalalabad for killing five Arab fighters who fled town a little too slowly when the Taliban fell. Just before taking his usual place leading the charge on Monday, Crazy found a white coat left by al-Qaeda fighters who had held a forward ridge the day before. "This is Osama bin Laden's coat!" he yelled as he pulled in on, twisted a white headscarf around his head, and called his commander, Haji Zahir, one more time on the wireless. "I told him, 'If you return unsuccessful, I'll kill you,' " says Zahir. "It was sort of a joke, to push him further."
>
> It worked. The *mujahidin* shoved far enough into the craggy Tora Bora landscape on Monday and Tuesday to drive the last al-Qaeda fighters in Afghanistan so deep into the mountains that they're offering to surrender. Small-arms fire crackled through Tuesday morning, but by afternoon the caves were secure, both sides had declared a cease-fire and the attackers were combing the area that once

seemed unassailable for war booty. One of three top commanders, Haji Zaman, spoke with an Arab leader by wire-
less. "He said don't fight, we want to surrender," says
Zaman. He ordered them to give themselves up by 8 a.m.
Wednesday or face a renewed assault.

There was no sign of Osama bin Laden himself. The
bombing and the two-day attack had destroyed the last
of the al-Qaeda training camps which were located above
the caves. Matthew Forney:

The area is a picture of devastation. Strewn across the
terraced slopes that climb a tight valley are torn strips of
Arabic training manuals, some shreds of clothing, a set of
parallel exercise bars and a shooting target printed by the
National Rifle Association. Trees blown from the earth lie
with their roots twisted into clumps like charred driftwood.
Bomb craters 50 feet across and 20 feet deep are filled with
rubble and cross beams. "I think yesterday he was around
there," says commander Zaman. "I don't know if bin Laden
is dead or alive," he added, saying he's waiting to see who, if
anybody, turns themselves in on Wednesday morning.

For the first time, the infamous man-made caves of Tora
Bora were thrown open. These weren't the five-star accom-
modations with internal hydroelectric power plants and
brick-lined walls, areas to drive armored tanks and children's tricycles, and tunnels like capillaries that have captured the world's imagination. Such commodious quarters
might exist higher in the White Mountains, but these were
simply rough bunkers embedded deep into the mountain.
They were remarkable nonetheless.

I entered my first cave by walking through a narrow 20-
foot passage chiseled into a 60-degree mountain slope.
The effect was of walking through a deep cavern open to
the sky. I walked down the passage, stepping over two
rows of sandbags that blocked my way, and came to a
three-foot opening. I ducked into the mouth and dared go
no further. Not even the *mujahidin* would follow, and

several were making "boom" noises and gesturing about flying body parts. Everybody expected booby traps or mines.

After my eyes adjusted I saw a chamber of about eight square feet and high enough for a tall man to stand in. The floor was dirt and rubble, but there were signs of habitation. It contained two empty white boxes decorated with palm trees and the words, "Sherjah Dates." Scattered on the floor were a few green metal boxes of ammunition with Russian writing on them, and a canister about the size of an unexploded cluster bomb but the wrong color – red instead of yellow. Another cave next to it was about the same size and filled with ammunition, mostly bullets for Kalashnikovs and rocket-propelled grenades. Another nearby was much bigger and also filled with ammunition. Its cavern sloped up and back and seemed to lead to a passage, but nobody ventured in.

The caves faced a narrow valley that twisted its way through mountain ridges that seem to overlap as they rise toward the White Mountains. As Tuesday afternoon waned and it was clear that the al-Qaeda fighters had accepted the cease-fire, the area took the appearance of an archeological dig. Across one ridge 20 *mujahidin* fighters scratched at the ground with sticks looking for fragments of US bombs, which they loaded into a huge cooking pot and carried to a pickup truck. One fighter handed me a rubber jug with a strap. "Al-Qaeda," he said with a nod. Arabs drink water too. Another fighter with pale green eyes carried a backpack that he had taken from a cave. It contained a stick of Mum Cool Blue roll-on deodorant. He wouldn't let anyone touch it, but he would let them sniff.

The victory they were celebrating came with relative ease – one *mujahidin* fighter died and seven al-Qaeda fighters, according to commanders. Gul Karim led a group of about 30 fighters, including Crazy, in the Monday assault on the caves and a cluster of mud-earth houses nearby. The first thing he did was raise the enemy on a walkie-talkie. "He said they don't want to fight us, that we all are Muslims.

They said leave us the Americans and we will fight them."
It had no effect. "Our troops had orders to attack," he says.
His soldiers, most of whom had spent the past five years
living in Pakistani refugee camps and had never fought
before, first occupied the ridges above the caves and swept
down the hills. The defenders withdrew quickly. One
fighter with a yellow flower in his hat said his friend had
killed two as they fled up the mountain.

By Tuesday morning nearly all the Arabs had followed to
higher ground, where they fired mortars and machine guns
at the advancing *mujahidin*. Three fighters on a strategic
ridge held off the advance for much of the morning before a
volley of small-arms fire and rocket-propelled grenades
blew them apart. Two were later dragged to a command
post and dumped on the ground for *mujahidin* fighters to
gawk at. One was so mangled that his torso faced the sky
and his legs faced the ground.

If they choose not to surrender by the Wednesday deadline, the al-Qaeda remnants will have to fight or flee. They
still control the highest ground and it's not known what
kind of fortifications they maintain there. "We can't say
they are completely surrounded; they have many ways to
escape," says a commander named Atiqullah. "They could
cross into Pakistan by traversing the snowy passes along the
border a several miles away, but that way is very difficult."

By December 17, the last cave complex had been taken and
their defenders had been overrun.

US forces continued to search the area into January, but
there was no sign of Bin Laden or the al-Qaeda leadership.
They had probably slipped away into the tribal areas of
Pakistan to the south and east. It is estimated that around
200 of the foreign jihadis were killed during the battle,
along with an unknown number of anti-Taliban tribal
fighters. No US deaths were reported.

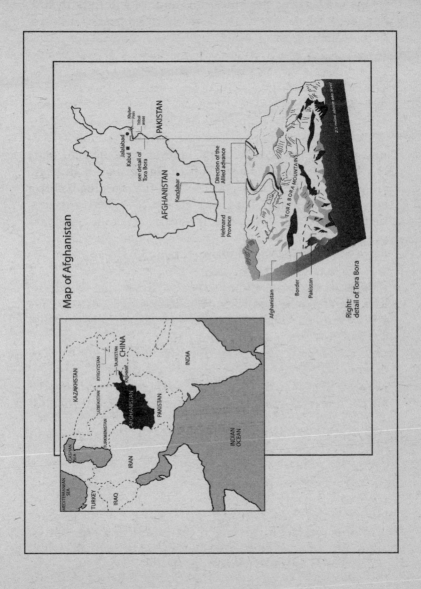

Map of Afghanistan

Right:
detail of Tora Bora

# PATHFINDER'S NIGHTMARE (1967)

*Richard R. Burns qualified as a Pathfinder on 10 August 1967. He arrived in Vietnam, soon afterwards, when the main part of the One Hundred and First Airborne Division joined its first brigade.*

*The Pathfinder's job was to land first and take control of the Landing Zone (LZ). An element of One Hundred and First Airborne Division's second brigade requested Pathfinder support. All the Pathfinders in Burns' detachment volunteered and drew straws to find out which of them should go. Burns and another Pathfinder, Joe Bolick, won the chance to be the detachment's first operational team on a combat mission. They would stay with the second brigade unit from insertion to extraction. Burns:*

A furious wind blew through the chopper's cabin, offering a welcome reprieve from the heat. Unbuttoning the top buttons of my jungle-fatigue jacket, I let the gale blow through my shirt, causing it to flap frantically.

I felt secure sitting on the floor beside the door gunner on the right side of the helicopter. Joe was seated on the other side, across from me. Turning my head, I yelled over to ask how he was doing, but he couldn't hear me. The only sound was the whopping of the chopper's blades.

The doors of the helicopter remained open to allow a quick exit when we hit the ground. Although I was close to the edge of the opening, I didn't have to worry about falling out; my rucksack was so heavy, I felt anchored to the floor. My M-16 rifle rested on my lap. It was locked and loaded with a twenty-round magazine. (Though our magazines were equipped to hold twenty rounds of ammunition, we packed them with only eighteen to lessen the tension on the magazine spring and help prevent the bullets' double feeding.)

The Vietnamese countryside was beautiful from a thousand feet up. Miles of lush vegetation ranging from pen meadows to thick jungle spread across the whole region. The landscape was decorated with every shade of green imaginable. Small ponds and soggy rice paddies speckled the area. The sun's brightness temporarily blinded me every time I caught its rays as they reflected off the water. Although the view was breathtaking, I had to remind myself that a menacing, deadly enemy lay concealed beneath all that lavish undergrowth.

I heard the blades of the helicopter changing pitch just as the door gunner tapped me on the shoulder, signaling our descent. Joe and I were on the lead bird, accompanying a flight of five helicopters onto the LZ. We were only a few minutes out. I had controlled numerous combat assaults in training, but this was completely different; this was for real. In my mind, I rehearsed the plan Joe and I had devised for when we landed.

Once we were on the ground, two other flights consisting of five helicopters each would follow at approximately two-minute intervals. It was imperative that we keep them abreast of the enemy situation, wind velocity, terrain, and any obstacles on the LZ. Based on those factors, we would also recommend the best landing formation (staggered left, staggered right, wedge, etc.) to utilize. (If possible, it is always desirable to land aircraft in the same formation in which they are already flying.)

We each carried a PRC-25 radio and had performed commo checks before our departure to ensure that both radios were operational. Joe's radio would serve as the ground-to-air radio. He would control the aircraft and issue instructions to the lead pilot of each flight. I would check the winds, throw smoke, and provide security. My radio was also set on ground-to-air so I could listen in and take over if Joe was hit or if his radio went dead. Furthermore, I could switch frequencies to the command-and-control net to request or control artillery or gunship support without interrupting control of the flights.

Approximately thirty seconds out, I could see the LZ off to our front, a huge, open, grassy field surrounded by thick jungle and trees. My heart started thumping violently; my hands began perspiring. I searched the faces of the three grunts sitting to my right. They were lost in their own thoughts. One guy, who appeared to be of Hispanic descent, was making the sign of the cross. He then held a religious medal to his lips. Somehow it was comforting to know that I wasn't the only one who was scared.

Suddenly the fear seemed to swell in my gut. I felt extremely vulnerable sitting there with the wide-open space to my front, like one of those moving metal targets at an amusement park booth. I thought about all the kids my age back home. Their biggest problem was trying to figure out what party to attend or what movie to see. I started to question myself. What the hell was I doing here? I could be sitting at home, safe, in a comfortable chair, watching TV or going to a movie. Maybe I really wasn't tough enough for the job after all.

The fear intensified. My mouth and lips dried. I wanted to reach for my canteen to get a drink of water, but it was too late. We'd be landing any moment. I could feel my heart beating in my throat.

Deliberately, my eyes glanced down to my left shoulder at the white screaming eagle with the yellow-and-black Airborne tab arced above it. Damn it! I'm a paratrooper. A proud member of the 101st Airborne Division. The finest

Airborne unit in the United States Army. I thought about all those who had served before me, and who had fought in places like Normandy and Bastogne. I thought about my family being safe back home and my friends having the freedom to choose what movie they wanted to see.

Burns made up his mind to do his job: to go in first and safely guide his fellow Airborne soldiers into battle. Burns:

Abruptly, my thoughts were interrupted as our helicopter skimmed just above some tall trees and went sailing toward the middle of the LZ. The door gunner beside me opened up, his M-60 rapidly spitting bullets. I watched the red streaks of tracers stream into the trees. He screamed over at us, "Shoot! Shoot!"

I flicked my weapon from "safe" to "automatic". I didn't observe any enemy, so I aimed at the door gunner's tracers and squeezed the trigger in short bursts. The grunts immediately followed suit. Suddenly my chest was on fire. It continued to burn all over. Glancing down, I watched in amazement as the door gunner's spent hot brass from his M-60 whipped down the front of my fluttering shirt, scorching my chest.

"Oh, shit!" I jolted back and watched the brass zoom by me just as the chopper flared into a quick hover.

I was fumbling to change magazines when the door gunner screamed, "Go! Jump out!"

I stared up at him. My mind was swirling. Everything was happening too quick.

Thrusting my torso toward the edge, my eyes gawked at the ground below. The long blades of elephant grass were pressed down from the chopper's blades, disclosing a drop of about ten feet.

I shouted back, "We're too high up!"

The door gunner stopped shooting and grabbed the frame of my rucksack in an attempt to shove me forward. "Get the fuck out of here!"

All eight of us seemed to leap at once. It felt like I was in the air for a long time. There was a mixture of moans, thumps, and equipment clanking as we slammed into the earth. I was stunned. I hit hard on my tailbone, and it took a moment for my legs to work. Glancing up, I witnessed the last of the helicopters abandon the area. A lonely feeling spread over me, like when your mother waves goodbye to you on your first day of school.

There was shooting everywhere. The sound resembled thousands of firecrackers going off all over the place at once. Leaders were shouting commands, and everybody took off running toward the tree line, which was at least fifty meters away. Joe and I moved with them for about ten meters, then sat down. Bullets were zinging by us as we took off our rucks and turned on the radios. We were sitting ducks out there in the middle of the LZ, but we had to stay and control the choppers.

God, those were real bullets zipping overhead.

Someone was actually trying to kill us. A soldier about twenty meters to our left toppled over; I didn't see him get back up. I heard the familiar sound of M-79 grenade launchers, followed by explosions. Maybe being a coward and sitting at home wasn't such a bad idea after all. I must have been insane to volunteer as a Pathfinder.

Part of me felt like there was a little boy inside just wanting to cry. I was hoping that I was living a bad dream, and if I was, I wanted to wake up right now. I'd heard somewhere that a person used only a small portion of their brain; I thought that maybe, if I concentrated real hard, I could use my whole brain and will myself out of here.

A voice barked over the handset. "Pathfinder Control! This is Black Widow Lead with a flight of five, approximately one minute out. Request landing instructions. Over?"

I looked over at Joe to see if he had heard the transmission as well. He was about five feet away and, like me, was hunkered down low behind his equipment, his handset to his ear. Bullets continued piercing the air around us. A few made a loud *crack* as they whipped by.

He seemed to be in his own little world, so I tried to shout above all the noise. "Joe, the choppers are inbound!"

He looked angry and snapped back, "I know, damn it! Cover me!"

For an instant I got pissed. This was the first time Joe and I had spoken since departing on this mission, and he was already barking orders at me. Right! Cover him? Who the hell was going to cover me?

I noticed something very unusual about Joe's face, however. Staring into his eyes, I recognized that Joe Bolick was as terrified as I was. At that moment I felt a peculiar alliance with him that I could not explain. He was also right. It was my job to provide security and cover him while he brought in the birds.

I brought my weapon up to my shoulder. "No sweat, Joe. I got you covered. Bring them in."

The elephant grass was so high I had to stand up to see above it. Searching the tree line, I spotted a few gray puffs of smoke from enemy weapons. Making sure I had a clear field of fire, I let go some short bursts at them. I was amazed at how fast the weapon emptied. As I changed magazines, I could hear Joe giving instructions to the pilot.

"Black Widow Lead, this is Pathfinder Control. Land one five zero. Staggered left formation. Winds calm at this time. Receiving enemy small-arms fire from the south and southwest. Continue approach. Over!"

"Pathfinder Control. This is Black Widow Lead. Roger! Continuing approach!"

Joe and I took a moment to remove our helmets and don our black hats so the pilots could distinguish us from the grunts. We hated wearing steel pots anyway. They limited our vision and were hot and uncomfortable to wear. (We hadn't wanted to bring them, but we were ordered to because of some division policy when in the field.)

Anticipating Joe's next request, I grabbed a yellow smoke grenade from my LBE [load-bearing equipment] and ripped off the tape that secured its lever. (Each smoke grenade had its color painted on the top for easy identification. The colors were yellow, green, violet, and red. Red was used only to identify enemy or danger and to abort missions and aircraft landings.)

We could see and hear the aircraft in the distance. Joe called out, "Richie, pop smoke."

Selecting a spot far enough away from us and downwind, I pulled the pin and threw the smoke grenade. There was a metallic *ping* as the lever flew off, followed by a loud popping sound, an eruption of sparks, and a resounding *whoosh* as the smoke roared out of its container. (Deployed improperly, a smoke grenade could cause a fire that would be spread by the rotor wash of helicopters, thus endangering future landings and soldiers on the ground. If thrown too close and upwind, the smoke would encompass us, hindering our vision. Luckily, our position was surrounded by wet, damp elephant grass. The likelihood of it creating a fire was low.)

Joe waited until the smoke had time to billow up from the grass. "Black Widow Lead, this is Pathfinder Control. Smoke out! Identify!"

It was extremely important never to inform the pilot ahead of time what color smoke you were using. At times, the enemy monitored American radio transmissions. Early in the war, incidents occurred in which pilots were instructed to land on a certain color smoke, for instance green. From monitoring the transmission, the enemy would understand ahead of time what color was being used and would release green smoke at a different or multiple locations. This either confused the pilots or caused them to land in the middle of an enemy ambush. Therefore, the practice was to pop smoke and then have the pilot identify the color.

"Roger, Pathfinder Control. I spot yellow smoke!"

"That's affirmative, Black Widow. Yellow smoke. You are clear to land!"

The flight of helicopters darted onto the LZ laden with troops. Door gunners carefully scanned the area for enemy; however, none could fire their machine guns because they might accidentally hit Americans already on the ground. By that time most of the fighting was occurring closer to the tree line. More paratroopers bounded from the choppers, tumbling into the elephant grass. Their leaders quickly began to bark orders. So much had happened since we landed on the LZ with the first lift, it was hard to believe that only a few minutes had passed.

Joe had just completed relaying landing instructions to the third and final flight of helicopters when a different voice crackled over the radio.

"Pathfinder Control! Pathfinder Control! This is Medevac One-three, approximately five miles to the northeast. Request landing instructions. Over."

Joe called out, "Richie, there's a dustoff inbound!"

"Yeah, I heard! I was monitoring! The unit commander must have called it! I'll find out where he wants it to land."

Turning the knob on my radio to the command-and-control frequency, I contacted the unit commander. I learned he was assembling casualties who needed evacuation on the southwest portion of the LZ near the tree line. There were six in all, one critical, another KIA.

Since one man was critically wounded, it was essential that we land the dustoff as close as possible to the injured. Joe would continue to control the flight of five that was on its way in while I trekked over to the approximate spot where the commander wanted the dustoff to land, roughly seventy meters away.

"Hey, Joe! When the medevac comes on station, tell him that I'll be there to guide him in visually. I'll link back up with you once he leaves."

"Okay! I'll instruct him to guide in on you when he gets about one mile final. You better get going."

I needed to get there quickly. The dustoff would be inbound in minutes. Searching for a prominent tree in the distance, I located one that I could easily recognize above the others in order to keep my bearings. I had plenty of smoke and ammo attached to my LBE so, leaving my rucksack and radio behind with Joe, I grabbed my weapon and plunged through the thick elephant grass.

Pushing through the dense grass required a great deal of exertion. Movement was rough. It was extremely hot, and my jungle fatigues were drenched from moisture and sweat. Besides my being eaten by insects, blades of grass sliced at the exposed portions of my skin. I couldn't see three feet in front of me, so I kept moving toward the tree I had selected. Hearing the last flight of helicopters approach, I turned and watched them land on the LZ next to a stream of green smoke. Damn, the medevac would be next on station any minute.

About ten meters from the tree line, the elephant grass ended, and it was as if the whole world came into view; I could see again. Noticing a small group of soldiers off in the tree line to my right, I called out, "Hey, where's the wounded?"

Someone from the group replied, "Over here! Are you the Pathfinder?"

I heard another mutter, "Of course he's a Pathfinder, man. Can't you see the black hat?"

As I ventured toward them, one of the group walked hastily in my direction. He seemed especially concerned.

"I'm a medic! Listen! We got to get these guys out of here ASAP [pronounced "ay-sap"]."

I touched him on the shoulder. "I know! No sweat! There's a chopper inbound, and it should be here any moment."

I proceeded with him over to the group. Gazing at the injured, my eyes fell upon a still, lifeless body covered with a poncho. Mud-soaked jungle boots protruded from beneath it. The scene was like something out of a movie, but it wasn't a movie; it was reality. A fellow paratrooper was dead. Forever. I wondered if he was one of the guys that had been on my helicopter coming in. I remembered the Hispanic kid praying and kissing the medal. I was grateful the soldier's face was covered, because I didn't want to know who he was.

A deep feeling of sadness encompassed me. I thought about how terrible it would be for his family when they received the news. I also wondered if the people back home could even slightly fathom the immense sacrifice the soldier and his family endured for the preservation of a people's freedom.

I pushed those thoughts out of my head and redirected my attention to the mission. Stepping out from under the trees, I searched the skies. Sure enough, off in the distance a lone chopper was heading our way.

I was certain Joe had already informed the dustoff pilot to proceed to the southwest portion of the LZ and guide on me, so I had to move fast.

I shouted to the group, "Okay, guys! We got a dustoff inbound. Let's get the wounded out into the field." I instructed the medic to load the litter on first, then the ambulatory, once the bird landed.

Running about twenty meters out into the LZ, I snatched a violet smoke from my web gear and tossed it off to the side. (Joe was in contact with the pilot and, once he saw the smoke, would ask the pilot to identify.)

Raising my arms straight above my head, palms inward, I faced in the direction of the aircraft. That was the signal for him to guide on me.

The dustoff was coming in fast. When it was approximately twenty-five meters to my front, I extended both arms out to my side, horizontally, palms downward. That signaled the pilot to hover. Once I had the helicopter at the desired spot, I moved my arms in a downward motion. Then, crossing my arms to the front of my body, I signaled him to land.

Racing around to the side of the medevac, I assisted in loading the wounded, then ran over and tapped the right-side window of the helicopter, catching the pilot's attention. I knew that the best departure route for him would be to his ten o'clock, thereby avoiding some tall trees as well as possible enemy fire. Making a circular motion with my right hand above my head, I then pointed in the direction I wanted him to depart. This also signaled him to take off. He acknowledged with a thumbs-up. Immediately the aircraft bolted skyward.

The medic and the others expressed their thanks. I didn't have time to converse; I was worried about Joe, who was all alone in the middle of the LZ. Besides, we still had to gather up our equipment and be ready to travel with the unit. With my weapon at the ready, I thrust back into the thick vegetation.

After trudging about fifteen meters, I discovered a path leading in the general direction I was moving. It had been created by our guys treading off the LZ during the assault. The trampled grass sure made the going a lot easier.

Eventually reaching the section I thought to be Joe's approximate location, I called out softly, "Joe! Hey, Joe!"

"Over here!" To my surprise, his voice sounded fairly close.

Proceeding about twenty feet, I stumbled upon a small opening. Joe had his equipment packed and was attaching his helmet to the back of his rucksack. I felt a profound sense of relief.

"How's it going, Joe?"

"Good! The pilots reported that the whole operation went real smooth."

Joe placed his arms through the shoulder straps of his ruck and struggled to his feet. "Did all the wounded get out okay?"

"Yeah!" I headed toward my equipment. "Everything went like clockwork."

"Airborne?" He seemed genuinely pleased.

While I secured my gear, we discussed the success of the operation. Joe and I certainly worked well together as a team. Something had changed in the way we interacted, something I'm sure neither of us could explain. Somehow a strong feeling of trust and camaraderie had developed between us in that short period of time.

We decided to keep Joe's radio operational while we moved off the LZ to link up with the unit. Staying in communication with them was vital to our survival. The last thing we needed was to get wasted by our own troops while entering their perimeter. Moreover, if we ran into any enemy along the way, we could summon help.

It was remarkably quiet on the LZ. I couldn't hear the faint voices off in the distance anymore. An eerie feeling came over me, that kind of feeling I used to experience when I was a young boy all alone in the house while watching a horror show on TV. I could tell Joe felt it, too.

Joe's voice interrupted my thoughts. "We better get going! They're probably waiting on us."

"I'm with you. Let's get the hell out of here."

Examining the area to make sure nothing was left behind, we set out for the tree line.

Since I had already crossed the LZ once, I took point. As we moved through the elephant grass, my mind began to race. What if the unit had already left the area and forgotten about us? What if the gooks saw me returning to the LZ and were waiting to ambush us? Damn, what if we ended up getting captured?

They found the paratrooper company. The Pathfinders spent the rest of the seven-day mission with the company Command Post (CP). There were no villages in their patrol area but they discovered an abandoned enemy base camp complete with booby-trapped tunnels.

When they reached their Pick-up Zone (PZ), they discovered that it was a Pathfinder's nightmare. It was strewn with obstacles such as stumps, bushes and bamboo thickets. Several tall trees blocked the approaches. They told the company commander that pick-up would have to be delayed while the PZ was cleared. The company commander took the news gracefully and they radioed back to postpone the pick-up for three hours. Most of the work of clearing the area was done using explosives. Burns was glad he had brought his steel pot because of the chunks of wood, dirt and stones hitting his helmet.

It was Burns' turn to control the aircraft. A Charlie Charlie bird (command and control helicopter) carrying the battalion commander landed. The battalion commander, a colonel, was furious about the delay. Burns told him the PZ was unsafe. Unfortunately the battalion commander had picked the spot himself, on an overflight. He insisted that the pick-up would take place in one hour.

An hour later there were still jagged stumps sticking up all over the place. Neither Burns nor Bolick thought that it would be safe for five helicopters to land and load troops without the possibility of something like a branch puncturing an aircraft's fuselage. The battalion commander refused to accept this.

Burns was still insisting that it was unsafe when the approaching helicopters called in. He told them to "Wait one." The battalion commander ordered him to land the helicopters. Burns refused. The battalion commander relieved him and Joe Bolick when he, too, refused to do it.

The battalion commander tried to bring the helicopters in himself but the helicopter pilots refused to take instructions from him and demanded to talk to one of the Pathfinders. Burns told them that the PZ had not been cleared properly so the ground commander had relieved them. The pilot of the leading aircraft asked how long it would be before the PZ could be cleared. Burns told him: "If everyone cooperates, approximately one hour."

The pilot told the ground commander that they would come back once the ground had been cleared on condition that the airlift was controlled by the Pathfinder. The pilot also told the ground commander that he was in contact with his own CO who supported his decision. He warned the ground commander he would be contacted by his own higher headquarters.

Ten minutes later the ground commander ordered his men to cut down and level everything to a foot or lower. When the work was finished. Burns and Bolick checked the PZ and approved it. They called in the pick-up. Before the pick-up the ground commander came and told them that the incident had gone all the way up the chain of command to divisional level. Burns and Bolick were surprised but pleased that they had been supported. The ground commander told them that everyone in command seemed to agree with them as Pathfinders. He apologized and praised their competence and ability as soldiers. He told them: "Don't ever stop standing up when you are right. Just make sure you are, like you did today."

# OPERATION FALCONER (2003)

*In 2003 the Australian contribution to the US-led Coalition was built around a Special Forces Task Group. The Australians named their military effort Operation Falconer.*

*The Australian Special Forces Task Group was manned by personnel from Headquarters Special Operations, the Special Air Service Regiment (SASR) based in Perth, 4 Royal Australian Regiment (RAR) Commando, the Logistics Support Force, the Incident Response Regiment and the Fifth Aviation Regiment. Support personnel came from the Australian army and the Royal Australian Air Force (RAAF). Australian SF Headquarters was part of a chain of command which ensured that Australian Special Forces were always commanded by Australians.*

*In February 2003 the main Australian contingent began to arrive in the Middle East. It immediately began to acclimatize and work-up. Their work-ups covered co-operation with US Delta forces and British SAS. This would be critical in relation to air operations as the Australians would have to rely on British and American Close Air Support (CAS).*

*If the Iraqis had possessed any weapons of mass destruction it was from western Iraq that they would have fired them at*

*Israel or Egypt. The main role for the Special Operations component of Central Command (CENTCOM) was to deny Saddam Hussein the ground space from which to launch missile attacks.*

*An Australian SASR operative described:*

In all there were around 80 of us operating in western Iraq, but to the Iraqis it must have seemed like 800. Our primary role was to stop weapons of mass destruction from being launched from the 1991 "Scud Line" in the western Iraqi desert, while our secondary role was to raise merry hell – "Digger Style". Basically we were like an enormous itch that the Iraqis could not scratch, as we were everywhere and anywhere. One day we were in the desert, the next in a giant cement works – in this case the one at Kubaysah, about 60km north of Highway One between Baghdad and Amman and 20km south of the huge Al Asad air base. This massive civilian infrastructure was nicknamed by us the "Temple of Doom", and was captured without us firing a single shot – and with 40 prisoners as well.

However it was not always like this for us, as in several contacts we engaged enemy forces on an ongoing basis for a number of days – fighting running battles with them that were as good as any I experienced in Afghanistan. Along the way we even treated wounded enemy, fed and watered prisoners and then sent them home with a simple message: "The war is over for you."

During our 42-day incursion, we took on more than 2,000 Iraqis, including elite Republican Guard troops and counter Special Forces troops – although not at the same time – and suffered no casualties – that's got to be a ripper result.

During our mission we found no Scuds, but we left our own calling card – 46,000kg of bombs and missiles in the first week of combat alone to be exact. The overwhelming success of the SAS mission to deny the enemy any ballistic missile launches was due to technology, training and superior communications basically. The fact that the squadron suffered no casualties did not surprise me, as we minimized the risks to our own people and to the Iraqis. Despite the lack of casualties and the string of victories, this was no picnic as the Iraqis were well organized and well equipped. It was one-on-one and it was tough.

The first SAS patrol to cross into Iraq by night spent 96 hours in open desert terrain without being spotted by anyone, including local Bedouin herdsmen and enemy forces. For them not to get compromised in that dead flat terrain was a significant effort. Although we never saw any Scuds during our deployment, the fact that we were operating as if they were there made a real difference as the Iraqis were always trying to second-guess us. It is called manoeuvre warfare and is designed to put pressure on the enemy and to unmask them. We were a small force element creating quite a disproportionate effect – by means of shock and surprise. Also we were completely unpredictable in our actions which were the key components of our tactics. We also had to deal with an unpredictable enemy, who would on occasions raise his hands in surrender yet resume firing as we approached. We even have one of their flags that bears proof of this as it has both powder burns and bullet holes from being fired through. Adding to our operational experience we also had the weather to contend with, as temperatures often ranged from −5C to 43C – and we thought Oz varied. All in all it was a magnificent effort, and a ripper achievement.

Australian Special Forces joined the American Rangers, US and British Special Forces at the FOB at Azraq in Jordan. As soon as the war began their first objective would be to seize the airfields in western Iraq. These were designated H1, H2 and H3.

On the night of 20 March, MH6 Little Bird assault helicopters started attacking Iraqi border defence positions.

The Iraqi border defences were quickly overcome and the Special Forces began to deploy. If they encountered heavy resistance they called in CAS. Mobile Land Rover patrols of British and Australian SAS went into action immediately.

After the airfields were secured, the Special Forces' next objective was to take control of the main roads linking Baghdad with the Syrian border and Jordan. A half squadron of Australian SAS moved northwards following an intelligence report that Iraqi Scud launchers were attempting to "run" their mobile launchers. This involved hiding across the border in Syria where they would be safe from Coalition air attack. When they wanted to fire they would cross the border and fire from positions in Iraq's western desert. Then they would retreat back to Syria.

The two main dual-carriageway motorways into Jordan and Syria were being kept open and protected by small groups of Iraqi commandos so that senior members of Saddam Hussein's regime could escape. As the Australian and British patrols moved eastwards and northwards they began coming into contact with these groups.

On 22 March a troop of Australian SAS in six-wheeled Land Rovers were ordered to destroy an Iraqi command and control installation. The installation consisted of a small number of vehicles and some entrenched, well dug-in positions. There were reported to be fifty soldiers and five vehicles. As the Australians approached the centre of the facility appeared deserted.

A two-vehicle element was surprised by an unexpectedly well-aimed burst of gunfire which the Australians reported as "determined and aggressive". The Australian patrol commander decided to make an aggressive move into the heart of the enemy position. He was hoping that the speed and surprise of the move would make the Iraqis give up. In fact the Iraqis returned fire as soon as the Australians broke cover.

Australian SAS trooper Bradley Vinnycombe was .50 calibre gunner on one of the Australian vehicles. As they charged the Iraqi position Vinnycombe noticed that at least twenty Iraqi commandos and two vehicles had placed themselves where they could keep the Australians pinned down. He opened fire. This scattered the Iraqi soldiers and hit some of them.

He moved to the shoulder-mounted Javelin missile system and fired a rocket at the first Iraqi vehicle, destroying it. This allowed the rest of his patrol to move. Vinnycombe continued to fire his .50 calibre machine gun, although his head and shoulders were exposed to return fire from Iraqi Kalashnikovs.

He fired another javelin missile into a second Iraqi vehicle. Then he noticed some Iraqis setting up an 82mm mortar tube. He grabbed his own assault rifle and opened fire. His first burst hit the mortar tube, which exploded into the faces of the men operating it.

With two vehicles and six men, the Australians killed twelve out of the thirty they fought. The rest surrendered.

For the next two weeks the Australians took a full part in the advance on Baghdad. With US Special Forces they called in air strikes on Al-Rutbah prison, 80km from Baghdad.

# OPERATION BARRAS (2000)

*There had been civil war in Sierra Leone since 1991. Other African countries and the United Nations sent peace-keeping missions.*

*At the beginning of May 2000 rebel forces were threatening Freetown, the capital of Sierra Leone. The main rebel faction was identified as the Revolutionary United Front (RUF). On Sunday 7 May 2000 the United Kingdom deployed a task force to evacuate British, European Union and Common-wealth passport holders from Freetown. Rebels had been reported as gathering in thousands north of Freetown. An advance party from C company of the first battalion of the Parachute Regiment was flown from Dakar in Senegal and inserted into Lungi Airport to ensure that the airport had not been taken by rebel forces. The Nigerian and UN troops at Lungi were surprised but happy to see them.*

*The rest of the Task Force followed. The task force's goals were to set up a headquarters, secure the airport and the peninsula around it. They also had orders to secure the British High Commissioner's residence and to establish Evacuee As-sembly Areas.*

*By the end of May United Nations Mission to Sierra Leone*

(UNAMSIL) and government forces had beaten back the advancing rebels. The Paras were followed by an Amphibious Ready Group from 42 Commando Royal Marines, which landed by boat from a naval taskforce including the assault carrier HMS Ocean.

Once the situation stabilized the task force was withdrawn.

In June a company of Jordanian Special Forces which was part of UNAMSIL was engaged in a fire fight with about 200 RUF fighters. They were trying to cross Rokel creek by canoe. The West Side Boys (WSB) were a local militia sympathetic to the RUF. They had about eight bases, including Magbeni and Gberi Bana in the Okra Hills. Foday Koroma filed an account for a Freetown newspaper:

Lightning swept across the dark cloud and there was a heavy noise. There was a thunderbolt that saw the West Side Boys in disarray. Quickly, very quickly, they were dislodged from their Okra Hills base.

This was the picture painted of the operation carried out by the United Nations.

Peacekeepers in Sierra Leone, UNAMSIL, have tried to get rid of the nagging renegade soldiers. Everybody had hoped it was the end of the harassment, extortion and intimidation perpetrated by the self-styled West Side Boys along the Freetown/Masiaka highway.

Nobody would have thought the renegade soldiers would ever again show their faces along the highway. Some reports spoke of how [attacks by] the helicopter gun ship had drowned hundreds of WSB in their desperate bid to escape the wrath of the ferocious peacekeepers.

But just a few hours after the "successful" operation, the West Side jungle boys were back at their checkpoints, doing the same things they were always doing. As a way of manifesting their presence, two of their commanders, including Commander Kallay, the new leader, went to Masiaka and had a tête-à-tête with the Jordanian troops stationed there. Not long after, a government-owned Road

Transport Corporation bus was ambushed and the passengers were dispossessed of their belongings.

The driver of the bus reported the incident to the Jordanian troops but nothing was done.

The West Side Boys are still at their Okra Hill base. This brings into question the success of "Operation Thunderbolt". It also heaps the question of the use of force to resolve our decade-long civil war.

Various forces have come and gone, but none have been able to end the war. From Executive Outcomes to Sandline International, from ECOMOG to UNAMSIL, the war is still on. "The people are still suffering," says Musa Kamara, a displaced man from Makeni.

The West Side Boys were once again a menace to traffic. They continued to set up random roadblocks to extort money and goods from vehicles and pedestrians.

A Freetown-based aid worker fell victim to one of these roadblocks. He gave an interview to the BBC on 30 August 2000; he was still frightened that members of the gang might track him down. He described the events:

We had a lot of materials in the pick-up, some of it underneath plastic sheeting. They searched the vehicle and we asked if we could continue. They refused to let us go and told us to wait for further instructions. Then suddenly they put us in the vehicle and drove off the main road into the jungle. They said we were going to a village about five miles away. We stopped halfway and then they took everything from the vehicle.

We were later taken to a village about seven miles from the main road and held in close detention until about 8 p.m. that evening. After that we were taken in a boat to the group's main base in a village called Gberi Bana and that is where we were held for ten days.

In Gberi Bana, we were allowed to move around because there was no way to escape; there were guys with guns everywhere.

They had taken this village over completely, chasing out the people who originally lived there.

At the beginning, they threatened to execute us because they said the United Nations was planning to attack them. This was during Operation Thunderbolt, which was aimed at getting rid of the West Side Boys' checkpoints on the main road.

There were lots of the group in the area, despite the UN's claims to have secured it.

They never made any demands. They only asked that they should be allowed back in the government army and that the government shouldn't use force against them.

You know, these boys are just there to cause trouble. They're very unpredictable – they could be nice one moment and nasty the next. At the base, there were men and women – some of them very young. Their number varied.

At one point, they said they were mobilizing and at that point there were between 200 and 300 armed people there. In another location, there were 60–100 people.

They have a reputation for being drunk, but actually they don't have access to much alcohol. They do smoke a lot of marijuana and they also take some cocaine. There are many marijuana plantations.

Basically they act like highway robbers; when they run out of things they seize vehicles and steal the contents.

They are capable of committing atrocities. While I was being held, six women suspected of witchcraft were executed by firing squad. They used their AK-47s.

I only heard the firing, but a colleague saw three dead bodies.

Aminatta Forna is a London-based journalist who grew up in Sierra Leone. She described a road block manned by the West Side Boys:

It became evident that we were in rebel teritory when we passed through the first checkpoint: a wooden pole, lowered and raised by means of a length of rope. To the side of the road stood the operator: a boy of ten or eleven, bandy legged and barefoot, wearing a pair of ragged shorts and nothing else, save a large machine gun strapped to his back.

On 25 August 2000 a patrol of three Land Rovers manned by eleven British soldiers was passing through the village of Magbeni. They were on their way back from an authorized liason visit to a Jordanian battalion at Masiaka, about 100km east of Freetown.

The British patrol was from the First Battalion of the Royal Irish Regiment. They were in Sierra Leone to train government forces at the Benguema Training Centre (BTC).

The Jordanian battalion was serving as peacekeepers with the UNAMSIL. During their meeting the CO of the British patrol had learnt that some of the West Side Boys were beginning to surrender to the UN as part of a disarmament programme. They drove into Magbeni to investigate further.

When they reached Magbeni, twenty-five men and women from the West Side Boys gathered around the British patrol. One of the West Side Boys, Ibrahim Koroma, described the situation: "They got down from their vehicles and talked with the Boys. We didn't know they were coming but everything seemed calm."

They asked the CO of the British patrol, Major Alan Marshall, to wait for their leader, Foday Kallay, to return. He was twenty-four years old and had been a former sergeant in the Sierra Leone Army. He regarded the area as his teritory and was angry because there had not been any request for British troops to visit Magbeni.

Foday Kallay arrived and began to give orders. The mood of the group around the British vehicles changed. A captured Sierra Leone Army truck armed with a heavy machine gun came out from among the huts, blocking the road south of the village.

The Royal Irish soldiers were so hemmed in by the crowd that there was little that they could do. They had a heavy machine gun mounted on one of their vehicles. But if they had opened fire they might have started a massacre or hit their own men. One of their other vehicles had a radio, and the radio operator was able to send a message reporting that they were being detained.

Major Alan Marshall tried to reason with the West Side Boys. They tried to grab his SA80 5.56mm rifle. When he resisted, they hit him with their fists and rifle butts. Then they attacked the Sierra Leone Army officer who was with the patrol as liaison. Attacking the officers showed the rest of the patrol that the West Side Boys did not respect rank and could be brutal. West Side Boy Ibrahim Koroma stated: "They had no chance to resist."

Five minutes later the Royal Irish soldiers had been disarmed. They were stripped down to their olive green T-shirts and underwear. Their wedding rings and watches were removed. They were herded down to a ferry point and taken across Rokel Creek to the militia's headquarters at Gberi Bana.

In London the Ministry of Defence (MOD) said that negotiations had begun to secure the release of the soldiers from a renegade faction which had a reputation for kidnapping and robbery.

Incidents of "hostage and ransom" had become normal in Sierra Leone. In fact, many of them went unreported. At first "hostage and ransom" kidnappings had been directed against foreign missionaries and aid workers, but by May 2000 UN peacekeepers were among the victims. A MOD spokesman in London reported that "they are in the hands of the West Side Boys, although we have not received any ransom demands."

The first contact between the West Side Boys and the staff at BTC took place over the patrol's radio. The CO of the Royal Irish, Colonel Simon Fordham, arranged a face-to-face meeting.

On 27 August Colonel Fordham and a small team met with the West Side Boys. Colonel Fordham's team included the regimental sergeant major (RSM), who observed a seventeen-year-old girl. She was carrying an RPG-7, which she put down before she paced out the distance to their

Land Rovers. Then she walked back, picked up her RPG-7 and adjusted the sights to cover their vehicles.

Two police negotiators from the Metropolitan Police Hostage and Crisis Negotiation Unit had been sent out from London. They advised Colonel Fordham before and after his meetings.

The West Side Boys demanded the release of a rebel leader, Foday Sankoh, plus food and medicine, in exchange for the British troops.

On 29 August the Regimental Signals Officer (RSO) who had been captured, accompanied by Foday Kallay, met Colonel Fordham and the Hostage Negotiation Team at the UN camp at Masiaka. The RSO assured them that he and his fellow hostages were being well treated and that no one had been injured. Before he was taken back he managed to hand over a map of the West Side Boys' camp hidden in a ballpoint pen.

Two days later five of the captured soldiers were released in exchange for a satellite phone and medical supplies.

During their debriefing, the soldiers who had been released described how, several days after their capture, six of them had been marched down to a swamp area where they were tied to wooden posts. Their bodyguards had lined up, pointing their AK-47s at them. The patrol commander, Major Marshall had tried to reason with Foday Kallay, who had screamed, "I will kill you! I will kill you!" The threats had continued for half an hour before they were marched back to the main camp. The released soldiers related that Major Marshall and the Sierra Leone Liaison Officer had been beaten.

Now that the West Side Boys had a satellite phone they became more pretentious. They called up the BBC's African Service and began to make political demands. However, the satellite phone was a Trojan Horse. Electronic warfare specialists were able to track its exact location and even turn it on and off by remote control.

A rescue mission was being prepared. The First Battalion of the Parachute Regiment was ordered to prepare a company for a "find and fix" role. Their role would be to tie down the West Side Boys while Special Forces went in to rescue the hostages.

"A" Company was chosen because it had recently undergone jungle training. "A" Company's CO, Major Matthew Lowe, began to organize his combat group. It would consist of a Company HQ and three Rifle platoons. They would carry two 7.62mm GPMGs per section. He chose the heavier belt-fed version. Each platoon was issued with 6,550 rounds of 5.56mm ball and 6,000 rounds of 7.62mm ball, 170 grenades (high explosive and red phosphorus smoke) and 50 bombs for their 51mm mortar. (Live ammunition had been called "ball" since the days of musket balls.)

The village of Magbeni was identified as the objective for the company group. Since the inhabitants had left, some of the buildings had collapsed and the jungle had encroached on the vegetable gardens. SAS patrols were already observing the village and had reported a Heavy Machine Gun (HMG). The HMG would prevent helicopters landing in the village or across the river at Gberi Bana. Lynx attack helicopters would have to destroy it at the start of the operation.

News that the paras were being deployed was allowed to get out as a piece of psychological warfare. The SAS had discovered that the hostages were being held on the north side of the creek in some mud and cement buildings in Gberi Bana. There were five buildings; one held the British captives, and next to it was one which held seventeen Sierra Leonese hostages who had been captured a week earlier. Kallay and his commanders lived in the other three buildings.

The SAS teams observing the West Side Boys concealed themselves in the swamps. Their hides were less than 250m from Gberi Bana. They reckoned there were about 50–100 West Side Boys in each village. Their weapons included the twin ZPU 214.5mm HMG which had blocked the Royal Irish patrol. They were also armed with 60mm and 81mm mortars, RPGs, Kalashnikovs, Medium Machine Guns (MMGs), anti-personnel mines and grenades.

In Magbeni they had "Technicals". These were pick-up trucks with machine guns mounted on the cargo floor. They also had the Royal Irish Regiment's Land Rovers. The vehicles gave them mobility and fire power.

The decision to launch a rescue operation was taken on 9 September. British officials did not think the West Side Boys were going to release the hostages.

The hostage extraction team came from D Squadron 22 SAS. The most likely plan would have been to "fast rope" twelve-man fire teams. Fast roping is a technique in which soldiers slide down a rope as fast as possible wearing leather gloves to protect their hands. They would fast rope at two Landing Sites (LS). The maximum number of ropes would be deployed from the rear ramp of a Chinook.

The patrols already on the ground would engage any West Side Boys who tried to shoot at the helicopters or engage the hostages. The attack would be before dawn to make it more likely that the West Side Boys would be sleeping and the hostages all in the same place. The fire teams would hold off the West Side Boys while a third Chinook landed on a football pitch 150m north of Gberi Bana. The Chinook would take the hostages out to the Royal Fleet Auxiliary *Sir Percivale*, which would be anchored offshore.

They expected that after sixty seconds, once the initial shock of the assault had worn off, the West Side Boys would begin to fight back. One advantage was the fact that the Royal Irish soldiers could be expected to obey orders and act as a disciplined group. As a precaution against any of the West Side Boys hiding among the Sierra Leonian hostages, all the freed hostages would be plasticuffed.

At 0500 hours the paratroopers of "A" Company were forming up in their sticks. The crew and gunners of the MK7 Lynx helicopter made their final checks. The troopers from D Squadron checked their fast roping equipment. Engines were started and the men filed aboard. Under subdued red lighting they moved down the interior of the helicopters and settled into the canvas seats. The pilots were flying with night vision goggles (NVG), which made the jungle below look luminescent.

Mohammed Kamara was a West Side Boy who heard the rotors of the approaching helicopters. He ran and took cover in the swamps. The Lynx came in first. Kamara said, "The helicopters were almost on the water. They fired again and again until there was no more shooting."

The West Side Boys at Gberi Bana opened fire as the Chinook carrying the SAS hostage snatch and fire teams came in and hovered above the palms in the half light of dawn.

Another West Side Boy said: "We never experienced anything like this . . . we saw the soldiers coming down to the ground. I fired my RPG two times but the helicopter balanced [swerved] and I missed." The teams had got down safely and the helicopters could move out of range.

Before the West Side Boys started firing, the SAS patrol lying up about 55m from Gberi Bana burst from the jungle. They made straight for the huts where both the British and the Sierra Leonian hostages were being held. They "discouraged" any interference until the main body arrived.

Only two people escaped alive from the West Side Boys' huts in the firefight that followed. One of them was Foday Kallay, who had hidden under bedding and bodies. Afterwards a British officer said, "We didn't even realize we'd got Kallay. Those who fought we killed. Those who surrendered we captured. It was only later we identified him." Kallay's wife fought and died.

One of the Sierra Leonian hostages, Emmanuel Fabba, saw SAS men blast buildings apart with grenades fired from their M203 rifles. He saw shapes descending from the helicopters. He thought at first that they were bombs. It was only when he looked again that he realized they were men – it was the SAS fast roping team.

It was probably during this initial exchange of fire that SAS trooper Bradley Tinnion was hit by a 7.62mm round which passed through his body, exiting through his shoulder. His colleagues dragged him to the Chinook and treated him as best they could until he was evacuated. He died as a result of his wounds aboard *Sir Percivale*. It had been his first operational mission.

As the Royal Irish soldiers were being rescued the other Chinook was inserting two platoons and the HQ of 'A' Company of First Paras. They knew it would be marshy but the first two soldiers down the ramp were surprised to find that they had landed chest-deep in a swamp. The reeds looked like grass, and they had thought the terrain would be firm enough. The SAS team had not been able to get close enough to see this because of a lack of nearby cover.

It should have been a sprint to the treeline but it became a 100–150m slog through mud and grass. A soldier from "A" company praised the corporals who urged their men on:

That was where the young NCOs were fantastic and that is where they really started gripping people. With the best will in the world the company commander and platoon commanders couldn't control it. They just wanted to focus on getting to the right point in the jungle.

The paras pushed forward until they felt the ground becoming firmer as the swamp became shallower. They moved to their left until they reached the tree line. The company was quickly into position for the break into the village. Command Sergeant Major (CSM) Chiswell and his party had to wait in the swamp on the side closest to Magbeni before they could secure the LS. CSM Chiswell had to wait for the Chinook to fly off again before he could even join his men.

While the SAS men across the river were holding off the West Side Boys in Gberi Bana, the Lynx helicopters were hitting the West Side Boys' positions in Magbeni. Corporal Simon Dawes said, "We came under fire at first, then it was taken out. We had helicopters and heavy guns that suppressed the fire."

The company shook out and began to move through the village from west to east. The leading platoon took its objective but 2 Platoon came under heavy fire as it reached the second objective. Corporal Dawes said, " This was the first fire fight I had been in where the rounds were coming my way. I don't like to talk about that sort of situation but it was scary. But once we got into the fighting the training took over."

A hard core of West Side Boys were standing their ground and fighting back. As the Company HQ group moved forward to join up with 2 Platoon there was an explosion in front of them. It injured seven of the soldiers; but for their helmets and body armour it might have been fatal. Private Julian Sheard said: "There was a loud explosion and we could hear these agonizing screams."

The CO, Major Lowe, was wounded in the legs by shrapnel. The 2 Platoon commander and three of the HQ group, including two signalers, were among the wounded. Captain Danny Matthews said, "The OC called me up and said I was to take command of the company."

Weapons, ammunition and radios were removed from the wounded and they were dragged clear. Sergeant Fitzwater took command of 2 Platoon. An unwounded signaller transmitted the casualty evacuation request.

It had been decided that radio messages would be in clear. Even if the West Side Boys intercepted their signals, they wouldn't have enough time to react. Besides, it was unlikely that they would find the right frequency on their captured radios.

The casualty evacuation was so fast that the company aid party were still running towards the scene when the helicopter lifted off. The first casualties arrived on board *RFA Sir Percivale* at around 07.00 hours. The surgical team began to try to save Trooper Tinnion's life.

All the casualties had been treated and stabilized by 18.30.

"A" Company kept up the momentum of its attack, despite the setbacks. The GPMG gunners struggled to clear stoppages. These were caused by mud getting into the linked ammunition. After they had cleared the stoppages, they had to fire their weapons from their shoulders because it was impossible to see any targets from a prone position. They had realized that the thick vegetation would make this necessary and had practised this during their work-up.

Under cover of smoke from red phosphorus grenades, 1 Platoon dashed across the open track. By about 07.00 hours the West Side Boys could be seen withdrawing eastwards.

"A" Company continued attacking its various objectives. They found the West Side Boys' ammunition dump at one of them. It was professionally dug in with a poncho stretched above it. 3 Platoon cleared the remaining buildings south of the track and took up a blocking position against any counter attack from the direction of Laia Junction.

Despite their radios being affected by immersion at the swampy LS, the action had been unaffected by communication problems. Within the small area of the village shouted commands could be heard and the action was fought by small well-led groups of soldiers.

1 Platoon pushed out clearance patrols into the outlying jungle but after 20m it was too thick to get any further. By 0800 Magbeni was secure.

A patrol went through the village. They destroyed the vehicles, including the Bedford truck with the ZPU-2 and the three "technicals". They also destroyed ammunition including mortar and RPG rounds with PE4 plastic explosives, and burnt down the buildings.

Across the river in Gberi Bana fifteen male and three female prisoners were taken. They were handed over to the Jordanian UNAMSIL battalion, who in turn handed them over to the Sierra Leone police.

The raid had freed twenty-two Sierra Leoneans who had been held prisoner for weeks or months. Five were women who had been abducted and forced to become "bush wives" or "sex combatants". The men had been used for forced labour. One of them, Emmanuel Fabba, revealed some details of their captivity:

The only lavatory had been a hole in the ground in a metal hut. It was used by both the captives and the militiamen. They were allowed to wash once a week in the Creek.

Usually the British kept very quiet. They spoke to each

other in low voices and sometimes shared a cigarette. The major did the talking for them if he needed to speak with the West Side Boys.

The British ate tinned "compo" rations which were sent in by the hostage negotiators. These were mixed with local produce such as casava leaves and coconuts.

Emmanuel Fabba explained that Major Marshall had warned the other hostages how to behave if a rescue was made:

> He came to talk to me in a low voice, he pointed at the wings on his uniform and said the Paras were coming. He did not know exactly when but he said we should not leave the house when we heard the helicopters. We knew the British were our only hope and had prayed that they would come soon as the West Side Boys had threatened to execute us.

When they heard the helicopters the Sierra Leoneans lay prone inside their hut. During the gunfire and the thump of the Chinooks' rotors, one captive panicked and ran from the hut. He was killed in the crossfire. Fabba:

> There was so much shouting and shooting it was terrible. We saw a British soldier outside so we called out, "Civilian hostages, don't shoot." They brought us out of the back of the building, tied us up and made us lie face down in case we were West Side Boys. The major confirmed our identity later.

The pregnant wife of one of the West Side Boys hid under a bed when the SAS attacked Gberi Bana. She said: "I was very afraid but the soldier spoke to me quietly. He brought me water, lit a cigarette and asked me if I wanted one. He was a friendly man."

By 10.00 the Chinooks began to ferry West Side Boys' prisoners and dead out of the area. In Magbeni the Paras discovered the Royal Irish Land Rovers. They were driveable despite some bullet holes and flat tyres. Spare keys were brought in by Chinook and they were underslung and lifted out by Chinook.

About 11.00 the last helicopters lifted the men of D Squadron and 1 Para out. Survivors from the West Side Boys began to emerge from the jungle around Gberi Bana. Sixteen-year-old Unisa Sesay had been a member of the West Side Boys small boys unit. He described the situation:

> There were many corpses and wounded people lying on the ground. One commander was standing and his friend was trying to remove a fragment from his shoulder. The rest of the people were on the ground.

One of the hostages explained about the West Side Boys' small boys unit:

> They were used as servants by the bigger members of the West Side Boys and as bodyguards because none of the older members of the group, especially the leaders, trusted one another.

SAS trooper Brad Tinnion died as a result of his wounds. The wounded paras recovered. Later in September, the Sierra Leone army swept through the area that had been dominated by the West Side Boys. They "encountered no resistance from the West Side Boys at Magbeni". Soon afterwards more than thirty former West Side Boys turned up at a Jordanian demobilization camp.

By 22 September a total of 371 West Side Boys, including 57 child combatants, had been disarmed.

The UN disarmament programme in Sierra Leone was formally concluded in January 2002. The training programme helped to transform the security situation. Democratic elections took place in May 2002.

# RAID ON THE PLO (1968)

*The Israeli Defence Forces (IDF) defeated their Arab neighbours in the Six-Day War in 1967. Another threat to Israel's security emerged in the form of the Palestinian Liberation Organization (PLO). The PLO tried to do what the Arab armies had failed to do in 1967 but it used different tactics. By 1968, terrorist incidents were daily events in Israel.*

*The PLO set up bases in the Jordan Rift valley of the Hashemite Kigdom of Jordan. The IDF sent special forces to look for the PLO's main base, which they found in the Jordanian village of Karameh. Muki Betser was in the Israeli Paratroop Brigade's reconnaissance unit. The unit was an Israeli elite unit known as a "sayeret". Sayeret means "tip of the spear" in Hebrew . . .*

*Muki Betser began his military service as a conscript. The Six-Day War extended his military service. After a bus full of schoolchildren was blown up by a landmine in the Negev, the IDF mounted a raid on the PLO's base at Karameh. The codename was Operation Inferno.*

On 21 March 1968 at 05.30 Betser and his detachment of thirty men from the IDF Paratroop Brigade reconnaissance unit should have been in an ambush position east of the PLO camp.

At dawn IDF jets would make a leaflet drop. The leaflets announced:

> The IDF is coming. You are surrounded. Surrender. Obey the army's instructions. Drop your weapons. If you resist you will be killed.

IDF tanks and halftracks had crossed the Jordan river over the Allenby bridge. IDF engineers had to provide temporary bridges over the Jordan north and south of Karameh. Artillery in the foothills of the Judean mountains would provide fire support. The IDF expected the PLO fighters to withdraw eastwards into the ambush set by the Paratroop Brigade detachments, which were due to land at 05.30. Before the helicopters reached the landing point they ran into fog and had to fly in holding pattern for at least fifteen minutes. The IDF command did not alter their schedule to account for this.

Betser's detachment landed an hour's jog away from their ambush position. As soon as they began to jog westward they ran into numbers of armed Palestinians, who were mostly wearing black and white keffiyeh headscarves. This suggested they belonged to the Fatah PLO faction which was loyal to Yasser Arafat.

Some of the PLO tried to fight but most of them tried to find cover in the sandstone gullies of the dried-up watercourses. The paratroopers chased them down to the dry riverbeds and over the ridges. They killed about twenty-five and took about twelve prisoner. They were harassed by mortar fire from the Jordanian army. The IDF had hoped that the Jordanians would allow them to cripple the PLO unmolested, because the PLO was challenging King Hussein's authority in the area.

Betser's detachment finally reached their position five hours later. The IDF raid was in trouble; the tanks had bogged down in mud caused by the winter overflow of the Jordan and the Jordanian army was reacting to the Israeli incursion into their territory with mortar and artillery fire. The other paratroop detachment was also in trouble. It had taken casualties and was under fire.

They were ordered to pull out. Betser took some of his men to help the other detachment, which was a mile and a half north of his position. When he reached them, he saw a wounded man who was pinned down by sniper fire. Then one of Betser's platoon commanders, Arazi, was hit. Betser:

"Get him to cover," I snapped at the squad to my left. They practiced for this situation hundreds of times. One soldier lofted a smoke grenade. It toppled through the air, exploding into a billowing cloud. Three ran into the smoke screen, racing to rescue their stricken officer, knowing the thick smoke only hid them but did not protect them from the bullets.

They knew the drill: to get Arazi to cover before anything else. But when the smoke cleared I saw my soldiers frozen by panic. They forgot everything. One soldier knelt by Arazi's side, a second fumbled with a packet of bandages and a third stood by fully exposed to the incessant enemy fire.

Bullets stormed across the wadi at us all. I shot back with my AK-47, my Klatch, as we nicknamed the Kalashnikovs captured from the Egyptian army in Sinai the year before.

Prone, at an odd angle created by the slope of the wadi bank, I noticed a tiny cloud of dust rise from the ground where a bullet struck just beside me. I ignored it, concentrating on Arazi and the three paralyzed soldiers.

"Get him to cover!" I shouted.

I heard a soft moan beside me. I looked to my right. "Betser, I'm hit," said Engel, a red-headed *kibbutznik* lying a few meters away. I looked him up and down. Blood darkened his green fatigues above the knee.

"It's your leg," I told him, offering a reassuring smile. "Not your shooting hand." He winced back a smile at me.

"Keep firing," I said. He did.

For the third time I shouted for the soldiers around Arazi to get him across the wadi to safety. But just then, one of the three fell soundlessly to the ground beside his wounded commander.

Only a few minutes passed since the shooting began, and we already lost two good fighters, not counting the wounded like Engel still shooting beside me. If we did not get out of there, we would all die.

"Hanegbi,"I called to a soldier about halfway between Arazi and me. "Get down there and tell them to move him to cover."

"No way I'm going down there," Hanegbi answered.

"Hanegbi . . ." I repeated slowly and sternly. More afraid of me, perhaps, than the enemy bullets, he started running toward Arazi. But after a few strides, Hanegbi flung himself to the ground, under heavy fire.

With nothing left to do but go myself, I plucked a smoke grenade from my web-belt and flung it into the wadi. Red smoke streamed from the can. As soon as it began billowing, I dashed down the slope toward Arazi. Firing over my Kalashnikov's sights toward the enemy, aware of my soldiers behind me doing the same, I raced to save my soldiers.

A freak gust blew the red smoke the wrong way, exposing me fully as I zigzagged across the wadi toward Arazi. Bending for my last strides, I saw the shock in his blanched face. Concentrating on the canvas strap of his web-belt, I reached for it on the run. I planned to grab it and pull him to the safety of a boulder jutting from the far bank of the wadi. My action would resolve the will of the soldiers who panicked. Indeed, bursting into their view, lead whistling in the air around us all, I became aware of my soldiers around me beginning to move. I reached for Arazi's belt.

And when I touched it, a blast exploded inside my head.

As if struck by a huge ax, my head felt like it burst open. The impact jerked me upright, while teeth flew out of my mouth. Blood cascaded from my face, a thick red waterfall pouring over my torso.

Instinctively, I grabbed my throat where the bullet ripped into my head. But as the blood poured out of me, so did my strength.

Still on my feet, I realized I was dying. The thought echoed inside me, reverberating into a singular serenity that quickly overcame all my other thoughts.

A soldier goes into battle thinking it won't happen to him. That's what makes it possible to face death. It should not happen to anyone. "But if it does, at least it won't be me." That's what I thought. Now I knew better.

As the officer in charge, I was the last person here who should be wounded. But as my strength ebbed away, and the sensations of my body diminished, I let go of those thoughts. The shooting around me continued, but nothing mattered anymore. I said farewell to the world, ready to die. Still on my feet, I let my hand finally drop the futile effort to stem the bleeding at my throat.

A hot blast of desert air seared my throat, surprising me as it filled my lungs, shocking me with the realization I would live – if I survived the swarm of bullets around me.

Even if I reached cover, I intuitively knew that I should not lie down, certain that if I did, I would drown in my own blood. I must stay on my feet, I thought. Not dead – at least not yet – and still the officer, responsible for my men; getting help for them became my primary concern.

I walked straight ahead, dimly aware of the shooting behind me, and started up the slope leading out of the wadi, knowing that only a few hundred meters away, Matan and his soldiers waited for us, oblivious to our predicament.

Gunshots snapped in the air like crazed drumming. "Betser, get down! Muki! Get down!" Soldiers shouted around me. But I marched on, alone, directly up the slope.

As Betser marched back to the other detachment's position, he realized that his boots were full of blood. It had soaked down through his uniform, into his socks and his lace-up paratrooper boots.

He made it all the way on his own. He couldn't speak because he had been hit in the jaw and the blood in his boots came from a wound in his thigh. He was picked up by a medevac helicopter.

# THE RESCUE OF JESSICA LYNCH (2003)

*Jessica Lynch joined the US Army because, as her father said, "They offered a good deal." She began her service as a supply clerk. She was assigned to the Five Hundred and Seventh Maintenance Company. The unit consisted of welders, repairmen and clerks.*

*On 23 March 2003 a convoy from the Five Hundred and Seventh Maintenance Company crossed into Iraq, heading for Baghdad. They were following up in support of the First US Marine Division, who had crossed over the border from Kuwait three days earlier.*

*Brigadier General Rich Natonski was OC of a Marine Air and Ground Task Force (MAGTF) following up first Marine Division. Natonski's MAGTF was responsible for taking Nasiriyah and opening up a supply route through the city.*

*Natonski was following the progress of his lead element, First Battalion of the Second Marine Regiment (1/2 Marines), who had reported being held up by incoming fire. He had come forward in person to see what was really going on: armoured vehicles should not be held up by small arms fire.*

*When he landed from his Huey he saw four US servicemen lying on litters. They were recognizable as army soldiers from their equipment and desert-pattern camouflage uniforms. They had bloody bandages on their arms and legs. He ran over to them and asked: "Who the hell are you?"*

The lost US soldiers from Five Hundred and Seventh Maintenance Company were officially posted as missing. A few days later five of the missing US soldiers were shown on Iraqi television but there was no sign of Jessica Lynch.

Nothing was heard for several days until an Iraqi approached a US Marine checkpoint. He told them that he had seen an American woman in a hospital in Nasiriyah. The Iraqi's wife was a nurse who worked at the hospital and he had gone to meet her. He said: "I went to the hospital to visit my wife. I could see much more security than normal." He asked a doctor he knew about all the additional security. The doctor told him: "There was an American woman soldier there."

After he had told the Marines, the Iraqi returned to the hospital to find out more about the security arrangements: where the injured American's guards were and when they slept. He reported back to the Marines on 30 March. By that time the Iraqi's own wife and daughter had had to flee from their home because they were in danger from the Iraqi regime.

The Iraqi was able to give the Americans information about the setup in which the captured soldier was being held, including the precise details of the security layout and the times that shifts changed. US forces planned a rescue operation based on this information.

US forces in Nasiriyah were on the opposite side of a river to the hospital, so a diversionary operation was required. On 31 March an assault force moved in to secure the hospital grounds while US Marines opened fire on Iraqi positions across the river. Special Forces landed and entered the hospital building where Jessica Lynch was being held.

A sympathetic Iraqi doctor showed the Special Forces exactly where she was. He also told them that there were the remains of several other US soldiers in the morgue or buried outside. The Special Forces called out her name as they entered her room. US Air Force Major General Victor Renault remembered:

> She had been scared, had the sheet up and over her head because she didn't know what was happening. She lowered the sheet from her head, but didn't really respond. One team member repeated: "Jessica Lynch, we're United States soldiers and we're here to take you home." Jessica seemed to understand that. And as he walked over and took his helmet off, she looked up at him and said, "I'm an American soldier, too."

A Ranger doctor checked her condition before the team evacuated her. She still seemed to be in some pain. Renault:

> Jessica held up her hand and grabbed the Ranger doctor's hand, held on to it for almost the entire time and said, "Please don't let anybody leave me." It was clear she knew where she was and didn't want to be left in the hands of the enemy.

Jessica's injuries included fractures to her right arm, both legs, right foot and ankle and lumbar spine. She also had a head laceration. Later the medical team stated that she had been wounded by a low-velocity small calibre weapon.

She was airlifted out by helicopter. Other members of the rescue team were taken to a site where eleven bodies were buried. Some of the bodies were thought to be American. Renault:

> The rescue team did not have shovels so they dug up those graves using their hands. They wanted to do that very quickly so that they could be off the site before the sun came up.

They recovered the bodies of eight American soldiers who

had been with the Five Hundred and Seventh Maintenance Company when it was attacked.

By 11 April, Jessica and forty-nine other wounded soldiers were landed at Andrews Air Force base outside Washington DC. They were taken to a nearby military hospital.

# RAID ON ENTEBBE (1976)

*Moshe "Muki" Betser was in the pit on 27 June 1976 when it was reported that terrorists had hijacked Air France Flight 139. The commercial flight had left Tel Aviv en route for Paris via Athens. Minutes after it took off from Athens it was hijacked.*

*The pit was a communications centre in an underground bunker beneath the Israeli Ministry of Defence. Betser was there because he was duty officer for Sayeret Maktal, Israel's elite counter terrorist unit. Betser expected the hijacked plane to return to Tel Aviv airport so he drove out there.*

*But the plane landed at Benghazi where the terrorists demanded that its fuel should be topped up. Betser was trying to work out a plan but this was impossible until they knew where the plane was going. Soon after 10 p.m. the plane took off from Benghazi. It would have taken three hours to fly to Tel Aviv. By 1.30 a.m. the plane had not arrived. By dawn there were reports that the plane was heading south into Africa.*

*Finally they learnt from a foreign radio report that the plane had landed at Entebbe airport, where Ugandan President Idi Amin offered his services as a mediator.*

The British Broadcasting Corporation (BBC) reported that the terrorists had hustled the hostage into the old terminal building, which was surrounded by Ugandan paratroopers. These were soldiers that Betser himself had been training four years previously.

The terrorists demanded five million dollars in cash and a hostage-for-prisoners exchange. The prisoners were to be released from jails in Kenya, France, Switzerland, Germany and Israel. From these demands the authorities could tell that it was clearly a case of co-operation between international terrorist groups.

Betser knew both Entebbe airport and Ugandan troops from personal experience. He knew that Ugandan troops were not good at operating at night and that they lacked motivation. He also remembered that an Israeli building contractor had built the terminal where the hostages were being held.

The Israelis called in all available information to try to build up an accurrate picture of the situation. They considered all the military possiblilities. It would be an eight-hour flight within radar range of hostile countries. The most unpredictable element in the whole situation was Idi Amin. What were his intentions?

A woman with dual Israeli-British citizenship was allowed off the plane. She had tricked the terrorists into believing she was in the middle of a difficult pregnancy. Back in London she contacted the Israeli embassy and was able to describe the terrorists in detail. They were led by a German man and a German woman; there were also two younger Arabs. The German was identified as Wilfried Boese, a member of the Baader-Meinhoff gang.

Among the military possibilities they considered was a major airlift of 1,000 troops. Betser was very much against this; he believed an attack on that scale would lose them the element of surprise. Betser thought that they needed to arrive in as compact a formation as possible with as few elements as possible. He was adamant that the more elements were involved, the more that was liable to go wrong.

The terrorists gave them a deadline of 1 p.m. on Thurs-

day 1 July. On Wednesday 31 June the terrorists released
some of the hostages as a gesture of goodwill. In fact they
released the 42 passengers who were not Jewish. The Air
France crew chose to stay with the remaining hostages,
while those who had been allowed to go free returned to
France.

One of the returning passengers was a retired French
army officer, who provided detailed information about
the hostage situation. The hostages were kept under a
twenty-four-hour guard, and the critical moment was
possibly midnight when the hostages were told to lie
down on mattresses. By one in the morning most of
the hostages were asleep. The Ugandans were definitely
working with the hijackers, and were there to prevent the
hostages escaping – but they were not expecting the IDF
to appear.

The most viable option looked like an intervention by the
IDF rather than one which involved rescuing the hostages
and then surrendering to the Ugandans.

Just before the hijackers' deadline, the Israeli government appeared to be reversing its policy of not making
concessions to terrorists. It asked that the deadline should
be delayed to give them time to make the arrangements for
the exchange. The hijackers announced a new deadline, 72
hours after the first one, at 1 p.m. on 4 July.

The rest of Entebbe airport was operating normally from
around the new terminal. Scheduled flights were still flying
in and out, which presented opportunities to sneak in.

The Israelis had already devised a plan involving four
C130 Hercules aircaft. Betser was adamant that they could
succeed if they could reach the terminal where the hostages
were being held before their attempt was discovered. His
plan was that the first Hercules would carry the "break-in
crew" from the Unit (Sayeret Maktal). It was one and a half
km from the new terminal to the old terminal. He announced to the planners: "We're going to drive." He
explained:

I know the Ugandan soldiers. I trained them. We don't

need hundreds of soldiers. Instead we use a Mercedes. Every battalion commander in Uganda rides around in one. A soldier spots a Mercedes, he snaps a salute. They'll see us in the Mercedes with a couple of Land Rovers carrying soldiers and they'll assume a general's about to drive by. They aren't going to shoot to stop us. You know it's possible I'll run into one of the soldiers I trained.

Betser emphasized that the vital thing was to avoid alerting the hijackers to their arrival.

The second Hercules would land seven minutes after the first, bringing more troops who would act as a "back-up crew". They would secure a perimeter around the aircraft and hold the Ugandans at bay if necessary. The third aircraft would bring more reinforcements and the fourth would provide medical facilities.

The Chief of Staff approved and took a team to present the plan to the Defence Minister, Shimon Peres. The minister approved but full governmental approval was required before they could go ahead.

The raid would involve soldiers from the unit and paratroopers. Betser briefed the officers from the unit, the paratroopers, signal corps and medical corps.

As soon as the first Hercules had come to a stop, a dozen paratroopers would run down the rear ramp and place large electric lanterns along the side of the runway in case the Ugandans turned off the runway landing lights.

The "break-in" force would be from the unit, disguised as a company of Ugandan troops under the command of a Ugandan officer, in a Mercedes and two Land Rovers. They would drive off the plane to the old terminal building at normal speed with their headlights on, which would take five minutes. After they arrived it should take them two minutes to free the hostages and secure the building.

Exactly seven minutes after the first Hercules had landed, a second Hercules would land and bring a second group from the unit aboard two BTRs, which were Soviet-made Armoured Personnel Carriers (APCs). The Soviet-

made APCs had been captured during the Yom Kippur
war. They had the advantage of being lighter than the
Israeli APCs. This force would act as a perimeter guard
around the old terminal.

One minute later a third plane would land. This would
bring two more BTRs manned by men from the unit, plus
more paratroopers and some additional troops. This force
would take the new terminal, the refuelling station at the
airport and guard the new runway. One of the BTRs would
move over towards an adjoining airfield where some Libyan
MiG fighter aircraft might be stationed. The fourth BTR
would patrol around the old terminal. The additional
troops would cover the area between the terminals and
stand by to help the hostages aboard the first Hercules and
guard any casualties as they were ferried to the plane by
Land Rover.

Medical crews would arrive aboard the fourth plane,
which would evacuate any casualties.

A command and control plane would be in the air overhead, keeping communications open with Tel Aviv.

A second medical plane would land at Nairobi airport in
Kenya, where the Kenyans would be asked for permission
for the four Hercules to land after the mission.

The unit's own base would be the headquarters and
operational centre for the mission. Betser insisted that he
should be a member of the "break-in crew". The key to
success would be delivering the "break-in crew" quietly to
the front door of the terminal.

As soon as the plan was approved by the Chief of Staff,
they built a full-size mock-up of the old terminal building at
the Unit's base. They used two-by-four strips of wood to
build doorframes, burlap and canvas for the internal and
external walls and practised their roles all night. As soon as
the paratroopers and air force technicians arrived, they, too,
began to practise their parts. The air force technicians
would be responsible for refuelling the planes. A Hercules
was brought in to practise the disembarkation and embar-
kation parts.

The right type of Mercedes was found on a used car lot in

Tel Aviv. Betser told them to paint it black and to put in a second ignition system. He stressed to his troops that the Ugandans wouldn't shoot at an officer. If they were in any doubt as to the identity of the "break-in crew" they would hesitate.

Recently, at Ma'Alot, the IDF had experienced an incident where they had failed to rescue some hostages before one of their captors had sprayed them with his automatic weapon. They were aware that their priority was to take out the terrorist guards.

From the information they had gathered they expected between two and four terrorists to be guarding the hostages and another two to four terrorists to be in a room nearby. The "break-in crew" would concentrate on eliminating the guards and defending the hostages. The other troops would be a "back-up crew" which would be responsible for holding off the Ugandans.

One of the "break-in crew" would be equipped with a megaphone. He would tell everyone, in Hebrew and English: "Everyone lie down! This is the IDF. Lie down!"

The "break-in crew" would be wearing leopard-spot fatigues like those worn by the Ugandan paratroopers. Once they got into the terminal building they would put on white caps to identify themselves.

Twenty-four hours before the terrorists' final deadline, they were shown an aerial photo of the eleven Libyan MiG jet fighter aircraft on the ground at the airfield next door. They flew down to Sharm el Sheikh on the Red Sea, the southernmost point in Israel, and encountered severe turbulence on that stage of their flight. The troopers were vomiting into air-sickness bags. They landed in 40 degrees but the fresh air was a relief. One of the "break-in crew" was too sick to continue and had to be replaced.

They took off at 1 p.m. Luckily, there was no turbulence over the Red Sea. They flew low to avoid being detected by Egyptian radar, and received their government's decision to go ahead while they were in the air. They flew through thunderstorms over Kenya.

As the plane began its landing approach, Betser and eight

others climbed into the Mercedes. The rest of the "break-in crew" sat in the first Land Rover. The "back-up crew" would follow in the other Land Rovers. Their first job would be to take out the control tower, which had a commanding view of the tarmac in front of the old terminal. Betser was only the reserve commander of Sayeret Maktal; its CO was Yonni Netanyahu.

When the Hercules came to a stop, the flight crew released the blocks and lashes holding the vehicles in place. The rear door met the ground. Yonni Netanyahu gave the command to "go". Betser:

> The car lunged forward and memories poured into me as we came out of the Hercules into the fresh night air of Africa right after rain. I felt calm, almost serene, looking out into the darkness as Amitzur drove slowly but steadily, like any convoy of VIPs in the Ugandan army, not too fast to attract attention, not too slow as to cause suspicion. The silence of the night was absolute. Far ahead, the old terminal was but a glow in the dark.
>
> I turned to look over my shoulder. Right behind us, the Land Rovers did indeed look like Ugandan troop carriers – though the soldiers' faces were white, not black. Nonetheless, everything felt right.
>
> I broke the radio silence between the three vehicles with the code word to my break-in crews to prepare their weapons. The ratcheting sounds of seven assault rifles clicking their first round into the chamber filled the car. I used the code to order the break-in crews to set their weapons to single-shot mode for selective shooting.
>
> The distant halo of the old terminal's lights sharpened into detail as we rolled closer. I could see the canopied entrances to the building, just as we expected, and began the countdown in my mind to the moment when the car would stop in front of the building. And we'd rush out into action.
>
> Out of the corner of my eye, I noticed two Ugandan soldiers. One of them was walking away from his comrade,

disappearing into the dark. But I concentrated on the building ahead. We could ignore the Ugandan guards – that's why we were in the Mercedes.

The lone Ugandan sentry noticed our arrival and, in the standard operating procedure of a Ugandan soldier, raised his rifle and called out, "Advance."

It was nothing to get excited about. Just routine. I used to see it all the time in Uganda. We could drive right by him. That's why we were in the Mercedes. "Eighty, seventy, sixty," I was saying to myself under my breath, concentrating on the first canopied entrance, where I would push through the doors and enter the hall where the terrorists held the hostages. When I reached zero, the action would begin.

"Amitzur," Yonni suddenly said, breaking the silence in the car, and my concentration. "Cut to the right and we'll finish him off." The car swerved to the right. "Leave it, Yonni," I said quietly but emphatically. "It's just his drill."

There was a moment of silence. Then Yonni repeated his order. Like me, he and Giora were carrying silenced .22 caliber Berettas, useful for very close quarters shooting. Giora Zussman cocked his Beretta, and aimed it out his window to the Ugandan. The car continued veering toward the Ugandan, away from the terminal.

"Giora, let's take care of him," Yonni said, cocking his own gun.

"No," I tried again. The entire effort of the last week was to deliver us to the front doors of the terminal in peace and quiet. The memory of Ma'alot raced through my mind. We were making a mistake, even before we reached the terminal. "Forget it, Yonni," I tried again. But I was too late.

Yonni and Giora both fired from the moving car from 10 meters away, using the silenced .22s. They were the only guns at the time that could carry silencers. I knew them well from my El Al air marshal work. It was a shot I wouldn't have tried to make. But it was too late. The silencers turned the crack of the small handguns into bare whispers. The Ugandan fell.

I sighed with relief. We could still get there and get our job done before he caused us any trouble. I tried to resume my focus on the terminal building. Amitzur continued driving toward the old terminal, now barely 50 meters away. The Land Rovers kept to the path behind us.

Suddenly, from behind us, came a terrifying sound – the long burst of a Kalashnikov. I jerked my head around, just in time to see the Ugandan, back on his feet and aiming his rifle at us, cut down by a burst of fire from the Land Rover.

The order was clear and simple. No shooting until the operation starts, but then heavy fire to keep the Ugandans away. Someone in the Land Rover behind us saw the Ugandan soldier get up, and take aim at us. Instinctively, he wanted to protect us. But now all of us were in danger, as shooting erupted all around us.

Fifty meters from the target, I was seeing the entire element of surprise evaporate in front of my eyes. The rattling gunfire certainly alerted the terrorists. At any moment the terminal building might turn into a fireball of explosions as the terrorists followed through with their threats to blow up the hostages.

From the very start of the planning, I recited the lessons of Ma'alot. "We failed there because of our own mistakes," I warned. And now it was happening again.

"Drive!" Yonni shouted at Amitzur, who braked instinctively with the first burst of Kalashnikov fire from the Land Rover behind us. "Fast!" Amitzur sped ahead another 10 meters. Fire came at us from the darkness around the tarmac.

Crammed together in the car, we became sitting ducks for the Ugandans. Yonni realized it, too. We shouted at the same time, "Stop!" Amitzur braked hard. The car slid to a stop, the Land Rovers behind us screeching to a halt.

I flung open the door and began running toward the building, still at least 50 meters away, instead of the 5 meters we planned for. I flanked left to avoid the pool of light on the tarmac directly in front of the terminal, hearing the thumping of the fighters' boots behind me. Long bursts of fire shattered the night air. But I continued running, still focused on the canopied entrance to the terminal building, my target, aware that I was pulling the fighters behind me in the same direction.

Some Ugandan fire blasted toward us from my right, screaming lead past my head. Still running, I flicked the Kalashnikov to automatic, and aimed a long burst at the source. I needed to create cover for all of us – myself and everyone in the column behind me. It was just like this in El Hiam, I thought for a second, as I raced ahead at the front of the column, creating as much fire as possible. The African flew backwards and I ran on, followed by all the fighters.

Finally I reached the building, directly below the control tower, barely a dozen meters away from the entrances to the building. The rattle and crack of rifle and submachinegun fire shook the air, kicking up bits of asphalt at our feet. And behind me, thirty-three Sayeret Maktal soldiers bunched up, instead of heading to the assigned entrances. It was a complete contradiction of the battle plan, indeed of any combat formation.

But then I realized that no explosions yet rocked the building. We still could prevent another Ma'alot. I was first in line, and the only way to proceed was forward. I took a deep breath and resumed the race to my assigned entrance, knowing that my example would spur the fighters behind me to follow suit.

Half a dozen strides into my run, a terrorist came out of the building from the second canopied entrance. I knew I had used up most of the magazine creating the cover fire in order to reach the control tower. But I also knew that once inside I only needed a few bullets to do the job.

Now, surprised by the terrorist, I aimed and fired. Only a couple of bullets spat out of the barrel. And I missed. He ducked back into the terminal building.

Racing forward, I pulled out the empty ammo magazine, and flipped it over, reloading on the run, all the while keeping my eyes on my target – the canopied entrance to the building a few meters away. Still, no explosion racked the building. The plan could still succeed.

Instead, a second disaster struck.

No glass doorway opened at the end of the canopied path into the hall. I found myself facing a blank wall. We planned according to Solel Boneh's original architectural plans, and they clearly showed an entrance. Somehow, we lost one of the most crucial pieces of information the Frenchman gave Amiram.

Withering machine-gun fire poured down at us from the control tower. Yonni's back-up fighters were supposed to take out the machine-gun nest up there. But obviously, the fighters were still confused by the bad start. The 50–meter run from the cars, instead of the few meters we practiced, threw everything off. At any second, I feared, the terrorists would ignite the explosives they planted in the hallway. I had no choice but to get inside, to prevent that from happening.

With my pre-assigned entrance blocked, I began running to the second entrance, where I saw the terrorist duck inside. Amir, a fighter from my second break-in, suddenly ran past me, followed by his team leader, Amnon. Later, Amir said that in the confusion he lost his crew and thought they already made it inside. Meanwhile, he became the first of us to get into the building.

He immediately spotted a terrorist and cut him down with a burst. Just then, Amnon ran in, and saw the German man and woman terrorists kneeling side by side, aiming guns at Amir's back. Amnon fired at the two Germans, sending them flying, just as I came in through the door, with Amos Goren on my heels.

I immediately added my own shots to the two German terrorists, to make sure they were out of the action.

For a second, silence fell over the room. Then suddenly, shooting erupted again from the outside, and screaming began inside the hall. I stood in the doorway, Amnon to my left and Amos and Amir on my extreme right, totally focused on the fully lit hall, searching for more terrorists.

People were lying all over the floor on mattresses. Some froze with fear, others screamed and shouted. People covered their heads with blankets as if to protect themselves from the bullets.

To my left, about 15 meters away, a man came out from behind a column, bringing a rifle up to firing position. Amos and I fired simultaneously, the terrorist dropping. Again we scanned the hall. A dark-haired young man jumped up from amidst the hostages. Bullets from all four Kalashnikovs cut him down.

The shooting continued outside. Suddenly, Amir remembered the megaphone he carried. "Lie down, we're the IDF. Don't get up!" He shouted the instructions in Hebrew and English. We stood that way in the room for a long moment, ready to fire again.

Hesitantly, one of the hostages raised his hand. "You got them all," he said. "All of them. But that one," he added sadly, pointing at the body of the young man we just shot, "he was one of us. A hostage."

The radio clasped to my web-belt gave me no time to respond. "Muki, Muki," it squawked.

"Muki here."

"Giora here. Mission accomplished." He took the VIP room, which the terrorists made into their dormitory. "Two terrorists down. No casualties on our side."

Betser tried to call Yonni Netanyahu but it was the signals man from the CO's Command and Control team who replied. He told him that Yonni Netanyahu was "down". Betser went outside to take a look at him and assessed the situation. The second and third Hercules had landed. Their perimeter was secure. The BTR was heading towards the MiG airfield. Betser radioed back to tell IDF command that he was taking over.

The passengers had been taken aboard and refuelling was in progress.

Three hostages had been killed during the rescue. One hostage had been hit by IDF fire because he was too close to an armed terrorist. A second hostage had been killed by the terrorists' return fire. The third had died because he jumped up and four IDF men, including Betser himself, shot him, thinking he was a terrorist. Another hostage, an Israeli woman, had been taken to a Ugandan hospital because she had choked on some food. She was never heard of again.

The casualties were put on the Land Rovers and driven to the planes.

As they were boarding, a burst of fire came from the control tower. Betser told one of the BTRs to take out the tower. The other BTR blasted the MiGs with machine gun and RPG fire on his own initiative.

They took off 59 minutes after the first plane had touched down.

They all stayed aboard as the plane was refuelled in Nairobi.

Betser analysed their mistakes: they had shot the sentry unnecessarily. This had resulted in the long blast of AK-47 fire that had alerted both the terrorists and the Ugandans. The soldier from the Land Rover who had fired said that he saw the Ugandan get back on his feet and take aim at the Mercedes.

Yonni Netanyahu had died by the time they reached Nairobi.

Betser left the unit and retired from the army when he was forty – just as his son Shaul joined it.

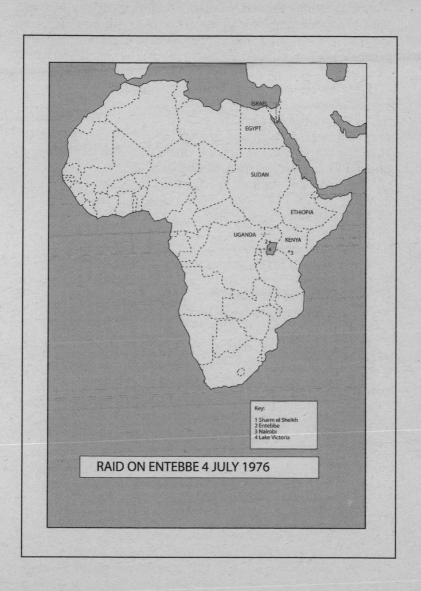

Key:

1 Sharm el Sheikh
2 Entebbe
3 Nairobi
4 Lake Victoria

RAID ON ENTEBBE 4 JULY 1976

# IED ALLEY (2004)

*On 18 October 2004 Sergeant Andy Wilkinson, of the Third Regiment Royal Horse Artillery (RHA) was on a foot patrol in Basra when he suffered the shock of seeing a comrade killed by a roadside bomb. While he was leading a midnight foot patrol in the same area of Basra, Sergeant Wilkinson recalled:*

We had dismounted from our vehicles and had gone ahead to check for IEDs (Improvised Explosive Devices). Sergeant Hickey was in front of me and our lieutenant was there too. To the right was a large waste ground area.

They had reached a point about a mile down "IED Alley" – a straight road that runs southwest out of the city from the Basra teaching hospital. Wilkinson:

The officer, who was only just out of Sandhurst, and was also behind Sergeant Hickey, bent down to examine what he thought might be an IED, and at that moment there was a huge explosion where Sergeant Hickey had been standing.

Sergeant Wilkinson had been standing just a few feet away when Sergeant Hickey took the full force of the blast. He died instantly. Wilkinson:

> This happened ten days after I arrived in Iraq and it was a shocking experience for all of us. I tried to give him first aid but it was too late.
>
> We did all we could for Sergeant Hickey but he was dead. The lieutenant was hurled backwards by the blast and both his eardrums burst. He also had a serious eye injury.

Sergeant Wilkinson did not realize that he had also been injured until he returned to base: "I was sitting on the steps outside when I felt pain in my ankle and when I took my boot off, it was soaked in blood," he said. A piece of shrapnel had pierced his boot and embedded in his ankle.

Sergeant Hickey, 30, of the First Battalion, the Coldstream Guards, was the ninth British soldier since May 2004 to be killed by a new sophisticated type of bomb consisting of a shaped armour-piercing explosive charge and an infrared triggering device.

Sergeant Wilkinson explained that the waste ground running beside IED Alley had provided the perfect line of sight for the attackers to wait their moment before detonating the bomb by remote control. Like the rest of the patrol, he was devastated by the sight of one of his comrades blown up in front of him. All of them were offered counselling. Wilkinson:

> It was a shocking event. When the explosion happened I thought of my wife and two kids. I was very lucky. I wanted to speak to my wife, Joanne, to reassure her, but I wasn't able to until later.
>
> I was offered two weeks' rest and recuperation but I wanted to be with my men and return to my job. The ones to feel sorry for are the families. They hear on the news that a British soldier has been killed in Basra but they don't know who it is until someone comes knocking on the door.

The patrol's regular interpreter, an Iraqi, admitted that he fears for his life every time he joins a British military patrol. He was there on the night of 18 October but was not injured. The 30–year-old interpreter, who earns $250 (£140) a month, said the rest of the British soldiers on the patrol became angry after the explosion. He said: "It was a terrible thing. They told me to go away. I think because I was Iraqi."

# A "COME ON" (1979)

*British soldiers on peacekeeping duties in Northern Ireland called a riot organized by the Provisional Irish Republican Army (PIRA) a "come on". The PIRA's purpose was to get the soldiers into a situation where they could snipe at them while they were trying to control the riot.*

*In 1979 Nigel "Spud" Ely was on his first tour of Northern Ireland with 2 Para. At that time the British Army's Armoured Personnel Carrier was a vehicle called a Saracen – a large armour-plated six-wheeled vehicle capable of a top speed of about 30 miles per hour. "Brummie" was the corporal in command of the patrol. Ely:*

On one occasion I was out on a mobile just coming in to Newry from Bessbrook Mill. The only route into town was down the Monaghan Road, notorious for getting a good stoning from the locals, followed by the occasional burst from snipers who used the nearby housing estate as a sanctuary. We were four up in two half-ton, cut-down Land Rovers; no roofs or armour plating, just a riot shield for windscreen protection.

Checkers was driving the lead wagon and I the rear. As

we approached the downward slope of Monaghan Road, which took us past "sniper alley" and then into Newry, we saw quite a large crowd of kids gathering on the playing fields on the left-hand side of the road some 50 metres away. Then they started showering us with rocks and stones, bits of wood and milk bottles filled with shit and piss. The brief was to drive straight through. Checkers put his foot down and I followed suit. He got by, but I had trouble controlling the Land Rover: 50 downhill was as much as the wagon wanted to do. I was also late in pulling up the riot shield. Brummie was screaming for me to get a move on whilst the guys in the back were doing their best to cover themselves from the barrage raining down. The windscreen shattered; I swerved to keep control of the wagon. Braking heavily I brought us to a halt, the kerb and a lamppost being our saving grace. We debussed rapidly and took cover behind the wagon.

By this time Checkers had seen what had happened and came screaming back up the hill. Brummie sent a "contact report" back to Newry as Checkers reached us and gave cover. There was no way the four of us could fit in the lead wagon: all eight had to sit it out and wait for the QRF. Apart from that, we couldn't leave the smashed wagon for the rioters; that would have been unPara-like, and I would have got a fearsome slagging from the rest of the platoon.

". . . Roger, about 150. The whole place has erupted. Send ETA, over," Brummie screamed into the radio.

"November Two Charlie. With you figures five, over."

"November Two Charlie. This is Mike One Alpha. Roger that. Be aware that the mob is now on the road and blocking your entry. We are located halfway up the hill opposite the school crossing, over."

"Mike One Alpha, November Two Charlie. Stand by for your crowd to bomb burst. With you, figures two. Wait, out to you. Zero acknowledge, over."

"Zero acknowledged, out."

Zero was the Ops room back at Newry, where the duty signaller was logging the exact movements of all the call

signs out on the ground and plotting the route of the QRF
to target.

The tension was growing second by second. I felt my
heart beating |n quick time. I had heard of many stories in
the past where the mob would just engulf a patrol that
didn't respond by firing to protect themselves. Patrols had
been ripped apart by these mobs, weapons and kit stolen,
the bodies found later, throats cut. What had started out as a
routine mobile patrol had turned into a full-scale riot and
the "full Monty" of the Security Forces were being mobilized. Choppers were flying above us, and RUC wagons
appeared and were racing across the playing fields on their
way to cut off the rioters in a pincer movement with the
QRF.

Brummie shouted orders to the others, then turned to me,
grinning. "Hey, Spud, we're gonna have to put you on a
driving course, you wanker, what do you reckon?"

I couldn't tell if he was serious or just taking the piss. In
two years, I could never get to grips with his accent. So I
said nothing.

Ely saw the Royal Ulster Constabulary (RUC) trying to
arrest a couple of the ringleaders. The QRF was two
Saracens, known as "cans", and four Land Rovers. When
it arrived the crowd fled as quickly as they had appeared.
The stoning stopped as soon as the QRF appeared. Ely:

The boss man came over to see the damage. It was the first
time in ten minutes we were able to stand up. A security
cordon was put up around us.

Looking around, the boss made his mind up. "Hey,
Brummie, get your patrol together, get in the cans and let's
get the fuck out of here – NOW. Leave the wagon, it's
fucked. This smells like a 'come on'."

We all piled into the two cans and screamed off to Newry.
That's when I found out how unstable these vehicles really
were. The RCT driver was good, but not that good. As we
came hurtling down towards Merchant's Quay, the main

drag through Newry, he went out of control, mounted the pavement and took out a parked Morris Marina, squashing it flat against a brick wall before stabilizing. Brummie ripped into him big style back at the compound. It was then the unwritten law amongst us all that can drivers were not to go over 30 miles an hour, even though the clock went up to 80. The riot was another move up the learning curve of being in Northern Ireland. I learned that I had to be more confident within myself. I could now control my fears and anxieties. I was a better soldier for that riot, although I didn't do anything. All I did was to get under cover and watch. I was lucky, I thought. Blokes in the early 1970s did not have the chance I had. I had time to think and take in all that was happening around me: how Brummie reacted; how the other patrol adopted good fire positions when they came up to help. I took it all in.

The riot was a "come on" set up by the local PIRA. Twelve shots were fired during that incident: seven at us by the damaged Land Rover, a couple at the RUC during their arrests, and the rest at the QRF. The can that I was picked up in had a 5.56mm Armalite strike, smack bang centre of the driver's glass viewing prism – a ten-by-four-inch slit the driver used to look through. Normally it was held in the "open" position, but that day the driver had accidentally snapped off one of the retaining brackets so it could not stay open. You can talk about Murphy's Law, but I reckoned we had had our fair share of luck as well.

An Armalite was a copy of an M16 made by the Armalite company. It was the characteristic weapon of the PIRA.

# AMBUSHED BY THE PPK (1991)

*In April 1991 Peter Mercer was on leave from the Special
Boat Service. His original unit had been the Royal Marine
Commandos. He was offered the chance to join a Commando
Brigade going to northern Iraq to protect the Kurdish
minority from Iraqi forces, which needed his helicopter skills.
He was trained to call in helicopters, set up and secure
landing sites. He had missed the First Gulf War because
he had been on duty elsewhere so he jumped at the chance.
Not long afterwards he was out patrolling the hills and dry
dirt valleys of northern Iraq with his fellow Royal Marines.
Mercer:*

Our 16–man patrol of 40 Commando had been tasked to
cover around six square miles stretching towards the Kurdish encampments hidden in the mountain ranges above our
Tactical Area of Responsibility. As the day continued to sap
our lagging energy, the heat enveloping our tired bodies in
lethargy, we spent the hours examining our watches, waiting patiently for the sun to go down, so we could make our
way back to camp to rest, drink and enjoy a cold shower and
some scran.

Then the "net" – the communications network – crackled into life.

"Two motor vehicles are heading towards your position," said the voice in a cool monotone. "We need you to set up an ambush by a roadblock. The occupants of the two vehicles are engaged in a firefight and they must be stopped at all costs. Use minimum force."

We all understood that the order to use "minimum force" meant that we should only attempt to stop the vehicle by shooting out the tyres and the engine, rather than take out the driver, the occupants and the whole bloody car.

"Shit," said one of the patrol, "let's go." Headquarters had given us no indication of the vehicles or the identities of the men involved in the firefight. And we had no idea how well they were armed or, indeed, what weapons they were carrying. We split up, two men standing by the improvised roadblock, four men behind cover on both sides of the road and the remaining two Royal Marines acting as cut-off some yards down the road towards base camp. We were all dressed in camouflage fatigues and armed with SA80s and two light support weapons with bipod legs.

Fifteen minutes later, as we waited anxiously, our fingers on the safety catches, the net crackled into life again.

"The car you must stop is a white Peugeot." Nothing else. No further information. We all watched the bend in the road about 200 yards away, waiting for the white Peugeot to appear, wondering whether the car contained members of Saddam Hussein's crack Presidential Guard or the rebel force.

Suddenly, the Peugeot rounded the bend and came careering down the road at about 60mph towards the two Marine Commandos waiting by the roadblock. They put up their hands, indicating to the driver to stop, but he took no notice. As the Peugeot accelerated towards the two Commandos, the men in the car opened fire, spraying their AK-47s at the two sentries. The driver obviously had no intention of stopping. I was one of the four men in the second line of defence and when we saw what was happening we just opened up, firing at the tyres and the engine. Within seconds, the tyres had been cut to ribbons and the car was forced to a halt. We continued to pour rounds into the engine to ensure that the car could not take off again. But the stupid bastards inside the vehicle continued to fire at us and so we returned fire.

Suddenly the firing stopped. I wondered whether we had shot the drivers. I could see no one in the vehicle, not even the driver. We ran towards it, and then saw the occupants lying low inside the car. We grabbed their weapons, pulled them from the vehicle and threw them away. Then we opened the doors, grabbed the four men and hauled them out by the scruff of the neck, making sure they were lying face down. Two of us stood over them with our S80s aimed at their backs as two others frisked them to see if they had any other hidden weapons. They were clean. But we were taking no chances with men who, only a few seconds earlier, had tried to shoot our mates at the roadblock. Two of the occupants were wounded but we soon ascertained that neither wound was life-threatening. We then went through their pockets in a more thorough search, looking for ID cards or driving licences, trying to discover any clue as to their nationality. We found nothing.

We called Headquarters and reported what had happened. We were ordered to remain, guard the men and await the arrival of the Military Police. The four men regarded us warily, glancing at our weapons, but didn't move a muscle. After a day in that desert sun, we must have looked mean and nasty. They sensed that and remained motionless.

Later, we heard that the four men were members of Saddam Hussein's Presidential Guard who had decided to desert and escape to Turkey. They knew that if any Iraqi soldiers had found them, they would all have been executed on the spot. But as they sped in their Peugeot towards the border, they had been spotted by Kurdish fighters of the PPK, who had given chase. The firefight continued as the vehicles raced along the scorching tarmac road towards the Turkish border. Fearing that they would be taken out as the chasing PPK gunmen came closer, the Iraqi guards decided to make a fight of it.

Having rounded a bend, the Iraqi guards pulled off the road and hid behind some trees. Three leapt from their vehicle and took up positions waiting for the PPK. Twenty seconds later, the four PPK gunmen came hurtling along the road, to be met by a fusillade of bullets. The driver was killed instantly, a bullet through the head. Their car careered off the road and crashed into a rock. Before any of the PPK gunmen had time to react, the Iraqis raced to the vehicle and poured round after round into the occupants as they struggled to escape. Within seconds it was over. Without bothering to examine the men they had just murdered, the Iraqis ran back to their car to continue their desperate escape.

They were asked by Arabic-speaking British Intelligence officers why they hadn't stopped when ordered to do so by the British Commandos. The men replied that they had been warned by Saddam Hussein that if they ever surrendered to any Allied forces they would be summarily executed – shot by firing squad, without trial. They had chosen to try to fight their way through any Allied roadblock rather than face a firing squad.

Those four Iraqi guards never realized how lucky they had been coming across the Royal Marine Commandos, for many soldiers would have been tempted to take immediate action against such bastards after seeing the number of innocent kids who had been killed and maimed by the deliberate and despicable actions taken by the retreating Iraqi forces. They had left booby-traps everywhere. There were booby-traps in all the houses, attached to weapons and even toys, kettles and buckets, furniture and chairs, spades and machinery, as well as the detritus of smashed vehicles and artillery pieces.

We saw countless kids without hands, arms or feet, lost as a result of picking up booby-traps. Some of the booby-traps contained home-made explosives, others high explosives (HE) and some contained white phosphorus which burned the skin to a cinder. The results were truly horrific and we wondered how grown men could leave such traps for innocent young kids of whatever nationality. And, on occasions, as we patrolled along the metal roads, we would see numbers of children lying dead by the side of the road.

# BLACK HAWK DOWN (1993)

*In the late 1980s severe droughts rendered Somalia unable to feed itself. Its infrastructure collapsed to such an extent that there was no effective government. An international relief effort was mounted, authorized by the United Nations. The international relief effort was escorted by UN troops, including the First US Marine Division.*

*Somalia was dominated by either brutal dictators or warring clans. By late 1992 two Somalian warlords and their clans were struggling for power. One of their tactics was to hijack the aid convoys and to sell the grain for profit.*

*On 5 June 1993, twenty-four Pakistani UN peacekeepers were ambushed and killed by militia loyal to the warlord Mohammed Farrah Aidid. The UN Security Council passed a resolution that those responsible for the attack on the peacekeepers should be brought to justice. US Special Operations Command formed a Task Force for the sole purpose of capturing Aidid, designated Task Force Ranger.*

*On 26 August 1993 Task Force Ranger landed at Mogadishu airport. Mogadishu was a city with a population of over a million people. There had been so much fighting in Somalia that, on average, a Somali militiaman had ten*

*years' combat experience and belonged to a long-lasting
warrior tradition.*

Task Force Ranger consisted of Special Forces Operational
Detachment Delta Operators and US Army Rangers from
Third Battalion, Seventy-fifth (3/75) Ranger Regiment. It
was based in a hangar at the airport.

The UN Security Council Resolution upgraded the
intervention from peace enforcement to peacekeeping.

On 3 October 1993, Operation Gothic Serpent was Task
Force Ranger's seventh mission. It was an attempt to
capture some of Mohammed Farrah Aidid's lieutenants.
It was undertaken at short notice, acting on reliable information. US Air Force Sergeant Dan Schilling was a
combat controller attached to Task Force Ranger:

At approximately 1430 hours on 3 October we received
Intel that two targets from our primary hit list were meeting
near the Olympic Hotel in the Black Sea district. The Black
Sea was adjacent to the Bakara Market, one of the largest
arms markets in East Africa, and was saturated with Somali
National Alliance (SNA) regulars and sympathizers. The
plan was the typical template used on our other raids: helos
with Ranger blocking forces and assaulters departed sepa-
rately for the target followed by our ground reaction force
(GRF) convoy as an exfil platform for the "precious cargo"
(PC) and all task force personnel. Aside from the challenging target location, right in the middle of town, this raid
was mostly indistinguishable from the previous raids we'd
conducted.

The GRF on this day was comprised of seven Kevlar
armored High Mobility Multipurpose Wheeled Vehicles
(HMMWVs, known to both military and civilians as Humvees), two cargo (unarmored) Humvees, and three five-ton
trucks. The convoy was manned by Rangers, assaulters,
SEALs, and me as the combat controller. I was located in
my usual spot, the C2 vehicle, third in the order of march.
My job, as usual, was to provide mobile command, control,

and communications in addition to fire support direction for the convoy or other forces as needed.

The targets were Abdi "Qeybid" Hassan Awale, Aidid's ostensible interior minister and Omar Salad, Aidid's top political adviser. They were thought to be meeting in a building in downtown (south) Mogadishu. The target building was on the Hawlwadig Road almost opposite the Olympic Hotel, in the Bakara Market area of the city. The area was home to hundreds of thousands of Aidid's supporters who mostly came from the Habr Gidr clan.

Mike Kurth was a 22–year-old African American. He was Radio Telephone Operator (RTO) in First Platoon, Bravo Company of the Ranger Battalion. He was in the assault on 3 October and described the Bakara district:

We had all heard about the Bakara Market before. It was dead in the center of Aidid's territory – which meant that everyone who lived in that area supported Aidid. On all of our previous missions we had dealt with only a few bad guys at a time. We'd gone in and done our jobs in the midst of a lot of curious onlookers. In that sense, we'd just been practicing riot control. This was going to be a lot different. We all knew it without talking about it. Everyone in the Bakara Market would either have a weapon or the ability to get a weapon. Watson told us that we could very well see some action on this one. I don't think anyone knew what to say to that. We knew the drill.

The plan was for the D-boys (Delta Force) to go in first and hit the building. Once they were inside, the four Ranger chalks were to fast-rope in, each one on its respective corner.

Special Forces operatives would enter the building to capture Aidid's men while four chalks (squads) of US Army Rangers surrounded the building. The Ranger chalks were from Bravo Company, 3/75. Sergeant Matt Eversman was the leader of Chalk Four, which was responsible for the blocking position on the north west corner.

Eversman was a staff sergeant with five years' military experience. He had been in the Rangers since March 1992.

The plan was to fly both the assault and blocking forces to the target and insert them. Then the ground reaction force (GRF), a convoy of Rangers in Humvee vehicles and 5-ton trucks, would extract them.

The Rangers would be inserted by fast rope from the helicopters. Once they had reached their assigned position, their job was to isolate the target building so that no one could get in or out.

At 3:32 p.m. they lifted off from the airport for the three-minute flight to the target. They flew in MH-60 Black Hawk helicopters, accompanied by AH-6 and MH-6 Little Birds. (The Little Bird has a crew of two. The AH-6 is an armed version, while the MH-6 is a version able to carry up to six personnel for insertion and extraction.) The helicopters were from the One Hundred and Sixtieth Special Operations Aviation Regiment (SOAR). Four of the MH-6 Little Birds were fitted with benches on either side to carry the Delta Operatives.

Four of the Black Hawks carried the chalks from Bravo Company, while two more Black Hawks carried additional Delta assaulters. One of the Black Hawks carried a Combat Search and Rescue (CSAR) team and the eighth Black Hawk carried the Command and Control (C2) team: Lieutenant Colonel Tom Matthews, was co-ordinating the One Hundred and Sixtieth SOAR pilots and Delta Lieutenant Colonel Gary Harrell was responsible for the men on the ground.

The ground convoy consisted of nine wide-bodied Humvee military vehicles and three five-ton trucks. They were manned by Delta operatives, Rangers and four members of the US Navy's SEAL team (Sea, Air, Land).

Altogether there were 160 men, twelve vehicles and nineteen aircraft, including three surveillance helicopters and the Orion navy spy plane circling overhead.

Eversman and his chalk were flying in a Black Hawk

which had been given the call sign "Super Six Seven".

When they reached the target the chalks would simultaneously rope out from both the port and starboard sides of
the helicopter. Once they had landed the ropes were released from the helicopter, which would continue to fly
overhead to provide cover with its minigun. A minigun
could fire four thousand rounds of 7.62mm ammunition per
minute.

Once it had reached the ground, the Ranger chalk would
set up an L-shaped perimeter around the corner of a
building or block. The ends of the "L" could make visual
contact with two of the other blocking positions. In this way
the perimeter was linked all around the target.

Eversman anticipated that the insertion would be dangerous for two reasons. First, it would be a long rope, about
70 feet down. Second, there would be two- and three-storey
buildings on either side of their insertion point.

They made their way towards their target from the north.
They could see that the Somalis were burning tyres in the
streets. At the "one minute" signal Eversman took off his
headset, put on his goggles and his Kevlar helmet and
moved to his rope.

They came to a halt over their insertion point. There was
more "brownout" than usual. The helicopters' rotors were
churning up clouds of dust from the dirt roads below, and
there were seventeen helicopters in the formation. Eversman heard the pilot complain, "I can't see shit."

The four Little Birds had already dropped off their
Delta Operatives immediately south of the building. It
was probably the Little Birds that had begun to "kick up
the dust".

The Delta Operatives succeeded in capturing their targets and about thirty other clan members.

Super Six Seven remained stationary for what seemed to
Eversman like ten minutes. He later realized it was probably only about thirty seconds; then the Rangers were told
to throw out their ropes. The last thing Eversman was told
before he left the helicopter was that they were two or three
blocks from their assigned position.

Eversman's chalk was Specialist Kevin Snodgrass, machine gunner; Private First Class Todd Blackburn, ammo bearer; and First Sergeant Glenn Harris and Sergeant Scott Galentine had come as riflemen. The Squad Automatic Weapon (SAW) gunners were Specialists Dave Diemer and Adalberto Rodriguez. The 40mm grenadiers were Privates First Class Anton Berendsen and Marc Good. Staff Sergeant Jeff McLaughlin was Forward Observer or Fire Support Officer (FO). Specialist Jason Moore was the Radio Telephone Operator (RTO) and Private First Class Marc Good was the medic. Eversman:

As I started my descent I was looking up toward the belly of the helicopter. I wanted to make sure I knew the direction of flight and therefore the target. I remember the air was so cloudy and thick with dust, and without the benefit of eye protection it was hard for me to see. The seventeen other aircraft also stirred up debris, so it was no wonder we couldn't see anything. Bless those pilots for holding our Black Hawk steady while we were on the way down. Despite my leather gloves, the nylon of the rope made my hands burn, so I looked down to see how much farther it was to the ground. It seemed like I was on the rope forever.

When I saw the ground, my heart sank. At the bottom of the rope was a crumpled tan-clad body. My God, someone's been shot. Who is it? And is he dead? were the first thoughts through my head. That was my first real feeling of fear, a feeling of helplessness, as if I couldn't defend myself. I had always thought that making a combat parachute jump must be scary as hell since you are floating down into harm's way, watching a firefight in a hot drop zone all the while. This was as close as I got to what that situation must feel like, except I couldn't see or hear any shots. Thank the Lord, I finally got my feet on the ground, literally straddling the body. The medics were already working on him. It was Todd Blackburn. As I made a quick check for the rest of the men it dawned on me that we were under fire.

We were in the middle of a four-way intersection and were taking fire from the north, the east, and the west. The fire wasn't that accurate at first but, unlike during previous missions, the Somalis were not just spraying their weapons at us with reckless abandon; this time they were aiming. The objective was only a few blocks to our south, but Murphy was with us again; we wouldn't be making the movement to the objective as quickly as we had planned.

Private Good was busy giving first aid to Blackburn. I couldn't believe that Blackburn was even close to being alive. He was bleeding out of his mouth, nose, and ears, and his body was horribly contorted. It was one of those surreal moments – there would be many more that day – and one that never in my wildest imagination would I have thought I would witness. Good and another medic had opened Blackburn's airway and were stabilizing his neck when the fire started to get heavier. As I checked the intersection to see where the men were, I realized that we had definitely landed right in the middle of the worst part of town, and the Somalis seemed none too pleased with our intrusion. As I checked the men I asked my RTO to call the commander, Captain Steele, to give him a sitrep and request an immediate extraction. All Specialist Moore got was nothing – no response, no acknowledgment. We had no communications with headquarters.

My first thirty seconds as the leader of Chalk Four sucked, plain and simple. We were in the wrong spot, had no commo, had an urgent casualty, and were being shot at from three directions. Things were going south in a hurry. The good news was that the Rangers from Chalk Four were performing phenomenally. I had no combat experience other than the previous missions, but watching them fight was a thing of beauty. They hit the ground running and were doing their job. We were dealt a bad hand of cards, but what really amazed me was just how fast the Somalis started to fight. It seemed that we were on the ground for a few seconds and then *bam* – the heavens opened up with small-arms fire. It really was like the movies, with the dust kicking up in the road as a hail of bullets ripped open the dirt. It was actually kind of wild to watch.

They moved the wounded man to the east of the intersection and set up a command post. The RTO was unable to get through because he had broken a connecting wire while he was roping down. He was still trying to get through while Eversman tried his own handheld radio. It wasn't very powerful, so Eversman had to shout, which didn't help. Finally he understood that they would have to take Blackburn, the wounded man, to another position where he could be picked up.

Two Delta medics came running in response to Eversman's radio call. They examined Blackburn and told Eversman that the wounded man needed to be extracted "right now or he's gonna die".

Eversman told Sergeant Casey Joyce to form an aid and litter team to take Blackburn to the ground convoy, which was at the target building. Sergeant Joyce gathered some litter-bearers and began to move towards the Humvees.

Whenever the individual Rangers engaged a Somali gunman, another just took his place. Eversman was incredulous that the Somalis would not even keep away from their perimeter. His feelings of incredulity were as strong as his fear, even though he was in the middle of an intense firefight.

Eversman noticed that one of his grenadiers, Berendsen, had been hit in the arm. Berendsen crossed the street to Eversman's position and they were under fire while Eversman put a dressing on Berendsen's arm. Berendsen was trying to manipulate the breech of his M203 grenade launcher with one hand, so Eversman opened the breech for him. While Eversman continued bandaging his arm, Berendsen fired a grenade into the corner of a building. The firing stopped.

Sergeant Scott Galentine was hit in the hand in front of Eversman's eyes. He crossed the street to Eversman's position; Eversman bandaged his hand and told him to keep it above his heart.

Ten seconds later Eversman saw Sergeant Telscher attending to Snodgrass, who had been hit. Moments later the RTO told him that he had heard on the command net that they should be ready to "collapse" on the objective before they moved out in a few minutes.

Eversman was told that a Black Hawk was down. All he knew was that: "a few blocks away I could see a big pile of rubble. No way was that a Black Hawk."

Specialist Shawn Nelson was one of Chalk Two's M-60 machine gunners. He had seen the flash of an RPG launcherand followed the smoke trail of the grenade as it rose towards the tail of a Black Hawk. Black Hawk Super Six One was directly overhead. Its tail boom cracked and its rotor stopped spinning. It kept moving forward but it shuddered and began to spin.

A Somali gunman known as "Little Ears" was credited with shooting down one of the Black Hawks with an RPG. His comment on American tactics was: "The Americans will always crash into things around them. They do not know how to move with things, only against them."

The pilot of Super Six One was Chief Warrant Officer Cliff Wolcott. He was flying the helicopter low over the target area at speeds of between fifty and seventy knots. Four Delta snipers and the two crew chiefs, Dowdy and Warren, were selecting targets for their sniper rifles and miniguns. Crew chief Dowdy felt a jolt. For a second or two it seemed all right but then the helicopter began to spin. Wolcott made a last radio transmission: "Six One going down."

The helicopter clipped the side of a house. Then it tipped over and crashed into an alleyway, nose first. Finally it tilted over onto its side.

Abdiaziz Ali Aden, a teenage Somali boy, had seen a Somali militiaman with an RPG tube step out of an alley, kneel and fire up at the helicopter overhead. He watched as the grenade exploded into the rear of the helicopter, cracking its tail. He continued to watch as the pilot struggled with the controls. Then the helicopter had tilted towards him. It hit the roof of a house with a loud crunch, then finally crashed into an alley in a thick cloud of dust.

Moore, the RTO, confirmed that he had been told by radio that a helicopter had gone down and that they were ordered to move to the crash site. Eversman was told that the other chalks would link up there. They were still being engaged from three sides, and hostile Somalis were between them and the crash site. Eversman's problem was how to get there.

Little Bird Star Four One found Super Six One within minutes. The pilot, Chief Warrant Officer Keith Jones, landed further along the street. If he had landed on the intersection he would have been a target from four directions.

One of the Special Operators from Super Six One came over to Jones' window. "I need help," he said. One of his arms was hanging limp. Jones got out and followed the operator, leaving his co-pilot to provide cover up the alley. Just then the first Rangers from Bravo Company began to arrive at the crash site. The other surviving Delta sniper from Super Six One was more badly wounded than the man who had asked Jones for help.

The air commander in the C2 helicopter immediately ordered Little BirdStar Four One to get out. Jones and his co-pilot loaded the wounded Delta operators aboard and took off.

Eight minutes after Super Six One crashed the CSAR helicopter, Super Six Eight dropped its fifteen-man team on the crash site. Super Six Eight hovered about 30 feet above the street where Super Six One had gone down. There was a delay as they kicked out some kitbags containing equipment. The pilot, Dan Jollata, felt the aircraft rock in response to an exploding RPG on his left side. He radioed: "Coming out. I think we have been hit."

The Little Birds confirmed: "You have been hit. Behind your engines. Be advised you are smoking."

There were still men on their ropes. Jollata kept the helicopter hovering until they reached the ground before Super Six Eight flew off, then radioed: "All systems are normal right now, just a little whine in the rotor system. I think I can make it back to the field."

Jollata nursed the damaged helicopter slowly across the city, trailing a thin grey plume of smoke. He began to look for an open field, near the port, where he could land. Then he called: "I've got the field in sight. All systems normal. I am losing transmission pressure right now."

He radioed for emergency crews on the ground after he had crossed the boundary fence of the airport. Then he landed the helicopter hard on its wheels.

Black Hawk Super Six Four was circling barren land north of Mogadishu in a holding pattern when Super Six One went down. The pilot was Chief Warrant Officer Mike Durant. He knew that the CSAR helicopter and the ground troops would begin moving towards the crash site. Super Six Four had inserted Chalk One earlier; Durant expected to be ordered to replace Super Six One as air cover for the men on the ground. He heard the expected call for Super Six Eight.

Then Durant heard that Super Six Eight had been hit but was still flying. He was ordered to join Super Six Two in the air cover orbit. He could see Rangers and darting Somalis everywhere. He was orbiting when his Black Hawk was hit by an RPG.

Mike Goffena was the pilot of Super Six Two. He was flying in the air cover orbit behind Super Six Four when it was hit. He saw a chunk come off Super Six Four's tail rotor, then oil flow out of it in a fine mist. A Black Hawk can fly without oil if necessary and, at first, Super Six Four seemed to be all right. Durant could see their base in the distance and Super Six Four seemed to be flying normally.

Then Durant felt a very strong vibration as the main crankshaft began to run dry. There was a very loud bang as it blew apart. Without the top half of its tail fin, Super Six Four's centre of gravity had been drastically altered. It began to spin. Durant managed to shut off one engine and throttle the other one down to half-power, which slowed the rate of spin. He was able to pull up the nose just before impact. He shouted into his radio: "Going in hard! Going down!"

Super Six Four crash-landed in an upright position in an area of huts and shanties. Durant blacked out.

Goffena, in Super Six Two, could see crowds of Somalis converging on the second crash site. Super Six Two and two Little Birds tried to hold them off with gun runs. There were three Delta operators still on board Super Six Two. They told Goffena they would be more effective on the ground. He asked for permission to insert them and was told to wait until they were certain that there were survivors from the crash. Goffena made a low pass and saw the pilots moving in the cockpit. He reported this but was still told to wait. They made sniping runs, which drew a lot of fire.

One of the Little Birds reported:

We've got to get some ground folks down here or we're not going to be able to keep them off. There are not enough people left on board the aircraft to be able to do it.

They were told that elements were on their way. One of their Delta snipers had been wounded manning one of Super Six Two's miniguns. Goffena again requested that they insert the remaining two Delta snipers. From the C2, Harrell eventually decided to put them in.

The Delta operators became a little disorientated as they roped down. One of the crew chiefs had to throw down a smoke grenade to mark the location of the crashed helicopter.

When Super Six Four's pilot, Mike Durant, regained consciousness he found that there was something wrong with his right leg. He and his co-pilot had been knocked out for at least several minutes. Their seats were mounted on shock absorbers, which had protected them from part of the impact. Despite this, his co-pilot's left leg and his own right leg were broken. They had landed on a flimsy hut, and some of its tin roof was projecting through into the cockpit. Goffena had seen Durant pushing it away.

Then the Delta operators appeared and helped him out of the cockpit. They sat him down on the right-hand side of the wreck. He had a 9mm machine pistol and could cover that side. He squeezed off rounds whenever Somalis appeared, to keep their heads down.

Super Six Two was directing the runs of the smaller attack helicopters at the larger gatherings of Somalis. But the Black Hawk was in increasing danger: RPG smoke trails were arcing up regularly from the crowds around the crash site. As he flew over Goffena saw one of the Delta operators get shot. He radioed that crash site two had "no security right now".

Super Six Two was making a steep turn when Goffena heard and felt a resounding crash. All his screens went blank. An RPG blast had deafened him temporarily. When his hearing returned, he could hear all his emergency alarms going off. They were telling him that his engines were dead and his rotors had stopped but they were still flying.

His co-pilot was slumped in his seat, head hanging down. Goffena thought they were going down. They were only 20 feet above a row of poles when the co-pilot came to and started shouting grid coordinates. Goffena pulled back on his control stick. The helicopter responded and Goffena looked ahead. He could see friendly ground. He touched the helicopter down safely and saw the reassuring shape of a Humvee driving towards them.

At Super Six Four's crash site the surviving Delta operator tried to hold off the Somalis on the left-hand side of the wreck. Eventually, Durant, on the right-hand side, heard a continuous fusillade that lasted for about two minutes. Then there was a cry of pain and no more shooting. When Durant's weapon was empty, some Somalis came around to his side. One of their leaders took charge of Durant. He was stripped down to his T-shirt and treated roughly. As the crowd took out their anger on him he lost consciousness.

Lieutenant Colonel Harrell in the C2 Black Hawk told McKnight in the ground convoy:

We just had another Hawk go down to RPG fire south of

the Olympic Hotel. We need you to get everybody to the first crash site. Need QRF to give us some help, over.

McKnight replied that he would "recon and see what we can do after that".

McKnight was supposed to get to the first crash site (Super Six One) with his convoy, which was already carrying prisoners and wounded. Then he was supposed to pick up everyone there and turn back south to the second crash site (Super Six Four) and secure it.

Due to inexperience, the Ranger Humvee drivers were stopping after they had crossed an intersection. This trapped the vehicles behind in a crossfire.

The two crash sites were confusing the crews of the helicopters flying above. They were trying to give directions to the drivers of vehicles on the ground. The communications chain meant that instructions from a helicopter reached the drivers after they had passed turnings they were meant to take. McKnight realized this when they saw the original target building in front of them. He could hear voices from several helicopters offering him instructions.

On the convoy, US Air Force Sergeant Dan Schilling muttered to himself: "We're going to keep driving around until we're all fucking dead."

After forty-five minutes of trying to reach the first crash site, there were more dead and wounded on the convoy than at the crash site. McKnight called up to Harrell: "We've got a lot of vehicles that are almost impossible to move. Quite a few casualties. Getting to the crash site will be awful tough. Are pinned down."

Harrell insisted that he continue to the crash site. McKnight and his force had had enough. McKnight called: "Gotta get these casualties out of here ASAP."

Matters were made even more complicated when a second convoy was despatched from the airport to the second crash site. The second convoy was from the Quick Reaction Force (QRF), provided by Tenth Mountain Division. The QRF convoy was a full company of 150 men from second battalion, Fourteenth Infantry, on two-and-a-half-ton trucks with a dozen Humvees.

Although they could see pictures of the second crash site at Joint Operations Command (JOC), the pictures couldn't tell them how to reach it. The US Commander, General Garrison, ordered that another emergency convoy should be assembled from whatever was available at the airport.

Tenth Mountain Division had replaced the US Marine Division as back-up to the UN forces, which consisted of Malaysian, Pakistani and Saudi Arabian troops. The Malaysians and Pakistanis agreed to help but it would take hours to get the larger convoy organized.

The observation helicopters guided McKnight's convoy towards the second crash site before he had reached the first. The original ground convoy had reached the target building and began to move towards Eversman's chalk.

Lieutenant Colonel Danny McKnight, the Ranger battalion commander, was walking behind the door of his Humvee. He told Eversman to get his men mounted onto the convoy. Blackburn, the wounded man, was loaded onto a Humvee carrying wounded. This was detached back to the airport. Two more Humvees went with it as escort.

Sergeant Struecker, in command of the three vehicles, expected to be back at the hangar in five minutes, but roadblocks and barricades began to appear in their path. As they turned onto the National Road, Struecker's M-60 gunner, Sergeant Dom Pilla, was shot in the head and killed.

The ground convoy was ordered to the first crash site to pick up the men there.

Eversman made sure his wounded and all his men were aboard before he tried to climb aboard himself. As he did so, he noticed some fragments of green plastic on the street. At the time he assumed they were from a broken coffee cup and wondered how they had got there. Later he found out that they were the broken earpieces from his own headset, which had snagged on his equipment when he roped down.

Eversman lost his balance as he was climbing aboard a cargo Humvee and fell flat on his back. He was unable to move because of the weight of his equipment and body-armour. Unable to shoot, he had to wait until the vehicle stopped before he could get off. They were not yet at the crash site but had stopped at a four-way intersection. Eversman:

The next thing I knew, I was kneeling behind a Humvee with a wounded Ranger on the ground, his head resting on my knees. One of my team leaders, Sergeant Casey Joyce, had been shot. He had been with Telscher across the street from me and was engaging the enemy down the road to the right when he was hit. Unfortunately, as Casey had been engaging the enemy to the right of the vehicles, he had been hit by a bullet from the unprotected side. Despite the Kevlar vest he was wearing, the round entered his body right under his arm where it was not covered by the vest. This was the first life-threatening gunshot wound I had ever seen. The wound was small, almost the size of my pinky nail. So small, in fact, that I almost overlooked it as we tried to assess its severity. Jim and I followed the first aid procedures just as we had been taught. It's going to be okay; it's going to be fine, I told myself. Casey did not seem to be in any pain, and he did not move or make any sound; he just looked up at me. As I tried to reassure him, Jim and I frantically worked on the wound to his chest. I had no idea what was happening around us until the senior medic bent over and checked Casey's vital signs. He already knew. He checked the vital signs and told us to put the litter on the vehicle. I don't think it registered with me that one of my men had just been killed. Nothing in my training had prepared me for that. There is nothing that can replicate that feeling of loss. But the reality of the events all around me kicked back in. We loaded back onto the vehicles and began the process of turning the convoy around to head back in the direction from which we came.

Eversman checked that no one was left on the street then he boarded another Humvee. He was lying on top of a wounded man and someone was screaming and yelling at him. It was Sergeant Chris Schlief, the Humvee's machine gunner. When Eversman had jumped in he had landed across the kneeling Sergeant's ankle and lower leg. As soon as Eversman realized this he also noticed that the Ranger he was lying on was dead. Eversman:

The sound of metal being torn apart was deafening. Much like the sound of a burst from miniguns, you know that something real bad had just happened when you hear it. We had just driven through an ambush and some vehicles were hit by small-arms fire and rocket-propelled grenades (RPGs). It was so loud that it hurt. I saw a Humvee behind us swerve and pass us on the right as we came to a screeching halt just past an intersection. There were soldiers wounded and lying in the street. One of our Humvees had been hit by a rocket, and the men riding in the back had been literally blown out of the vehicle. Several of us immediately jumped from the convoy to help the wounded. As I started to climb out from the back of my Humvee, I watched as a Somali pipe grenade landed between one of our wounded Rangers and my vehicle. It looked like one of those old World War II potato mashers that the Germans used. Regardless of who made it, it was going to hurt. There was no place to go. The vehicle was stopped, and there was this grenade right in front of me. I tucked in my head and waited behind the tailgate. A couple of seconds later there was a puff of white smoke, and that was it. It was a dud. What a lucky bastard.

We began to take care of the wounded, but the bad news was that we were still pretty much in the kill zone. All we could do was move the wounded to a good vehicle, police all our equipment, and get ready to move again. Most of the men in the vehicles were engaging the enemy, while those on the ground attended to the wounded. We began to take heavy gunfire from down a street. In one of those vivid moments, I watched Sergeant Aaron Weaver appear out of nowhere and toss a grenade with the grace and accuracy of a Nolan Ryan fast ball. It was awesome. Like Berendsen's one-handed M-203 shot back at the blocking position, Weaver threw that grenade with all the confidence of a major leaguer, and the grenade sailed right in the direction of the firing. The grenade detonated a few seconds later, buying us some time to load our casualties onto the remaining vehicles.

How many Rangers were wounded? I had no idea. All I knew was that we were taking fire from every direction and were in a fight for our lives. We had lost a vehicle or two in the ambush. In concert, all the Rangers on the ground were taking care of business. Watching men like Weaver jump into the mix was so reassuring to us all. We were reacting to the events all around us and doing, like the old Shaker adage, "the next thing". In this case, the next thing was taking care of our casualties, policing all our men and equipment, and fighting the enemy with all our might, though not always in that order.

It wasn't too long after we began moving again when we ran into yet another ambush. Again, the wretched sound of metal crashing through metal slapped me back to the moment. We stopped and had to begin another round of fighting, aiding the wounded, and policing the battlefield.

Eversman described the Somalis' tactics:

The Somali battle drill was very simple. They would race down both sides of the street, turn toward the center, and start pulling the trigger, waiting for us to drive through the wall of bullets. *Macabre* would be the adjective that best describes this tactic. There was no way of telling how many of their own people they killed. I could only focus on the right side of the street, and I knew that the Rangers on the other side of the vehicle were doing the same. The only person that I remember being in the vehicle with me was Sergeant Marc Luhman. He was sitting in the front passenger seat, riding shotgun. As we raced down the street, we were following an unwritten rule: pull the trigger faster than the bad guy. With the window down, I had to contort my body in order to get a good shot. Because I wanted to engage the enemy to the front, I decided that I would open the door and lean out. That way I was not restricted by the door frame and would have more room to traverse my barrel. Plus, being a right-handed shooter, it would give me more room. Good initiative, bad judgment.

Eversman noticed that the convoy was going slower than the Somalis running on the sides of the street. He was also running low on ammunition. He had brought thirteen magazines: 390 rounds of 5.56mm ammunition.

He noticed a Somali man shuffling towards them. He was hunched and clutching a shawl or cloth around himself; his hands were hidden. According to the rules of engagement they had been given, if you could not see his hands there was no evidence that he had a weapon. Therefore there was no evidence that he was a threat. Several other soldiers saw the same man who was, apparently, unaware that he was in the line of fire. None of them fired.

Soon afterwards they stopped again and turned around, heading back into the fire fight. Eversman saw the same shuffling Somali man again. Eversman was told that they were heading back to the airport. He was facing the rear, looking for guns. He was yelling to one of his men who thought that he had just been hit when they crested a hill and saw the ocean in the distance. That meant that they were almost safe.

When they reached the airport Eversman helped his wounded into the aid station. He found himself in tears. A medic reminded him that he couldn't let his men see him cry. The medics kept asking him questions because his trousers were covered in blood; they did not know it was not his own. He found Scott Galentine on a litter and had to tell him that his friend Casey Joyce was dead: "He is home in heaven." Then he had to identify Joyce's body.

Eversman went to the JOC to get information. He learnt that the QRF from Tenth Mountain Division was putting together another convoy to link up with the men still in the city and the crew of the second helicopter.

Raleigh Cash was a twenty-two-year-old sergeant from the Third Platoon of Bravo Company. He was Third Platoon's principal Forward Observer (FO). He was in charge of a resupply detail when they heard over their radio the codeword for the mission to go in. They immediately started back towards the hangar. They could hear over their radio what sounded like "utter confusion" over a loud volume of fire.

They were reassured when the questions were answered in order so they assumed the situation was under control.

When their section of four vehicles reached the hangar they were told to prepare to form part of General Garrison's emergency convoy. As they were preparing their vehicles they heard the radio report, "Black Hawk Down!". Cash started "scrambling to get as much ammo as possible". He got two crates of 5.56, two more of .50 calibre and 100 to 150 rounds of ammunition for the SAW. In addition he had his personal weapon, a CAR-15–203, a Remington 870 sawn-off shotgun, two hand grenades and the standard amount of 210 bullets for his CAR-15. His web gear held three ammo pouches, his first aid kit and night vision goggles (NVGs). He was aware that a second helicopter had gone down and the men on the streets were moving to the crash sites.

Cash helped unload the wounded from the Humvees which had been detached from the convoy, and the body of Sergeant Pilla who had been killed as the detachment came out.

One of Cash's men, Dale Sizemore, had injured himself and was wearing a protective cast on his arm. He was a SAW gunner. Cash told him he couldn't come with a cast on his arm; Sizemore just went and cut it off. Sergeant Struecker had been in charge of the detachment that had brought Blackburn back. He led them back out. Cash:

Every time we were on a mission in the city, the Somalis would get the word out and all the locals would run out into the middle of the street, grab a bunch of tires or whatever else they could find, and build a roadblock to mark what was going on. I think they also wanted to keep us from where we were attempting to go. We ran into one of those roadblocks and were trying to navigate our way around it, receiving fire the whole time. A roadblock would cover the entire street – like a giant speed bump made of rubber and wood or any type of debris the Somalis could pull out into the street. They'd build them up till they were about three feet high. Then they'd set it on fire. All we'd see would be the flames and the black smoke from the burning rubber.

Lieutenant Moores was trying to talk to the commander to figure out which way we needed to go. Behind him sat Major Nixon, who was in the right rear seat. I sat in the left rear seat behind Milliman, and in the back was Specialist Velasco, our RTO. Velasco had just graduated from Ranger School. I was talking to the Little Birds, trying to find out if there were any near us that could give us better directions. I had access to what was called the helo common, or the helicopter common net, where all the helicopters talk among themselves to coordinate airspace. Obviously the Little Birds were tied up with what they were doing – supporting the men from the initial assault.

Cash described the difficulties they had finding their way to the crash site:

When I did get directions from the helicopter, I would tell Lieutenant Moores, who would tell Sergeant Struecker, who was up in the lead vehicle; but by the time it got to him, it was too late – we had missed the turn. We'd get turned around and have to drive right back through an area we'd just received fire from. I'd yell to take the left, and the lead vehicle would miss it. I can't tell you how many times we did this. It seemed like a hundred.

At about 1700 hours the driver of Cash's Humvee was driving with his right hand and shooting out of the window with his left hand. Cash himself was sitting behind the driver engaging targets in front and left. The turret gunner was engaging targets at the rear.

They had put the doors on the Humvees only that day. On their previous six operations they had gone without any doors. Cash suddenly realized that his door had been hit.

They hopped out when the convoy stopped and received some incoming fire. Cash shouted out a target to Sizemore. He yelled: "Where?" Cash put a couple of rounds of tracer into a tree, and Sizemore's burst of fire from his SAW brought down a sniper and half the tree.

They turned around several times until they joined up with the ground convoy on the National Road. It was on its way back to the airport. They had to make a 15–point turn to follow the ground convoy. Cash:

Then we started receiving more fire. Lepre began shooting again. That's when a Somali jumped out from behind one of the stone walls and shot an RPG at the vehicle in front of us. Milliman slammed into the back of the stopped Humvee. All of us got smashed up inside, bouncing our heads off things. I remember looking at my strangely oriented pinky and thinking it might be broken. I grabbed some electrical tape off my web gear and taped it up in case it started swelling. I then went back to pulling security on the vehicle.

The RPG blew a lot of sand into our vehicle, and it was hazy for a second. I couldn't tell if we were being fired at or not. I couldn't really hear anything – my ears were ringing. Then it cleared up and we started moving again. We had to drive some crazy crisscross pattern back toward the hangar – *turn left here, turn right here* – to avoid the burning roadblocks and piles of debris. We started receiving fire again, and this time they were shooting from the windows, from the alleyways, the doors, everywhere. I could hear the alleyways erupting like crazy as we were going past them. We were picking off onesies and twosies as best we could, discriminating among those who had a weapon and those who didn't. We were still following the rules of engagement as written. But as we were driving farther it was getting crazier; more and more people were coming out. I was seeing more and more weapons and fewer and fewer civilians until it seemed we were engaging everybody. There were so many of them. I recall hitting another roadblock and having to back up to go around it. Finally, as we got closer to the airfield, the fire began letting up a little bit. The vehicles in front of us were still firing sporadically, engaging targets as best they could. I think at this point the very front of the convoy was getting hit hard, but by the time we got to their position, it was only sporadic fire.

I remember pulling back into the airfield and it was like we had crossed an imaginary line to safety. As soon as we crossed that line everything stopped and it was quiet. It went from crazy noise and shooting and RPGs blowing up all around us and people yelling out directions and orders to – nothing. You could hear some chatter on the radio but it was only background noise.

They unloaded the wounded and tried to clean up the vehicles. They changed some of the tyres on the Humvees and reloaded with .50 ammo and 40 mm grenades for the MK19 grenade launchers, then checked the radios.

At sunset they heard that another rescue mission was being prepared. This time the Malaysians and Pakistanis would help. The Malaysians had 38 Russian BTR Armoured Personnel Carriers (APCs) and the Pakistanis had four American M-28 tanks. The problem was each force used different types of radio. They agreed that the Malalasians would provide the drivers and gunners for their APCs but that the infantry aboard would be American and that they would equip each vehicle with an American radio. The Pakistanis were reluctant to use their tanks to crash through the barriers but they agreed to clear the way through the initial roadblocks and obstacles outside the base, then they would fall back in the convoy. The convoy would consist of about one hundred vehicles.

They set off several hours later. There were roadblocks at every intersection and sporadic small arms fire. According to Cash it was "a moving firefight, pretty much a nonstop engagement, all night long" . They drove past the burned out hull of one of their APCs. Cash's vehicle lost radio and visual contact with the vehicle behind.

They stopped midway between the two crash sites. For two hours they pulled security on the adjoining alleyways. When they began moving again the convoy split up between the two crash sites.

They began to receive more intensive fire. A Pakistani tank fired its main gun and it was the loudest sound Cash had ever heard. Cash was using tracer rounds to locate targets for his turret gunner and other machine gunners. They began to hear reports that there were problems cutting the bodies out of one of the wrecked helicopters. They heard progress reports from the Combat Search and Rescue (CSAR) helicopter.

As night drew on towards morning the incoming fire slackened to occasional potshots and now and then a burst from an AK-47.

At dawn on 4 October the firing began to pick up again. They arrived at the intersection of the Marehan Road and an alleyway. Most of the stranded chalks were still holding on there. The CSAR team had finally released the bodies from the wreck. Cash took charge of the situation around him. Cash:

We'd loaded up a lot of the men onto the vehicles, but there wasn't much room left. I told Specialist Milliman to back up our vehicle to get close to some of the guys who were running from their positions. We filled up the back of our Humvee. There must have been four or five guys in the back, maybe six. They jumped in, and grabbed some of the Kevlar that we had lying back there for added protection in case we hit a mine. While we stopped and the guys were hopping in, I started organizing who would shoot where – who had what. Everybody seemed to be working well together. As the ranking NCO, I was in charge of my vehicle.

I looked around and began to see the damage to the

vehicles around us, to the city, the streets themselves, the
buildings, and the bodies of the dead – the casualties taken
by our opposition. There were quite a few on the ground in
various positions around the vehicles. We found out that
many of the Somalis had been a lot closer to us than we
would have liked to believe. All night we'd been engaging
targets that we could only guess at how close they were.
Now, during the day, we could *see* them. Some bodies were
as close as four or five meters away. In the night we'd fired
at muzzle flashes or outlines of bodies; now we were seeing
the result. The utter destruction to the city and the sheer
number of Somalis that had been taken out by our firepower was mind-numbing. As we pulled forward, it seemed
like the city erupted on us again. Maybe they knew that we
were leaving. The vehicles in front of us were shooting
down alleyways, shooting everything that posed a threat.

The sun was coming up, and the sky had that beautiful
reddish-orange glow it gets before turning to blue. We
continued to drive and then, like the abrupt ending of a
spring shower, the noise just stopped. It was around eight in
the morning. The sun had been up a couple of hours. It was
as though we'd crossed a line that marked the exit point of
the battle, and then all at once you could hear on the radio
all the guys yelling at all the different vehicles: "Cease fire!
Cease fire! Cease fire!"

The Pakistanis were using an old football stadium as their
base. It was the nearest safe haven. As soon as they reached
it Cash looked for his fellow Forward Observers. They had
to drive all around the city to get back to their own base at
the airport. When they got back to the hangar, Cash found
that his fellow FO, Carlson, was alive: "I got shot but I'll be
okay."

That night Cash wondered why his right shoulder was
aching. Lepre, his turret gunner, told him later that he had
been shoving whole cases of ammunition – each weighing
about 50 pounds – up to him with one hand. Cash had been
so pumped up with adrenaline that he hadn't noticed.

Mike Kurth was in Chalk Three which was led by Sergeant First Class Watson. Because he was an RTO, Kurth packed extra batteries for the radios and Chem-lites into his Load Carrying Equipment (LCE). Kurth had taken part in several missions in which he had carried a great deal of equipment that he had never used. This time he decided to leave behind his two-quart water canteen.

As soon as his helicopter flared out for insertion he began to hear AK-47s firing. This alarmed him because it was so much earlier than on any of his other missions. Kurth was held up by something in the helicopter catching on his LCE so that he could not reach his rope, but Sergeant Watson pulled him free. Chalk Three did not land at a corner of the block. Kurth:

> Our chalk was going to be a little different; we would be roping down in the middle of the block. There were some power lines at the intersection that hindered the helicopter from dropping us directly on the corner so, when we hit the ground, we knew we'd have to run 15 or 20 meters to the corner in order to set up our positions. After Delta secured the building and captured the personnel, we would be there to extract them all. They would call for the five-ton trucks that the Ranger ground convoy would escort on the drive up National Road. The enemy detainees would be loaded onto one of the five-ton trucks, and the Ranger chalks would be loaded up on the rest of the vehicles. This was the game plan.

Kurth hit the ground running; he kept running towards the corner of the building with Sergeant Watson. When they reached the corner, the squad leaders were setting up fields of fire for their men. Kurth called in that Chalk Three was in position and okay. The volume of incoming fire was becoming more intense, the longer they stayed. Kurth was waiting for the convoy to arrive when he saw that Sergeant Boren had been hit. Kurth:

You could hear the convoy firing their guns from blocks away as they rolled toward our position. They hadn't arrived more than a few seconds before one of the .50 cals cut loose again, and everyone at the blocking position, including the Delta boys, started cheering. Staff Sergeant Boren wasn't wounded too badly. He'd caught a ricochet round in the neck, and it had just barely grazed him. They slapped a field dressing on him and he was fine.

Our first priority once the convoy arrived was to get Blackburn loaded up and back to the airfield. The next task was to load the enemy prisoners of war onto the five-tons. I must have counted anywhere from fifteen to twenty prisoners. I'd been sitting there with Ramaglia, still pulling security, and I noticed one of the Black Hawks circling a little lower than normal. It was weird, because it looked like it was drifting somewhat. They were just about finished loading the bad guys when I saw the bird go down. At first I thought the pilot was doing some strange maneuver in order for one of the snipers on board to get a clean shot at someone. But the bird continued to spin and kept losing altitude. After almost another full turn, the bird completely disappeared behind the buildings. I couldn't hear the crash, but I knew what had just happened.

It was Kurth who made the first radio call reporting that a Black Hawk had gone down. He judged that the sooner Higher Command knew about it the better.

From all the radio traffic, Kurth was aware that everyone in Bakara was trying to find the crash site. Hostile Somalis were also converging on the area. Bravo Company commander Captain Steele was asking if anyone could see the downed Black Hawk. Kurth replied that he did not have a visual but that he knew the general location. Lieutenant DiTomasso replied that they were perhaps only a couple of blocks away from the crash site. DiTomasso told Steele that he was going to take a party to the site and remain there until either the Rangers or the CSAR helicopter arrived.

Higher Command decided that Chalks Three and Four should link up and proceed to the crash site together.

Meanwhile Chalks One and Two should do the same, proceeding on parallel routes. Chalk Four was still out of communication. Command asked for a visual to see if they were still there. Sergeant Watson told someone to stick his head around the corner to see whether they were still there. The answer was affirmative.

Lieutenant DiTomasso called in to say that he had reached the crash site but that one of the crew had been killed. One of his Rangers was wounded a minute later and two more men went down in quick succession.

Kurth's chalk moved in single file on either side of the street at a slow, deliberate pace. Kurth had to monitor his radio at the same time as pulling security. He saw one of his comrades take a round in the leg but the Ranger was able to scramble to some cover with a little help.

The Somalis were beginning to work out how to get closer to them. It was becoming a race to the crash site. Private First Class Neathery was chalk three's M-60 machine gunner. Kurth:

I squeezed off a couple bursts. I heard Neathery fire a burst, so I got up and ran back to him and covered his rear. I had just turned around to cover Neathery when he fired, his muzzle right next to my left ear. The last thing Sergeant Watson wanted was a radio telephone operator who couldn't hear.

Our chalk was pretty much intact. The only casualty was Sergeant Boren, and he was walking wounded. I looked ahead at the next corner, and the battle going on there was incredibly fierce. I looked to our rear and saw a small road — more like an alley than anything else. If we had continued on the major road, we would have gone straight into the alley, but instead, in order to get closer to the crash site, we'd taken a left. I noticed that the road we were on had a slight elevation to it, which gave us a slight advantage, but at the same time it was crowned, so it was hard to get a really clear field of vision all the way across the street.

Our chalk and part of the CO's chalk were all within

about a block of each other. We were in a kind of a U-shaped courtyard. To our rear was a house with a small patio, and to our front was a pretty large intersection. The fiercest part of the battle was taking place there. The volume of fire had grown so intense that it had been a little while since anyone had crossed the street. In our immediate area the major threat was coming from a small road that veered away from the crash site – somehow the enemy had managed to backtrack away from us and had found small alleys to make their way down the road that led to our chalk. We were between them and the crash site, but we didn't know exactly how close our position was to it.

At an intersection, Kurth saw a Ranger cross the street unscathed; then one of the Delta operators took a round in his helmet. He was wearing a different type of helmet, not a K-pot (the standard Kevlar reinforced helmet). Kurth saw the operator's head snap back and a red mist spray out of the back of his head and hit the wall behind him. Another operator began to pull him to safety almost as soon as the wounded man had hit the ground. They requested an aerial medevac, which was refused.

They were told that the area was too dangerous for helicopters to operate. Then Steele told Kurth that the ground convoy had sustained so many casualties that it had turned around and returned to base, where it would link up with the Tenth Mountain Division Quick Reaction Force.

Kurth was beside Neathery when he was hit. Errico took over on the M-60, then he, too, was hit. Kurth realized that someone had the M-60 position locked in. He warned the next man on the gun: "Be careful. Someone has a bead on that gun." Finally Sergeant Watson told the new M-60 gunner to use the Light Anti-tank Weapon (LAW) that he had slung on his back. He put down the M-60 and fired the LAW but the respite did not last long.

Kurth went over to help their medic, Doc Strauss, with Errico's wound. Then Kurth noticed a smoke trail out of the corner of his eye. It was "an old time pineapple grenade". He yelled a warning and they all rolled away. He lay with his K-pot nearest to the grenade and his arms between his body and the ground. He felt the earth punt him in the chest. He was coughing and spitting up dirt but he was able to make a roll call. Only one of them had been hit (by shrapnel in the leg). Kurth concluded that grenades blow up and out and they had been so close that this one had blown up and over them.

It was starting to get dark. None of them had brought any night observation devices (NODs).

They were very close to the first crash site. Sergeant Watson decided to take over an adjacent house. They pulled their wounded inside and settled in the main living room. The house was the home of a family of three Somalis whom they kept under guard. Kurth didn't know that members of Chalk One were in the house with them. The medics set up a Casualty Clearing Point (CCP) in the house. Kurth found Goodale, the Chalk One FO, in the CCP. Since sunset, the firing had died down to the occasional burst, when suddenly there were thirty to forty-five seconds of intense firing then silence. Occasionally, Kurth heard the Little Birds coming in for gun runs. He didn't know that they were only 50 metres from the crash site.

The C2 helicopter warned them that they had twenty to thirty Somalis armed with RPGs approaching from the east. None of their doors or windows faced east. The Little Birds made a pass with their rockets. Command reported that the threat had been "neutralized". Then Command said that they wanted them to consolidate at the crash site. At first their CO, Captain Steele, wanted to obey but Sergeant Watson persuaded him that it would be disastrous to try to move with their wounded. Finally they decided to stay where they were.

Kurth was given guard duty over the Somali family.

Sergeant Atwater, the CO's RTO, asked me if I had any extra batteries, as his were beginning to die out. I said I had extras in my rucksack, and told Hawley I'd be back in a minute. I hadn't even gotten up on one knee when a Somali opened up on the house and rounds peppered the wall just above my head. The burst wasn't even over before I slammed myself into the floor sideways so that the radio didn't come crashing into the back of my K-pot and crush my nose, which had happened on many occasions throughout my RTO career. I was lying on the floor scared shitless and not moving, trying to catch my breath. My initial thought was how in the hell that Somali had seen me move around inside the house. That's when I heard Hawley yell, "Kurth's hit! Kurth's hit!"

How does he know I'm hit? Did my blood splatter him? Am I hit? It had happened so fast, I hadn't even checked myself out. I gave myself a once-over and piped up, "Negative! Negative, I'm good." I could hear the Delta medic make his way back through the CCP; I'm sure he was relieved – one less casualty for him to worry about.

Hawley was dumbfounded. "Holy shit, Specialist, you hit the floor so fast I thought for sure you got hit!"

I moved up toward the front of the house about two feet, on my belly this time. I was right behind a small concrete divide that was about a foot and a half tall, so I made that my new home. Hawley decided that he wanted to move up with me. I couldn't say that I blamed him. Hawley was sitting next to me. "Damn, Specialist, I've never seen anyone move that fast before!"

Kurth told Hawley that he thought it must have been survival instinct. His CO told them that the convoy would be moving out in twenty minutes. Half an hour later they were again told that the convoy would be arriving in twenty minutes.

Kurth spent the time in the CCP helping prepare the casualties for evacuation. He could still hear the Little Birds making gun runs, so he deduced that there was still plenty of hostile activity. They were running low on medical supplies and ammunition. A Black Hawk flew over the alley between Chalks One and Three to make a supply drop. The convoy was forty-five minutes away but when it arrived at the crash site they were still trying to cut the body of one of the pilots out of the wreck.

Kurth and his comrades could hear the convoy's fire-fight. Then it began to move away. Then there was nothing on the net.

Sergeant Watson had set up his command post in a small courtyard. Kurth heard the CO tell Sergeant Watson to keep a look out for the convoy. The CO got word that the convoy's point man had spotted some of their Infra Red Chem-Lites. Finally it came into sight and Kurth could hear his CO telling them where the chalks were. The APCs were backed up to the doorway. They were filled up with wounded "pretty quickly". The convoy had their perimeter secured so they could get some sleep before they left. Kurth fell asleep until Sergeant Watson woke him, saying, "Time to go". He was one of the last to leave but the APCs were full. Sergeant Watson said, "It looks like we're taking the Heel-Toe Express."

When he stepped outside, Kurth was "dumbfounded" that it was daylight. Sergeant Watson told him:

All the APCs are filled with casualties, and some of the chalks, including the rest of us, are going to walk out beside the APCs and use them as cover. We're going back the way we came. About four-fifths of a mile past the Olympic Hotel there is a secure intersection with more vehicles, and we will load up there.

By the time they reached the first corner they were already jogging. Once they turned the corner the APC drivers just left them behind. Kurth:

We were going out with guns blazing! If they *were* still hanging around by this time, you knew they were up to no good. There were about twenty-five of us out there fighting for our lives. I turned the corner and started laying down some heat. I got about six rounds off and my M-16 jammed.

I yelled, "Jam!" as loud as I could about three times and pulled back from the corner. I took a few steps back to fix my weapon. I completely forgot I had traded my M-16 with Kent at some point in the night, and I didn't know he had fired it so much. The carbon buildup caused a double feed, a real nasty one. I couldn't get the rounds out to save my life. I was slamming the butt of my weapon on the ground, trying to force the round out, but no luck. Finally the last guy told me to go, so I hauled ass across the street. I made it about halfway down the block before I stopped to try to unjam my weapon again. Nothing was working; those two rounds were so wedged in that I couldn't pry them out. I needed to find someone carrying two weapons and fast. I couldn't believe how badly this was going. It's daylight, there's no room on the APCs, we have to walk out, the APCs leave us, and now I'm running out of this thing naked with no weapon!

Kurth tried to clear his weapon until they reached the original target building. At that point, Doc Strauss got hit crossing an intersection. He was hit on a "flash bang" grenade in one of his ammunition pouches. There was a big cloud of dust and smoke. When the smoke began to clear Kurth saw Doc Strauss getting to his feet.

Kurth saw Sergeant Elliott carrying a spare M-16. He explained that his own weapon was jammed. As soon as Elliott gave him the spare weapon, he found a target and began to fire.

At one intersection they were held up by a sniper. Kurth was only five feet from one of the Pakistani tanks when it fired its main gun: "one way to take care of a sniper."

They reached the building that had been designated as the link-up site. They were told more vehicles were coming back to get them. Kurth wondered how long that would be but before long the vehicles arrived. The driver of Kurth's vehicle was just following the vehicle in front. Kurth kept the back door open with his foot to look for targets but the people on the street weren't even throwing rocks. They were obviously out of the Bakara market.

After about ten minutes they pulled into the Pakistani stadium.

Aidid bought Mike Durant from his original captors. He was fed and given medical treatment. After five days a representative of the Red Cross was allowed to see him. Then two journalists were also given access to him.

On 8 October the US Ambassador to Somalia, Robert Oakley, told Habr Gidr leaders that the US mission against Aidid was over and Task Force Ranger's mission had ended. He also told them that President Clinton wanted Durant released immediately without conditions.

The Rangers were still holding sixty or seventy of Habr Gidr's top men, including those taken on 3 October. Oakley promised that he would talk to the President about releasing the Habr Gidr men, "but only after you've released Durant."

Aidid himself was in hiding. He agreed to hand over Durant. The next day, Durant was handed over to the Red Cross. He was the only man from Super Six Four to come back alive. The Somali leaders were released later.

The survivors of the battle were home within a month.

Task Force Ranger suffered 18 killed in action and 75 wounded in action. TV pictures showed the dead bodies of Americans being dragged through the streets by a mob. Conservative estimates of Somali casualties were five hundred dead and more than a thousand injured.

The US Marines, Rangers and Delta Forces were pulled out followed by the entire UN mission.

Aidid died in 1996 without having ever gained full political power in Somalia.

Immediately afterwards, the United States was less inclined to make risky military interventions. It was unwilling to intervene in Rwanda in 1994. Other nations followed its example. This resulted in the collapse of the UN initiative.

The disaster in Rwanda stiffened international resolve. The international community intervened to prevent another wave of killing in the former Republic of Yugoslavia. The Daytona Peace Accords were signed in 1995. By that time between 200,00 and 250,000 Croats, Bosnians, Serbs and Muslims had died.

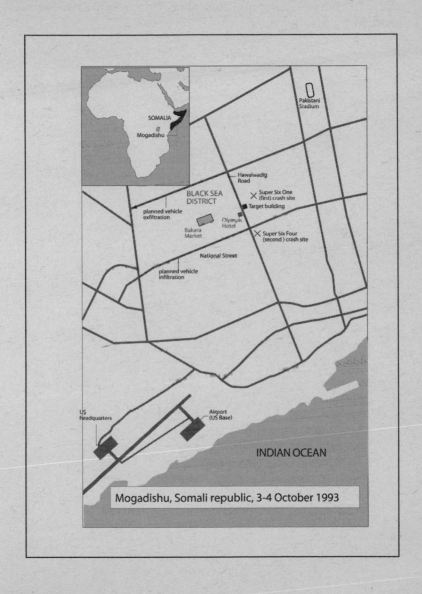

SOMALIA

Mogadishu

Pakistani Stadium

Hawalwadig Road

BLACK SEA DISTRICT

Super Six One (first) crash site

Target building

planned vehicle exfiltration

Olympic Hotel

Bakara Market

Super Six Four (second ) crash site

National Street

planned vehicle infiltration

US headquarters

Airport (US Base)

INDIAN OCEAN

Mogadishu, Somali republic, 3-4 October 1993

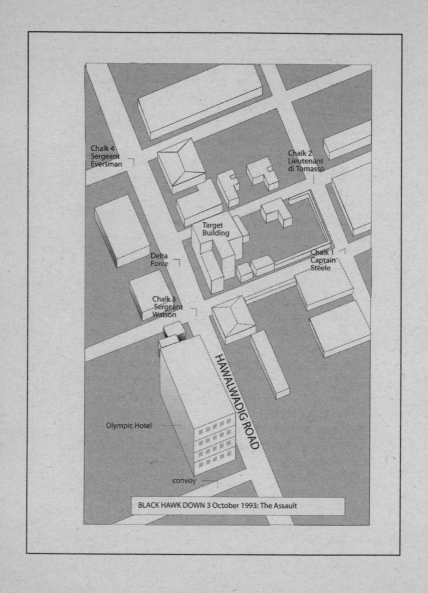

BLACK HAWK DOWN 3 October 1993: The Assault

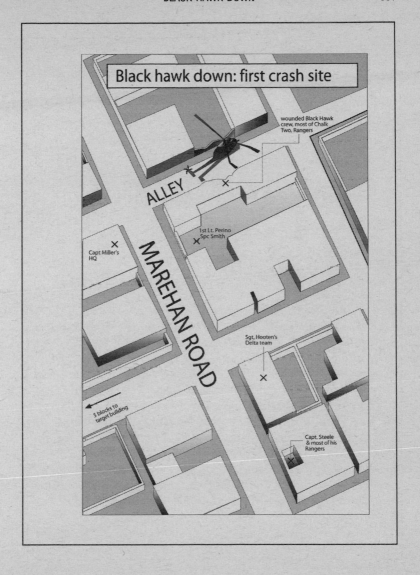

Black hawk down: first crash site

wounded Black Hawk crew, most of Chalk Two, Rangers

ALLEY

MAREHAN ROAD

1st Lt. Perino
Spc Smith

Capt Miller's HQ

Sgt. Hooten's Delta team

3 blocks to target building

Capt. Steele & most of his Rangers

# AMBUSH ALLEY (2003)

*When Operation Iraqi Freedom began on 20 March 2003, the main attack on Baghdad was to be made by the thirty thousand soldiers of the US Third Infantry Division (Third ID) from the south west. The attack by Third ID was to be supported by a second attack by the First US Marine Division, which would approach Baghdad from the south east.*

*The First US Marine Division would bypass Nasiriyah to the west then move directly towards Baghdad via Route one. The two attacks on Baghdad would split Saddam's forces.*

*After the First US Marine Division had bypassed Nasiriyah, a Marine Air and Ground Task Force (MAGTF) would be responsible for taking the city to open up a supply route for the Marines. The MAGTF was named Task Force Tarawa.*

*Brigadier General Rich Natonski was in command of Task Force Tarawa, which consisted of First Battalion, Second Marine Regiment, (1/2 Marines), Alpha Company, Eighth Tank Battalion and a Marine aircraft group. 1/2 Marines was commanded by Lieutenant Colonel Rick Grabowski (call sign: Timberwolf). It consisted of three infantry companies: Alpha, Bravo and Charlie. Each Marine infantry company was transported by a platoon of Amphibious Armoured Ve-hicles (AAVs, amtracks or tracks, as the Marines called them).*

*As well as taking Nasiriyah, Natonski's MAGTF would be responsible for opening up the supply route through Nasiriyah.*

The intel Task Force Tarawa had received from CEN-TCOM, US Central Command, had led them to expect a friendly reception from the local population who were predominantly Shia. Grabowski had tried to find out about Nasiriyah. He had learnt that it was a military town with several large complexes around its northern edge. Intel had only been able to tell him that the large complexes were "military compounds" but they did tell him that the soldiers of the Iraqi Eleventh Infantry Division were carrying civilian clothes so that once they saw the Americans they could disappear into the civilian population. CENTCOM didn't expect much resistance. By the time the MAGTF reached Nasiriyah it had been reported that the Fifty-first Iraqi Mechanized Brigade had already given up.

The vital part of Task Force Tarawa's mission would be securing two bridges and the road between them. The southern of the two bridges ran over the Euphrates river. The northern bridge ran over the Saddam Canal. The road between them ran for 4.6km right through the city of Nasiriyah. They didn't want to get involved in urban fighting because it would slow them down and because it might result in civilian casualties and collateral damage. At a planning meeting on 6 February Natonski had been shown an aerial map. He was told: "Army planners call this stretch of road Ambush Alley." Officially they referred to it as Route Moe but some of Natonski's marines were already calling it Ambush Alley.

Natonski's battalion commander, Lieutenant Colonel Rick Grabowski, planned to move up from the southern bridge to the northern one by finding a route around the eastern side of the city.

On 23 March 2003 Natonski's Marine task force was advancing towards Nasiriyah. The tank detachment was leading.

About 7 a.m. Major Bill Peeples, the commanding officer of the tank detachment, called Grabowski: "Timberwolf. This is Panzer 6. We are receiving mortar and small arms fire."

The leading vehicles of the column, Combined Anti-Armour Team (CAAT) Humvees, began returning fire. The tank detachment's executive officer (XO), Captain Scott Dyer, saw a truck heading towards them. His gunner called out the range and requested permission to fire. Dyer thought there was something odd about the truck; then he noticed that it had US Army markings. He called Peeples to tell him about it. The tank detachment should have been the leading element of the Marine Task Force.

Then three more vehicles appeared; two of them were large trucks, which accelerated towards them. As the trucks came closer they could see that they were shot up and trailing smoke. The third vehicle was a Humvee with bullet holes in its windshield. It screeched to a halt just behind Major Peeples' own tank. A soldier told him: "We've got people north of here. Soldiers. US soldiers. They are pinned down and they're getting shot at."

The soldier explained that he was the CO of an army maintenance convoy that had got lost during the night. They had mistakenly driven into Nasiriyah. Just as they realized their mistake they had been ambushed and chased through the city. Some of his soldiers were wounded and others were caught in a firefight further north.

Peeples reported to Grabowski that he was going to investigate and rescue the US soldiers if necessary.

A few kilometres up the road, Peeples found a column of battered and shot-up US Army trucks. Many of them were in flames. He could see muzzle flashes through the smoke. US soldiers were returning fire at the surrounding buildings. Peeples drove his tank in front of them to give them cover. He could not traverse his turret to engage because his tank was carrying bladders containing one hundred gallons of spare fuel. He had to jettison the spare fuel and the rest of his company did the same. It was Standard Operating

Procedure (SOP) to drop the bladders if they became engaged in combat.

The tanks and CAAT Humvees dealt with most of the hostile forces. They called in artillery support to deal with the hostile artillery positions. A track from Alpha Company, 1/2 Marines came up to evacuate the wounded from the Army Maintenance Company.

The tank detachment's XO, Captain Dyer, called the battalion Command Post (CP) to ask for permission to refuel. The tanks had used up to half of their fuel in the rush to extricate the survivors from the Army maintenance company. At full speed they consumed fifty-six gallons an hour. Major Sosa, the 1/2 Marines Operations Officer, reluctantly gave permission for the tanks to come back to a Refuelling Point (RP).

This created a series of problems. First, all eleven of Major Peeples' tanks had to come back. They were supposed to lead the advance and be at the spearhead of any attack, providing fire support for the infantry. The problem was made worse by the fact that the RP would have to be at the rear of the column when the tanks were supposed to be at its head. Second, the tanks should have provided fire support at the southern bridge over the Euphrates; now the infantry would have to advance unsupported.

At about 7 a.m. Natonski had been following the progress of his lead element, 1/2 Marines. They had reported being held up by incoming fire. He went forward in person to see what was really going on. He knew that armoured vehicles should not be held up by small arms fire.

When he landed from his helicopter he saw four US servicemen lying on litters. They were recognizable as Army soldiers from their equipment and desert pattern camouflage uniforms. They had bloody bandages on their arms and legs. He ran over to them and asked: "Who the hell are you?"

The soldiers were in a state of shock. They were part of US Army's Five Hundred and Seventh Maintenance Company. They were supposed to have been following an army convoy but they had taken a wrong turn in the dark. They had planned to bypass Nasiriyah but they had gone right into the centre of it and been ambushed by Iraqi forces.

Natonski tried to appear calm. US army units should not have been there at all. What Iraqi forces had they encountered? Natonski had expected the Iraqi Infantry Division in Nasiriyah to surrender rather than fight. The Brigadier General promised the wounded men that the Marines would get them out of there as soon as possible. Natonski went further forward to find the battalion commander of 1/ 2 Marines. When he found the battalion commander, he also found six more army soldiers gathered around an army vehicle. They, too, were from Five Hundred and Seventh Maintenance Company.

At the junction of Routes Seven and Eight, the Maintenance Company convoy should have turned sharp left to head around Nasiriyah to the west; instead they had gone straight on into the centre of the city. Iraqi soldiers had waved them through several checkpoints until they emerged on the other side of the city. Only then did the men of the US army convoy realize that they had made a mistake.

The sun was rising. They had just turned around to retrace their route when they were attacked. The convoy's eighteen vehicles came under fire from Iraqi fighters as they drove back through Nasiriyah, trying to avoid roadblocks and debris in their way. Only a few of the vehicles got through. Most of them were hit and disabled somewhere in the city.

Natonski asked them: "Is that all of you?" "No, some are still missing," he was told.

An army captain was almost crying as he explained that twenty soldiers and thirteen vehicles were still unaccounted for. The missing included Private First Class Jessica Lynch.

As Natonski talked to the men from Five Hundred and Seventh Maintenance Company, Lieutenant Colonel Grabowski and his operations officer, Major David Sosa, were trying to work out how the army convoy had got in front of them.

In the early hours of that morning, Grabowski had been aware of an army convoy overtaking his vehicles 60km south of Nasiriyah. At the time his only concern was that the two convoys shouldn't get mixed up with each other's vehicles.

The Five Hundred and Seventh Maintenance company had not only got themselves shot up, they had compromised the entire US plan. This relied on speed and stealth to keep the Iraqis guessing as to whether they were going to bypass the city or march into it. At an opportune time Natonski intended to seize the crucial bridges across the Euphrates and the Saddam Canal. Now the Five Hundred and Seventh had alerted the Iraqis to their arrival before his Marines could reach the bridges.

Natonski decided to attack immediately. He told Lieutenant Colonel Grabowski: "We've got to find those missing soldiers and get to those bridges before they're blown." Natonski's final words to Grabowski were: "Rickey. Those soldiers are in the city. Try to find them if you can. The army would do it for us and we need to do it for them."

Natonski saw the tanks coming back to refuel as he was deciding what to do about his attack. Because of the Army Maintenance Company, he had lost the element of surprise. If he did not move quickly the bridges might be blown. The First Marine Division's advance on Baghdad might be held up by a lack of supplies. He ordered Grabowski to accelerate the attack.

They had planned that Alpha Company 1/2 Marines would take the southern Euphrates River bridge. Bravo and Charlie companies were to follow in trace, cross the bridge then go around to the east and head towards the northern Saddam Canal bridge. Alpha Company would hold the southern bridge until relieved by the Second Battalion Eighth (2/8 Marines). Once relieved, Alpha Company would follow Bravo and Charlie Companies. This was how they had planned the operation on the ship to Kuwait.

But now that the tanks had gone to the rear, it was Bravo Company that was in the lead. Captain Tim Newland, CO of Bravo Company, called Grabowski on his radio: "This is

Mustang Six. Sir, we are on Euphrates Bridge." He had made a navigational error. He was on a railway bridge south of the Euphrates Bridge. Grabowski corrected him and told him to push on.

Corporal Neville Welch was a fireteam leader in Bravo Company. As they moved forward in stops and starts, in and out of their tracks, he saw a road sign, half written in English: WELCOME TO NASIRIYAH. At that moment small arms fire began to ricochet off the side of the track.

After they had crossed the railway bridge, Bravo Company came into contact with dug-in Iraqi T-55 tanks. The Combined Anti-Armour Team (CAAT) in their Humvees engaged the Iraqi positions with .50 cal machine guns and Tube-launched Optically-tracked Wire command-link guided (TOW) anti-tank missiles. They reported: "Five T-55s engaged and killed."

Grabowski was a couple of hundred metres south of the railway bridge in his Humvee. He was alarmed by the contact with the enemy tanks. He called his XO, Major Jeff Tuggle, who was at the main battalion Command Post (CP) at the rear. He was also in charge of the RP. Grabowski told him: "If we don't get tanks up here we are not going any further."

Tuggle was having problems at the RP. He could only give each tank 100 gallons and his fuel pumps had broken down. They were having to refuel the tanks by gravity. It was taking fifteen minutes to give each tank its 100 gallons because there was only one hose. Tuggle told Peeples: "Bill, we need those tanks up there as soon as possible." Peeples told his second platoon commander, Gunnery Sergeant Randy Howard: "You need to get the hell up there." Howard's tank platoon cut short their refuelling and moved off at full speed to join Bravo Company.

Just before 1200, Grabowski ordered: "We got to take those bridges. Alpha, take the southern bridge. Charlie, take the northern bridge. If we don't take those bridges now, regiment will give the mission to LAR." (Light Armoured Reconnaissance.)

Howard led his tank platoon from the RP at their full

speed of over 40 miles per hour. They caught up with Bravo Company at the railway bridge where the tanks moved up to the head of the column. It was 2km from the railway bridge to the Euphrates river bridge. By 1245 Howard had crossed the southern Euphrates river bridge. When he came off the bridge, he was in the city looking straight up the road to the northern bridge.

The road which would earn its nickname of Ambush Alley began as a four-lane highway criss-crossed by telegraph and power poles. It had a concrete strip down the middle. Gunnery Sergeant George Insko in the third tank saw a group of Iraqis running towards a stash of weapons. His crew sprayed them with the coaxial machine gun, while the survivors ducked into cover in an alleyway. A machine gun on the roof of a mosque opened up on them. They took it out with an MPAT (Multi Purpose Anti-Tank) round from the main gun.

After Howard had gone about three blocks, he was ordered to make a right turn. He found an opening to his right and turned off the main highway. Followed by the rest of Bravo Company, they weaved through narrow streets towards the open ground on the east side of the city.

In the gaps between the houses were pools of stagnant water. Howard's tank had just arrived at what looked like a hard-packed mud road. He felt his tank come to a halt; then his driver said: "Gunny, we're stuck."

The M1A1 tank sank in the mud until its treads were almost completely covered. Both tanks behind also became stuck in the mire. Insko, the commander of the third tank, warned the commander of the fourth tank, Staff Sergeant Aaron Harrell, to stay away. Harrell had approached by a different route and could see that what might have looked like hard mud was just a thin layer of hard crust over a bog of watery mud and sewage. The tank crews began to call the area the "shitbog".

As well as the three tanks, three Humvees and three tracks became stuck in the "shitbog". Hitting the gas just dug them in deeper. Other vehicles trying to tow them out became stuck themselves because the tow-ropes were too short.

Grabowski and his forward Command and Control team were advancing with Bravo Company about 1km behind the leading tank. One of the stricken tracks was the C7, the battalion forward Command and Control vehicle.

Grabowski preferred to travel in a Humvee. His Humvee was just turning east off Ambush Alley when he heard: "The tanks are stuck. We've got tanks down."

When Grabowski caught up with the leading vehicles he saw the C7 up to its axles in deep mud. His forward movement had come to a halt. He jumped out and ran over to the C7.

*Fedayeen* were trying to get close enough to overrun the stricken vehicles. The CAAT Humvees were weaving in and out trying to keep them back. The tanks were taking out technicals (pick-up trucks with machine guns or RPG launchers mounted on them) with MPAT rounds.

Grabowski was having trouble getting comms with his subordinate units. Although they were in relatively open ground, the nearby two-storey houses masked the VHF signals. Grabowski's most urgent need was to prevent Charlie Company from taking the same route as Bravo and sharing its fate.

Comms were flooded by an incoherent mess of radio traffic. Too many people were talking at once and some of them were "hot miking": keying in their handsets even when they weren't speaking. This cut everyone else out.

Captain Brooks' Alpha Company crossed the Euphrates river bridge behind Bravo. His Marines dismounted and took up positions around the bridge. By 1315 Brooks was satisfied that they had secured the bridge. He called Grabowski: "Timberwolf, this is Tomahawk 6. We have secured the bridge but we are under increasingly heavy fire."

Charlie Company had pulled out from the fields and onto the road as Bravo and Alpha crossed the Euphrates river bridge. They passed the burnt-out remains of the army Maintenance Company's vehicles at the foot of the railway bridge. The Charlie Company commander, Captain Dan Wittnam, was in the fifth track from the front of his convoy.

He saw crashed Humvees and two US army trucks with their trailers still on fire.

Track 209 from Charlie Company broke down. The commander of the AAV platoon attached to Charlie Company decided to "bump" the crew and the infantry from 209 into Tracks 210 and 211. Charlie Company pushed on with eleven troop-carrying tracks, a medevac track and three Humvees.

Lieutenant Ben Reid, commanding officer of Charlie Company's weapons (fire support, mortars and heavy machine guns) platoon, could see Alpha in a firefight at the foot of the Euphrates bridge. Captain Wittnam told his subordinates by radio: "We're going to move along the MSR (Main Supply Route)." They were going straight up the road towards the northern Saddam Canal bridge. Since briefing sessions on board ship on their way to Kuwait, the Marines had been calling that stretch of road Ambush Alley.

Lance Corporal Edward Castleberry was the driver of Charlie Company's leading track, 201. He could see hundreds of Iraqis and realized that they were under fire. The commander of the AAV section including 201, Sergeant William Schaeffer, saw Iraqis running across the street and trucks moving back and forth. The sound of bullet strikes on the side of the AAV grew from a few "dinks" on the sides to a louder and more insistent clattering.

Private First Class Casey Robinson, firing his Squad Automatic Weapon (SAW) from 201, sprayed hundreds of rounds into houses wherever he saw a muzzle flash. Marines below were linking ammunition and passing it up to him. A Rocket Propelled Grenade (RPG) hit a pack on the outside of the track. Robinson called down to get more Marines up to return fire.

Schaeffer was in 201's gun turret. He was alternating between the .50 calibre and the MK19 40mm grenade launcher. He saw a sandbagged machine gun pit on the corner of a two-storey building. It was manned by three men in black. Castleberry manoeuvred the AAV so that the MK19 could bear on the machine gun pit. Schaeffer aimed and fired the MK19 at it. The 40mm grenade hit just under the sandbags and the position exploded.

The smoke trail of an RPG careered past 201. Castleberry saw something like a school bus stop in the middle of the street ahead; black-robed fighters with RPGs got out. Schaeffer saw them and used the foot control to turn the turret towards the bus. He hit it with a round from the MK19 and it exploded. One of the black-robed fighters aimed an RPG at the track. Schaeffer switched to the .50 cal machine gun and hit the man with a burst. Castleberry tried to call out targets: "Fifty metres to the right. Hajji on the roof. Hajjis in the ditch by the road. Port side. Machine guns down alleyway. Hajjis coming from east."

There were too many to call out. He steered with one hand and fired his M203 with the other. He stopped the track and turned it to face the targets as he had been trained, but the AAV platoon commander, Lieutenant Tracy, radioed him: "Quit fucking stopping. Push, push, push."

Tracy was in 204 with Captain Wittnam. They were fourth in line. Behind them was Lieutenant Reid in 208. They were a couple of hundred yards into Ambush Alley. The convoy received a barrage of RPGs, though most of them missed. One embedded itself in the line of trucks suspended on the outside of the AAV, but failed to explode.

Track 211 was carrying Marines who had been offloaded from 209. Lance Corporal Thomas Quirk was one of the Marines lying on the roof of 211. He saw Iraqis in windows, on roofs and darting out of alleys. He fired his first combat shot. As he realized that the Iraqis were not taking full advantage of their positions, his training began to take over. He began yelling: "Changing magazines. Machine gun position behind the wall. Guys with AKs on the roof. RPG in the alleyway, nine o'clock."

201 had nearly reached the northern canal bridge. Castleberry reported two men in the middle of the road with RPGs. Schaeffer told him to run them over. The Iraqi fired the RPG, which hit the concertina wire protecting the front, angled slope of the track and ricocheted off to the side. The second fedayeen prepared to fire and Castleberry

drove straight at him. He felt the bump as the treads went over the man's body.

Robinson saw the whole incident and the empty bridge ahead. On top of 211 Quirk saw a black-robed fighter jump out from behind a house on their right-hand side. The fighter fired an RPG which hit the side of the track. The explosion threw Quirk onto his back and he blacked out for a second as the track actually lifted into the air. The RPG had been hit under the wheel well, which protected the men above from the blast. Quirk recovered in time to walk his rounds into the RPG fighter. Inside 211 there had been a blinding flash. The ear-shattering explosion was followed by a rush of hot air. Sergeant Joe Torres had been in the rear of the overcrowded track, which immediately filled up with black smoke; he screamed because his eyes felt as if they were burning. The driver, Sergeant Michael Bitz, had been slightly wounded and stunned by the explosion. He slowed the track down to a crawl. Someone yanked Torres out through the rear hatch. Hospital Corpsman HM 3 Robert Ritchie told him: "You're gonna be fine but that you got real bad shrapnel wounds to your right leg."

The RPG hit had caused a second explosion, which had scattered chunks of hot metal fragments under the benches on which the marines inside were sitting. Combat medics reached 211 and began treating the wounded. The marines on top jumped off over burning rucksacks. It was a 10–foot drop down to the ground, and they were laden with 30 pounds of gear. Marine Fitzgerald from 211 screamed out that he had broken his ankle jumping down. Quirk reckoned that if they had not been so full of adrenaline they would never have risked jumping off the track.

The damaged 211 was in an exposed position on the middle of the raised highway. Sergeant Schaeffer from 201 had run over and opened 211's rear hatch. Fire was spreading across the top of the track. Five wounded men were helped out of the vehicle; they had all been injured by hot metal fragments below the knee. They were placed at the side of the road, out of the line of fire.

Second Lieutenant Michael Seely, commander of Charlie Company's third platoon, had been in 211. He had been in the first Gulf War. He shouted at the men from 211 to get over to a berm (a manmade earth wall) on the east side of the road to provide some security. Quirk was one of the men who was still able to obey.

Lance Corporal Trevino was driving 208. He brought it to a halt 125 metres north of the Saddam Canal bridge. The command track, 204, had stopped nearby. Lieutenant Reid crawled out of 204's command hatch, threw his helmet and maps down to the ground and jumped down after them. He landed hard but safe. He ran around to the rear and banged on the rear hatch. When it opened, Second Lieutenant Fred Pokorney, the Forward Air Controller (FAC), was first out, followed by mortarman Corporal David Johns. Reid told them: "Fred, get comms up and let Arty know our position. Help Corporal Johns with the 81s. I'm going to get the 60s up and firing."

The 81mm mortars were still south of the Euphrates river bridge but if they were within range they could be directed to give Charlie Company some fire support. They had brought the 60mm mortars with them.

Reid ran over to where his 60mm mortarmen were setting up. He saw track 211 out of the corner of his eye. The rucksacks on top contained ammunition which was still burning. He noticed that some Marines were still trying to cut the rucksacks free and ordered his staff Sergeant, Philip Jordan, to stop them.

They were under small-arms fire. It was hard to identify the direction from which it was coming. Once his mortarmen had set up, he told them: "Line it up on that fucking big-ass white building. Charge 1. Elevation 1420." He didn't wait for the first round to land before he told them to keep firing at what he was sure was a military compound.

Lieutenant Fred Pokorney, the FAC, grabbed him to tell him that they had no comms. Until they could find a way to get through, the 60mm mortars were all the fire support they had. Reid redirected one of his mortar squads to fire to the west, where they could see Iraqis and vehicles in an exposed position by a big berm.

Staff Sergeant Jordan reported to Reid that Sergeant Torres, who was in charge of Charlie Company's M240G machine guns, had been wounded. Reid told Jordan to sort out any machine guns he could find and have them facing back towards the city to their south west. Reid still did not know where the rest of Charlie Company was. He could see the first platoon on the other side of the road but he had no idea whether the second and third platoons had even crossed the canal. He was so involved with directing the fire of his mortars that he was unaware of how much small-arms fire they were receiving. He actually stood up to watch the fall of shot from his mortars, but Lieutenant Pokorney immediately tackled him to the ground.

Lieutenant Swantner from First Platoon called him to ask for fire support as they had come under mortar fire. Reid desperately needed comms but none of his four radios were able to get through as the radios in the tracks were not set to the firenet frequency. All Reid could do was reposition one of his 60mm mortars to the south.

Lance Corporal Castleberry had lowered the rear ramp of 201. Robinson and his fellow Marines from first platoon dismounted and took cover in an irrigation ditch. The ditch lay in fields east of the northern Saddam Canal bridge. They were 200 metres from Charlie Company's tracks. The men of Charlie Company could see fedayeen crawling towards them through reeds and scrubland. They were laying down a hail of fire, which the Marines were returning with aimed shots at anything that moved.

Captain Wittnam had thought that he was following Bravo Company when he headed straight up Ambush Alley. It was only when he was actually over the canal bridge that he realized that he had been mistaken. He could see that the land either side of the road to the north was impassable to his heavy vehicles. He called battalion on the tactical net with his position: "Timberwolf 6, this is Palehorse 6. I am on the bridge." There was so much chatter on the net, he couldn't tell if Grabowski had received his message. He dismounted and began to organize his defences facing both north and south.

Lance Corporal Quirk had taken cover behind a berm. None of the men beside him were from his fire team. Rounds were cracking and whizzing all around them. The incoming rounds were mainly exploding ammunition from the burning track (211), which was only 50 metres away.

Grabowski had been stuck with Bravo Company for thirty minutes. He was still worrying that Wittnam might follow Bravo Company into the mire to the east of the road. Then he received Wittnam's message that he was on the bridge and immediately demanded to be told which bridge. They were cut off. The battalion fire support officer reported that he had heard a message that Charlie Company was on the second bridge. He had been monitoring radio traffic from the sinking C7 Command and Control vehicle.

Grabowski was relieved but he still needed to get his tanks up there. The C7 vehicle was the heart of the battalion's Command and Control system. The Intel, Fire Support, Forward Air Controller (FAC) and the battalion commander himself were forced to dismount to try to get comms up outside the vehicle. In their efforts to get their radios to work, they had become so far apart that they needed to use their radios to contact each other.

After conferring with his operations officer, Grabowski decided to leave a small force to protect the enmired vehicles and push on with the rest towards Charlie Company on the northern bridge.

Command and Control at battalion level had broken down but at small unit level the men were doing what they had been trained to do. Corporal Neville Welch of Bravo company was lying in an alleyway with his fire team when he was told: "The helos have found a way out. They'll lead us out of here. Back to the tracks."

Ten Bravo Company vehicles snaked through a labyrinth of dusty streets and alleys, trying to avoid water holes that threatened to suck them back into the mud. Some Marines dismounted, pulling security at the intersections. Welch saw white pick-ups with machine guns and RPG teams shadowing them down alleyways. Whenever they appeared in the open the .50 cal machine guns or MK19 grenade launchers on the AAVs would destroy them.

North of the Saddam Canal bridge, Lieutenant Reid was still trying to deploy his mortars when Lieutenant Pokorney reported that he had managed to relay some fire missions. Suddenly Reid was aware of an explosion behind him; then he felt a searing pain through his right arm. When the dust cleared he could see and feel that his arm had been broken. He didn't receive much sympathy when he announced this, because Lance Corporal Brian Buesing, Lieutenant Pokorney and Staff Sergeant Jordan had all been hit. His radio operator was wounded. Reid ran for help.

After 20 metres he found himself lying in the dirt. He could only see with one eye. He struggled to his feet and staggered to one of the tracks. He managed to crawl inside. It was 208, Trevino and Elliot's track. Reid moaned at them: "We got casualties. We need to get them evacuated. You get up on that fucking gun and I don't care what you shoot but if there are hajjis you fucking kill them." As soon as he had got them to react he stumbled away from the track to find his remaining mortar teams.

From track 201 Castleberry had seen the incoming shells getting closer to Reid's mortars. He saw Pokorney blown into the air. As he was calling out targets for Sergeant Schaeffer on the .50 in the track's turret, Castleberry saw Iraqis who seemed to be collecting RPGs and AKs from huts and shacks in the fields around them. Standard Operating Procedure (SOP) for the crew of tracks was to stay with their vehicles in case they needed to move.

Captain Dan Wittnam, CO of Charlie Company, realized that his men and vehicles were in a form of kill zone, surrounded by artillery and mortar positions. The Iraqis had been expecting them and the volume of incoming fire was becoming a threat. If they could not match it, they would be in danger of being overrun.

At Charlie Company's medevac track, the casualties were mounting. There were five from track 211. Michael "Doc" Robinson, a Navy corpsman, cut away the chemical suit around Sergeant Torres' right leg. He did what he could and tried to reassure Torres, who urged him to attend to the others. Robinson moved from one wounded Marine to the next. First Sergeant Hennao got through from the medevac track to the main battalion CP south of the Euphrates bridge. They asked him for grid co-ordinates. Hennao needed to look at his map and dismounted to look at it. The track was hit by something which smashed a hole in its side, so he decided to take the wounded out of the track.

They began to lay out the wounded in the ditches beside the highway. The position was clearly too hot to be a Landing Zone (LZ) for helicopters and comms were still difficult. When Wittnam's RTO got through he was asked: "When was the last time you took fire and from what direction?" "We're taking fire from all directions and we're taking it now."

Back at the Euphrates river bridge, Captain Mike Brooks, CO of Alpha Company, saw Iraqi fighters pressing in on them along a number of routes. He, too, realized that the Iraqis must have been waiting for them, because they had stockpiled weapons in the area. He had two of his platoons dispersed around the foot of the bridge, with one further north at the beginning of Ambush Alley. His marines were picking off Iraqis whenever they appeared in windows or emerged from doorways to fire their RPGs. Huey and Cobra helicopters were firing into a line of houses on the opposite side of the road.

Captain Brooks managed to get through to the main battalion CP. He requested tank support.

7km south of the Euphrates bridge, Captain Scott Dyer, XO of the tank detachment, was still trying to refuel each tank by gravity. Major Tuggle, the battalion XO, came back in a track and demanded to know what the tanks were still doing there. "All units are in contact. We have to deploy the reserve. We need to get all those tanks up there." Dyer replied: "First it was Bravo in contact and now you are saying that everyone is in contact. What the hell is going on?"

The first platoon of the tank detachment was struggling

to remove some anti-mine ploughs, which slowed them down. Major Tuggle was so desparate that he sent the two remaining tanks from Third Platoon to help Bravo Company. They were only partly refuelled. They were led north at full speed by Captain Romeo Cubas. Only the tanks of First Platoon and the Headquarters element were left behind at the RP. Major Tuggle came up to Major Peeples and told him: "We need all your tanks up there now." Peeples was still unaware that Grabowski had ordered the seizure of the bridges without tank support. He immediately told his men to stop refuelling the last tanks and to head north. He had five tanks with him: three from First Platoon and the two from the Headquarters element, his own "Wild Bill" and Dyer's "Dark Side".

Peeples listened to the battalion net to try to find out what was happening. His own tank, "Wild Bill", had a problem that would only enable it to move at five miles an hour. He left "Wild Bill" and switched to one of First Platoon's tanks, which had been named "Desert Knight". They had to change the radio in "Desert Knight" to the battalion net. As they reached the railroad bridge, they sighted some Iraqi T-55s. The turret of one of them was moving. Peeples in "Desert Knight" ordered his gunner to fire a SABOT. This was an armour-piercing projectile with stabilizing fins and a uranium rod which could pierce and melt armour. The T-55 exploded and its turret spun off.

Dyer, in "Dark Side", ordered his gunner to engage the remaining T-55s as the US tanks approached the Euphrates bridge. The sky above was still dark from the smoke from the damaged US army vehicles and the Iraqi tanks which had all been destroyed. The US tanks were getting closer to the city. It is not conventional for tanks or armoured vehicles to operate in an urban environment where they could be hit from above. Armoured vehicles are most vulnerable to a top-down attack, and tanks are best used engaging targets at a distance of 1km or greater.

In the original plan, the tanks were to support the infantry at the bridges. Dyer saw the men of Alpha Company pinned down near the foot of the bridge. Their AAVs were spread out on the road in front of them and the air was thick with smoke and flying metal.

East of Ambush Alley, the Bravo Company convoy was unable to make any progress. Each time they tried to go east their way was blocked by irrigation ditches and treacherous ground. They had reached halfway between where their vehicles had become stuck and the northern canal bridge. Despite this, by 1400, Grabowski had to concede that the eastern route was not going to work. But the more open ground was better for comms. Grabowski decided to pause there while he tried to get a clearer idea of what was happening. Sosa, the battalion operations Officer, realized that they were involved in several different fights, not a single coherent battle. Grabowski had Close Air Support (CAS) overhead. Back at the main CP he had an air support officer whose job was to put the pilots in touch with the Forward Air Controllers (FACs). But the main CP was south of the Euphrates bridge. Grabowski had two FACs, which he had assigned to Alpha and Bravo Companies. Charlie Company was supposed to be behind them so they didn't have an FAC attached.

The call sign of the FAC attached to Bravo Company was "Mouth". Mouth had been controlling the supporting helicopters during their advance to the Euphrates bridge and beyond. He was ensuring they continued to provide supporting fire for the enmired tanks. Grabowski had told his air support officer to get on the guard net and to pull in any air support he could contact. The air support officer was having difficulty with his comms, so he called Mouth, who was only 100 metres away from Grabowski's forward CP. Going on the guard net meant using the emergency channel to pull in any air support which was both in the area and available. This included Air Force assets as well as the Marine aircraft and helos with whom they had trained. Mouth called: "On guard. On guard. This is Mouth. We have troops in contact and need immediate air support."

Several thousand feet above Nasiriyah, two USAF A-10 Thunderbolts were flying on a bombing mission towards targets in southern Baghdad. The pilots were from the

Pennsylvania Air National Guard. Before the war began they had been flying in the area, enforcing the no-fly zones imposed since the first Gulf War. Their call signs were "Gyrate 73" and "Gyrate 74". The pilots were monitoring their radios in case they received a call for emergency CAS.

The A-10s carried five 100–pound bombs, high-explosive rockets, Maverick and Sidewinder missiles. But their most effective ground attack weapon was their Avenger 30mm gatling gun. These were twenty-two feet long, two-ton, seven-barrelled weapons that could fire 3,900 armour-piercing or high-explosive rounds per minute.

Several fixed-wing aircraft checked in with Mouth, including Gyrate 73 and his wingman. Mouth consulted Bravo's CO, Captain Tim Newland, to find out where CAS was most needed. They agreed to send the aircraft north of the Saddam Canal bridge. Although the battalion commander was not far away, Mouth still thought Bravo was the unit furthest north, as they had planned. He was unaware that the battalion was no longer following the plan. Mouth told the A-10 pilots about the fight they were involved in and the tanks stuck in the mud. Then he told them: "I need you to take out targets north of the canal bridge. That's the northern bridge on the eastern side of the city."

The aircraft searched for the targets Mouth had referred to. Eventually they sighted some vehicles on the ground. Gyrate 74 thought they looked like dark pick-up trucks. The Air National Guard pilots had practised Close Air Support but they were unfamiliar with US Marine Corps vehicles.

There were three types of Close Air Support. Type 1 was when the FAC could see both the aircraft and the target. Consequently he could guide the pilot onto it. Type 2 meant the FAC could not see the aircraft. This was usually because of bad weather or when the attack would be made from high altitude. Type 3 was when the FAC authorized a pilot to operate in a geographical area but the FAC could not see either the aircraft or the target. The battalion commander had written in the operations order that any type 3 clearance had to be approved by him: "We will not authorize a Type 3 CAS unless approved by the battalion commander."

Unfortunately, with their comms proving so difficult, the battalion commander was the hardest person to contact. The difficulty was even greater because he wished all such decisions to be referred to him.

Gyrate 74 fired a smoke rocket to show Mouth where they were. Mouth couldn't see it. The A-10s spotted some helicopters and smoke north of the canal bridge. In fact, it was the burning Charlie Company track 211. They reported it to Mouth, who confirmed that the smoke was in the target area. The A-10 pilots thought that the helos were attacking the vehicles they had seen. Mouth checked with Captain Newland, Bravo's CO, that there were no friendly units north of the canal. Neither Mouth nor Captain Newland knew that Charlie Company were north of the canal bridge.

Charlie Company was in danger of being overwhelmed by incoming artillery, mortar, RPG and machine gun fire. Captain Wittnam and Lieutenant Tracy, CO of the AAV platoon, had got the tracks spread out in a fan-shaped formation about 200 metres north of the northern Saddam Canal bridge. Several of the tracks had been loaded with wounded. Wittnam and Tracy were hoping to see Bravo Company's vehicles coming towards them over the bridge. Wittnam thought that if they could not match the sheer volume of incoming fire they would be overrun.

Comms was still a babble of confused radio transmissions. Captain Wittnam ran along the lines of his positions. He saw the four dead mortarmen and tried to encourage his infantrymen by appearing to remain calm and by showing his face.

Corporal Elliott in track 208 had been wounded in the neck by shrapnel and called for help. Sergeant Hennao in the medevac track called the battalion main CP: "We need a medevac. It's urgent. We need a helo. But we're in a hot LZ."

Mouth decided that with comms as they were, if he tried to get the battalion commander's authorization he would lose the CAS opportunity. The A-10 pilots did not realize that he was giving them a Type 3 clearance; they asked for permission to attack the target according to the procedure for types 1 and 2. Mouth wondered why but he let them get on with it.

Lieutenant Reid had told his mortarmen to load the wounded onto the tracks. He was in a ditch on the east side of the road and could only see out of one eye when he saw the A-10s line up on the AAVs. The Marines had taken the orange identifying panels off their vehicles because they didn't want anything on them which stood out from their green and tan camouflage.

A group of Marines was running towards 201 to avoid mortar fire when they heard the A-10s overhead. Lieutenant Seely recognized the sound from the first Gulf War when he had been strafed by A-10s. With him were Lance Corporal David Fribley and Lance Corporal Jared Martin. They were both hit, Fribley so badly that Lieutenant Swantner, his platoon CO, didn't recognize him. Martin and Seely were trying to get him into track 201 when his back was blown out.

The Marines tried all the signalling pyrotechnics they had, including green and red smoke, to get the A-10s off them. Lieutenant Seely tried to call battalion on the net: "Timberwolf. Cease that damn A-10 fire. Cease fire. It's hitting friendlies. Cease fire. You got to turn off that air."

As soon as Major Peeples' tanks arrived at the Euphrates bridge, Major Peeples looked for the Alpha Company CO. Captain Brooks came running up to him. Peeples asked him: "What the hell is going on? What do you need?"

Captain Brooks showed him on a map: "I've got a platoon up to the north here and we're taking fire from buildings on the east of the road about here. I want two tanks orientated that way up to the north and another tank to the east." "Roger that."

Peeples deployed his tanks as requested. It was highly unconventional to allow his tanks to become involved in close-quarter urban fighting. Brooks' voice came over the radio: "I want you to shoot that building with the blue door." Peeples stuck his head out of the turret. He could see three buildings with blue doors. "Gunner MPAT. Shoot all the fucking buildings with blue doors."

Dyer found that his tank was attracting Iraqi small-arms fire. It was ineffectual but it kept the small arms fire away from the Marines. His driver wasn't responding because every time they stopped he kept falling asleep. He had been driving for thirteen hours.

Dyer wanted to manoeuvre his tank into a position where they could shoot at long range. He was leaning out of the turret, directing his driver: "There are grunts all over the ground, so be careful. I want you to pivot to the right. Okay, move forward, hard left."

He yelled down to the Marines on the ground: "Where do you need fire?" A Marine fired two rounds of tracer down an alleyway. Dyer told his gunner to fire the co-axial machine gun into the alleyway.

The Marines were reinvigorated by having the tanks with them. Captain Brooks could see the tank crews were out of their turrets, manning their guns and looking for targets.

At first Wittnam and Tracy thought that the air support had come to help them. Beside them was the wounded Sergeant Torres, who looked up and was hit in his left side by shrapnel. Wittnam and Tracy kept down but were hit by an eruption of dirt and stones from the strikes.

Grabowski was still in open on the east side of the city. His staff had heard that Charlie Company had requested a medevac but their LZ was too hot. Then they heard Seely's message. Forward CP received another call: "Cease that damn fire. Abort air. Abort air." Grabowski himself recognized the voice. It was Seely.

Corporal Matt Juska had just reached 203 when the A-10s attacked. He jumped into the parked track and closed the hatch. Corporal Randal Rosacker was already inside. He saw white sparks hit the top of the track and felt a blast of hot air sweep through the track. 7.62 and 5.56 ammunition on the left side and 40mm grenades on the right exploded and blew the sides out. Lance Corporal Radley Seegert in the top hatch felt his arm burning. Juska didn't know what had happened but grabbed the Marines with him and baled out into a ditch.

Sergeant Schaeffer in track 201 tried to contact his platoon commander, Lieutenant Tracy, as the wounded were being brought to his track. He heard Corporal Elliot in 208 scream for help when he was wounded in the neck by shrapnel. He saw the other tracks manoeuvring to get out of the way of the incoming fire from the A-10s. Unable to contact the AAV platoon commander, Sergeant Schaeffer yelled to Castleberry to drop the ramp and recall the Marines back to his track. They did not make an orderly retreat; neither did they hear the A-10s overhead. They struggled to get in, pushing the body of a man killed in action (KIA) into the vehicle. Shrapnel came in through the top hatch as they tried to close the rear hatch. Schaeffer could see 205 was already heading across the bridge back down Ambush Alley. Schaeffer hoisted a US flag up on the turret and called the other AAV commanders: "Let's go watch for the flag."

The driver of 205 had driven off, heading back down Ambush Alley without any orders. Track 205 was carrying two wounded Marines and a Navy corpsman.

After he had baled out of 203, Juska had climbed into Sergeant Michael Bitz's 206, which was following behind 201. Track 210, carrying 25 marines and Staff Sergeant Anthony Pomposs, followed 206. Corporal Brown's 207 carrying uninjured Marines brought up the rear of the impromptu convoy.

203 had been destroyed by the A-10 attack. 205 had left on its own. Then came 208 leading a convoy. 201 followed close behind and was followed in turn by 206, 210, and 207.

Corporal Elliott in 208 reached the mouth of Ambush Alley. He was heading for the battalion aid station south of the Euphrates bridge. 208 was carrying the injured mortarmen, Sergeant Brendon Reiss, Lance Corporal Donald Cline, Lance Corporal Thomas Blair, Corporal Patrick Nixon, Lance Corporal Michael Williams and Private First Class Nolan Hutchings. Elliott was in the commander's hatch looking for threats coming from down Ambush Alley

when another explosion rocked the vehicle, which filled
with black smoke and came to a halt. Elliott ordered everyone out and pulled himself out of the turret. The driver,
Trevino, pulled himself out of a forward hatch. All the
Marines aft, in the troop compartment, had been killed by
the blast.

Gyrate 73 called Mouth: "Vehicles from northern target
area progressing into the city." Mouth cleared them to take
out the vehicles, provided they attacked from the direction
of the city not towards it.

Gyrate 73 had aimed at the leading AAV, 208. In 201,
Schaeffer actually saw the underside of 208 when it was hit
and lifted into the air. Castleberry, driving 201, steered
hard right to avoid running into 208. When he swung back
left he found the steering was not responding. Track 201 hit
a telephone pole, bounced off and headed towards some
houses on the east side of Ambush alley. Castleberry braked
and the track came to a halt outside a two-storey concrete
house. At that moment something ripped open Castleberry's hatch, shredded his CVC comms helmet and blew him
right down into his seat. Schaeffer felt heat come up
through the turret; he could tell that 201 had stopped so
he ordered everyone to get out.

Gyrate 74 had fired a Maverick, which had blown 201's
rear hatch open. Inside, Casey Robinson was sticky with
blood from wounded Marines.

The pilot of Gyrate 73 was coming round to fire his last
Maverick when he heard the ceasefire order. They questioned "Mouth", who didn't want to discuss it over the
radio. The A-10s left for their base in Kuwait shortly
afterwards.

Wittnam, Charlie Company's CO, had seen a small
convoy of his tracks disappear over the bridge. He guessed
that they were carrying wounded but he was disturbed that
they had left without reference to him. Lieutenant Seely ran
up to him and told him that they had been hit by "friendly
fire".

After Castleberry had heaved himself out of the driver's
hatch of his AAV, he fell to the ground on the left of the

track. Casey Robinson had climbed out of the top hatch. He took cover in a courtyard, behind a wall. From 201's turret, Schaeffer saw the other two tracks steer around them and disappear towards the southern bridge. He climbed out and dropped down on the right hand side of the vehicle. He saw a crowd of Iraqis closing in from the alleyways on the other side of Ambush Alley and for a moment he thought he was going to be overrun.

He turned and found Lieutenant Swantner and another Marine beside him. Then they heard the sound of an AAV. It was Corporal Brown's 207, which had turned around to pick them up. The three of them sprinted 100 metres under fire and threw themselves into the open hatches of the AAV, which turned again and continued south.

Elliott and Trevino limped away from 208. They had survived because they had been in the front, not in the troop compartment at the rear. They made their way towards the wreck of 201. Robinson was surprised to be joined by Martin, Castleberry, Wentzel, Doyle, Milter, Ortiz, Doran, Honmichl, Matteson and Olivas. They were all young Marines without any officers or senior NCOs.

Robinson looked over the wall. He noticed another burning track about 70 metres away. Two figures limped out of the smoke, evidently trying to reach their position. Robinson and his fellow Marines put down a spontaneous burst of fire as Elliott and Trevino climbed over the wall. Then Robinson heard someone calling out. He saw Corporal James Carl was still lying against the side of the track. Robinson and Doran jumped over the wall. Jake Worthington had been in the troop compartment of 208. He was still by the track, trying to help Corporal Carl, when Robinson and Doran arrived. Worthington and Doran were able to drag him back to the wall, while Robinson provided covering fire. They forced open a gate, which opened into the courtyard of a house. A middle-aged Iraqi man with his hands up came out, shouting. One English word was intelligible from his Arabic: "family". The Marines told him he could get his family out. A young girl and a woman came out. The Marines motioned for them to leave, then cleared

the house room by room, using the room entry techniques
they had learnt in their Military Operations in Urban
Terrain (MOUT) training. Robinson got all the way up
to the flat roof before he called down to the other Marines,
who were still sheltering behind the wall to the courtyard.

In addition to Carl there were three other serious casualties and twenty more or less able-bodied Marines. They
had a chance to assess where they were. There were crowds
of Iraqis in the alleyways but the house was like a fort.
Iraqis kept trying to pull the rucks from the track. The
Marines shot them but they kept trying. One of the Marines, Sena, was an RTO but he couldn't get comms because
his battery was dead. The most senior corporal was Wentzel, but he wouldn't allow one of them to go back to the
track to try to get some batteries. They repelled the first
wave of Iraqi attacks.

At this point they agreed that Robinson should try to
retrieve whatever he could from the track. Robinson,
Milter and Olivas gathered at the gate. It was only twenty
strides to the track. Robinson and Milter fired while
Olivas dashed to the track and began throwing out whatever he could. His first attempt produced some ammunition and the Command Launch Unit (CLU) thermal-
imaging night sight from the Javelin Missile system, but
no batteries.

Robinson asked Milter for cover while he hopped onto
the track himself. He turned over the debris until he found
batteries for the radio.

Back at the northern bridge Captain Wittnam had less
than two platoons of infantry to hold it. He only had a
couple of tracks with functioning weapons systems. His
mortar section had received a direct hit and was low on
ammunition. He managed to get a direct message through
to the forward CP. He could hear that Bravo and Alpha
were heavily involved, and told them that he would stay
until they could link up with him.

Lieutenant Tracy, CO of the AAV platoon, reckoned that
he only had two fully functional tracks left out of the twelve
they had started with that morning. One had broken down

by the railway bridge, six had gone back down Ambush Alley and three others were disabled or destroyed. That left 202 and 204.

From one of the remaining tracks he tried to get through to the battalion forward CP. He picked up the voice of the battalion's assistant operations officer (AS3). He told him: "This is Tracy. I'm with Charlie. We need some help." The AS3 told him: "There is anti-aircraft fire and enemy forces on the northern bridge." "I know. I'm north of that bridge." "Yes, Tracy, I understand. You are north of the south bridge." "No, I am north of the fucking north bridge." There was a pause. "Oh, shit." Tracy was appalled: no one in command seemed to know where they were. He crawled over to Wittnam to report.

Wittnam told him: "We are going to hold the bridge and stay here until we get back-up."

Men from Alpha's second platoon saw the first two tracks from the impromptu convoy come down Ambush Alley. One of them was dragging its rear ramp and being hit by AK-47 fire and RPGs. As it came to a halt at the foot of the Euphrates bridge, an RPG flew into its top hatch and detonated the ammo inside. It burst into flames. It was Charlie company's 206. Track 210, carrying the uninjured Marines, was so close behind 206 it had to brake and swerve to avoid crashing into it.

Marines from Alpha's third platoon rushed up to try to pull any survivors out of 206. They found Juska unconscious but alive.

At first, Captain Brooks, Alpha's CO, thought that it was one of his tracks. He was supposed to be relieved by units of second battalion Eighth Marines (2/8 Marines). He was getting frustrated. He now had Peeples' tanks with him and he thought that his best place was with Charlie Company. He asked Grabowski when he would be relieved by 2/8 Marines.

Grabowski told Brooks to hang on in there until 2/8 Marines reached him. 2/8 Marines were moving slowly because they were clearing the route into the city for the service support units following behind. They were being transported in soft-skinned trucks rather than AAVs.

From the open area just to the east of Ambush Alley, Grabowski could actually see the two disabled tracks to his north. His operations officer, Sosa, had seen Corporal Brown's 207 sweep past him. Lieutenant Swantner recognized him and told him: "Captain Wittnam is dead. Charlie is taking casualties." Sosa ran over to Grabowski: "Sir, we've got to get north. We've got to send Bravo up to the northern bridge to help Charlie."

Grabowski's regimental commander, Colonel Ronald Bailey, had moved his CP towards the railway bridge. Grabowski had twice asked him to get 2/8 Marines up to the Euphrates bridge. Colonel Bailey knew 2/8 Marines hadn't reached the railway bridge yet but he could get 1/2 Marines some air assets.

Captain Eric Garcia was the pilot of a CH-46 twin-rotor helicopter. Garcia and his CH-46 were based at the Task Force's CP, 65km south of Nasiriyah. Reports had come in that 1/2 Marines were taking casualties in Nasiriyah and needed a medevac. Captain Garcia had been briefed that the enemy threat was medium to high and that the LZ was hot. Another CH-46 flew as his wingman – they always flew in pairs. Two gunships accompanied them as escort and they were brought into an LZ south of the Euphrates bridge.

As soon as Track 207 reached the Euphrates bridge, Sergeant Schaeffer jumped out. He was desperate to get some help for Charlie Company. He saw a track bristling with antennae and presumed that it was a command track. He wrenched open the back hatch and explained who he was and what was happening to Charlie Company on the northern bridge. A captain shook his head and said: "There's nothing we can do to help you right now."

Sergeant Schaeffer ran over to one of the tanks and banged on the hatch. An officer popped his head out. "What do you need?" It was Major Peeples. Schaeffer told him. Peeples replied: "I'll see what I can do."

Peeples knew that he was not the only one having difficulty communicating with the battalion staff. Captain Dyer had told him about the distress call he had received. It confirmed what he had just heard from Sergeant Schaeffer: Charlie Company was in trouble and the battalion commander had no idea what was happening.

Peeples had never been in action before, but he had been taught that a large chaotic battle could be won by breaking it down into smaller fights. He ran over to Alpha Company's CO and said: "Charlie Company is having a rough time. They are taking a lot of casualties. They need some tanks up there."

They agreed that two tanks would stay with Alpha Company while two went to help Charlie Company. He told Dyer to follow him in his tank.

After Schaeffer had spoken to Major Peeples he didn't think that Peeples was going to do anything, so he decided to go back himself. He felt that the Marines from 201 were his responsibility. Brown was prepared to take him back in 207. Brown said: "I think we're going to die." "Probably so." "Let's do it."

After the Charlie Company Marines had been in the house off Ambush Alley for about an hour, they began to feel as if they had the situation under control. From the roof they could see any Iraqis who got close enough to become a threat. Robinson saw a white pick-up truck which could have knocked down the wall which protected them from being overrun. He took aim with his M249 machine gun; when he fired the truck veered off the road and exploded.

With the batteries from the track they were able to get a weak signal on their radio. Castleberry wanted to try to fix the radio himself. He could hear Sena trying, without success, to contact Captain Wittnam. When he got his turn he managed to get through to the AAV platoon commander, Lieutenant Tracy.

On the northern bridge, Lieutenant Tracy had just climbed back into his track when he heard a faint noise on the radio. Through the static noise he recognized the name of Castleberry. He tried to reply: "Castleberry, this is Tracy. Where are you? Over."

But Tracy could not hear what Castleberry said. Tracy told Castleberry to click once for yes and twice for no. All

Tracy was able to learn was that there was at least one Marine trapped in the city without support.

Up on the roof of the house off Ambush Alley they noticed "something big going on over there." South of them, they could see Cobras circling the buildings to the east of Ambush Alley. They tried to attract the helos' attention with laundry and an orange recognition panel.

Major Peeples' tanks drove up Ambush Alley at 45 miles per hour with small arms fire pinging off their sides. Major Peeples hardly noticed it but halfway along he saw a Marine officer step out into the road and flag him down. It was Major Sosa, with his pistol in his hand. He yelled: "Charlie company needs you up north." Peeples replied: "I know. That's where I'm going." "Well, get going, then."

Major Peeples realized that he must have just passed the 1/2 Marines' forward CP.

It was about 1600 when Wittnam and Tracy saw the two M1A1 Abrams tanks rumbling over the canal bridge. Peeples headed for the track with the diamond symbol that identified the unit commander's vehicle. Captain Wittnam came up to him. "What do you need?" asked Peeples. Wittnam pointed out the positions from which the heaviest fire was coming. The tanks destroyed the positions with their main guns.

Dyer took his tank over to where Lieutenant Seely and his platoon was receiving heavy fire from the north. They were returning fire which was coming from a large white building to the north. It was one of the Iraqi military complexes which Dyer had been briefed about. He told his gunner: "Put some rounds into those buildings. Fire into the high points. And hose down the whole complex with the coax."

After Major Peeples' tanks had reached Charlie Company, Lieutenant Tracy remembered the radio message he had received from Castleberry. He also remembered that he had seen figures running along the bank of the canal when one of the tracks going south was hit. Tracy found Major Peeples and told him: "We have Marines in the city."

Peeples remembered that Sergeant Schaeffer had told him there were some Marines in the city. He told Captain

Wittnam: "I'm going to leave my XO here, but I'm going back into the city to find those missing Marines."

Alpha Company's CO got through to the main battalion CP to ask about 2/8 Marines' progress. He heard that they, too, had mistaken the railway bridge for the Euphrates bridge and had reported that they had arrived. Brooks decided to move north to help Charlie Company as soon as Garcia's casevac lifted off.

"The shitbog" was covered in pools of green mud and slime. The tanks of third platoon, led by Captain Cubas, had charged straight into it. Sergeant Alan Kamper was even more horrified to see flames coming out of the rear of his tank. The filters of his Nuclear Biological and Chemical (NBC) system had caught fire.

Staff Sergeant Aaron Harrell came up with an idea to make a longer towing cable by joining two cables with a piece of scrap metal and a clevis (a U-shaped piece of metal). Harrell tested the two lengths of cable together for strength and attached a third to give them length. They attached the improvised cable to one of the enmired tanks commanded by Staff Sergeant Insko, and slowly sucked it out of the mud. They were successful in pulling out a second tank.

At the house off Ambush Alley, they had heard the rumble of the tanks going past them. They tried to wave the tanks down but the tanks thundered by without stopping. They had been in the house for two hours and there were only two hours of daylight left. Then the Marines on the roof heard another vehicle coming up Ambush Alley.

But as 207 passed their position, an Iraqi aimed an RPG at it. The AAV accelerated past them and continued towards the northern bridge.

Castleberry, as an AAV driver, recognized that it was Corporal Brown's 207.

Back at the LZ south of the Euphrates bridge, the casevac was taking longer than anyone expected. The loading was taking place under a hail of fire. The corpsmen on the CH-46 were working on the wounded as they were loaded aboard. When corpsman Moses Gloria and his buddy had finished stabilizing the wounded men, Garcia finally took off.

Alpha's Marines took this as the signal to get in their tracks. Staff Sergeant Pomposs, who had come back down Ambush Alley with 25 other Charlie Company Marines, came up to Captain Brooks to demand rides for his men. By the time Captain Brooks had assembled his convoy there were up to thirty Marines packed into each of the AAVs. The two tanks led, followed by sixteen troop-carrying AAVs. Next came the 81mm mortar section in nine Humvees and the four CAAT vehicles. Another AAV brought up the rear. As he looked behind, Captain Brooks could see no sign of a relieving force from 2/8 Marines.

About thirty minutes after the tank had gone past the house off Ambush Alley, the clattering sound of a Huey woke Robinson up. He was up on the roof, dozing off. It was horrifying to see the Huey bearing down on them with all its guns aimed at their positions. They put their fists on their heads to signal they were friendly and yelled, "Friendly. Friendly." The helicopter came in for a closer look and gave them thumbs-up signs.

They all felt better; then they heard the roar of a tank again. Peeples had crossed the northern bridge and was looking for signs of the Marines when he saw the torso of a dead Marine. He spotted a disabled AAV on the east side of the street and ordered his driver to pull up alongside a building near the wrecked AAV. He jumped off, ducking because he was under fire. When there was no sign of the missing Marines at the building, he tried next door. The Marines from Charlie Company were waiting for him. He asked, "What the hell is going on? How can I help?" "There are guys who've been bleeding for two hours. If we don't get them out of here right away, they're gonna die."

Peeples turned the turret of his tank sideways so that the wounded could be laid on the flat, exposed part of the tank and be driven back to the position north of the bridge. He offered to drive slowly with the tank protecting the Marines on one side. The Marines decided not to walk back alongside the tank. Peeples thought that they could hold out a little longer. He climbed back aboard and promised: "We'll get the rest of you out of there soon enough."

Grabowski, at his forward CP, heard that a Huey had seen some marines on the roof of a house off Ambush Alley. He began to plan a rescue which he would put into operation as soon as the vehicles had been pulled out of the bog. As he was explaining his plan, Major Sosa could see Iraqi civilians walking around the edge of the open area where they had stopped. Other Iraqis were waving flags from rooftops. He didn't know if this signified hostile intent or if they were acting as a screen for *fedayeen*.

As Captain Brooks' convoy passed the house, Ortiz was hit on the helmet by a round which had ricocheted off a wall. The round went round the back of the helmet and penetrated it, but came out of the top without touching his head. Ortiz blacked out. Robinson had seen him drop and realized that someone in the convoy had shot at them.

But as the last vehicle in the convoy drew abreast of their position, a gunnery sergeant in a Humvee spotted them. He drew up to the house. It was gunnery sergeant Jason Doran. "What do you need?" Worthington replied: " Water. We need water. And radio batteries."

The gunnery sergeant ran around to the back of the Humvee to fish out what they had asked for. He threw a five-gallon can of water and a pack of batteries into the house. "I'll be back."

The can was empty and they were the wrong batteries.

Robinson tried another trip to the track. His efforts to find supplies came to an end when Fribley's body got in the way. When he tried to move it, it just came apart in his hands, spilling intestines all over the floor and his hands and arms. It was getting dark.

When the Alpha Company convoy crossed the northern bridge, Captain Brooks looked for Captain Wittnam. Captain Brooks began to set up a stronger defence with his FAC and 81mm mortars. The tanks quickly suppressed the incoming fire, as they had done as soon as they arrived

at the Euphrates bridge. Staff Sergeant Pomposs was looking for the rest of his men when he ran into Gunnery
Sergeant Jason Doran. Doran told him: "There are some
Marines inside the city. I just drove past them. They are
from Charlie Company. Help me clean this Humvee up."

Castleberry saw five Humvees coming towards them.
They were the CAAT Humvees, led by the same gunnery
sergeant they had seen earlier. Gunnery Sergeant Doran
ran to the house and shouted at Worthington: "Hey, man,
why didn't you say you needed out of here the first time?"

Worthington couldn't think of an answer. "Well, let's get
the fuck out of here now."

The Marines piled into the Humvees. As they left they
fired off all their remaining ammo. During the three-minute drive back to the northern bridge a wall of lead flew out
from both sides of the convoy.

At the "shitbog", M88 tank retrievers had arrived. This
time a couple of tank crew reconned the route on foot. But
just as they pulled out the last enmired tank out, the tank
retrievers began to get stuck. Just before nightfall the C7
Command and Control vehicle and an M88 tank retriever
were still stuck.

Grabowski, at his forward CP, had seen the Alpha convoy pass. He gave permission for his artillery liaison officer
to target the areas of the city which were the sources of
hostile fire. Until then they had not been firing into civilian
areas unless a target was positively identified. The fighting
of the last five hours had changed that. The artillery fire
had the required effect.

Grabowski finally abandoned the stuck vehicles and
moved out. As they drove up Ambush Alley they stopped
by the wreck of AAV 201. They recovered Fribley's remains and loaded it onto a Humvee.

As soon as the Alpha Company convoy had arrived the
situation north of the bridge had been transformed. To
Lance Corporal Thomas Quirk it was as if someone had
called a "time-out". He started looking for the other
members of his team, Fribley, Martin and Olivas. Helicopters were coming in to collect casualties. Quirk saw

Fribley's body covered by the Stars and Stripes, then saw a TV cameraman filming and screamed at him. Private First Class Brian Woznicki tried to calm him down: "It's okay. Leave it. He's just doing his job."

The vehicles that had gone into the city to rescue the stranded Marines pulled into the reinforced position. Martin had just got out of a Humvee when he met Quirk. A Marine next to him asked: "Do you know we've been doing this shit for over six hours?"

Captain Dyer was several hundred metres north of the foot of the Saddam Canal bridge. For the past thirty minutes combined arms had really worked. It was conventional warfare again as Dyer took out targets with his tank's main gun and the FAC called in F-16s and A-10s to take out targets to the north. The pilots identified dug-in positions, which enabled the tank crews to call in targets for artillery fire. These took out the mortar and artillery batteries that had been firing at them from within the complex Dyer was facing.

Dyer noticed that the battalion's vehicles were concentrated too tightly around the foot of the Saddam Canal bridge. They could have been wiped out by a single direct hit. He called back to the main CP. He received another frustrating response from the battalion staff.

Dyer felt that at least it was quiet enough to let his driver open his hatch. As soon as he did, a mortar round landed close enough to splatter his face with mud. The driver ducked back down and closed his hatch.

Sergeant Schaeffer met up with Lieutenant Tracy. They shared a cigarette. Schaeffer was close to breaking down. Tracy reassured him: "You did what you thought was right. At least you were able to let them know of the situation at the northern bridge."

When Grabowski assembled his company commanders, only Charlie Company reported casualties: nine dead, twelve wounded and nine missing. The full count would be eighteen killed and over thirty-five injured.

Captain Newland of Bravo Company and his FAC "Mouth" came towards Grabowski. They told the battalion commander what they thought had happened. He said:

"We are going to report this, and there will be an investigation. You did what you thought was correct, but war is a confusing bloody mess."

The investigation cleared the A-10 pilots of any wrongdoing. "Mouth", the Bravo Company FAC, was held responsible for the incident.

Grabowski had to use the satellite radio to reach Colonel Bailey at regimental headquarters. The VHF radio would not reach that far. He gave him the latest estimates of dead, wounded and missing. He added: "Tell General Natonski that we've got his damn bridges. Timberwolf 6 out."

The Iraqi infantry Division in Nasiriyah had fought in an unconventional way, but the MAGTF's individual units had responded in an equally unconventional manner.

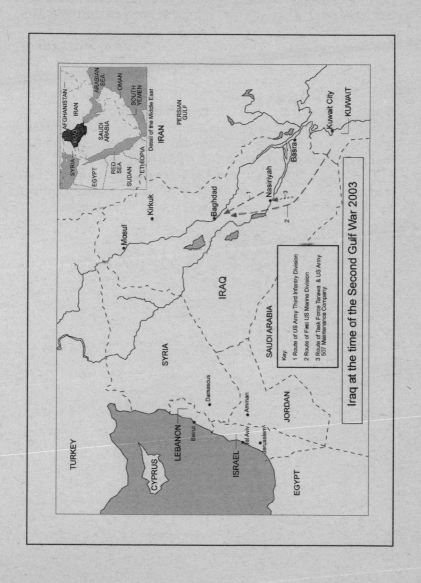

Iraq at the time of the Second Gulf War 2003

Key:
1 Route of US Army Third Infantry Division
2 Route of First US Marine Division
3 Route of Task Force Tarawa & US Army
507 Maintenance Company

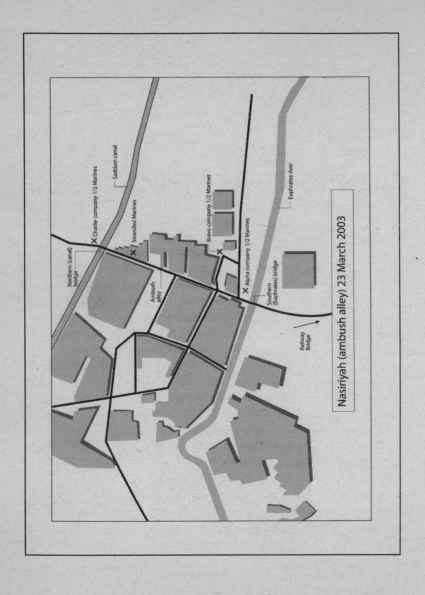

Nasiriyah (ambush alley) 23 March 2003

# FACE TO FACE WITH THE IRA (1970s)

*During the 1970s Duncan Falconer was a Special Boat Service (SBS) operative. Although the SBS operatives are specialists in maritime operations, they have been frequently sent for undercover duty in Northern Ireland.*

*In Northern Ireland SBS operatives served under cover with Military Intelligence detachment 14. They called it "the Det". While on a tour of duty with the Det, Falconer was manning an Observation Post (OP) in South Armagh, near the border with the Irish republic.*

*An Active Service Unit (ASU) was a Provisional Irish Republican Army (PIRA) unit.*

*It was early in the morning. Falconer was on foot, on the border, not far from the village of Crossmaglen. He had been watching a farmhouse, which they suspected was being used as a staging post for arms smuggling across the border. It was a two-man patrol; Falconer's partner was an operative called Max.*

*At dawn Falconer emerged from his hide in snow-covered bushes. He was wearing a donkey jacket over a thick woolly polo-neck and jeans with thermal underwear and long johns. His clothes were grubby and his long hair was matted. He still had bits of food in his beard from the previous night's meal. He had eaten the food cold in a frozen ditch.*

*They were moving out at first light rather than in the dark because they suspected that the area was booby-trapped. Falconer was heading for the pick-up point a hundred yards away. His job was to make a reconnaissance of the pick-up point while Max packed up their optical equipment and brought in the explosive devices they always placed around their position. These were miniature Claymore mines: shaped charges that fired hundreds of tiny fragments of metal outwards. Their purpose was to prevent the operatives from being caught unawares.*

*Falconer had left his M16 and back pack in a ditch where they could wait for their pick-up. He was moving through a thicket hedge because they always avoided gates, stiles or easy paths in case they had been mined. The international border was marked by a sagging three strand barbed-wire fence on the other side of the road. The countryside was divided into small fields. Falconer was looking for somewhere to place a signal marker which their pick-up driver would recognize. As he crouched to place the marker he noticed a movement a hundred yards away. He saw two men climbing through the hedge directly in front of him. They had seen him too. Falconer:*

I scanned in search of others. There was no sign. They could have been farmers, but there was something about them, the way they were watching me. A ripple of concern passed through me, but ripples of concern were always doing that in this job. You learned to do nothing unless the skin broke and you were drowning in the stuff. I stood to face them and put both hands in my coat pockets. I did not want to go back for my M16 because it would mean turning my back on them, nor did I want to risk getting stalled by the thicket – if these were boyos they were close enough to run forward and take a shot at me. Anyhow, one of the tricks of undercover work was never to overreact. They might just nod "good day" and pass me by. My left hand went to my hidden radio and my right was through the pocket of my jacket, which I had removed, to grip my 9mm

Browning pistol in its holster underneath. I could fire it without having to draw it out of my pocket if I had to, not the most accurate but definitely the quickest method to get off a shot, which was often all that counted. I wondered where Max was.

The two men also had their hands in their coat pockets. I didn't recognize them – if they were boyos they were none I had worked against before. They headed directly for me and stopped a few feet apart at the waist-high border fence, their eyes never leaving me. Their breath, like mine, was a thick steam. The width of the country lane was the distance that separated us – them in the Republic, me in Ulster.

They were older, in their forties I reckoned, their faces craggy and weathered. They scanned around, looking to see if I was alone. Both were cool and cordial but I could sense an arrogance and a malevolence. They were definitely suspicious of me.

"How yer doin'?" one said.

"Fine," I replied.

"What ye doin' out here?" said the other.

"I'm waiting for some mates," I said.

When they heard my London accent any doubts they had as to who or what I was disappeared. There was only one kind of Englishman who hangs around the Irish border in bandit country at dawn wearing civvies and looking as if he'd been out all night. I could not disguise my English accent – it was pointless trying to. A professional actor would have trouble fooling these people with a put-on accent. That's why this job was the most difficult intelligence-gathering of its type in the world. You could not ask anyone questions or strike up an innocent conversation without revealing you were not one of them. I felt certain they were boyos, if not official, then highly prejudiced sympathizers. If they did suspect I was a British undercover man – an SAS man, as they called all of us – they would also expect me to be armed. If so they were too confident not to be armed themselves.

"You're a long way from home, Englishman."

As I answered I triggered my radio, which transmitted

everything I said. "My home goes all the way up to that fence you're standing behind."

My voice boomed over the speaker in South Det operations room, some 80 miles away, and jolted out of his reverie the only occupant of the room, the duty bleep (signaller), who had been sitting back reading a book.

As it was early and my operation, which was closing down, was the only one going on that morning, everyone else in the Det was in bed or having breakfast. The duty bleep wheeled his chair over to the operations wall, which was covered with a giant map, and looked at the only operation marker on it, on the border, indicating my location. I never met a signaller assigned to the 14 Int Dets who wasn't as sharp as a razor. They were not trained as operatives, but knew all there was to know about our side of it. He realized I was having a conversation with a local and knew we avoided this type of contact. If I was transmitting the conversation it meant I was trying to tell the Det something.

He punched an intercom which connected him to the rooms of all relevant personnel and said, "I think we've got a standby! I repeat, standby, standby."

Bodies dived out of beds or from the cookhouse or TV room and rushed to the ops room. Within half a minute every member of the operations staff was there. "Standby" was the most serious transmission you could send over the radio. Everyone else on the net automatically went silent to clear the airwaves. It meant an operative was about to unavoidably engage with the enemy. The next thing the ops room expected to hear was shooting. The ops staff always felt helpless in these situations because they could hear and talk to a lone operative in trouble, but could do little else to help. And it was not as if the man on the other end of the radio was a stranger, either. We drank, ate, worked, mourned and celebrated together, and all they could do now was listen and hope that when the shooting stopped, it was the familiar voice that came back over the speaker to say he was OK. This was not always the case.

"Who are you?" I asked.

There was no doubt in my mind now that they were boyos. The aggression was seeping from their pores. One of them was clenching his jaw, holding himself back, waiting. They had either not quite decided if I was alone, or they were carefully choosing their moment.

They had no idea they were being listened to 80 miles away, and they no doubt intended to dust me anyhow. They felt in control. As they talked, I kept my radio on "send" and their voices were picked up by the highly sensitive microphone and transmitted to the operations room.

"Michael's the name."

Michael, the one who was clenching his jaw, did not appear to be the leader of the two, but he looked the most eager to have a go. The other quietly stared at me, more intelligent and calculating than Michael. The comms room didn't quite catch the name and I repeated it, at the same time stepping slightly forward so the men's voices could be picked up better. I found myself repeating much of what they said.

"You shy?" I asked the other man, who did not appreciate being talked to like that.

"Cassidy. Jimmy Cassidy," he said confidently.

In the ops room our intelligence officer, still in his pyjamas, jotted down the name and hurried off to check it.

"Where's your mates?" Cassidy asked.

"They'll be along," I said.

"Will they, now?" asked Michael.

Our pick-up car was still some 20 miles away and the driver was going like the clappers to get to me, fully aware of what was going on as he listened to the transmissions. I was feeling edgy. Whoever started the shooting would have the advantage. I was daring myself, looking for an excuse to start. My adrenaline was rising. Things were starting to seem like they were taking for ever. I decided to move first and destroy the bastards, but something was holding me back. A doubt, perhaps, that I was all wrong about what was going on. I rehearsed the move in my mind. I would hit Michael first. All I needed was a tiny excuse to start. Then the intelligence officer's voice came through my earpiece and brought me back.

"I've got two possible Jimmy Cassidys of South Armagh. How old is he?" Then, quickly realizing I couldn't talk directly to him, he said, "Is your man in his twenties, would you say?"

I kept silent.

"In his forties?"

I clicked the radio twice.

"That's a yes," said the bleep.

Michael and Jimmy could not hear the transmissions, obviously. They said something to me, but I just stared at them, concentrating on what the intelligence officer was telling me.

"One of the Jimmy Cassidys I have is forty-seven. His hair is thinning – a high forehead."

I clicked twice.

"He's five-ten, stocky, round-faced, about eleven stone."

I clicked twice. Cassidy said something to me during the transmission. I heard myself say, "What?" and continued to listen to the intelligence officer and Cassidy at the same time.

"If it's our Cassidy he runs his own ASU."

"I said, what are you doing out here?" asked Cassidy, repeating his question.

"The other man is more than likely one of his team. Try Michael Doherty."

"Are you deaf? Cassidy asked.

"I told you. Waiting for some friends."

Michael moved away from Jimmy, stretching the gap between them to a few yards. They were dividing up – getting closer to making their move. I decided if one of them made an attempt to climb over the fence I'd take advantage of his hands being occupied and engage the other first.

"Doherty is thirty-five. Dark curly hair. His eyebrows meet."

I clicked twice and decided to take a different tack.

"You're Michael Doherty, aren't you?" I said.

Michael's reaction confirmed it.

"Yeah, it is Doherty, isn't it?" I was speaking to the intelligence officer in reality.

Michael was staring at me, wondering how I knew him. I'd stalled him.

The intelligence officer started to rattle off information from his file.

"What are you doing here yourself, Jimmy? Bit early for you, isn't it? Don't you live in Armagh? Hall Street, I believe . . . number seventy-seven."

Jimmy's eyes narrowed.

"Two-twenty-four Saggart Road. That's where you live, Michael – when you're this side of the border, that is. Isn't that right? With your sister and her husband."

Michael flashed a look at Jimmy. I talked to the two men as if I were recalling their details from memory, repeating what was said to me over the net.

"How's your brother doing, Jimmy? Another five years and he's out . . . perhaps."

Both men were off balance.

"And how's the bomb-making school doing?" I continued to Jimmy. "I understand you're specializing in mortars these days."

"Who the fuck are you?" Michael asked.

I had nowhere else to go with this. They were no doubt stunned that I knew so much about them. Then I heard a familiar voice break over the radio.

"I'm twenty yards behind you, Duncan, on your left."

It was Max. He had heard everything over his own radio and had run then crawled as close as he could without being detected. He would have his M16 pointed at them.

"If they show armour I'll unzip the fucker on the left," he said.

I now felt in control. My confidence in Max was total. Their lives were in my hands. A desire to goad them into a fight nickered across my mind. Max would take out Michael. I would take out Jimmy. But that's not the way I am. I'm not a murderer, which is what it would have been had I gone for it. We could have got away with it, too. I could have said they had drawn first. We could have upped our score. I could have killed them for Jack and several other friends who had been killed by the IRA over the years. But body counts don't win wars. They are won by convincing the other side they cannot succeed.

"There's a rifle pointed directly at you," I said. "Either one of you takes a hand from his pocket and you'll both lose your heads."

They took this information well and I could see by the subtle change in their faces that they had no doubt I was telling the truth. Perhaps they read the booming confidence in my threat.

"I'm gonna do you a favour today. Now fuck off the way you came."

They communicated to each other with silent looks. Jimmy nodded to me, then they stepped back and walked away.

# FREED BY CHANCE (2006)

*A hostage no one knew was missing was freed by US forces looking for insurgents. On New Year's Eve of 2006 a British reporter kidnapped in Iraq was rescued by US forces. Two weeks later he described his captivity and his unconventional rescue.*

*The kidnapped reporter described how his captors threatened to behead him before he was freed by chance when US soldiers raided the farmhouse where he was being held.*

A British reporter, Phil Sands, was working for the Dubai newspaper *Emirates Today,* when he was kidnapped and held for five days on the outskirts of Baghdad.

At the time of his rescue on New Year's Eve he had not been reported missing and his family was unaware of his plight.

During his captivity he had been forced to make a video calling for British withdrawal and the release of all detainees in Iraqi prisons, but his captors had not distributed it before their arrest.

Throughout his captivity Mr Sands, 28, was convinced that he would be killed. At one point he was led to a deep pit and assumed that he was about to be shot. US soldiers found a large sword and an orange boiler suit similar to those worn by other murdered hostages.

He is the only British hostage to have been freed during a military operation and whose captors have been caught. Captain Eric Clarke, a US military spokesman, described his case as "frankly amazing".

Mr Sands was kidnapped on Boxing Day on his way to interview academics in Baghdad. About ten armed men in masks forced his car to stop in a desolate suburb and bundled him into the boot of another car. The reporter, who has covered the Iraq conflict for three years, said: "From the moment I was taken hostage, I was certain I would be killed. A strange calmness fell over me. I thought, 'What is the point in panicking? I am dead'."

He was taken to a house where he was handcuffed and blindfolded. "They asked who I was, what I was doing there. I told them my name. I told them I was a journalist," he said. His captors said that they would check and, if he turned out to be a soldier, they would kill him.

They said that they were Sunnis, the minority to which most insurgents belong. They gave him a bed and fed him well. He worried about his parents, David and Jackie, who live in Poole, Dorset, and tried not to think about dying.

About 2.30 a.m. on New Year's Eve, he heard helicopters. The door flew open and two US soldiers burst in, yelling at him and his guard to stand up. Only when he saw how surprised the Americans were to see him did he realize how lucky he had been. They were on a routine search for insurgents and had found him by chance.

He was flown to Dubai where British security services questioned him for seven days. "We went very thoroughly through what happened. They've got all those outstanding hostage cases in Iraq," he said, referring to hostages such as Norman Kember, 74, the British peace activist who was snatched with three other foreigners on November 26.

Mr Sands was in Poole with his family when he said: "One of the things I am most glad about is that my parents did not know that I had been kidnapped. It was a weird phone call, to say the least. Dad picked up the phone and was amazed that I had bothered to call. They are always complaining that I do not get in touch enough."

He had no immediate plans to return to Iraq, but when he did it would be as an embedded reporter with the military. He said: "I feel fine. I was lucky. I'm definitely taking a stiff-upper-lip approach. I don't feel traumatized, just humbled."

# DRUGS BUST BY THE
# SPECIAL BOAT SERVICE (1995)

*The Special Boat Section (SBS) was originally formed for special operations of a maritime nature during the Second World War. After the war the Special Boat Section was maintained as a special operations unit. It recruited its members from the Royal Marines and continued to undertake maritime special ops. Later the title of the unit was changed to the Special Boat Squadron. Its current official title is the Special Boat Service.*

*Peter Mercer joined the Royal Marines in 1988. After his basic Marine training, he completed Royal Marine Commando training. This entitled him to wear the green beret. After serving with 40 Royal Marine Commando (battalion) he volunteered for the SBS. He was selected after passing first SAS training and the SBS' own induction process.*

*In 1995 Peter Mercer was taking part in an SBS anti-terrorist exercise in Essex. He was told to report to a secret location near SBS headquarters in Poole, Dorset. Their CO told them that it was a rush job, a drugs bust off the south coast.*

*A police escort was on its way but they needed to get moving. A full briefing would follow later. Mercer:*

We ran over to the armoury and picked up all our weapons. Whenever we left Poole to go on exercises, we always took with us a complete kit because we never knew where or when we would be needed. It was assumed that most of the operations would call for immediate action, where minutes were vital, and we needed to have everything with us so we could be on the road within an hour, ready for action.

Not only did we keep our personal weapons in the armoury, but everything else as well, including explosives, entry charges, linear cutting gear and ammunition. As always, we stored our weapons in one van, our ammunition in the second and the explosives in a third. We always travelled in convoy like this for safety reasons. We clambered into a fourth van and set off. Police cars and outriders, with sirens blaring and blue lights flashing, took up positions ahead and behind the convoy. We sped through red traffic lights, the wrong way round roundabouts and the Dartmouth tunnel had been closed so that we could swoop through at high speed. They didn't want to risk us being held in some traffic jam halfway into the tunnel. Most of the time, we sped along at about 90mph in the specially adapted Ford Transit vans, equipped with 2.9 litre V6 fuel-injection engines churning out 165 brake horse power.

It was great racing along at such speed, knowing that we were breaking the speed limit every mile of the way – and with the police urging us on to go faster. But we did have one serious scare. Paul was driving flat out at the time when a car pulled out unexpectedly, a few seconds after the police vehicles had flashed past. Without giving any signal or warning, the car edged out into the centre of the road. Paul took immediate action, swerving to avoid the car that was only travelling slowly. But he could not react quickly enough and we clipped the side of the vehicle. We drove on, followed by the other three team vans. We looked back to see the driver shaking his fist at us, grimacing angrily. We didn't stop, nor did we even contemplate stopping. I have no idea what damage we did to the car but, thankfully, we never heard anything about the smash.

As we drove down the M3, it was decided to launch the raid on the unknown vessel from our Poole headquarters. On arrival, we learned that this mission was a major drug bust but that no helicopters would be used, only three RIBs. This was going to be fun.

It took two hours of dedicated, hard work to prepare the three RIBs for the mission. In addition to SBS personnel, each RIB carried police officers from SO19. These officers would be the first to jump from the boat, to lead the assault and make the arrests. It was intended that we would be on hand as back-up, but fully armed and in our traditional all-black SBS kit with balaclavas and, of course, our handguns. The SBS officers had argued with the police that it would be better to let the SBS go in first, capture the drug-runners and then call in the police units. The police decided, however, that this drug bust was their responsibility and they wanted to make the arrests, keeping the SBS as back-up if trouble arose.

We looked at each other and winked. We knew the police officers fancied making the initial arrests to enable them to take the glory. We weren't worried because we preferred to play the background role, stealthily going about our business with ruthless efficiency, without anyone realizing that the SBS had been involved.

With everything packed and ready to go, the CO walked in to give us a full briefing. "We know that the drugs gang we are going after tonight is a serious, international group of men who have been involved in drug smuggling over a number of years. They are not only involved in drugs but they are also wanted for other serious crimes committed across Europe."

Then we were briefed by an army lawyer. His words of wisdom, which we were given before every single mission, warned us of the legal problems we could face if we became involved in a gun battle.

"If you get involved in a gunfight and people get injured or killed, then on no account must anyone say a word until I get to the scene. Answer no questions whatsoever; no matter if you are being questioned by Army or Navy officers or even high-ranking police officers. It is vital for what might follow those shootings that you say nothing until I have debriefed you in full. OK?"

We all nodded. We knew the score. In effect, the army lawyer was telling us to "trust no one".

At 2200 hours, we made our way down to the RIBs, along with our police officers who were all dressed as we were. There was one important difference, however. They insisted on wearing extensive body armour, which was very effective in stopping high-velocity rounds but totally useless in practice because the armour was so heavy and cumbersome, making movements slow and ponderous. On such missions, we only ever wore light body armour because we were then able to move around at speed, climb ropes fast and, if necessary, tackle a gunman using unarmed combat skills. With full body armour we wouldn't have been able to carry out any of these skills with any speed whatsoever, thus putting our lives at risk.

Having carried out one further check, we were assembled waiting for the order to go. For two more hours, we gently floated around, the engines idling, waiting for the off. It was a cold February night and, despite the thermals we were wearing, we all began to feel the chill wind insinuating our bones. The swear words became more frequent as everyone grew increasingly pissed off with every passing minute. We kept checking our watches, which seemed to be ticking at a snail's pace. Some of us cracked open our flasks, and I took a few gulps from mine, which contained hot, strong, black coffee with lots of sugar to help keep up the levels.

There was one good point in our favour. The long wait enabled some of the lads who had considered joining the police force to talk with the two officers, asking their opinions, finding out the attractions and the down side of life as a police officer. But even that conversation eventually dried up and we were left to clock-watch once more. For three more hours we continued bobbing around Poole Harbour, the engines still ticking over quietly, gur-

gling away in the black water. By 0400 hours we had come
to the conclusion that this had been another boring, wasted
night and we expected to be "stood down" at any moment.

I had all but lost interest when over the "net" came the
news that the target vessel had been picked up by radar and
was on its way along the English Channel towards us. The
boss gave us 15 minutes to collect our shit and get everything ready once more. For one final time we checked our
weapons and ammunition, our communications equipment
and personal belongings. But this time we had to be ready
for instant action.

We knew that, high above the clouds, a Nimrod reconnaissance aircraft had detected the target vessel and that,
eventually, we would be guided to its location. Then we
would take over for the final, flat-out push to the ship and
the assault. We were given a heading to follow and then,
minutes later, the warning order came through. We were
within seconds of taking off. We pulled on our balaclavas
and cocked our weapons. We were ready. The intention was
to circle the target ship slowly and silently at some distance,
and then approach it, hoping that the crew and any lookouts
wouldn't notice us until it was too late. We set off.

Suddenly, the whole fucking area was flooded with
brilliant light, as the four RIBs were caught in the full
glare of a helicopter's powerful spotlight. We had been lit
up like a fucking Christmas tree, exposed to everyone on the
target ship who happened to switch their attention to a
helicopter suspiciously hovering around at some ungodly
hour looking for goodness knows what! We believed in that
instant that Customs officers in the chopper above had
unwittingly given the game away and exposed us. It tran-
spired that the stupid Customs men on board the Sea King
believed they were helping us because they had "lost" the
target vessel and had decided to switch on the spotlight to
find it. They hadn't focused on the poor SBS blokes below
who were risking their necks putting a raiding party on
board a ship that was under the command of dangerous and
armed drug smugglers.

Unbelievably, the Customs men had been unaware that

we had already located the vessel, knew precisely the course it was sailing, and were positioning ourselves to make the attack. It was obvious that no one had fully appreciated that such an action might alert the crew we were trying to catch off-guard. Such actions gave the drug-runners the option of making a run for it or simply dumping the drugs overboard and pleading innocent. We would have been able to prove nothing without the evidence. The curses poured from our mouths.

Jokingly, one of the lads shouted up to the chopper, "Why didn't you just phone the fuckers first and tell them we were on our way?" We all laughed, but it had been a serious error that could have put SBS lives at risk.

The boss got on to the "net" and radiocd Poole headquarters, telling them what had happened and emphasizing that the Customs men aboard the chopper had put the entire mission at risk. A message was immediately flashed from Poole to the chopper, telling them to shut off the light and piss off out of the area until called for. Seconds later, the spotlight was doused and the chopper flew away. We waited around for a few minutes, expecting the job to be called off and waiting for orders to return to base as the mission had been seriously compromised. But no.

Thirty minutes later, still awaiting orders, the "net" opened up.

"Target vessel has been lost to radar but understood it could be near your position."

We asked what type of vessel we were searching for.

"It's an RIB like yours but exact size or power unknown."

I shut off the engine until it was barely idling and we all strained our ears trying to pick up the sound of another RIB powering away not far from our location. Our three RIBs scattered, trying to cover as great an area as possible, as we searched for the target boat. I could see the other RIBs bobbing gently about, sailing along at only a few knots, searching for the missing boat. But within a few minutes I even lost sight of our black-and-grey RIBs because they blended in so well with the shore as a background.

Suddenly, a voice came over the "net". "Look over by the yacht club. Lights. They look like tail lights of a vehicle parked near the sea. That could be our men."

I grabbed the night-sights and peered into the darkness. Suddenly I caught them. It was the back of a $4 \times 4$ Land Rover or something similar. It seemed to be manoeuvring to get a boat out of the water.

That was all the evidence the boss wanted. "Go, go, go," he shouted, "I repeat, go, go, go."

I nailed the throttle and we took off towards the yacht club, weaving in and out of the yachts and boats moored haphazardly in the bay, swerving all over the place, missing some of them by inches as I tried to maintain our top speed and keep the bloody RIB upright. The last thing I wanted to do was overstew it and end up in the bloody water. I was concentrating hard, straining every muscle to keep the RIB going at a flat-out rate of knots. The lads were sitting in their positions, their hands gripping the grab handles for dear life, their feet under straps on the bottom preventing them being bounced around too much. Riding an RIB at that speed and throwing it around every few yards knocks the hell out of everyone on board. It's no picnic but hard, fucking work simply trying to sit still, riding the horrendous bumps and jolts as the boat crashes through the waves. Some SBS guys end up with serious back injuries riding the RIBs at speed.

Within ten minutes or so, all three RIBs were inside the marina and we could clearly see a group of men desperately trying to pull a boat out of the water and attach it to the back of a $4 \times 4$ vehicle.

There was only one way to capture this lot and that was to drive the RIB on to the beach, leap out and arrest the men who were surrounding the vehicle and boat. I slammed the RIB into neutral and the boat instantly slowed. We must have been travelling at around 20mph when we hit the beach, and the RIB came to an abrupt halt in the soft sand.

As ordered, the two police officers were the first out of our boat, leaping on to the sand. But the gear they were carrying, including their personal weapons, and the heavy body armour proved too much for them. As they landed, they simply fell head-first into the sand. That was the end of their parlour game; their glory days were over. The lads jumped from the boat and used the backs of the fallen coppers as a springboard to leap on to the sand. As each SBS guy leapt from the boat on to the backs of the coppers, they pushed the police officers deeper into the sand, ignoring their cries for help. There was no time to stop and help them. As far as we were concerned these smugglers in front of us may have been armed and dangerous.

Our only thought was to arrest them, grab their weapons and secure any drugs that might be on the boat or in the $4 \times 4$. The cops could take care of themselves.

"Lie down, get down," we shouted at the bunch of men who turned to face us. The men seemed too shocked to move. They simply stared at us, their mouths open, a look of fear in their eyes as 18 men all dressed in black overalls with machine pistols in their hands came racing towards them.

We screamed at them, "Get on the fucking floor now . . . lie face down . . . don't fuckin' move . . . stay still or you're dead."

At one time there were maybe five or six of us shouting and swearing at the men, deliberately shocking them, making them feel nervous and vulnerable. Other SBS men ran into the buildings and outhouses, searching for other accomplices, checking out the area in case there were others in hiding. At all times we had to presume that some men on that mission would be armed. What we didn't know was whether they would be stupid enough to use their weapons on us. If they had done so we would have taken them out without a second thought.

One man stood stock still looking at us, not moving a muscle, paying no heed to our orders, so someone went up to him and gave him a right cross, knocking him senseless. He crumpled to the ground and didn't move, so someone kicked him, yelling at him to lie on his face and keep still. Another man looked up to see what was going on, so he received a good, hard kick on the side of the head and was told to lie face down. Not surprisingly, he obeyed. As one SBS man went to put plasticuffs around a suspect's hands and feet, another man began to sit up. As if from nowhere, an SBS man sent him flying, catching him under the chin with the full force of his boot.

"When I tell you to lie down, I mean LIE DOWN," he screamed at him. "If you move another muscle you'll be a dead man." And he placed the barrel of his Heckler & Koch on the man's neck, pushing his face into the ground.

"Stay like that," yelled the SBS man. "Don't move a fucking muscle," he warned as the plasticuffs were placed tightly on the man's wrists and ankles.

One by one, we went around the six men, holding the barrel of the machine pistol to the backs of their necks as we asked each of them in turn, "Are you carrying a gun? Is anyone carrying a gun?"

When no one answered, we shouted louder, telling them to yell their answers aloud if they didn't want a bullet in the back of the neck.

"No guns, no guns," they all shouted, their voices quivering with fear.

While half a dozen of us stayed with the prisoners, others checked the boats on the marina, the yacht club, the beach huts, everywhere someone could possibly be hiding or where the prisoners may have stashed their drugs. We found nothing. We searched the $4 \times 4$, a Mitsubishi Shogun, as well as the 22ft-long rigid inflatable, which had a 150hp Yamaha motor capable of moving in excess of 50mph. Nothing was found.

Within five minutes of our arrival on the marina, about 30 police cars came screaming at speed into the yacht club car park and dozens of officers came running across to where we were standing, our guns still pointing towards the men on the ground lying motionless at our feet.

When the senior officers asked who was in charge, we pointed to the hapless cops, who had by now managed to climb to their feet and stagger to the marina where we were standing. Their gear was covered in sand and sea water and they didn't look very happy bunnies. One or two also gave us filthy looks, but they didn't say anything.

Over the following few days, police divers searched the Solent and eventually discovered two tons of cannabis, packed in hessian and wrapped in plastic that the crew must have thrown overboard when they saw the chopper's spotlight searching the sea earlier. As a result of that hit, 13 people from various parts of the country were arrested and tried at the Old Bailey. They were all found not guilty.

There were perhaps three or four major drugs busts every year in which the SBS were called in to take part. Drugs busting became one of our favourite activities because we never knew what reception we would receive whenever we raided a vessel. We were always prepared for the worst – a serious fire-fight – but thankfully that hardly ever occurred. On most occasions we received very little opposition from any of the crews ferrying the illicit drugs, but SBS senior officers believed the principal reason for that was the manner in which we had been trained to carry out such raids.

# WARRENPOINT (1979)

*Nigel "Spud" Ely joined the Parachute Regiment in 1978.
After being trained he was assigned to the second Battalion (2
Para) and was sent to Northern Ireland with 2 Para in 1979.
On 27 August 1979 he was part of the Quick Reaction Force
(QRF), which was on standby to respond to any major
incident.*

*Two four-ton trucks and a Land Rover from A company, 2
Para were on their way to help with a route clearance operation. As they approached the Warrenpoint-to-Newry dual
carriageway they passed a trailer loaded with hay, parked in a
lay-by. The trailer was parked at the nearest point to the
border with the Republic of Ireland along that stretch of road.
A 500-pound bomb in the trailer was detonated by radio
control. The explosion caught the rear four-ton truck, leaving
only a tangled mess. Six men from A company were killed. The
first reports from the scene suggested that there were only two
survivors.*

*Ely was told to get his vehicle ready for a fast drive to the
incident; then his orders were changed. The QRF was to be
taken in two Wessex helicopters. Ely:*

I had only been in the province a couple of months so, although I had seen a few things, nothing had prepared me for the next 24 hours. It was to be the rudest awakening to the consequences of terrorism.

The chopper blades were already turning when we made the short tab from the compound to the helipad, the only place where you had to leave the relative safety of the compound. It always struck me as strange and stupid to have the only means of transport to get you into "bandit country" detached and in a seemingly insecure site. (Some years later when I was back at Bessbrook with the SAS, things had not changed.)

As always, the Wessex strained to gain height to clear the high wire fencing which was the helipad's only protection from a rocket attack. Though it might be only for a short take-off time, we were now at our most vulnerable. The chopper shuddered and whined as it rose. The loadie was hanging out of the only door, directing the pilot over the top of the last part of the fence, a two-foot stack of razor wire. When he was sure the wheels were clear he closed the door. We were expecting an overnight stay so we had our bergens (rucksacks) as well as the usual complement of weapons, ammunition and webbing.

It was impossible to talk over the noise of the chopper. We were flying low-level and the pilot's actions indicated he was taking this particular task very seriously. He was flying into a hot DZ and we all didn't fancy being shot out of the sky by a fluke Rocket Propelled Grenade (RPG) attack.

Back at the incident, two Land Rover patrols from the Machine Gun Platoon, on patrol around Newry at the time, had also been dispatched. My mate Gerry was in that patrol. I remember hearing him on the radio, back at the Ops room, his voice full of seriousness at the thought of being first to arrive at the site.

The chopper ride lasted about 15 minutes, and I had time to reflect on what we were approaching. This was my first major incident and it was hard to deal with knowing that I was going to be confronted with my first sight of death. It could have been any of the Security Forces lying there. It made it harder when they were blokes you knew. Good mates. Paratroopers.

I gripped my SLR with both hands and squeezed my knees together, gaining some comfort from the thought that I had the protection of 100 7.62mm rounds to fire, should the shit hit the fan. The M79 grenade launcher I slung over my back gave me added security as it cut into my old parachuting wound. I could see Brummie becoming more agitated in a conversation with the navigator. He eased himself back down and shouted into Taff's ear. The message was passed along with a look of disbelief. "There's another bomb gone off in the same area. No word of any casualties. The pilots going to land us as close as possible, without ripping the arse out of it, and once he dumps us off he's fucking off, back to bring in more backup."

There seemed to be a tone of apprehension in his voice. The message had been passed down three blokes before it got to me, and I was just thinking what to make of it all when suddenly the loadie made a move to the door. The chopper banked violently and shuddered. The loadie was quick to slide the door open. The noise increased and the effect of cold air from the outside somehow seemed to dispel the fear that we were landing on one hell of a hot DZ. I could see the ground below as the chopper began to descend. With a heavy jolt we hit terra firma. We scrambled out to form an all-round defence position whilst the loadie and the last man threw all the bergens and other pieces of kit out as quickly as possible. Then, within seconds, the Wessex disappeared. The other chopper landed some way off in a different field. This was for security reasons rather than convenience; if the PIRA staged another ambush, two choppers together were a greater target.

When the second bomb had gone off, a Wessex that had landed on the dual carriageway to recover wounded from the first explosion had taken some of the force of the blast, making the pilot of our Wessex think very hard about our safety. This bomb was thought to be twice the size of the first: a 1,000-pounder.

I looked around to get my first real experience of a terrorist attack. The smell was incredible. The only way I could have explained it would be a fresh morning after Bonfire Night, mixed with an acrid barbecue odour – charred human flesh. I could see Brummie talking to a member of the Machine Gun Platoon who had run up on to the field when he saw the chopper land. Brummie beckoned half of us to join him; the rest were to remain at their defensive position. Moving towards Brummie I could see red berets and a couple of policemen who, I reckoned, had been called out from Warrenpoint RUC station, running around crossing the road and shouting to one another. Then more confusion as two other choppers landed. Both sides of the dual carriageway had been sealed off by the RUC. The debris of mangled Land Rovers, four-tonners and 18 soldiers covered the area for hundreds of metres. This scene of total carnage was never to leave me. It was probably the hardest introduction any of us could have had to the horrors of what had been, and quite obviously is still, happening in Northern Ireland. That was the only positive thing I could remember from what I learned that day, 27 August 1979.

Waiting for the rest of the Company to arrive, our immediate task was to secure the area on the far side of the dual carriageway and face outwards towards the Republic. Gerry, my mate in the Machine Guns, came running over to me to tell his account of the past two hours.

"We were out on a mobile." He stopped to get his breath. He was still shaking. "We were just outside Newry when we heard this fuck-off explosion. Jimmy sent the contact report at the same time as a Marine did. We drove like fucking nutters."

"Did you have a clue what was happening?"

"Yeah. We reckoned the PIRA had detonated a fuck-off device but we didn't know jack-shit else. We put two and two together and raced out here towards Warrenpoint to see what was what. When we got here, I mean, shit, there was crap all over the place, just like now, but it was still burning and the blokes were all running around, trying to do a body count and patch up the two survivors."

I asked if he knew any names. He said no, not yet. He only confirmed that it was a platoon from A Company. We were cut short when someone from his platoon called him. "Gerry, get your arse over here. The boss wants to know about the shooting."

"Shooting?" I said. "You've been shooting as well?"

"Yeah, give us a couple of minutes and I'll come back over. I reckon the fuckers are still over there somewhere, waiting to get us with a third bomb." Gerry shot off over towards what was left of an old, stone-built gatehouse, the lodge of a country house, and left me with a feeling of "Fuck, this isn't over yet, by far." The PIRA could have put bombs all over the place and it was possible they were just sitting back in the forest, 100 or so metres across the estuary that divided the North from the South. They could be watching every movement we made.

I quickly looked around to see what the rest of the blokes were up to. They were facing south, watching their arcs of fire. Trying to make myself as small a target as possible and get into cover from view as well as cover from fire, I reminded myself that I was wearing the biggest marker for any would-be sniper, a red beret. Better keep the head moving! I waited nervously for Gerry to come back with more news. The smell of cordite was still thick in the air. It was a hot summer's afternoon with little or no wind so the smell was going to be around for a while. I was breathing heavily, and tried to compose myself and make sense of what I was witnessing. I told myself that many soldiers had seen all this before, but as I lay there looking around at the dismembered bodies, limbs ripped off in a millisecond, guts ripped open by the massive amount of secondary fragmentation. I wondered, Has anybody in this country witnessed carnage on such a colossal scale? I doubted it very much then, and still do.

I tried to make out where the bits of debris immediately around me had come from. A piece of angled metal embedded into the dry-stone wall that I was using as protection I recognized right away: part of an SLR. I pulled it free and stuffed it down the front of my flak jacket. Everywhere I looked I could make out bits of body: the remains of a torso high up in a tree to the right; forward of me, on the estuary's beach, intestines and what looked like half a head, the face side. The explosion had cut the head clean off at the neck and had somehow bisected it from top to bottom. I looked for the back half, but didn't find it. Then Gerry rushed over to me again. I asked what he'd just done.

"Oh, I fired off a few rounds. We were taking incoming when the second bomb went off, so a few of us let rip into the forest over there. I saw two blokes, and taking them to be the firing point, I slotted one and then took cover, but as I did, I must have knocked my sight out of zero. I tried to slot the other fucker but he disappeared back into the forest. The boss wanted to know how many rounds I let rip."

I was looking out across the water but kept nodding, suggesting that I was taking it all in.

"Anyway, we managed to get the wounded into the Wessex which happened to be in the air at the time. He's flying them back to Bessbrook. He landed up there on the road, just past the gatehouse.

"Someone had established the CP at the gatehouse, and as we were all trying to help out, you know, secure the area, there was this horrendous explosion. It threw me over and stunned me for a couple of seconds. The place was covered in shit and stone. The dust didn't settle for ages. You couldn't see fuck all. Shit was still falling for at least half an hour. Well, you can see it's still in the air now." He was right – a cloud of dust and crap was still visible above us.

He went on. "We had a Gazelle landing with the CO QOH" – referring to the Queen's Own Highlanders. He pointed half right to where we were lying. "He was running down to meet the boss when it went up. It took out our Land Rovers which were parked down by the CP."

"Fuck me, Gerry! Who did you lose?"

"Well, we're not sure yet, but at least 15. And we haven't accounted for everybody yet."

Later on during the afternoon, I was detailed, along with the rest of 4 Platoon, to "area clean the incident of human remains". I picked up a pair of boots with the feet still in them, socks pulled up. The blast had neatly cut the legs off at the top of the socks. There was no blood. I could not find the rest of the body. Just a pair of booted feet with about 14 inches of leg still in them. Other blokes were assigned to stand guard over the remains of our mates. The amount of their remains grew and grew as the evening wore on.

Soon I was to learn the full extent of our Battalion's loss. Sixteen Paras and the CO and his signaller of 1 Queen's Own Highlanders. Six blokes that I had come through Depot at Aldershot with had been killed, including my good friend Barney. Another close mate from Depot was badly injured. He had 80 per cent burns and was not expected to live.

*Ely went to visit his friend when he got back to England. His friend recovered but was unable to resume his duties. He had to return to civilian life.*

*On the same day the PIRA killed Lord Louis Mountbatten. The 79-year-old uncle of Queen Elizabeth II was killed when a bomb was detonated on his boat while he was enjoying a holiday in the Republic of Ireland.*

# SPECIAL FORCES'
# FIRST SUCCESS (1991)

*On 23 January 1991 Special Forces achieved their first*
*success in the first Gulf War. At the time General Sir Peter*
*de la Billiere, the commander of the British forces, was still*
*wondering whether it was right to commit them or if they could*
*achieve anything that allied aircraft could not.*

*It was a Special Boat Service (SBS) force which included*
*Don Camsell:*

We were tasked to go into Iraq and sever the country's key
fibre-optic communications link. There was only one snag:
it was only about 25 miles south of Baghdad.

It was going to be a helicopter insertion, the only way of
getting that close to Baghdad and coming back out alive
again. We'd have to stay in there for perhaps as much as two
hours, locate the fibre-optic link, dig down the twelve feet
of sand it was buried under, and cut it with a shaped charge.
To increase our chances of survival, the two CH 47s would
have to remain on the ground with us, 'burning and turning, while we did the job. Which had the paradoxical effect

of making the whole operation even more hazardous, since it is quite difficult to conceal two Chinook CH 47s the size of a small house in the middle of the desert just outside your enemy's capital. And right next to a major access road.

We did our detailed planning and rehearsals at our FOB 19 miles outside Riyadh. The helicopter would have to skirt the big Iraqi armoured formations scattered about in the area. And it would be slow in the air: there would be 35 people on the two CH 47s, plus 3 long-range fuel bladders in the mid-section. Talk about putting all our eggs in one basket. Because of the fuel problem, the mission would be strictly time-limited. If we hadn't completed the task before the cut-off time, we'd have to EXFIL regardless, failed. And no one in SF likes failing.

The first phase was the insertion. Phase two was securing the area. Third phase was finding the comms line in the darkness and then placing the small charge that would blow the cable apart and cover the mess back-up. The fourth and final phase was the exfiltration – coming out!

Working for us was the fact that the task was relatively simple, and the fact that the terrain, where we'd be operating, was slightly undulating. There were low ridges and shallow wadis, and we might be able to at least partially conceal the Chinooks. And we'd have top cover in the shape of a squadron of A-10 tank-busting aircraft, standing off ready to jump any interference.

We had six-man protection groups for each element of the operation that was at risk: one group protecting the CH 47s and their crew; one covering the digging team; the rest of us either digging or providing perimeter security.

We left our FOB at about 2030, arriving on the target about two hours later. We flew at ground level, the aircrew wearing NVGs, flinging this great helicopter around the ridgelines in the darkness. It was difficult not to be airsick. We landed and piled out of the Chinook's tail. The initial security was to protect the big birds as they were our only way out. We cleared the immediate area and then quickly found the tell-tale signs of the cable. So far, so good. It was like a well-oiled machine: everything that we did in the rehearsals was being initiated; not one person had to be redirected; they all knew their jobs. We were all sweating, with nerves or just sheer excitement and we had not started digging yet.

I don't know which company laid the cable, but it must have been friendly to our side, because the location we'd been given for it turned out to be exactly right. There was even a small marker post sticking up out of the desert. We were very aware of the road off to our right, which was teeming with traffic, most of it military supply convoys headed south.

The CH 47 left its engine at idle, the rotors turning slowly, so that it needed only thirty seconds to get them up to full speed and take off. In a matter of seconds we were out, deployed and digging. In my six-man cut-off group, which was tasked with taking care of the diggers shovelling hard and fast in the night, we had three GPMGs, a full set of '66' anti-tank rockets, and 203s – enough to discourage all but a full-blown and very determined armoured assault. All the time, we had the distinctive smell of Avgas in our nostrils, and it struck me that this was our greatest concern. We could hear the faint *swish* of the CH 47's rotors as they were moving around. If one of the drivers on that road over there stopped for a piss and smelled the gas, we could be in trouble.

It seemed to be taking them an age to locate the three-inch black plastic-covered cable, even with the aid of the marker post. And it did take more than an hour after several holes were initially dug. But at last we found it, put the small shaped charge on the link, blew it, made sure it was ruptured, and sanitized the area as best we could. We grabbed a small length of the cable to be analysed on our return and also the marker post, which was presented to "Big Norm". It was a complete success and one that each individual who participated in it can be rightly proud.

A risky operation, but one that was feasible and worth the risk. Charging out into the barren waste in a Land Rover with no real objective? That's another matter.

*Sir Peter de la Billiere described it as: "our first success . . . a high-risk operation, separate from the SAS deployment, carried out by the Special Boat Service with great skill, determination and courage in a most hostile environment."*

*Sir Peter continued: "The first raid made a major contribution towards establishing the reputation and capability not only of our Special Forces but those of America as well."*

# TIGER COUNTRY (1968)

*In 1968 Franklin D. Miller was leading a Special Forces patrol in hostile territory looking for signs of enemy activity. Miller's patrol was mainly Montagnard tribesmen, the original indigenous people of Vietnam. The special forces who trained them called them "Yards" . . .*

Miller's patrol discovered a hilltop position which had been used by the enemy. The slopes of the hill were covered with thousands of puji sticks – bamboo sticks sharpened to a point at one end, and the other is stuck into the ground at an angle. Miller was puzzled. Although they were in South Vietnam they were deep in enemy-controlled territory. The enemy wasn't expecting regular troops to invade the area. What were the puji sticks for?

The next morning they cut a path through the thousands of puji sticks. Then they ran into an enemy formation thirty-five to forty strong. Miller's recon team was only seven men. The enemy put them under heavy fire. There was only tall grass, which gave no cover, so they had to run back the way they had come; despite enemy mortar fire falling ahead of them to block their retreat. They were doing okay until they got to the barrier of puji sticks. By the time his Yards had got through, the enemy had almost caught up with Miller. His Yards kept the enemy occupied as he tried to rush through the deep barrier of puji sticks. But he started too quickly and a puji stick pierced right through his calf. One of his men pulled out the puji stick; blood gushed everywhere and the pain was "indescribable". He knew that stopping would mean capture or death.

They reached the deep jungle and hid for the rest of the day.

The next day, just before daylight, they realized the enemy had found them and were just outside their perimeter. The recon team had set up their Claymore antipersonnel mines so they were prepared for them.

At a prearranged signal, the enemy started firing into the recon team's position, then after a minute or so jumped up to make their assault. The recon team blew up one of their antipersonnel mines and the assault stopped. The recon team waited until light and exchanged a few rounds with their attackers, who were evidently retreating. Miller and his men went to inspect the results of the Claymore explosion.

It was clear that the unit which had attacked them was not able to take on a small, highly mobile, well-armed reconnaissance team like theirs. They found bodies lying on the ground which were poorly armed with a variety of weapons and small quantities of ammunition of doubtful quality. One of them had a MAT-49, an old 9mm French weapon. They thought that it was probably a Pathet Lao tracker unit that was just trying to keep them there until the main element arrived

They discovered that one of the men hit by the Claymore was badly wounded but still alive. Prisoners could be valuable sources of information. Miller told his Yards to carry him but he slowed them down. They carried him for the entire day but the next morning he died, so they left his body.

The weather was "socked in" so they had to wait another day before they could be extracted. But the next day they found themselves in the middle of a storm. It rained heavily and constantly. They were chilled to the bone.

The storm lasted for five days. Miller's leg was hurting him and it looked as though the wound might be going bad. They were making their way to a possible extraction point when they saw some enemy troops. As they were carefully moving around the enemy troops, they came to the place where they had left the body of their prisoner. The body had gone. In the place where the body had been were paw prints. Big ones.

Several of Miller's Yards were excellent trackers. They squatted down beside the paw prints to study them. One of them pointed at the tracks, looked at Miller and said: "Tiger." Something in his voice told Miller that he was seriously spooked. Miller realized that the thousands of puji sticks were a barrier against tigers. It was so deep so that the tigers couldn't leap over it. What was worse was that his Yards considered that the encounter with the tiger was a bad omen.

Later that evening, they became involved in a firefight with a large group of enemy troops. Miller began to wonder if the omen was being fulfilled.Fortunately, they were able to break contact before the enemy had inflicted too much damage, despite firing RPG-7 anti-tank rounds at them.

They reached the extraction point the next morning after an alarmingly quiet night. Miller was relieved to leave tiger country.

# MISTAKEN FOR THE IRA (1993)

*Special Boat Service operatives were often sent to Northern Ireland for security duties. The Special Boat Service was responsible for intercepting arms shipments that were being brought ashore and across the border by boat. A Rigid Raider was a type of Ribbed Inflatable Boat (RIB). Peter Mercer described a incident in which his unit was mistaken for an Irish Republican Army (IRA) unit with consequences which were nearly fatal:*

In March 1993, we were on patrol in Kilkeel, Northern Ireland, detailed to carry out two weeks' patrolling on the streets of Belfast and then two weeks' patrolling Carlingford Lough. It was some time shortly after five o'clock in the afternoon and we were all dying for a cup of tea. We tied up the Rigid Raider and decided to stretch our legs after a nine-hour stint of duty in the boat. We were suffering from cramp and muscle stiffness. We were dressed in army fatigues and carrying our British Army-issue SA80 weapons. We were also wearing our famous black woolly hats.

Unknown to us, we had, in fact, just been sighted by a British Army patrol who believed we were an IRA active service unit on patrol. They reached this conclusion primarily because we were wearing our black woolly hats and old army fatigues, which many IRA active service units also wore. The British patrol were about to open fire on us and had, in fact, cocked their GP machine gun ready to take us out when there was an almighty crash near their position.

They realized that they themselves had come under attack from a totally different direction, with mortar bombs raining down on them as they had taken up their positions preparing to target us. The IRA was firing the mortar bombs at a Royal Irish Regiment [detachment] of about 60 men who were camped on a football pitch next to the local school where a detachment of [Royal] Marines were stationed.

Within a matter of minutes, the extraordinary situation had been analysed and some 24 [Royal] Marines and [Royal] Irish Rangers had been ordered to burst out of the camp and make for the spot where the mortars were being fired. They burst out, spreading into a "star" formation as soon as they were out of the school gates. Armed only with SA80s and MP5s, the men raced towards the spot and found the base plate of a mortar gun inside a Ford Sierra car with the roof neatly cut out. The intention was to track down and capture the IRA unit and, if they didn't surrender, take them out.

Other Royal Irish Rangers were ordered to throw a cordon around the school and secure the area. The bomb squad was called in because it was feared that some of the mortars had landed inside the school but had not exploded. Many such IRA mortar bombs were extremely dangerous because they were usually home-made and therefore very insecure, liable to explode at any moment. Understandably, British bomb disposal squads treated such bombs with great caution.

During the casualty assessment which followed, we suddenly realized that one of the lads was missing and no one had any idea where the hell he could have been. It was established that he had not left the camp and we feared that he may have been hit by one of the mortars that hadn't exploded on impact. Thirty minutes later, the bomb squad moved through the school, gingerly examining and clearing each room, taking no chances. We had not been permitted to enter the building for fear of accidentally setting off one of the unexploded bombs.

One mortar bomb had, in fact, gone through the gymnasium roof, but no one had recalled it exploding. Gingerly, the bomb squad moved in and they could see the unexploded bomb quite clearly lying on the floor. Only six feet away from the bomb was our missing man, lying naked under a sunbed with his Walkman clamped to his ears, utterly oblivious to the events of the last hour. Even now, as he lay there, soaking up the rays and sound asleep, he was unaware that an unexploded bomb was only a few feet away. If the bomb had exploded, he would have been killed.

Gingerly, the bomb squad moved in behind a protective, reinforced blast blanket, inching their way towards the sleeping Marine. Then, without ceremony, they grabbed the Marine, threw the blanket over him and dragged him forcibly out of the room while he screamed and yelled.

"What the fuck are you doing?" he was yelling over and over again. "What the fuck do you think you are playing at?"

"Shut up, keep quiet," the bomb squad yelled at him.

But he was wild, fighting and kicking at the men trying to save his life. Eventually, they succeeded in dragging him out of the room to safety and explained to him precisely what had happened. At first, he refused to believe their explanation, thinking they were simply having a joke at his expense. After all, he had heard nothing. Then they let him see the mortar bomb lying a few feet from the sunbed and he turned white. He never forgot that incident and neither did we. But he took it all in good heart and later bought the bomb squad lads a few pints of beer.

# THE LARGEST SPECIAL OP IN HISTORY (2003)

*Perhaps the largest assault in Special Operations history took place early in the Second Gulf War. On 28 March 2003, at 0600 hours, fifty Green Berets from Third Battalion SFG Alpha Detachment and between eight and ten thousand Peshmerga fighters attacked the secret mountain base of the terrorist organization known as Ansar al-Islam. It was east of As-Sulaymaniyah in north eastern Iraq near the border with Iran.*

*It was an uphill battle which lasted two days, resulting in the biggest victory in the Global War on Terror since the victories over the Taliban and al-Qaeda in Afghanistan. Although the terrain was rocky and rough, in places it was covered in ankle-deep mud.*

Intelligence had informed the Coalition forces that the areas off the roads were heavily mined. The attacking forces had to keep to the roads and mountain trails because of the fear of minefields. They also had to abandon their preferred wedge shaped attacking formation. They moved as "ducks in a row" in a two-pronged assault.

The Peshmerga fighters were armed with AK-47s and PKs. The latter were Russian Pulemyot Kalashnikova – general-purpose machine guns with 100 and 200 rounds per man. The Green Berets were armed with their M-4 carbines and M-240B SAW (Squad Automatic Weapon) light-machine guns.

A support force followed 300 yards behind the lead force of each group. These were Green Berets in trucks armed with fifty-calibre machine guns and MK19 belt-fed grenade launchers. The Peshmergas were supported by their own heavy weapons contingent, equipped with ZSU 23mm Soviet anti-aircraft machine guns and mortar tubes on wheeled trailers. There was no dedicated Close Air Support on this mission. Unless there was an aircraft in the area they were on their own.

The northern prong was led by the men of Operational Detachment Alpha 093. Operational Detachments Alpha 094 and 095 led the southern prong, 2 kilometres further south. The two prongs advanced parallel to each other.

Just after 0600 hours they approached the edge of the mountains. The enemy held the high ground. They came under machine-gun fire, which quickly became heavy. The enemy began to use their own ZSU 23mm weapons and Katusha rockets. Under this fire the attackers had no option but to charge straight at the defenders covered by their own supporting fire. They used their own ZSU 23mm weapons and Katusha rockets. To this was added the American fifty-calibre machine guns and MK19s. The grenade launchers were particularly effective in clearing dead ground – any low-lying depression which might conceal an enemy seeking cover or concealment.

The MK19s fired 40mm high explosive projectiles on a high trajectory. Within thirty minutes the first ridgeline was seized. It was only the first lookout post.

Next they had to move downhill towards the small village of Dekon. Dekon was where part of Ansar al-Islam had its headquarters. After that their second objective would be the village of Gulp. The road approaching Gulp followed a switchback course. It was a natural "ambush alley".

Their third objective would be another village called Varogat. The approach to the village was along narrow footpaths, and it lay in a depression surrounded on three sides by steep high ground. It was a naturally strong defensive position which could turn into a last redoubt. One Green Beret called it "the enemy's Alamo".

As the combined forces charged into Varogat and across the objective, they were pinned down by heavy fire from the heights above. The assaulting teams needed fire support to suppress the enemy fire. It was 0715 hours.

Fortunately there was an Air Force Combat Controller attached to one of the Operational Detachment Alphas. He was able to contact a United States Navy F/A 18 Hornet fighter bomber. The pilot was able to hit the hilltops with two 500-pound bombs. This reduced the incoming fire to a sporadic level.

None of the Green Berets had been hit yet but the level of incoming fire was still potentially lethal. United States Navy Standard Operating Procedure was to maintain a 35,000-foot ceiling. The pilot ignored this. He made a low-level attack on the remaining enemy positions with his 25mm auto-cannon. The accuracy of his fire not only amazed the Peshmerga, it ended the resistance of terrorists. The Peshmerga were able to take the high ground around the village of Gulp.

The remaining Ansar laid down their weapons and stood up in apparent surrender.

The Green Berets had learnt to be suspicious of this in Afghanistan the year before. They kept a safe distance and ordered the Ansar to drop to their knees and take their robes off. The few remaining terrorists who were left detonated their hidden suicide vests and vanished in puffs of smoke.

Any defenders who had not been captured or killed disappeared over the crest of the hill in the direction of Varogat.

Varogat was actually on the border itself. It was a dangerous trek towards the village. Seven Green Berets and about fifty Peshmerga led the way. About a mile further on, the lead force came under heavy fire, including mortar rounds, and had to dig in.

One Special Operator remembered that he could see his medic, Bobby, crouching in a small bit of cover nearby. The mortar fire lasted for over ten minutes. Bobby saw the Special Operator being splashed squarely in the face by a clod of wet mud thrown up by a near miss – exactly like a hit from a custard pie in a comic routine. They looked at each other and burst out laughing.

The Green Berets were able to suppress the enemy fire with their M-240B SAW light machine guns and the few MK19s they had been able to carry with them. It was enough to enable the Peshmerga to make a run for the side of the switchback. From here they began a flanking manoeuvre.

It worked. The Ansar al-Islam fighters withdrew back to their Alamo. Up to this stage the operation should have taken six to twelve hours. In fact, it had taken only two and a half hours. The 8–10,000-man force had hardly taken any casualties.

What was more, they had become so used to being under fire, they were relatively unperturbed by it. One Green Beret said:

> We literally didn't think much of it at all. Being shot at was normal to us at that point. We thought, "Hey, maybe this will be just a little burst of fire, and be over in ten minutes." Ten minutes of heavy enemy fire was no big deal at that point.

The Green Berets came round the corner, making short rushes known as Immediate Action Drills (IADs). They gained ground a few feet at a time.

At this point the first truck came round the corner carrying a fifty-calibre machine gun. This was dismounted and set up. It was soon "rocking and rolling", suppressing the enemy fire.

The fifty-calibre machine gun created lulls in the return

fire. The Peshmerga took advantage of these lulls to over-run the enemy positions. They could see mud huts dotted all over the slopes of mountain and over the crest down towards the Iranian border.

The attackers sheltered under the cliff face and ate a meal while Special Forces medics dressed wounds. The Special Forces and the Peshmerga chugged water and gulped down food. They realized that they were in the middle of the largest terrorist camp they had ever seen.

The Green Berets wanted to finish the job. They had pushed on so fast that they had left their heavy support vehicles behind. The final slope on the Iraqi side of the border was the steepest yet.

They faced the enemy fire once again. The Green Berets took cover behind the mud huts and laid down suppressing fire with their fifty-calibre machine guns and MK19s. The Peshmerga joined in with their DHSK (Dushka) Russian machine guns and fired mortars up the slopes. The enemy fire ceased for the last time.

As they mopped up, the multinational nature of this terrorist stronghold became evident. Few of the terrorists were left alive but one survivor was a Palestinian and another was a Syrian. Identification found on scores of bodies pointed to every country in the Middle East. Links to other organizations were found in the camp. The organizations included HAMAS, abu-Sayaf in the Philippines and al-Qaeda.

Not one Green Beret was wounded. Seventy-five to eighty Peshmerga were wounded and twenty-four were killed.

# FIRST SPECIAL
# FORCES PATROL (1968)

*Franklin D. Miller's first patrol with Special Forces in Vietnam was part of his appraisal to see if he was suitable for Special Forces. He had already served in Vietnam for two years with an Airborne Long Range Reconnaissance Unit. Then he decided that he would like to see what Special Forces was like. He spoke to his first sergeant, who had been in Special Forces himself. The sergeant sent him up to Nha Trang for an interview, where they decided they should try him out. They sent him to an "A" camp just outside Nha Trang.*

*Military Assistance Command, Vietnam (MACV) had an intelligence-gathering group called the Studies and Observation Group (SOG). SOG was a diverse organization which was divided into regional commands. The teams in Command and Control Central (CCC) were named after US States.*

*When he arrived at the "A" camp, Miller was assigned to Reconnaissance Team (RT) Vermont. The leader of a Reconnaisance Team was known as the "One-Zero". The second in command was known as the "One-One". Miller:*

So when I arrived at Kontum they immediately took me out on an intelligence-gathering mission to test my abilities. We were to recon a particular mountainous area and take pictures.

The team leader seemed like a very competent individual. I liked him. But I realized I was going to have trouble with the number-two man. He could see that there was quite a difference between my abilities and his own. He became very jealous and hostile toward me. In the field that's a dangerous situation.

We also had an American as the RTO. All told there were four Americans and four Montagnards on the Vermont team. We were "running heavy" on Americans. Normally we'd have a maximum of two US soldiers per mission.

It wasn't long into the patrol before I determined that the RTO was not what I wanted. I was running tail with one of the Montagnards. The RTO was between me and the team leader, and he made the sometimes-fatal mistake of letting the patrol break into two separate elements. He let the front four guys get about 500 meters ahead of us. They were long gone.

It just sort of blew me away when I realized what had happened. I wanted to jump dead in his shit. I was furious. There we were in the middle of the woods, and we had lost contact with half the team.

Immediately I got down on the ground and started tracking the lead element. Finally we got together with them, but not before we gave them a thrill. They heard us coming and thought we were the enemy when they saw that nobody was behind them. They got into position to hose us down. Needless to say, we were extra cautious as we approached. Fortunately they recognized us right away and we rejoined them without further delay. That was the first upsetting incident of the mission.

Number two came when we found an abandoned enemy camp. It had been vacated only minutes earlier. I could tell that they'd just moved out because the brush that they used to sleep on was still matted down and was still green.

It was getting dark and I told the One-Zero that we

should stay there because it was a secure area. I let him know the enemy just left and probably wouldn't return for a while. The One-One challenged my recommendation. That pissed me off, and we had a short verbal skirmish right there.

The team leader halted the conversation. He saw that I knew what I was doing and could lead the patrol myself. He was aware that I wasn't some "newbie" from Fort Bragg, and that I had twice his amount of experience at running patrols.

We stayed at the camp.

The next day we ran into a four-man squad of enemy troops and smoked them easily. I made the recommendation that instead of withdrawing we should go to a point where we could observe the bodies and hose down whoever came across them. We positioned ourselves and waited, but nobody came along. We left.

After a while the assistant team leader came to the realization that I was starting to run the patrol. I was making the most logical recommendations under the circumstances. But all he wanted to do was argue with me. I cut him off every time he wanted to dispute a recommendation.

I didn't want to argue with him. I wanted to successfully complete the mission. I wanted to survive.

When we got back to Kontum after the mission the One-Zero made the recommendation to the commander that I take over the team. That really pissed off the One-One. Right away I got rid of the RTO. He got another job within the unit. The One-One who argued with me all the time was immediately transferred out of the unit. They didn't fuck around with him. They couldn't afford to because they had high-level business going on. There could be no distractions at any time.

The command group saw that I had the experience to be a good team leader. I was now in charge of RT Vermont, and the next mission we ran was in the same mountainous area as before. We were very successful. We gathered some valuable information. I took some very good pictures of enemy soldiers moving along a trail. The pictures were so clear we could easily make out their unit. I used correct procedures for calling in reports and finds. I was making all the right moves.

After every outing we'd have a One-Zero meeting, where all the team leaders would gather together and listen to the people who just did their thing. Each One-Zero would give a blow-by-blow account of his mission. These meetings served to pass along valuable information to team leaders on new things the enemy was doing, and so on. Little tricks to give you the advantage were also discussed. They were very productive sessions.

Thus began my career with Military Assistance Command, Vietnam Studies and Observation Group (MACV-SOG).

# CENTRE STAGE (2003)

*In 2003 the US Coalition had permission to set up a Forward Operating Base (FOB) in Jordan, just over the border from western Iraq. A co-operative Jordan was not the only difference between the Gulf War of 1991 and the Gulf War of 2003. In the 1991 Gulf War, Special Operations had been regarded as a sideshow but in 2003 they were on centre stage.*

*There were the same Scud-hunting teams and road-watch teams as in 1991. In addition there were tactical reconnaissance and targeting missions. In both the north and the south of Iraq, targeting and reconnaissance were decisive factors.*

*The weapons were similar to 1991 but the precision of the guided munitions was considerably greater.*

*There were also more US Special Operations than in 1991. On 4 April 2003 Major General Stanley McCrystal, vice chief of operations on the US joint staff, said:*

Special operations forces are more extensive in this campaign than any I've ever seen. Probably as a percentage effort, they are unprecedented for a war that also has a conventional part to it.

The US and British special forces were joined on special ops by Australian and Polish special forces. A British special forces operative described the situation:

Unlike the rest of the guys who were hard at it in western Iraq, we were, for our sins, on a covert recce mission in the middle of nowhere – at least that's how it felt at first. Basically our team was a road-watch team, but to call what we were observing a road would be an insult – this was no M1. Our mission tasking was simply to watch, report and target, but with the type of traffic we had to observe targeting would have been a waste of time, as the munitions would cost more than the target itself. For the best part of the day, all that moved down here was smugglers and their ill-gotten gains – they carried oil, tyres, satellite dishes and just about anything else that would bring in a buck – or, in this case, a dinar. But for us this was good news, as the Iraqis tended to turn a blind eye to this sort of activity – making movement for us easier should we be compromised. Military traffic seemed limited to troop, artillery and armour movements – but no Scuds. Even at night, little changed apart from the volume of traffic, we certainly never saw any target of value that would justify compromising our position here. As boring and unexciting as our traffic was, it told us where Saddam's forces were moving to – so to somebody this was good intelligence. During our time here nothing really threatened our security as we were on a high embankment that only goats, or idiots like us would climb and visit. The only time we had a concern was when a camel caravan traversed across the side of our embankment about 80 metres away. However the herders had other things on their minds, as they were trying to transport the carcass of a luxury car downhill without losing it off the camels' backs. The saying "the straw that broke the camel's back" seemed to come to mind at the time, but in this case it was a Merc. For the others in my team it was a great laugh, as it helped break the monotony of the situation – but I had seen this stunt performed before, only in Afghanistan and not Iraq.

Once the herders had moved on, normality returned to the OP – but things were about to change. The war was well underway by now, and the military movements on the road were intensifying by the hour – first one way and then another – but still no Scuds or anything else that could pass off as a high threat. There were certainly no Weapons of Mass Destruction here. Barely a week later and there was clearly an exodus of Iraqi head sheds, as the pressure was mounting and they knew it. I personally had no beef with the rank and file Iraqi army – as they were as much victims of Saddam's regime as anyone else – it was the Republican Guard and the *fedayeen* I despised, as they persecuted their own people.

The only time that our lives were ever potentially threatened was during an over flight by American close support aircraft that just happened to be in our vicinity as a convoy was passing through. They lined up for an attack, but thankfully broke off. I say thankfully because we probably would have got malleted as well as the Iraqis, as we were very close to the road.

If things had really gone "Pete Tong" we could have tried calling them off by way of the TACBE, but then we would have risked being compromised. And I personally did not fancy trogging off into the Ulu, with half of Saddam's cousins on my tail . . . as they just might be a little miffed.

Another British Special Forces operative described:

From the time the balloon first went up we were busy, real busy. We were initially deployed close to Basra, and had the job of targeting Iraqi forces – both conventional and unconventional. Our position was such that we had a good field of view over the main urban area that led to the river, and as such we could observe everything that moved along the main line of communication. This vantage point gave us the ability to recce or target an area as circumstances dictated, as we had a commanding view over the city. On several occasions this vista provided us with good intelligence on Iraqi troop and armour movements, as we were able to predict their routes out of the city – thus enabling an intercept by friendly forces or a target mission.

Our team was one of several that had infiltrated the city of Basra – and between us we had all routes covered. In one action we spotted a small convoy of armed Toyota pick-up trucks heading for a warehouse complex that was located near to a bridge controlled by British and US forces. As we observed it, a group of Iraqis set up a mortar on the back of one of the vehicles and began bracketing the bridge with effective fire. Seeing the danger, we were able to provide target information on the convoy via our PAC – and within a very short time the threat was eliminated. In another action, we spotted a large force of some twenty Iraqi armoured personnel carriers and tanks heading for our forces surrounding the city. But our concern was short-lived, as the force was quickly destroyed by a squadron of Challenger tanks.

For the Iraqis this must have been an extremely frustrating time, as they could not move anywhere within the city without SF spotting them. Essentially we acted as a barometer for our own forces – gauging the right time for them to attack, and gauging the right time for them to withdraw, and only when we felt that the time was right did they advance. I believe that our actions saved many lives – both British and Iraqi alike – and I am proud of what we did.

# WHAT A BUMMER! (1966)

*When paratrooper Franklin D. Miller arrived in Vietnam in March 1966 he was a assigned to the recon platoon of Headquarters company, First Cavalry Division. He was taken by chopper to his unit. The chopper set down in a clearing. As he walked into the trees he noticed some well-concealed tents. A sergeant came up to him and said: "Let me take you over to meet the Bummer."*

*Miller had been told about his platoon sergeant at An Khe when he had passed through there on his way to his new unit. Staff Sergeant Bumstaten had the reputation of being the best. Miller never learnt why he had received his nickname, but presumed it was a contraction of his surname. Miller described the ironic aspect of the Bumstaten's nickname:*

An ironic aspect of Staff Sergeant Bumstaten's nickname was the fact that the phrase "What a bummer" enjoyed great popularity back in the States while I was in 'Nam. I left before the phrase entered the American vocabulary; consequently, I had never heard it, nor had anyone else in my platoon.

Anyway, after a firefight, everyone got together and

talked about who did what and who shot who. Most of the time none of us had shot anybody, yet there'd be two or three dead enemy troops at the scene. Each one had caught one or more rounds straight through the heart or square in the head. We'd look at each other, point at a body, and say, "That's a Bummer!", because the calculated, precise nature of the kill indicated Bumstaten had put him down.

As new guys rotated in from the States, the phrase took on a dual meaning, such as, "What a bummer for that dude, man, because that's a Bummer!"

When I finally met the Bummer he wasn't exactly what I expected. From everything I'd been told, I was looking for some supermacho individual. A Sergeant Rock type. What I saw instead was a small, wiry guy, about forty-five years old, with an extremely short haircut. His voice smacked of the country, and he had a ready, pleasant smile.

When we came upon him he was squatting over a burning block of C-4 explosive, heating a cup of coffee. The sergeant introduced me, and the Bummer told me to sit down.

They found out that they were both from North Carolina. Towards the end of their conversation the Bummer said: "By the way, there's an enemy village on the other side of this ridgeline here. We got in a fight with them yesterday. and we're going over there in about thirty minutes to kick their ass. Would you like to go?"

He asked the question so casually that Miller said yes. He was new and wanted to cooperate.

When they started moving, the Bummer came alongside him and whispered: "I don't want you to do a thing. Just take it easy. If you have a chance to fire your weapon, go ahead and fire it. It'll just add to the confusion, and that'll be good for us. Just make sure there are no friendly people in front of you. Be careful and don't worry about it. Just stay with us." Miller stayed with the sergeant, his RTO and some other men in his section. They forded a stream, which was chest deep.

Miller was about in the centre of the formation as they

moved into a deeply wooded area. All of a sudden he heard a
pop on the right flank. Then a couple more pops, then
three, four, five and then rounds were flying everywhere.

The Bummer had manoeuvred the platoon so that it
formed a semi-circle around the village. Miller did not
see any enemy but he squeezed off a few rounds from
his rifle. The encounter only lasted a few minutes. The
enemy had withdrawn, leaving five or six men behind to
slow the US troops down. The paratroopers killed two of
them and wounded another before the rest took off for the
"tall timber".

They burnt the village and killed the animals. When they
got back to their base Miller and his new buddies "shot the
shit for a while, swapping outrageous lies about our man-
hood."

Four months later he was involved in a small skirmish
with about seven people who had split up and were doing
their thing when they realized that they were outnumbered.
The recon platoon was only twenty-eight in number but the
enemy were about four times as many. The US troopers
started hosing them down so the enemy decided discretion
was the better part of valour. They began to try to disen-
gage.

Miller followed the Bummer's advice and aimed at a
point in front of them and fired on automatic. Before Miller
was aware of it he raised his M16 to his shoulder and was
firing. He was just getting his weapon under control when
he saw a man fall. He went over to look at the man's body
when a sergeant came over and slapped him on the back.
"You got that motherfucker! All right!"

Miller was exhilarated that he was alive and the other guy
wasn't.

The Bummer gave Miller another bit of advice which he
applied later. Miller:

I began to take stock of what I was getting out of my 'Nam
experience. For one thing, I was completely satisfied with
what I was doing. I finally felt I was doing something
worthwhile with my life. And I was good at what I did.

Now I wasn't the smartest guy or even the best shot. But the one quality that I possessed that set me above most of the guys in my platoon was my ability to keep very cool when the shit started flying. The Bummer always preached to us how it was absolutely essential to remain cool under fire and to keep a clear head. Easier said than done, believe me.

But I made it a point to practice what he preached. And surprisingly enough to me, I was able to follow his advice with a level head under adverse circumstances. That was one of the reasons I was put in charge of a squad early in my career. And let me tell you, leading other guys in critical and dangerous situations was pretty heady stuff for a Private First Class.

I loved it. I couldn't get enough.

# GOOSE GREEN (1982)

*By 1982 talks between Great Britain and Argentina had
failed to resolve the dispute over possession of the Falkland
Islands. On 2 April 1982 Argentinian forces landed near
Stanley, the capital. Their strength and numbers forced the
British garrison of 40 Royal Marines to surrender.*

*The British Government decided to retake the islands, by
force if necessary. A British Task Force was sent to the South
Atlantic, consisting of nearly 30,000 men, warships, merchant
ships, aircraft, helicopter squadrons, and supporting arms.*

*The British landed on beaches east of Port San Carlos on 21
May. The Argentinian commander, General Benjamino Me-
nendez, had been told that a landing at San Carlos was
unlikely, so he had done little to defend it. Major Carlos
Esteban was in command of an Argentinian outpost at San
Carlos:*

It was about ten to eight in the morning when one of my
advance observers came running down and told me that
there was a frigate coming in through the channel. I took the
binoculars, ran forward with him, took up his position and
observed that a considerable number of ships were entering.

There was a large white ship in the middle of the bay of San Carlos, many frigates were protecting it and helicopters were flying around.

Nigel "Spud" Ely was a private in C Company of the second battalion of the Parachute Regiment (2 Para). He had taken part in a selection course for the SAS but had been injured and returned to his unit. 2 Para had been attached to 3 Commando Brigade but it was the Paras rather the Royal Marine Commandos who would land first. Ely described the British plan:

The plan was that 2 Para was to be the first on shore at a pre-designated spot that came to be known as Blue Beach 2. The rest of the Brigade would follow as we pushed on to secure a base around and on Sussex Mountains, then waited until the rear echelons had established a secure beach-head. From that the Brigade could organize itself and start to bring the essential supplies ashore. The next thing would be to organize a plan and strike out towards the Argentine forces in the area and finally to the capital, Port Stanley, where the bulk of the Argentines were entrenched. C Company would be in the second Landing Craft Utility (LCU) of the first wave along with Colonel H. If it was an opposed landing, we were to fight through, secure a safe area and await reinforcements. If it was unopposed, our task was to push forward inland, securing the area as we went and wait for the bulk of the Battalion to get ashore, prior to going up to Sussex Mountains, establishing a series of OPs and reporting back to Battalion HQ any enemy movement we saw.

2 Para had been brought south by a North Sea ferry, *MV Norland*. They had to board their Landing Craft from *MV Norland* in full kit. Ely:

By now I could hear what I was to face for the next few weeks: the naval bombardment was in full swing. I pitied anyone underneath it. The noise was quite reassuring and as I waited to time the swell against the rise and fall of the LCU I caught sight of the steady stream of tracer and gun shells up in the night sky.

"Now, GO!" LCU Marine Corporal said. My timing was just right to clear the ship but the LCU came up a lot quicker than I had anticipated and my right leg jolted as 300 pounds of body and bergen weight met a 100-ton floating steel platform. I was in one of the first patrols to go. Basha the patrol IC, Buster, the LMG gunner, and Pops, the 2IC were already on the LCU. It was pretty black outside and I took a couple of minutes to get my night vision. My leg a bit sore, I made my way across the LCU to three dark shapes huddled up in the far corner by the ramp. We had all woken up to the fate that might be waiting for us the other side of that ramp. The entire Task Force was blacked out. Only the glare of a red light could be seen. There was not much to see or do whilst we waited for the LCU to fill up; a long slow process. Once everyone was on board, we drifted off to a semi-safe position and waited for the rest of the crafts to load. This would take a couple of hours. We had no life jackets on; it would have been impossible with the kit we were carrying, and I could not help thinking we would be sitting ducks just outside San Carlos Water.

The ultimate objective of the British Task Force was to recapture the capital, Stanley. San Carlos was 86 miles from Stanley. The advance to Stanley was to be quick, using helicopters. This had become a conventional tactic.

On 21 May, despite Argentinian air attacks, the British landed 3,000 men with their artillery and brought thousands of tons of supplies safely ashore. The Argentinian air attacks continued. On 25 May they hit and destroyed the merchant ship *Atlantic Conveyor*, a container vessel which was carrying the helicopters to be used in the advance on Stanley. Because of the loss of the helicopters, the advance would have to be by "tabbing". This was what the paras called marching in full kit. (The Marines called it "yomp-ing".) By 1982 this was no longer the conventional way to move from a base of operations up to a battle area.

On 26 May the British commander-in-chief in London ordered the advance to begin. Most of the British force marched out of San Carlos on a northern route towards Stanley. 2 Para marched south to attack Argentinian positions at Darwin and Goose Green. There was an airstrip at Goose Green where some Pucara light ground attack aircraft were based. According to Ely, SAS intelligence had told that them that there were about 400 aircraft crew for the Pucaras and a platoon of infantry to protect them. After a 15-mile night march 2 Para rested at an unoccupied farm at Camilla Creek.

Colonel H. Jones was in command of 2 Para, which consisted of four companies each of 110 men and a tactical Headquarters unit of 12 men, a total of 450 men. The British thought they were attacking a similar number of Argentinians.

There was high ground on either side of the route to Goose Green. The Argentinians held Darwin Hill to the east, above the small settlement at Darwin. They also held a ridge to the west at Boca House. On the night of 27 May, A Company of 2 Para was sent to attack Darwin Hill. B Company was sent to attack Boca House. D Company and the tactical Headquarters unit were to advance between them. C Company was in reserve.

The attack began before dawn. At first it went well but slowed down under heavy fire. At 8 a.m. an Argentinian captain, Jose Centurion, was ordered to take his men forward to help in the defence of Darwin Hill. They set up their machine gun positions in slit trenches in front of the hill. Centurion:

As the British tried to advance we opened fire. We fought a fairly intense battle, with some advantage because we managed to check the British detachment straight away and hold them back.

A Company was pinned down in a gully. Colonel Jones took charge of the attack himself. Barry Norman was a company sergeant major in 2 Para:

> Colonel Jones said: "Right, the only way we're going to do it is over the top." So we lined up in extended line, and we went over the top with mortar smoke coming down onto the position to provide a screen. But that particular day, even for Falkland standards, the wind was exceptionally strong.

The wind blew the smoke screen away. Three paratroopers were killed. Colonel Jones shouted to Norman that he intended to make a flank attack on an Argentinian machine gun position ahead. Norman:

> He said, "Follow me" which I did. We then turned right and the Argentinians were firing at us from the high ground to the left. We ran across the top feature, as fast as we could, and then down, into dead ground from the Argentinian position. And I thought he was going to stop, but he didn't. He just continued running.

Norman followed Colonel Jones. He heard a warning about another machine gun position. He dived for cover and started firing at it. Colonel Jones did not take cover but kept going. Norman tried to warn Colonel Jones:

> To my utter amazement I looked again and he was just checking his sub-machine gun, to make sure he had a full magazine on, and he went charging up the hill, to the trench which I was firing at . . .
>
> I shouted to him, "Watch your fucking back!" And he totally ignored me. Whether or not he heard me, I don't know. I think he ignored me, personally. And the higher he went up, the nearer he was to this fall of shot. All of a sudden his body and the fall of shot coincided and he was hit in the back. The momentum of the shot actually forced

him forward and he fell just within inches of the Argentinian trench he was actually going for.

Captain Centurion was amazed by Colonel Jones' participation in the attack:

He [Colonel Jones] found my detachment by chance; I arrived not ten minutes before him, and took up the advantageous position, really by a stroke of luck. I think of Colonel Jones as someone who proved himself to be an excellent commander. Although he possessed innumerable resources – 66mm rocket launchers, Milan anti-tank weapons, mortars, and some artillery support – he personally took part in a machine-gun battle fighting with hand grenades.

The second in command of 2 Para, Major Chris Keeble, was 1,500 yards behind with the tactical Headquarters unit. He heard a radio message "Sunray is down". He knew that meant something had happened to Colonel Jones and that he was in command of the battalion.

He decided that the Boca House ridge was the key to the battle.

Keeble changed tactics. He sent D Company to help B Company. Using the cover of the terrain they were able to crawl along the beach to attack the Argentinian position at Boca house from the flank. C Company was in reserve. Keeble brought up his supporting artillery (three 105mm guns).

Nigel "Spud" Ely was in C Company. During the earlier part of 2 Para's advance Ely's patrol had been the most forward OP. They had tabbed at night and laid up during the day.

By daylight, 28 May, C Company was "mopping up" the Argentinian positions at Burntside House, 9km north of Goose Green. At 10 a.m. C Company came under mortar fire. They took cover in some dead ground where the Argentinian Mortar Fire Controllers (MFCs) couldn't see them. Ely could hear an incredible amount of small-arms fire coming from where A Company was attacking the ridge at Darwin.

By 11 a.m. the Argentinian positions at Boca House and Darwin were taken but the Argentinians at Goose Green had not yet surrendered. When Nigel "Spud" Ely heard that Colonel Jones had been killed his reaction was: "Well, that's a real bastard and let's get on with the job."

The Argentinians had some 37mm anti-aircraft guns on a strip of land beyond the settlement which could be used to fire directly on 2 Para. During the afternoon, an air strike by Harriers knocked out the 37mm guns. Major Keeble decided to attack two positions: the School House, a strongly held position between Darwin and Goose Green and the airstrip. He ordered B Company to march south around the airstrip and approach Goose Green from the south. He ordered D Company to advance directly towards Goose Green, taking the airstrip on their way. He ordered C Company to attack the School House.

Nigel "Spud" Ely was C Company's point man.

C Company was less than fifty strong as they lined up at the start line. They had already been "on the go" for eleven hours.

They were lined up in four-man patrols. Ely's patrol was in front, then two patrols behind them, then three behind them, and so on until the whole company was lined up. The HQ element was in the last line of patrols.

When Ely's patrol came to 800 metres from the Argentinian positions, they began to advance using a technique called breaking cover. This involved crawling to a different position after you had gone to ground before getting up and zigzagging towards the enemy. They were ordered to hold their fire. Ely reached 500 metres from his target. There was a small bunker in a fold in the ground. Ely had become impatient with the delays and checks. He threw a white phosphorus grenade into the bunker. Ely:

Instantly I was up, safety catch off, firing into the now collapsed bunker. I had been right; it was flimsily built. As it burned a scream rang out. Fuck me, I thought, there's someone in there. Through the smoke and fire, I could see two bodies inside, one totally fucked, burning and obviously a goner. The other was about to be fucked. I shot him in the guts. The look on his face was total shock as blood spurted up from him and covered my right leg.

Were they asleep? Didn't they see us? Why didn't they defend themselves? I thought, fuck it, it's not for me to understand the personal behaviour of the enemy. Then I put two rounds in the other body for good measure. At the same time, all hell broke loose.

"INCOMING," was screamed out all over the place. Obviously we had disturbed something more than 400 aircraft technicians. For some reason I leapt out of the relative safety of the bunker and sprinted forward. I could hear Basha shouting something, but I wasn't aware if it was directed at me, Pops or Buster. I just kept on running, trying to zigzag and not get caught in the sights of the Argy fire. I spotted a fold in the ground directly ahead of me and made for that. I was aware that there were two blokes close to me on my left: Buster and Dick. What was he doing up with Buster? He had started off with another patrol. But I put the thought out of my head, and ran like a man possessed. I couldn't return fire, I was too concerned with reaching that fold and getting into cover. I made it! I dropped down out of the field of fire then quickly spun around to see who was with me, at the same time taking in all my immediate surroundings. Heart pumping, I lay face down on the peaty ground, my helmet just supporting my head and keeping my face from touching the ground. I closed my eyes tightly, took a couple of deep breaths. Jesus Christ!

C and D Companies were attacked by Pucaras. The paras shot one of the Pucaras down with a "Blowpipe", hand-held anti-aircraft missile. Ely and his fellow patrol members came under fire from one of the 37mm AA guns.

Ely was hit in the thigh by an Argentinian 7.62mm round. Fortunately it hit a pouch containing spare magazines and didn't even break his skin. Ely took cover in an empty trench, where he was able to check out his right thigh. Buster and Dick joined him in the trench.

They could see where they were: 200 metres from the schoolhouse itself. In front of the schoolhouse was a little bridge with some dead ground on the far side. To the left was one of the AA gun positions. They thought there were some of "our guys" on their left but apart from that they had lost contact with the command and control element of the company and had become separated from their other patrols.

They decided to attack the School House. Ely and Dick would use their 66mm Light Anti-tank Weapons (LAWs) while Buster covered them with his Light Machine Gun (LMG). They screamed their heads off to release some of the tension they had built up. Then they jumped up and ran towards the bridge. When they had crossed it they dropped down to prepare their weapons. Ely:

We had to be totally focussed because we had now entered no man's land and could be targets for our own blokes. I was breathing fast. The run had worked my lungs to full capacity. I made a positive effort to control my gasps for air as I crawled up the track on my side, trying to keep the 66 and my weapon off the ground as much as possible, and looking left, right and straight ahead every second. The track was even, making the going easy. We stayed about five metres apart. This gave us a fighting chance, should we get spotted by the Argies, to return fire; being bunched up close made us an easier target. I was approaching the top of the track now and signalled Buster behind me to get ready; he passed it on to Dick. Two more metres and I would break the skyline and be in full view of those in the schoolhouse. To take out the schoolhouse, all three of us would have to expose ourselves to the open ground. It was pointless just one going up and letting rip, then another; we had to hit the target with maximum firepower, all at the same time. Without any prompting from any of us it was obvious that that was going to happen.

Within seconds we were out from the safety of the side of the track and in full view of the schoolhouse, no more than 80 metres away. It looked a hell of a lot bigger now we were close. Buster let rip almost immediately, emptying a full magazine, raking the windows and the front door. I fired off a few rounds first and got down, ready to fire the 66. Dick was firing away trying to cover me while I got my shot off. I had one chance: the 66 is a once-only-fire weapon, light, small and relatively accurate. I was not aware of any incoming rounds, I was too busy concentrating on getting a stable fire position. With the launcher on my right shoulder, I tried to make out the sight pattern and remember what sight line to use. My mind blanked; a tremor of nervousness came over me. I was worried about being exposed. Then all of a sudden, I picked up the sight picture, aimed and fired. The rocket has a 15-metre back-blast, so you should always check no one is behind you. I forgot to, but it didn't matter; I knew Dick and Buster were to my left. The rocket whooshed off.

Meanwhile Buster was still putting massive amounts of fire power down. Windows smashed and doors and parts of the structure were being chewed up by 7.62mm. My rocket found the target. I had aimed too high; it hit the right-hand side of the roof, halfway up. The roof exploded as the HE sent secondary fragmentation whizzing around inside and out of the schoolhouse. I had now picked my SLR up and was firing into the blazing building while Dick fired his and hit it almost square on. This caused it to burst into flames, big style. The Argies didn't know what had hit them. One or two made the wrong decision and came out of the front door. They were slotted instantly. Some might have slipped out of the back door around the other side and out of our view, but many were slotted by the rounds Buster was putting down and many more were obviously taken out by the two 66 rockets. Because of the sheer amount of rounds Buster had used, Dick and I had to re-sup him with extra LMG mags which we carried for the gun. I remember him screaming out for more magazines even as we made our retreat back down the track. He was covering us, still firing at a rapid rate. Dick and I dropped off two mags each, ran a little way back down the track and waited for Buster to finish. He was just at top of the track and only had to drop down less than a metre and he would be out of view. When he was ready, all three of us made a dash back down the track to the bridge. From start to finish, the firing took less than a minute. We had achieved what we had set out to do: destroy the schoolhouse.

Three paratroopers were killed while taking the surrender of some Argentinians who had raised a white flag. Men from D Company were appearing from the direction of the airstrip. Ely met up with some other men from C Company who had been pinned down by the AA guns.

Ely found out that the 37mm cannon which had been pinning him down earlier had been taken out by some paras called Raz, Mal and Sean. They had been pinned down by its fire for over two hours but they took advantage of it changing target to rush close enough that it could not depress far enough to bear on them. Then they "let rip and took out the gunners".

After the schoolhouse had been destroyed, Major Keeble was prepared to besiege the settlement of Goose Green by firing at it with his artillery until it surrendered. A patrol reported that 112 civilians were being held in the community centre in Goose Green. Keeble took some time alone to decide what to do:

I thrust my hands into my pockets, because they were so cold, and my fingers caught a piece of plastic that I had in my pocket, a laminated prayer, from a French soldier. I had a kind of bargain with God, you know, I'll carry this prayer, if you look after me. I knew this prayer well. And I suddenly thought, I need to say this, and in that darkness knelt down, in this gorse, and I said this prayer, which was essentially abandoning myself to God and seeking his will and whatever the outcome was, I'd live with that. And a most amazing kind of transformation occurred. From feeling cold and fearful, and uncertain and frightened, I suddenly felt joyful, hopeful, warm and very clear about what we should do. And I turned round and went back to the boys. I said, "I'll tell you what we're going to do. I'm going to seek a surrender, tomorrow morning." And they were astounded, inevitably, and I said, "Trust me", in the way in which I felt I needed to trust my God, in this case.

He sent some prisoners to open negotiations. The Argentinians offered to surrender if they could have a formal ceremony. The British were amazed when 1,500 Argentinians marched out. The British had lost 17, including 13 officers and non-commissioned officers. They had learnt some lessons from the battle. All subsequent attacks were made at night.

On 14 June, the British reached Stanley. The Argentinian commander, General Menendez, surrendered.

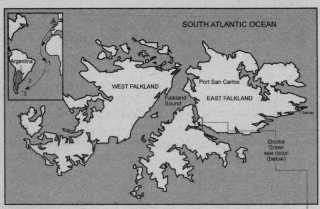

**FALKLAND ISLANDS Battle of Goose Green, 28-29 May 1981**

Key to inset map (above)

↘ route of British Task Force
1 Ascension Island
2 Buenos Aires
3 Falkland islands

Key to Goose Green detail (right)

1 Camilla Creek Farm

2 B company heading for Boca House

3 A company heading for Darwin Hill

4 D company & Tactical HQ

5 Colonel H Jones killed

6 D company attacks Boca House

7 & 8 attacks on airstrip & Goose Green

9 attack on School House by C company

10 airstrip

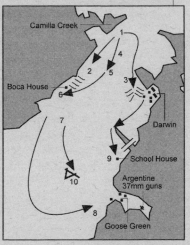

# APPENDIX I: THE ORIGIN OF US SPECIAL FORCES (1952–)

US Army Special Forces came into existence in 1952, when the United States was helping the French in their fight against Communist insurgency in south East Asia. The US Army had formed a Special Service Force during the Second World War but it had been disbanded.

On 20 June 1952 the first of the Special Forces groups, the 10th Special Forces Group, was activated at Fort Bragg, North Carolina; it became the nucleus of the Special Warfare Center, now known as the John F. Kennedy Center for Military Assistance, at Fort Bragg. The next unit to be formed was the 77th Special Forces Group, which was also activated at Fort Bragg, on 25 September 1953.

In spite of US support, in May 1954, the French Army was defeated by the Communist-supported Vietnam Independence League or Viet Minh at Dien Bien Phu, and under the Geneva armistice agreement Vietnam was divided into North and South Vietnam.

By July 1954 the US Military Assistance Advisory Group, Vietnam, had a strength of 342 men. In October of that year President Dwight D. Eisenhower promised direct aid to the government of South Vietnam, led by Premier Ngo Dinh Diem.

From 1954 to 1956 Viet Minh cadres were forming action committees to spread propaganda and to organize the South Vietnamese to oppose their own government. In July 1955 the People's Republic of China announced an agreement to aid the Viet Minh, and the Soviet Union announced aid to Hanoi.

In August 1954 Diem's government rejected for the third time Hanoi's demands for general elections throughout the two Vietnams, and in October South Vietnam was proclaimed a republic by Premier Diem, who became the first president.

US Special Forces troops actually worked in Vietnam for the first time in 1957. On 24 June 1957 the 1st Special Forces Group was activated on Okinawa, and in the course of the year a team from this unit trained fifty-eight men of the Vietnamese Army at the Commando Training Center in Nha Trang. The trainees would later become the nucleus, as instructors and cadres, for the first Vietnamese Special Forces units.

In 1959 and 1960 the Vietnamese Communist insurgents in South Vietnam became known to the South Vietnamese as the Viet Cong. As they grew in number their power to terrorize the people increased. Clashes between government forces and armed Viet Cong increased in number from 180 in January 1960 to 545 in September of that year. Thirty Special Forces instructors were sent from Fort Bragg to South Vietnam in May 1960 to set up a training program for the Vietnamese Army.

On 21 September 1961 President John F. Kennedy announced a program to provide additional military and economic aid to Vietnam. The government of the United States was by this time deeply concerned over the insurgency in South Vietnam. It was trying to take what it considered were the necessary steps to help the republic of South Vietnam to deal with the threat.

On 21 September 1961 the 5th Special Forces Group, 1st

Special Forces was activated at Fort Bragg. 5th Special Forces Group would eventually be charged with the conduct of all Special Forces operations in Vietnam. In the fall of 1961, President Kennedy himself began to display particular interest in the Special Forces. He was convinced that the Special Forces had great potential as counterinsurgents. This made him into a very powerful advocate for the development of the Special Forces program within the Army.

President Kennedy himself made a visit to the Special Warfare Center in the fall of 1961 to review the program. It was President Kennedy who personally authorized the distinctive headgear that became the symbol of US Special Forces, the Green Beret.

Until 1961 both the South Vietnamese and US Governments had concentrated on developing the regular military forces of South Vietnam. These excluded the ethnic and religious minority groups. Late in 1961 several initiatives began to broaden the counterinsurgency effort by developing the paramilitary potential of certain of these minority groups. These initiatives became known as the Civilian Irregular Defense Group (CIDG) program.

One of the original purposes of US Special Forces in Vietnam was the development of paramilitary forces among the minority groups. Franklin D. Miller joined US Special Forces later in the war:

A primary mission of most Special Forces troops in 'Nam was to teach the indigenous population how to fight, which was excellent public relations for our side. It really was a good plan. The Special Forces people would go out and establish a training base known as an "A" camp. There, about twelve Americans would teach the ways of war to anywhere from two hundred to three hundred Montagnards or South Vietnamese. The instructors simply gathered surrounding population under their wings and treated them well. They gave them food, first-class training, and weapons. The local inhabitants never had it so good. The feeding and training served to develop a strong alliance between Special Forces and the local people, especially the Montagnards which greatly enhanced our capabilities. So while many Special Forces missions involved ass-kicking, the majority were geared toward teaching.

At first the program was concentrated on an ethnic group known as the Montagnards. They lived in a strategic area, the Central Highlands of South Vietnam. Miller:

Montagnard (pronounced in English it sounds something like "Mountainyard") is a French word meaning "mountaineer" or "highlander", Montagnards, or "Yards" as we called them, are the original inhabitants of Vietnam. Like the American Indian, the Yards are composed of many tribes, each with its own unique personality and traits. And also like the American Indian, the Yards were run off their ancestral land. The Vietnamese, who are of Chinese descent, swept down from China and forced the Yards into the mountains of Vietnam. It was in their mountain retreats that the Yards stoked the fires of contempt for the Vietnamese.

I worked side by side with the Yards during my many years with the Special Forces. I found them to be the most dependable, hardworking, and loyal soldiers I've ever fought with, and I would welcome them into my unit any time without question.

The tribes in the major areas that I worked were the Rhade, the Halang, the Jarai, the Sedang, and the Bahnar. In many ways it was just like the frontier. The men ran around in loincloths and the women wore skirts with nothing on top. The Bahnar are the most educated of all the tribes. I always had members of the Bahnar tribe on my team because they were capable of speaking all the different Yard dialects. They also spoke Laotian, Cambodian, and Meo. The Bahnar were knowledgeable about languages because they were the traders among the tribes. So regardless of what area you were operating in, you could communicate with the people if a Bahnar tribesman was with you. That was an invaluable asset.

The most warlike tribe was the Sedang. They were the tallest, meanest, and most aggressive. This may or may not be true, but I was told that up until the middle sixties they still had human sacrifices. I wouldn't doubt that after being around these people. They were so tough and hard it was scary.

These people truly lived by the law of nature. Only the strong survive. If a baby has a defect, it dies at birth, or it's not going to live very long. Consequently, most of them were in excellent physical shape, very muscular, and built for endurance. Their knowledge of the woods was unrivaled by any American soldier. Face it, when you're born and raised in the jungle you become intimate with its essence. You learn about the sounds of the animals, how to track prey, what to eat, what to avoid. A Bahnar youngster can construct the little booby-traps you set up for people, because they are the same traps he uses to catch animals. By the time a Sedang child is eight years old he knows all the things they teach you in ranger school about the woods and tracking. All he'd need to do would be learn how to jump from a plane, and he'd be an airborne ranger.

At one time while I was operating with the Sedang, they wanted me to dye my hair black. They felt that if my hair was black we might not get so much shit brought on us because we would all look alike from a distance. I had a really dark tan but my hair was bleached blond from the sun. If the enemy saw us from a distance and we all had black hair and dark skin they might not open up on us. But if they saw that one guy had blond hair they might just want to hose everybody down without thinking about it. So I dyed my hair. I don't know if it did any good, but I stopped doing it after a while because I just didn't like it.

Most of them couldn't write at all. When I'd pay them they'd take their finger and push it down on a stamp pad to ink the tip and then sort of roll it on the pay sheet. Some would take a pen, which they held like a stick, and make an X.

But I'll tell you what. I'd rather have one of them in an asskick than an American, any day. That's not meant as a derogatory comment on American fighting men, but simply a compliment regarding the tremendous fighting abilities of the Yards. They are natural hunters, people born to the hunt. Many times we'd be in a fight and I'd look downhill or across from me and the Yards would be on the move. I very rarely had to tell them anything. I'd see them fix their eyes on the enemy and move like they were stalking game. Once they learned your personality and technique no words were necessary. Eye contact said it all.

One of the most interesting things to see was the way Yards were hired to work for us. We paid top dollar for our recruits. Most would get more than a staff sergeant in the Vietnamese Army. Big money for a guy straight out of the woods. We're talking anywhere from thirty-six to fifty dollars a month, depending on his position on the team. A Yard who was the lead soldier on a patrol – or the "point" of the element – got paid more because that was the most dangerous position.

The hiring procedure went something like this: my commander, knowing how many folks we were short, would put the word out that we needed X number of soldiers. There was always a camp of Yards located around our compound. Once they heard that we were recruiting, they'd go back to their villages and pass the word. From what I've seen, the villages would send their best people to the tryout. The Yards chosen by their communities had to be good because they represented a particular tribe or village. Pride and honor were at stake. They couldn't afford to send old Charlie who might fuck up bad and make the tribe look like a pack of assholes. So you could be guaranteed that the Yards who lined up for inspection were qualified to be there.

Believe me, some of the Yards who showed up on those occasions were primitive. They'd never held a rifle, let alone fired one. They'd stand there wearing a loincloth and nothing else. But, man, you'd see hunter written all over them. They had that look. They were hard as nails. Once one of my Yards got cut in the foot by a piece of frag. Later I took him to the dispensary to have the cut stitched, but the doctor couldn't get the needle through the skin on the bottom of his foot! His feet were tough as leather. The doctor finally resorted to butterfly clips and a tight bandage.

Sometimes the applicants would come with credentials. They'd have letters signed by American commanders–colonels and the like – saying that so-and-so was the best thing he'd ever seen, he was sorry to be losing him, he comes highly recommended, etc., etc. I'd jump on those guys right away.

So the Yards would gather in a big group, and the American team leaders would go through the selection process. I always selected tall people who looked like they could carry somebody if the situation demanded it. I'd move along the ranks, looking for men who had that look. The one that said, I'm an ass-kicker. I'm good. Let me show you.

When I found someone I wanted I'd tell my One-One to pull that guy from the group and have him fall in behind us. Soon I had my quota, and with the entire gang in tow I'd move off to conduct interviews. I'd get my interpreter and ask them if they'd ever been in a unit before, had they ever fired a weapon, and so forth. I asked these questions to determine where I was going to place them in my element. I wasn't going to reject anybody at this stage. I had already selected them; now it was just a matter of matching people to positions.

Once I had an idea of where I was going to put them, I'd run a recon mission in the area to test them out, to see if my assessment of their abilities was correct. The point man had to see things at any distance and detect movement instantly. He also had to be one of the best shooters because nine times out of ten he'd be the one who engaged the enemy first. He also had to have a sixth sense about danger. He had to be able to feel that something was wrong. He had to detect areas that might be traps ready to be sprung.

Running the "tail gunner" position was also critical. The last man in the element had to cover our tracks. He had to put things back the way they were prior to our passing through. When the situation called for it he'd sweep the trail of footprints, replace sticks and stones, reposition vegetation and do a number of other tricks. All these actions were done to slow down or stop the enemy from tracking us. It was an interesting contest because the Yards were experts at making an area look undisturbed, and the North Vietnamese, sometimes aided by turncoat Yards, were excellent trackers. An outstanding tracker could detect a doctored trail, but he wouldn't be able to determine how many people had passed through.

Another interesting observation I made about Yards is that they didn't waste ammo. Americans had a tendency to fire rounds in big bursts all over the place. But Yards really conserved their rounds, making sure that each one counted. That's why I was reasonably sure that some enemy troop went to the ground if I heard a shot fired by my point man or tail gunner.

Yards were basically your bodyguards as well as your killers. My point man was named Hyuk (pronounced with a silent *H* and long *U*). He was good. He was fucking dynamite. Even though he was a Yard, he had once worked as a squad leader in an NVA unit. I don't know if he had ever fought against Americans or why he came over to our side. I never bothered to ask. He was about thirty years old and I was about twenty-five. He always had this very businesslike look on his face. I wasn't afraid to question him about his past, but perhaps it was just as well that I didn't. The only important fact was that he always covered my back and he was always there when I needed him. I had nothing but respect and admiration for him, as I did for all the Yards.

The first step in the CIDG Program was taken in October

1961. It actually began with a project designed to prevent the Rhade tribesmen in Darlac Province from succumbing to Viet Cong control. Exploratory talks were held with Rhade leaders in Darlac to seek their participation in a village self-defense program. One Special Forces medical non-commissioned officer participated in that first effort.

Early in 1962 the government of the United States under President Kennedy began to set up the actual interdepartmental machinery for aiding South Vietnam. The Executive Branch, the Department of State, the Department of Defense, the Joint Chiefs of Staff, the United States Information Agency, the Agency for International Development, and the Central Intelligence Agency were all involved. Because of the nature of the growing conflict in Vietnam and because the Special Forces were designed for unconventional warfare, it was inevitable that the Special Forces would play a conspicuous role. It was also plain that the actions and suggestions of the various government agencies would heavily influence that role.

During the early years of Special Forces involvement in Vietnam, 1961–65, the concept of how best to employ the forces was developed, put into practice, and adjusted as they went along. The government of the United States and the government of South Vietnam were dealing with a Communist-inspired insurgency, and for the United States it was a new experience. Many local tactics were attempted on a "let's-try-it-and-see-what-happens" basis. If something worked, then it became an acceptable counterinsurgency tactic; if it did not, it was dropped.

During these formative years, it became clear that the part the US Special Forces was to play would differ from the role foreseen for it when it was created in the 1950s. At that time, the troops of the force as organized were capable of waging unconventional war under conventional war conditions. The war in Vietnam, however, never fell smoothly into the conventional category. In Vietnam "enemy or enemy-controlled territory" was the countryside of South Vietnam, the government of which had invited US military presence. The enemy insurgents were guerrillas themselves. Instead of waging guerrilla warfare against conventional forces in enemy territory, the US Special Forces troops were to find themselves attempting to thwart guerrilla insurgency in "friendly" territory.

At first the Civilian Irregular Defense Group program was concerned with what was called area development. The goal was to provide an area with security from Viet Cong influence and terror, to help the people develop their own self-defense program, and, if possible, to enlist support for the government of Vietnam from its own citizens. Operations took an offensive turn only because many of the areas involved were already effectively controlled by the Viet Cong.

In late 1960 United States' military involvement consisted of the presence of a Military Assistance Advisory Group. The US and South Vietnamese governments were trying to meet the mounting Communist insurgency by increasing the size and effectiveness of Vietnam's conventional military forces. For the most part, these did not include the ethnic and religious minority groups in the highlands of the central and northern portions of South Vietnam and in the rural lowlands of the Mekong Delta. Under the sponsorship of the US Mission in Saigon several programs were initiated in late 1961. The programs were intended to keep these minority groups from falling under the control of the Viet Cong. US Special Forces detachments were assigned to the US Mission to provide training and advice for the programs, the first of which was among the Montagnards.

The pilot project with the Rhade tribe in Darlac Province was successful. The next step was to set up area development centers in remote areas where there was little government control. The development centers were bases of operation. Special Forces detachments, working through Vietnamese Special Forces counterparts, assisted in the establishment of village defense systems. They gave them elementary training in small arms and mortars. They taught them minimum tactics designed for squads and occasional platoon manoeuvres.

From September 1962 to July 1963 US Military Assistance Command, Vietnam (MACV) and the Army gradually took over responsibility for operations. From July 1963 to the spring of 1965, when the conventional US build-up began, MACV bore full responsibility for the Civilian Irregular Defense Group (CIDG) program.

From 1961 to 1965 more than eighty CIDG camps or area development centers were established. Many of them were built in areas where the government had no effective control.

Each camp was a self-contained and comprehensive counterinsurgency effort. US Special Forces men provided advice and assistance in all aspects of camp administration and operations. They were involved from the initiation of each site until the camp and its paramilitary assets were turned over to local Vietnamese authorities.

# APPENDIX II: VIETNAM CHRONOLOGY

## 1930

Ho Chi Minh and his followers began the Indochinese Communist Party. This was opposed to French colonial rule.

## 1932

Bao Dai returned from France to reign as emperor of Vietnam under the French.

## September 1940

Japanese troops occupied Indochina, but allowed the French to continue their colonial administration of the area. In July 1941, the Japanese moved into the southern part of Vietnam. In reaction, the US and Great Britain restricted Japan's supplies. The resulting oil shortage added to Japanese motives towards war with the US and Britain.

# 1945

An OSS (Office of Strategic Services, forerunner of the CIA) team parachuted into Ho Chi Minh's jungle camp in northern Vietnam and saved Ho Chi Minh who was ill with malaria and other tropical diseases.

## August 1945

Japan surrendered. Ho Chi Minh established the Viet Minh, a guerilla army. Bao Dai abdicated after a general uprising led by the Viet Minh.

## September 1945

Seven OSS officers, led by Lieutenant Colonel A. Peter Dewey, landed in Saigon to liberate Allied war prisoners, search for missing Americans, and gather intelligence.

## 2 September 1945

Ho Chi Minh read Vietnam's Declaration of Independence and established the Democratic Republic of Vietnam in Hanoi. Vietnam is divided.

## 26 September 1945

OSS Lieutenant Dewey killed in Saigon, the first American to be killed in Vietnam. French and Vietminh spokesmen blamed each other for his death.

# 1946

Ho Chi Minh attempted to negotiate the end of colonial rule with the French without success. The French army shelled Haiphong harbor in November, killing over 6,000 Vietnamese civilians. By December, open war between France and the Viet Minh had begun.

# 1949

Communists won civil war in China.

# 1950

The United States recognized Boa Dai's regime as legitimate. United States began to subsidize the French in Vietnam. Chinese Communists began to supply weapons to the Viet Minh.

# 3 August 1950

A United States Military Assistance Advisory Group (MAAG) of 35 men arrived in Saigon. By the end of the year, the US was bearing half of the cost of France's war effort in Vietnam.

# 7 May 1954

The French were defeated at Dien Bien Phu.

# June 1954

The CIA established a military mission in Saigon. Bao Dai selected Ngo Dinh Diem as prime minister of his government.

# 20 July 1954

The Geneva Conference on Indochina declared a demilitarized zone at the 17th parallel.

# 24 October 1954

President Eisenhower pledged support to Ngo Dinh Diem's government including military forces.

# 1955

Ngo Dinh Diem organized the Republic of Vietnam as an independent nation; he declared himself president.

# 8 July 1959

The first American combat deaths in Vietnam occurred when Viet Cong attacked Bien Hoa billets; two servicemen were killed.

# 1960

The National Liberation Front (NLF), called the Viet Cong, was founded in South Vietnam.

# 1961

The United States' military build-up in Vietnam began with combat advisors.

# 1 November 1963

Ngo Dinh Diem was assassinated.

# 4 May 1964

Trade embargo imposed on North Vietnam in response to attacks from the North on South Vietnam.

# 2 and 4 August 1964

North Vietnamese torpedo boats attacked the United States destroyer *Maddox* in the Gulf of Tonkin. (The Gulf of Tonkin Incident.)

# 5 August 1964

President Lyndon Johnson asked Congress for a resolution against North Vietnam following the Gulf of Tonkin incident.

# 7 August 1964

Congress approves the Gulf of Tonkin Resolution which allowed the president to take any necessary measures to repel further attacks and to provide military assistance to any South East Asia Treaty Organization (SEATO) member. President Johnson ordered the bombing of North Vietnam.

# 8–9 March 1965

The first American combat troops arrived in Vietnam.

## 6–8 April 1965

President Johnson authorized the use of United States ground combat troops for offensive operations. The next day he offered North Vietnam aid in exchange for peace. North Vietnam rejected the offer.

## 17 April 1965

Students for a Democratic Society sponsored the first major anti-war rally in Washington, D.C.

## June 1965

Generals Ky and Thieu seized the South Vietnamese government.

## 15–16 October 1965

Anti-war protests were held in about 40 American cities.

## 14–16 November 1965

The first major military engagement occurred between United States and North Vietnamese forces.

## September 1967

General Thieu was elected president of South Vietnam.

## 21–23 October 1967

50,000 people demonstrated against the war in Washington, D.C.

## 21 January 1968

The battle of Khe Sanh began. It lasted six months.

## 31 January 1968

The Tet Offensive. Communist forces launched attacks on Hue and other major South Vietnamese towns, and military bases. One assault team penetrated the walls of the United States embassy in Saigon but was driven back.

## 16 March 1968

My Lai massacre: 150 unarmed Vietnamese civilians were killed by members of a United States Army platoon led by Lt. William L. Calley Jr.

## 10 May 1968

The Paris peace talks began between US and Vietnamese officials.

## 10–20 May 1969

The battle for Ap Bia Mountain, known as Hamburger Hill. Ap Bia Mountain is in the Ashau valley near the border with Laos. It was being used as a base by the North

Vietnamese Army. The terrain and heavy rain nullified the United States forces' technological and air superiority. After ten days' fierce fighting United States and South Vietnamese troops finally captured the hill. Fifty-six Americans were killed. Four hundred and twenty were wounded. Five hundred and ninety-seven North Vietnamese were killed.

## 8 June 1969

President Richard Nixon announced the first troop withdrawals from South Vietnam.

## 3 September 1969

Ho Chi Minh died.

## 15 November 1969

250,000 people demonstrated against the war in Washington, DC.

## 1970

The draft lottery began.

## 30 April 1970

The armies of the US and South Vietnam invaded Cambodia.

**4 May 1970**

Four students were killed by National Guardsmen at Kent State University in Ohio.

**6 May 1970**

More than 100 colleges were closed due to student riots over Kent State.

**February 1971**

South Vietnam and the United States invaded Laos in an attempt to sever the Ho Chi Minh Trail.

**December 1972**

Christmas bombing of Hanoi.

**27 January 1973**

United States, South Vietnam, and North Vietnam signed Paris Peace Accords, ending American combat role in war. US military draft ended.

**29 March 1973**

Last US combat troops left Vietnam.

**21 April 1975**

South Vietnamese President Thieu resigned.

# 30 April 1975

North Vietnamese forces took over Saigon, South Vietnam surrendered to North Vietnam, ending the war and reunifying the country under communist control. Washington extended embargo to all of Vietnam.

# BIBLIOGRAPHY AND SOURCES

*Soldier Five*, Michael Coburn, Mainstream Publishing (2004)
*The Real Bravo Two Zero*, Michael Asher, Cassell (2002)
*Operation Barras*, William Fowler, Cassell military paperbacks (2005)
*Eye of the Storm*, Peter Ratcliffe, Michael O'Mara Books Limited (2000)
*Hunting Saddam*, Robin Moore, St Martin's Press (2004)
*Midnight in Some Burning Town*, Christian Jennings, Cassell (2004)
*Black Hawk Down*, Mark Bowden, Corgi (2000)
*The Battle of Mogadishu*, ed. M. Eversmann & D. Schilling, Ballantine
   Books (2004)
*Last Round: the Battle of Majar al-Kabir*, Mark Nicol, Weidenfeld &
   Nicolson (2005)
*Ambush Alley*, Tim Pritchard, Ballantine Books NY (2005)
*First Into Action*, Duncan Falconer, Time Warner Books UK (2003)
*Black Water*, Don Camsell, Virgin Publishing Ltd (2003)
*Pathfinder*, Richard R. Burns, Ballantine Books (2002)
*Not By Strength, By Guile*, Peter Mercer, Blake Publishing (2001)
*The Khyber Rifles*, Jules Stewart, Sutton Publishing (2005)
*The 13–cent Killers*, John J. Culbertson – selections used by permission
   of Presidio Press, an imprint oof the Ballantine Publishing Group, a
   division of Random House Inc (2003)
*Secret Soldier*, Muki Betser / R. Rosenberg, Simon & Schuster (1996)
*Reflections of a Warrior*, Franklin D. Miller & E.J.C. Kureth, Pocket
   Books /Simon & Schuster, (2003)
*For Queen and Country*, Nigel "Spud" Ely, Blake Publishing Ltd (2002)
*Special Operations in Iraq*, Mike Ryan, Pen & Sword Military (2004)

**Extract from the Mammoth Book of**
*SAS & Special Forces*
**Published by Robinson, £7.99**

# THE COLOMBIAN JOB

## Gaz Hunter

*Since the early 1990s, 22 SAS has trained and advised anti-narcotics police in Colombia, the global centre of the hard-drugs trade. One of the first SAS teams sent out was commanded by Staff Sergeant Gaz Hunter (a pseudonym) of B Squadron.*

WE PICKED UP our weapons and ran to the waiting Hueys, a dozen men to each one. Tucked in close behind one another, the helis took off, dropped their noses, and snaked out low over the jungle, weaving constantly in case of ground fire. Climbing steeply to get out of small-arms range we turned south. The Hueys had 7.62mm M-60D machine-guns mounted on pintles in their port-side doors, one to each helicopter. A thin layer of high cloud blocked the sun and as we climbed it grew bitterly cold. I shivered inside my DPM combat gear. It was our third week in Colombia. We were way down in the south of the country now, with a different regional command group. Our mission was to seek and destroy the local cartel's main airstrip and processing centre. Acting on information received, we were hoping to catch them with their next shipment ready to go.

After twenty minutes airborne, we came on a small coca plantation, several acres across, with a small hut at its heart: the captain in charge told one of his men to note it for future attention. The coca bushes were planted in neat rows, a few feet apart, in land that had been slashed and burned out of the jungle. This little farm was a good sign: it meant we were probably getting near one of the cartel's main operational nodes. Sure enough, we saw a second, larger, coca plantation below us almost at once.

We plunged down to tree-top height. The captain turned in his seat and waved at me. "Danger area," he said.

I nodded enthusiastically. "Great." I locked and loaded. I had that tight feeling you get when there's the chance of a contact, half fear, half anticipation.

A broad river appeared below us, gleaming like a mirror in the light. The pilot dropped the helicopter right down on to it. Now we were below tree-top height, flying very fast and very low, skimming the surface of the water. There was a massive sensation of ground-rush, the brilliant green walls of the jungle flashing past in a blur on either side. The thump and clatter of the Huey grew louder still, echoing back up off the river, the machine bucking and yawing in the low-level turbulence.

We shot out over a small mud village. The captain shouted something I couldn't hear. He pointed at the ground. We looped into a tight turn, and set down hard on a scrubby little football pitch. You can go just about anywhere in Colombia and never be more than a click from a kick-about pitch. The policemen bundled out, trotted over to a nearby hut and squeezed inside. I took a good look around, then followed them. Obviously we weren't going to be staying long: the pilot was still turning and burning. When I reached the door of the shack I found the men arguing over a map. Gradually the locals from the village wandered up, in singletons and small groups, to have a look at the strangers who had landed from the sky.

"Is it usual for helicopters to come this way?" I asked the captain.

"Oh, no," he assured me. "It's very unusual."

Christ, I thought, another sneak attack. After about ten minutes of map-wrangling we took off, flying back up the river we had just been following. Then the pilot turned the machine back

on to its original heading, coming back down over the water for
the second time. This was bad operational practice and, with the
map business, it meant only one thing: we were lost. We started
circling. "It's here somewhere," the captain shouted. It was his
job to pin down the location before we got airborne. He hadn't
bothered doing his staff-work.

But I still had the feeling this was going to be our lucky day.

We were dead low, clipping the tops of the trees. I wasn't the
only one there with that feeling in my gut: the door-gunner
cocked and made ready. I grinned at the policeman opposite.
Like me, I could tell he wanted to get out there and do the job.
Then, suddenly, there was the airfield, right below us, a scrubby
rectangle blown out of the virgin jungle. Someone shouted,
"Armed men! On the ground." The captain looked at us, giving
us the thumbs down. Oh, no, I thought, you're not backing out of
this one now. I tapped the stock of the Armalite with the heel of
my palm, giving him some teeth and pointing down at the strip.
"Let's go get them," I shouted. He looked at the door-gunner.
The gunner waggled the barrel of the M-60 up and down and
nodded vigorously. He, too, was raring to go.

The Huey bucked and lurched. I wondered if we had been hit.
There had been no thumps, but I was acutely conscious of the
fuel-cells under the floor of the cabin: 844 litres of high-octane
aviation fuel. "Incoming!" the pilot screamed. Through the door
I could see bright orange tracer floating up at us from the edges of
the trees. Everyone went very quiet. I tapped the gunner on the
shoulder and pointed at the flashes. "*Si*," he said. We were
within range. He squinted briefly along his sights. The gun
roared as he opened up.

I couldn't hear or see the captain giving any commands.
"Down!" I signalled to the pilot. "Get us down! Lower!" He
pushed on the Huey's collective and we screamed in along the
edge of the field. Our gunner hosed down the tree line, M-60
hammering. Glancing back out of the door, I saw the second
gunship swoop in behind us, spraying the other side of the strip.
There was a hot smell of cordite, and big brass cartridge cases
flying everywhere. Fumes whipped around the cabin and back
out into the slipstream.

I could feel my heart pumping hard and my blood running.
There was the deafening noise of the M-60 and the rotors, the
smell of hot engine oil and gunsmoke. Everything was bright and
pin-sharp.

We peeled off out of the attack, but our own pilot turned the wrong way, putting us directly into the path of any ricochets from the following Huey, and stopping our own gun from bearing on the target. I shouted at him and pointed, but he looked blank. We turned sharply at the end of the strip and came back in for a second pass. I couldn't see any return fire from the ground now. We shot back along the runway again, then banged down hard at its northernmost end. In a second we were all out and down, firing into the trees where we had last seen the muzzle flashes. There was no return fire. After one short burst of three I quit firing to save ammo.

We started pepper-potting: one man forward, down, observe and fire, next man forward, down, observe and fire, the first on his feet again making a short zigzag dash forward. Matt's group in the second Huey had landed right behind us. The police started running along a narrow track to our left, spearing its way into the dense jungle. There was only enough room for them to run in single file. Against all my instincts and training, I followed. There wasn't much choice. At once we came under fire from the trees to our left. I could hear rounds slapping and whacking into the surrounding bush, the heavier thud of the tree-strikes.

I had closed right up on the leaders of our group. I got down on one knee and waited. A burst of fire came in close to my position, the bullets whistling through the undergrowth, the air pressure parting the leaves, and buzzing past like huge wasps. Another burst rapped into the trees just above my head: *Thwock! Thwock! Thwock!* The fat punching sound in the dense, moist wood was exactly like that of a round going into a human body. One bullet came right out of the other side of an atap palm directly in front of me: a huge chunk splintered out towards my face. I ducked aside. There was the high-pitched *ping!* of a ricochet, and I saw yellow-orange muzzle flash in among the dark green. I could tell where that one had come from. I swivelled slightly, took aim at the blue haze in the bush, and blasted back, firing controlled double-taps, moving the Armalite in a slow arc to cover the location.

At my back, Matt was firing at the same spot. There was a high-pitched scream as someone made a hit. At that it was up and on. The jungle ahead of us suddenly opened up: I saw a clearing with some buildings dead in the centre. The policemen swept up and around these shacks, then stopped.

"Clear through, clear through," I yelled in Spanish. "Follow on and fire!" The men had regrouped at the far edge of the clearing. They stood there, looking pleased with themselves, instead of going in pursuit. As far as they were concerned, the job was done. I thought we had just started. I could still hear the distant sounds of cartel gunmen crashing off into the jungle. "They're running away," I said. "Let's get after them and finish the job."

"No, no," called the captain, lighting a cigarette. "They've gone now."

I looked around. All over the clearing and in atap-covered lean-tos around the central hut there were big fifty-gallon oil drums, filled with a mixture of fermenting coca leaves and petrol. The smell was putrid, rank and disgusting in the hot air. Boxes and crates of chemicals, sulphuric acid, acetone and the rest, all stacked ready for use, lay next to what looked like a huge washing-machine. Some of the police had started searching, and there was a sudden shout. They had found three drugs workers cowering under the beds in a long wooden accommodation hut. They dragged these men out by the scruff of the neck and began to interrogate them, shouting in their faces and slapping them.

The rest of us got busy destroying the processing plant. There was too much equipment and cocaine paste to ship out on the helicopters, so we made a big pile of it, doused it in fuel, and burned it. Next we carried all the chemicals into the huts, threw in anything else lying around that looked like it might be useful, and set fire to them. There were cracks and whizzes as it went up, and sharp snaps from the blazing wood. Columns of oily smoke billowed up into the air. We backed off and stood for a while, watching the firework display. Some of these labs, the really big ones, can produce as much as $1 billion a month in refined cocaine. This outfit wasn't quite in that league, but it was a start, the best drugs-enforcement effort I'd seen yet.

The captain came up and told us we were going off to hit another, even bigger, drugs camp: they had extracted its location from the prisoners. I decided there wasn't all that much wrong with our leader's commitment, it was just the lazy, haphazard way he went about things. We mounted up in the Hueys again.

With directions from the captured men, we were over the next target in no time. From the air, we saw that the strip was pockmarked with deep holes, as though it had been deliberately cratered. The Huey shimmied in, lifted its nose and we jumped off its skids from the hover. Fanning out, we skirmished around the main house. A woman with a small child on her hip came out, waving her arm and shouting abuse. The police charged past her and arrested a man inside.

After slapping this man across the face a few times, they rushed off across the airfield like a pack of dogs. The prisoner had told them something. Watching the tree line, I followed them across. Hidden in the tall growth were four huge metal barrels lined up in a row. They were filled to the brim with semi-refined coca paste. Bingo! We had found one of the major shipment points for the local operation. Alongside these barrels were dozens of wooden planks, which at first was a bit puzzling. Then I realized they went over the craters in the runway, so that the shipment planes could land. The craters were deliberate, designed to make us think that the strip was disused.

We were inspecting these finds when I heard two shots from the other end of the field. Two or three of the policemen had remained down there with the prisoner. It might be that they were trying to scare more information out of him. Or it might be something else. We made a new bonfire out of everything we could find, including the planks, set it alight, and went back to join the rest of the team.

The prisoner was on his knees. They had his hands tied behind his back, and they were really laying into him, slapping, punching and kicking. When they saw us, they stopped, stood him up and dusted him off. Things seemed to calm down a bit.

There was another shout, this time from the nearby riverbank. Someone had found a second cache of semi-processed cocaine, about eight drums of it, hidden near a small creek leading down into the river. Following this inlet back towards the camp, we found two rubber boats with powerful outboards carefully hidden in among the undergrowth: getaway craft. From the air, we had missed them. We poured petrol over them and left them blazing.

When I got back, the police were jumpy, scared looking. The prisoner had been talking. He was white and his mouth was running blood. "This is a very bad place," said the captain encouragingly. "Many narco-terrorists here."

The Hueys, which had been standing off at a safe distance, came whopping back in for the pick-up. "This is a big find," I said. "Why not use it? They'll be back to see what the damage is. Leave an OP in for a few days – say, three or four men. Let them watch what happens. If they do come back we'll extract the OP covertly, come back in with the Hueys, only this time we'll land clear and work our way in. Surround the bastards. Then we'll catch them all, just when they think they've got rid of us." The captain smiled back at me, shaking his head.

As we finished talking, there was a loud bang from the rain-forest and I turned with the Armalite up. Low velocity, I thought. Pistol round. Four policemen came out of the trees and started climbing into the helis. Last I'd heard, the man we'd caught was coming back to base with us for further questioning. "Where's the prisoner?" I asked.

"He was small fry," replied the captain. "They've let him go."